MUSIC IN THE ELEMENTARY SCHOOL

SIXTH EDITION

Robert E. Nye
Vernice Trousdale Nye
Gary M. Martin
Mary Lou Van Rysselberghe

University of Oregon

PRENTICE HALL, ENGLEWOOD CLIFFS, NEW JERSEY 07632

MUSIC
IN THE
ELEMENTARY
SCHOOL

Library of Congress Cataloging-in-Publication Data

Music in the elementary school / Robert Evans Nye . . . [et al.].—6th
ed.
    p.   cm.
  Rev. ed. of: Music in the elementary school / Robert Evans Nye.
Vernice Trousdale Nye. 5th ed. c1985.
  Includes bibliographical references and indexes.
  ISBN 0-13-607722-6
  1. School music—Instruction and study—United States. I. Nye,
Robert Evans. II. Nye, Robert Evans. Music in the elementary
school.
  MT3.U5N94 1991   91-32509
  372.87—dc20   CIP
                                          MN

Editorial/production supervision
    and interior design: **John Rousselle**
Acquisitions Editor: **Bud Therien**
Copy Editor: **Anne Lesser**
Prepress Buyer: **Herb Klein**
Manufacturing Buyer: **Patrice Fraccio**
Cover Designer: **Bruce Kenselaar**

 © 1992, 1985, 1977, 1970, 1964, 1957 by Prentice-Hall, Inc.
A Simon & Schuster Company
Englewood Cliffs, New Jersey 07632

All rights reserved. No part of this book may be
reproduced, in any form or by any means,
without permission in writing from the publisher.

Printed in the United States of America
10 9 8 7 6 5 4 3

ISBN 0-13-607722-6

PRENTICE-HALL INTERNATIONAL (UK) LIMITED, *London*
PRENTICE-HALL OF AUSTRALIA PTY. LIMITED, *Sydney*
PRENTICE-HALL OF CANADA INC., *Toronto*
PRENTICE-HALL HISPANOAMERICANA, S.A., *Mexico*
PRENTICE-HALL OF INDIA PRIVATE LIMITED, *New Delhi*
PRENTICE-HALL OF JAPAN, INC., *Tokyo*
SIMON & SCHUSTER ASIA PTE. LTD., *Singapore*
EDITORA PRENTICE-HALL DO BRASIL, LTDA., *Rio de Janeiro*

Contents

2 PLANNING FOR TEACHING 37

3 THE DELIVERY OF INSTRUCTION 68

6   TEACHING CHILDREN ABOUT TONE QUALITY   165

7   TEACHING CHILDREN PITCH, MELODY, AND HARMONY   209

8 *TEACHING CHILDREN TO SING* 233

Preface

During the past decade, elementary music has been at the forefront of innovative change in music education. Although past editions of *Music in the Elementary School* have provided timely methods and materials, this newest edition is notable for its clarity—a restructured design which fits current college courses for prospective elementary music specialists as well as for tomorrow's classroom teachers.

We have organized the book in two main parts. The first, Learning, Development, and Planning, gives the aspiring music teacher an understanding of the current theories of learning, and an awareness of learner characteristics apparent in today's children. Conceptual teaching in each chapter is based upon children's earlier experiences with music. Pictures of youngsters actively engaged in music making reflect the excitement in store for teachers of music. Specific adaptations of the music program are provided for exceptional students mainstreamed into the classroom. The chapter on evaluation is expanded substantially, and now includes examples of a variety of types of questions for student assessment, as well as sections on teacher self-evaluation and program evaluation.

The second part of the book addresses the topic, Bringing Children and Music Together. It presents the many aspects of music in a clear, conceptual sequence, and discusses the teaching of the musical skills necessary for their assimilation by students. Many new songs have been introduced as part of the instructional units in the text. Electronic keyboards and computer-based instruction are more thoroughly presented. A three-year acquisition plan for the purchase of electronic instruments is provided, along with our recommendations for equipment that facilitates music teaching in contemporary settings. Another innovation for this edition is a new chapter titled "Teaching Children to Listen to Music," complete with listening lessons that have proven appeal to young listeners. Numerous listening examples, reflecting a myriad of cultures, are featured, particularly in the section on music of other cultures. A thorough review of the major current approaches to elementary music is presented, and their integration into the curriculum occurs frequently throughout the book. We also endorse an integrated model of music taught in relation to other subject areas—a reflection of the current trend for integrated teaching in U. S. Elementary schools.

This book will serve as a unique resource: first, for its emphasis on the way children learn; second, for its discussion of how music instruction is planned; third, for its comprehensive approach to the teaching of music in the elementary school; and fourth, for its extensive, up-to-date references on related articles, publications, recordings, and films, provided at the end of each chapter. This last feature alone would make the book a valuable reference for the college professor designing a music fundamentals or methods course, as well as a permanent addition to the prospective teacher's professional library. Another helpful new addition is the chapter outline that appears at the beginning of each chapter. Finally, the number of appendices have been increased with a listing of recordings available in the Machlis's series, *The Enjoyment of Music,* and a newly created cross-reference of all songs in the book which appear in the three most recent editions of music textbooks published by Silver Burdett & Ginn, Macmillan, and Holt, Rinehart and Winston. When combined with the existing appendices—''Books for Elementary School Children''; ''Alphabetical Listing of Composers in *Adventures in Music*''; ''Compositions in the Bowmar Orchestral Library''; and ''Copyright Law''—the book provides significant assistance in locating materials to be used in the classroom.

Long after the toys of childhood are gone, the gift of music remains.

ANONYMOUS

Introduction

There are many theories justifying the inclusion of music and the arts in the schools. In these times of declining confidence in education, music teachers must clearly perceive their roles. They may be asked, for example, why music must be taught in the schools when it is so freely available in society.

Early in this century music in the curriculum was supported for its extolled values of encouraging cooperation, building character, raising morale, improving physical and mental health, and, later, for enriching the language arts and social studies curriculum. Today music is recognized as a content area in its own right that possesses elements of the values just listed and others as well. Strong claims are made to justify music as essential in the aesthetic development of each human being. Thus it is a component of arts education. Music and the other school subjects are perceived as mutually supportive, with some measure of integration desirable. However, music and all other subject areas maintain their separate identities.

From the standpoint of how children learn, and the skills and processes involved with learning, the necessity of music in the school becomes more apparent. Aesthetic experience engages cognitive processes as it fosters imagination and feelings. Art experiences can provide a foundation from which cognition (thought), concepts, judgment, and action spring. Developing the imagination influences thinking processes, the quality and quantity of ideas, values, and theories. Without imagination, creativity and intelligence are diminished. Music is a primary stimulus for such development in the schools, and with the other arts is essential in developing lifelong thought processes and in organizing and expressing feelings.

The final report of the National Commission on Excellence in Education, *A Nation at Risk: The Imperative for Educational Reform* (April 1983) contains repeated endorsements of the arts, stating, "A high level of shared education in these Basics (English, mathematics, science, and computer science), together with work in the fine and performing arts and foreign languages, constitutes the mind and spirit of our culture.'' Arts education on the elementary level is specifically endorsed. The College Board included the arts as one of six areas of basic learning in a report issued the same year. Among recommended skills in the arts are the ability (1) to understand and appreciate the unique qualities of each of the arts, (2) to appreciate how people of various cultures have used the arts to express themselves, and (3) to understand and appreciate different artistic styles and works from representative historical periods and cultures. ''College entrants . . . should be able to express themselves in one or more of the arts.''

Arts education can enrich experience in ways that other subjects cannot. Arts education gives order and definition to feelings and gives them meaning. It provides constant exploration of feelings that extend far beyond everyday experience. Aesthetic response is indispensable to much experience, and instruction in the aesthetic response is both possible and necessary (Broudy, 1977). Good teaching improves the sensitivity of the learner to aesthetic qualities in the environment. All teachers, not only those in the arts, have responsibilities for this area of learning. Aesthetic experience is basic to becoming an educated person. The schools must take serious account of this fact and act upon it. Teachers have the task of providing environments in which children respond imaginatively to the arts and other areas of the curriculum. As part of this process, the arts should have a permanent and central place in the school and in the the lives of children.

There are at least two quite different points of view about quality in the arts. These views have to do with the question of whether art is to be valued because of the personal satisfaction of individuals who experience the art, or because of standards of excellence determined by society or the so-called experts in society. This interesting issue can challenge older children to analyze a musical experience and to determine what about it is appealing, less appealing, or not appealing, and why. Children need not agree with the ''experts'' in these matters, but they should be able to defend their positions with clear statements about the experience.

Most persons would agree that the arts add quality to life. Through arts education children learn unique things about themselves and others. The arts are particularly useful in understanding other cultures and historical periods. By exploring the musical patterns of sounds and silence in their own and other cultures, and by experimenting with the creation of musical sounds themselves, elementary school children enjoy an increased variety of cognitive, psychomotor, and affective experiences.

Basic Education   Many years ago John Dewey said, in effect, that the arts were the cement that joined the curriculum. It has taken considerable time for American education to come to grips with this idea, but a growing number of educators have found that music is an excellent vehicle for cognitive development. Many experiences in music, both intellectual and psychomotor, provide data to be organized by conceptual thinking. Muscles, voices, ears, and eyes work in combination with the brain. The arts contain prerequisites to cognition such as interpreting symbols, coordinating muscles, stimulating imagination, and refining perceptions. Music and other subjects unite in the mutual goal of public instruction.

When arts are integrated into the general school curriculum, all education in that school is enhanced. The aesthetic, emotional, and cultural qualities of music add interest and meaning to other areas of the curriculum. It is also true that the subject matter of other areas makes the study of music more enjoyable. Music has always been one of the most natural mediums of human expression, and through its use, individuals continually interpret civilizations, past and present.

Charles Fowler (1978) says that when we try to identify the basics in terms other than describing subject areas, basic education refers to "skills that are prerequisite to learning, such as the ability to distinguish and interpret symbolism, to organize words into expression, to coordinate muscles, to harness imagination, to hone perception, and to grasp the essentials of cultural history" (p. 30). He further states that the infusion of the arts into *all* subject matter is mutually beneficial. The movement toward a new view of basic education and the crucial place of the arts in it requires new or revised college courses in education and the subject fields, and makes inservice education for all teachers necessary. Fowler continues, "To move from the periphery of the curriculum to its center means that the arts are no longer a separate realm but are woven into the fabric of daily life. When students see that most subjects have aesthetic components, they begin to see and accept the import of aesthetic considerations in the world about them—the decisions about the clothes they select, the way they furnish their homes, and the need for urban landscaping. The arts suddenly take on real importance; they have significant practical value . . ." (p. 33).

History Music education in the United States is an expression of the needs of the people rather than a product of an artistic elite. Its roots are in the singing schools of the early days of the nation when Lowell Mason, William Billings, and others responded to the desire of communities that church singing be improved by organized instruction in music fundamentals and note reading.

Among Mason's teaching principles were the following (our condensation):

1. Since students learn by seeing and hearing, and because what they learn should be an evident and logical deduction from well-established facts, a teacher guides the pupils to learn by their own powers of reasoning.
2. Educational steps are placed in a logical order that coincides with the natural development of the child, who learns a thing step by step when the necessary skills and background are acquired.
3. The teacher does not depend fully upon books, rules, or formulas, and thus will not teach by merely telling. The teacher depends upon present proof making its appeal to the mind of the pupil.
4. The primary values of music instruction will be social and moral.
5. There will be a strict but loving guidance of the pupil; music should be pleasant and agreeable; the pupil will be actively thinking and learning things constantly; gratification will come from the attainment of knowledge.

Mason's much quoted motto for teachers was

THINGS BEFORE SIGNS;
PRINCIPLES BEFORE RULES;
PRACTICE BEFORE THEORY.

Elementary school music began to be offered officially in some cities in the 1850s, but it was not until 1864 that music instruction was approved and financed in Boston's primary grades. Luther Whiting Mason joined the Boston music staff, specializing in elementary school music and becoming its dominant figure in that century. He was also called upon to assist the music programs of Japan.

Music Methods   In 1834 the Boston Academy of Music formed a class for instruction in the methods of teaching music, a short summer lecture course held for a few days in August. Each succeeding year enrollment increased, until there were 200 people from all parts of the nation being instructed in how to improve their teaching in singing schools, private schools, and public schools. As early as 1836 some of these students organized their free time to discuss other matters of concern to music education, church music, and performing groups. Lowell Mason encouraged them, and in 1840 he helped to form the National Music Convention. Because in those days colleges and universities did not offer course work in music education, other music conventions were organized throughout the country. These were brief, usually from three to five days in length. Their value and popularity created a demand for the *musical normal institutes* held in summers for two to three months duration, forerunners of the present-day college or university summer session.

Lowell Mason organized a normal institute in New York City in 1851. These continued into the 1920s, when teachers colleges began offering summer music courses. One of the most important figures in innovative elementary school music of that day was Satis Coleman of the Teachers College, Columbia University.

In the twentieth century, music education became an integral part of the teacher education program of the nation. The four-year degree in music education, first introduced at the Oberlin Conservatory, became possible in the teachers colleges of the 1920s. Thus music education can be traced from the singing school, music convention, and musical normal institute to the teachers college.

The term *music education* was an invention of the early National Education Association, which expressed the view that music was a part of general education. In the early days of music education in the United States there were two primary aims of instruction: to read music and to sing acceptably. Later there was additional emphasis on the performance of both vocal and instrumental music. Teachers assumed that by this contact with music, understanding of music and improved social and ethical behavior was somehow absorbed. Performance became the major emphasis of music programs. Still later, appreciation and understanding of musical concepts were assigned positions of importance

Photo by Juretta Nidever.

among the goals of instruction. The early attempt to realize these new goals usually resulted in learning facts about music rather than acquiring the ability to discriminate and analyze. A more recent aim has been to achieve musical responsiveness through the study of music as an academic discipline. This is aided by the development of instructional and performance objectives in the cognitive, affective, and psychomotor areas of learning. As a performing art, music has an *affective* component, based upon feelings that cannot be accurately assessed. Nevertheless, music also involves *cognitive* (intellectual) and *psychomotor* (physical) experiences and is learned through the integration of these three areas of learning, since no one of them exists in isolation.

In this decade the general goals include creating a learning environment and using teaching procedures that will develop the musical abilities of the musically gifted, the average child, and those students with special problems and styles of learning.

There has been from the beginnings of music education a cross-fertilization of ideas between the United States and European nations, and more recently among other nations of the world. The names of leaders from abroad are many, the most recent major figures being Dalcroze, Orff, Suzuki, and Kodály. In turn, American educators such as Lowell Mason, Luther Whiting Mason, and many others influenced music education in other nations. One American movement that attracted the attention of European educators was the Manhattanville Music Curriculum Project (MMCP), with its emphasis on exploration and improvisation. An earlier distinctly American influence was the school band movement. As events continued to unfold, the strong relationship between music education and education in general became an American distinction. The contributions in music education of two European composers of stature, Zoltán Kodály and Carl Orff, have increased understanding of and respect for elementary music education in the United States. Another healthy influence has been the interest of private music teachers in applying methods adapted from music education to their studio teaching. Still another positive response has come from the almost universal realization that the large majority of music graduates will become teachers, if not in schools, in private studios and in institutions of higher learning. A closer bond among all areas of music has resulted.

Relating the Arts   One of the popular ways of dealing with music in school settings is by relating it to other art forms under such titles as "Integrated Arts," "Comparative Arts," "Cultural Arts," or "Arts and Humanities." The underlying reason for such a curricular move is that certain principles are common to all of the arts: for example, repetition, contrast, unity, variety, and balance. Anderson and Lawrence (1982) describe the common theme approach and the historical era approach in which the arts reflect humanity at a given time. Some artistic works such as opera, theater, and dance also combine the arts. These approaches naturally relate music to the other arts, bringing a unique perspective through their association.

Significant generalizations can be made in correlating the arts:

Any work of art has a plan or form.

The arts are a source of satisfaction for people.

When people work creatively with the arts they arrange their materials in various combinations which others may contemplate and study.

Combinations of the materials of art provide interest and variety.

Everyone can experiment with original expression by arranging and combining the materials of the arts.

Application of artistic principles can affect daily living in varied ways. Artists bring fresh insights and perspectives to the experiences of life.

Humanity expresses universal and unique concerns through the arts.

The individual arts have some common elements and some marked differences.

EXPLORATORY ACTIVITIES

1. From statements in this chapter and elsewhere concerning the purpose and/or justification of music in the schools, prepare a defensible rationale of why music should be in the curriculum.
2. Discuss this statement: "In a world which compels men's minds to invent the machines of destruction, the arts must remind it of the beneficence of beauty and the worth of an individual." (Oleta Benn, in the 57th Yearbook of the National Society for the Study of Education: *Basic Concepts in Music Education*, 1958, p. 355.)
3. Role-play a situation in which a local school board is confronted by some disturbed taxpayers who want art and music eliminated from the educational offerings in order

to reduce the local tax burden. Include among the players a music teacher and a parent who want a good music program. The other class members can be the audience at the regular meeting of the board. Later, exchange the roles. Afterward, identify the ideas that become evident in the performance.

4. It has been said that certain school subjects have to do with *making* a living while others have to do with the *quality* of living. Discuss whether there is a reasonable priority of importance implied or whether these two aspects of education are equal in importance.

References

Alliance for Arts Education, John F. Kennedy Center for the Performing Arts, Washington, DC 20566. For information about arts-in-general-education projects.

ANDERSON, WILLIAM M., and JOY E. LAWRENCE, "Approaches to Allied Arts," *Music Educators Journal*, September 1982, 31–35.

BIRGE, EDWARD B., *History of Public School Music in the United States*. Philadelphia: Oliver Ditson, 1937. Reprinted by the Music Educators National Conference, Reston, Va., 1966.

BROUDY, HARRY S., "How Basic Is Aesthetic Education? or Is 'Rt' the Fourth R?", *Educational Leadership*, November 1977, 134–147.

CEMERL, Aesthetic Education Program. Write to The Viking Press, Lincoln Center for the Performing Arts, 625 Madison Ave., New York, NY 10022.

EISNER, ELLIOT W., *Cognition and Curriculum. A Basis for Deciding What to Teach*. New York: Longman, 1982.

FOWLER, CHARLES B., "Integral and Undiminished: The Arts in General Eucation, *"Music Educators Journal*, January 1978, 30–33.

GREENE, MAXINE, "The Art of Being Present: Educating for Aesthetic Encounters," *Journal of Education, 166/2*, July 1984, 123–135.

HOFFER, CHARLES R., *Introduction to Music Education: Section Two*. Belmont, Calif.: Wadsworth, 1983.

HOFFER, CHARLES R., and MARJORIE HOFFER, *Teaching Music in the Elementary Classroom*. New York: Harcourt, Brace, Jovanovich, 1982, 9–10.

JDR 3rd Fund, 50 Rockefeller Plaza, New York, NY 10020. Information encouraging administrators and teachers to adopt an arts-in-general-education approach.

JORGENSEN, ESTELLE R., "Philosophy and the Music Teacher: Challenging the Way We Think." *Music Educators Journal*, January 1990, 17–23.

LA CHAPELLE, JOSEPH R., "The Sociology of Art and Art Education: A Relationship Reconsidered," *Studies in Art Education, 26/1*, Fall 1984, 36–40.

LEBLANC, ALBERT, "Nation at Risk: Opportunities within the Essentials Report," *Music Educators Journal*, September 1983, 29–31.

LEE, WILLIAM R., "The Snedden-Farnsworth Exchanges of 1917 and 1918 on the Value of Music and Art in Education," *Journal of Research in Music Education,* Fall 1983, 203–213.

LORD, DONALD C., "The Slave Song as a Historical Source," *Social Education,* November 1971, 763–767, 821.

McNett, Ian E., *Charting a Course: A Guide to the Excellence Movement in Education*. Washington, D.C.: Council for Basic Education, 1984.

Miller, Bruce, "Artistic Meaning and Aesthetic Education: A Formalist View," *Journal of Aesthetic Education, 18*/3, Fall 1984, 85–99.

Music Educators Journal, March 1983. This issue highlights utilitarian versus aesthetic rationales for arts education.

Parker, Olin G., "Toward a Theory of Values Through Music," *Educational Research Quarterly, 9*/2, 1985, 3–7.

Reimer, Bennett, "Music Education and Aesthetic Education: Past and Present," *Music Educators Journal*, February 1989, 22–28.

_____, "Music Education as Aesthetic Education: Toward the Future," *Music Educators Journal*, March 1989, 26–32.

_____, *A Philosophy of Music Education*, 2nd ed. Englewood Cliffs, N.J.: Prentice Hall, 1989.

Smith, Tim, "The Aesthetic Heart of Education," *Music Educators Journal*, March 1984, 38–40.

Wilson, Frank R., "The Full Development of the Individual Through Music," *Update*, Spring 1984, 3–7.

Zinar, Ruth, "Highlights of Thought on Music Education Through the Centuries," *American Music Teacher*, February-March 1983, 32–38.

1 How Children Learn: A Basis for Music Teaching

One of the most important considerations in planning any music curriculum is the recognition of how students acquire, retain, and apply knowledge at various stages of intellectual development. Teachers of music must continually explore the various theories postulated by educational psychologists. These theories must be assessed before choosing those most pertinent to the learning needs of students. Concepts and skills to be learned must be identified, sequentially ordered, and introduced at chosen times for the development of optimum learning. For example, multiple and repeated experiences are necessary for young students to develop skills and knowledge in music. They must have many encounters with cause-and-effect relationships before they acquire a simple understanding of logical sequence.

Research has shown that the amount and quality of learning is in direct proportion to the individual's experiences. One of the most encouraging theories of our time is that intelligence scores can be changed significantly by increasing the number of quality experiences in a person's life.

Teaching and learning are different operations. Teaching consists of actions by one person to induce learning in another; learning consists of a person's acquiring knowledge, skills, and feelings by means of perceptions through the senses and reflection on those perceptions. Learning can take place without teaching. In the school environment it is assumed that learning occurs as a result of interactions between teacher and learner, although this may or may not be true. Teachers and learners engage in verbal and nonverbal interactions and practice psychomotor skills such as musical performance and body movement in relation to musical stimuli. They also experience affective reactions of a nonverbal nature that indicate their values, feelings, and ideas.

Learning and Thinking

Percepts and Concepts The human mind receives signals from the outside world through the five senses. Each of those signals is a percept. Many percepts are recorded in the mind, which discovers links between some of them and formulates appropriate concepts. These concepts in turn influence new and old perceptions. Music is an aural art, and the stimuli that bring forth musical responses are musical structures varying from a single percept of a sound to highly complex sounds. When musical perception takes place, the learner's mind becomes aware of many aspects of the music being experienced.

Musical percepts, when combined, become the musical concepts of the learner, the outgrowth of personal experiences which are processed by the learner. Because each person's experiences and mental processes are different, concepts differ from person to person. Concepts are very complex and are continually being developed and modified. They cannot be communicated verbally with precision because the one who attempts the communication is speaking from a personal interpretation of the events. Verbal communication of musical concepts can improve to the extent that those exchanging information hold similar concepts. However, many responses are covert, and cannot be communicated verbally.

To think conceptually, we progress from the level of perception of objects, situations, and events, to making associations, to forming concepts, to grouping two or more concepts to form a generalization, to applying the generalization to solve related or new problems. Previously formed concepts and generalizations can be part of the data used to form the learner's new and expanded concepts.

Cognitive Processes   Several types of thought processes are implied in the preceding paragraphs. Benjamin Bloom and others (1956) have identified the following six levels of thought processes (cognition) and placed them in a taxonomic hierarchy from simplest to most complex:

1. *Knowledge*: Recall of specific facts, terminology, principles, and practices. Shows little or no ability to manipulate these facts, restate them in a different version, or relate them to other knowledge.

2. *Comprehension*: Ability to manipulate and reconstruct knowledge in one's own language, and summarize or interpret it at a simple level.

3. *Application*: Ability to select appropriate information and bring it to bear on specific intellectual tasks.

4. *Analysis*: Ability to break down knowledge into its constituent elements or parts, and show the relationships between those parts.

5. *Synthesis*: Ability to combine elements or parts in new or original forms. The creation of unique plans or works of expression by reordering existing parts, or mixing newly created ones and extant ones.

6. *Evaluation*: Ability to make judgments about the value of processes or objects, especially on the basis of selected criteria.

In a good music program the teacher engages the students in all six levels, focusing when possible on the higher levels (numbers 4 through 6). Opportunities for such activities abound in music programs. For example, there can be analysis of performance and recordings in terms of pitch, tone qualities, tempo, dynamics, articulation, tension and release, form, and the balance of musical elements. When evaluating a song, the relationship of the words and the melody may be examined. Questions could include, for example, "Listen to the song we just sang as I play it back to you on the tape recorder. Have we used all appropriate ways for singing it expressively?" "Is the form of this recorded composition logical in terms of the composer's title, *Theme and Variations*?"

Students may also be asked to evaluate music with questions such as "Which percussion instruments are most suitable to accompany this music?" "Why?" "Does this melody make good sense in terms of what the words are communicating?" "Why, or why not?" Such questions cannot be answered by a simple *yes* or *no*. They always imply a logical defense of the *yes* or *no* based on appropriate criteria.

For example, when concerts are presented in elementary schools, it is useful for teachers and children to develop together a description of the standards of behavior for the concert. After the concert the students evaluate the behavior of the performers and themselves in terms of their stated criteria. This type of thinking involves value judgments and beliefs. As the learners reflect, refine, and test their beliefs they become more able to defend them on factual grounds rather than on an emotional basis. In this way values and beliefs acquire additional meaning and significance. The student develops the ability to make value judgments, to act on the basis of hypothetical propositions, to test, prove, and seek new data if needed, and to prize values.

In developing children's thought processes, the teacher begins by providing data-collecting experiences from which concepts can be derived. Then the process moves to a higher level where learners practice analyzing and synthesizing data, evaluating and judging as required by the experience or problem, and then applying this knowledge in solving new problems. It is important that thinking abilities that call for musical skills are emphasized.

Cognitive Process Skills. In studying cognitive processes it quickly becomes apparent that there is a very large number of cognitive skills related to any discipline. Although some of the skills are related, many of them are quite distinct and need to be taught if students are to master the subject matter.

I. *Concept Formation.* Concept formation is the process through which data are collected and organized. It is the necessary foundation for formulating generalizations, and is basic to other cognitive processes as well.

    A. Identifying and enumerating through use of the five senses musical characteristics such as pitch, rhythm, harmony, and instrumentation. (Through such activities students learn to identify, list, examine, and compare.)

    B. Grouping in accordance with common qualities, uses, and other characteristics. For example, type of chords, even and uneven meters, types of phrases, and classifications of instruments.

    C. Discriminating between the common features of these groups and the unique features of individual items within the group. For example, comparing and contrasting the meters of 3/4, 4/4, and 5/4.

II. *Interpreting Data and Generalizing.* After data have been assembled and ordered and an understanding of the relevant concepts has been achieved, it is possible to relate concepts and use them to form generalizations.

    A. Examining the same aspect of music in several different compositions. *Example:* What are the outstanding rhythm patterns in each of these songs?

    B. Comparing the same aspect of music in several different compositions. *Example:* Compare these rhythm patterns: How are they the same; how are they different?

    C. Generalizing. *Example*: This type of song tends to have a rhythm pattern characteristic of what country?

    D. Explaining. *Example*: The characteristic rhythm pattern is the result of each song's relationship to the same national dance.

III. *Application of Data, Concepts, and Generalizations.* Concepts and generalizations can be used for:

    A. Comparing objects, performances, activities, or phenomena. *Example:* What things do a stage play and an opera have in common? A ballet and a musical comedy?

    B. Predicting possibilities. *Example:* What would composers do differently if there were no woodwinds in symphony orchestras? If there were no percussion section? What would happen if there were no symbols to depict accidentals in music?

C. Supporting predictions. *Example*: What evidence can you give that the percussion section is important? How do you know that it would not sound better if all accidentals were abandoned?

D. Verifying. *Example*: How can we find out if instrumental music in Asia includes woodwinds? What makes you say that drums in Africa are more important than drums in Western classical music? Where can we find evidence to support your answers?

Psychomotor Skills

The term *psychomotor* unites mind and movement; it describes mental processes that result in movements, including musical performance. Psychomotor activities begin with a perception that calls for a physical action, followed by a *set*, which implies a readiness to act, and end with an observable physical action. Among the types of psychomotor skills are learned responses of habitual nature, more complex overt responses such as the automatic fingering on an instrument, the refinements of motions that result in adaptations or improvements, and finally, the ability to originate or develop new skills.

Motor skills can be evaluated in terms of observable performance. Class objectives based on musical behaviors may refer to individual or group performances, or other body movements. Checklists and rating scales can be used as criteria to evaluate the performance of individuals. Evaluation can focus on rhythmic skills, instrumental performance, vocal performance, improvisation skills, and conducting skills.

If students are to engage successfully in music learning activities they need to become involved in a variety of psychomotor musical skills that will assist them in their growing understanding of music. Appropriate objectives should be constructed for the following types of motor skills:

1. *Moving to music.* The most universal response to music is physical movement. Students learn about music by moving their bodies to its salient characteristics as they listen to it. They need to experiment with free interpretation, characterization, dramatization, fundamental movements, singing games, and dances.

2. *Singing.* Singing is one of the most satisfying of human activities. Students need to be able to sing on pitch with a tone quality suitable to the meaning of the words they sing. By the time they leave the elementary school they should possess the ability to sing independent parts of songs such as rounds, chants, and descants, the skills that build the foundation for harmonic part singing.

3. *Playing instruments.* Students ordinarily find great pleasure in playing instruments. Performing on pitched and nonpitched percussion instruments or the recorder can contribute to their understanding of rhythm, pitch, form, dynamics, tempo, and melody. By chording on the autoharp, guitar, piano, or synthesizer, they learn about harmony and chord construction. Improvisation and composition are related skills.

Attitudes   Good curricular planning shows concern for feelings, attitudes, appreciations, and values. Teachers should avoid indoctrinating learners, but rather assist them in making judgments with increasing independence. Since such judgments are highly personal, the learner's position should not be challenged. When students are reacting positively to music they are finding satisfaction in the experience, and will normally want to hear more of the same. Since such personal responses are often covert, teachers' objectives are more difficult to construct. Such affective goals as appreciating, accepting, choosing, and liking are not directly observable. However, under each of these goals must be listed several specific instructional objectives that indicate what students will do to reveal that they appreciate, accept, choose, or like.

Five learning categories to use as guides when constructing affective objectives have been identified by Krathwohl, Bloom, and Masia in the *Taxonomy of Educational Objectives, Handbook II: Affective Domain* (1964). These categories are as follows:

1. *Receiving*. Lowest level: student is simply willing to pay attention to a stimulus in the environment. Little recognition of value or importance, but at least the stimulus is not ignored.

2. *Responding*. Next higher level of valuing: point at which student is willing to do as directed, to respond, such as completing an assignment, even though, as far as the student is concerned, there is no importance to the work.

3. *Valuing*. Third level: point at which most people recognize that values are being developed. Here the person finds merit or value in what is being done. He or she may even be drawn to it sufficiently to say that some commitment to it exists.

4. *Organizing*. As individuals develop values they find it necessary to determine their preferences for some values over others. This sorting out of preferences ultimately results in a system of values that becomes apparent to the individual, even though the preferences change over time. On a mundane level, the individual may prefer whole wheat bread to white. On an aesthetic level the person may prefer Bach to Brahms, and Beethoven to either of the others. Thus, a system of values is established.

5. *Generalized set*. Person has come to value something to the extent that it is generalized throughout that individual's life. Individual will say without hesitation that he or she is a music lover, a sports enthusiast, or a history buff. In many ways that trait characterizes the person.

Every day teachers have opportunities to deal with some of the levels of the affective domain. Because the highest level takes so much time to develop, teachers will only occasionally influence that level. But because of the power of attitudes in influencing behavior, teachers should devise ways for students to express appreciation, attitudes, and values. Several examples follow:

CATEGORY OF LEARNING	BEHAVIOR
Receiving	When the teacher is describing various families of musical instruments, students are clearly attentive.
Responding	After several successful experiences in accompanying with the autoharp, the student, at the teacher's suggestion, takes the instrument to a practice booth on his or her own time to work with an individualized learning task (job card).
Valuing	After attending a school concert of the local symphony orchestra, the student voluntarily writes to the conductor, urging him or her to bring the orchestra to the school again for another concert.
Organizing	When given the opportunity to choose to participate or not participate in several types of group activities, the student prefers to join a recorder group.
Generalized set	When the teacher becomes acquainted with the student, he or she is already known as the school musician because of intense involvement in musical activities of a wide variety over the preceding years.

Research indicates that children's attitudes regarding music may reflect the attitudes of the peer group, the family, and other important adults. Thus it is possible that a child's musical attitude can be affected by contradictory musical influences emanating from adults and peers, and from radio, television, and recordings. Given this variety of experience, music teachers should not expect that all students acquire the same musical values. The teacher's personal attitudes toward music may also affect the musical values of students as much as formal class presentations. Teachers should therefore work toward a classroom environment in which the varied opinions of students on the many different types of music are welcomed and discussed with interest. Such an environment permits disagreements that can be expressed in ways permitting personal differences and expanding student tolerance. An intellectually sound position for a teacher is one that attempts to judge music in accordance with how well it performs its function, and to operate in a climate of openness that explores every type of music.

The cognitive and affective aspects of what a person learns *cannot be separated*. The affective domain influences every part of the learning and evaluation process. Teachers should not emphasize the intellectual aspects of the music curriculum to the detriment of its aesthetic and affective aspects. The current emphasis on conceptual and structural learning is laudable, but those are verbal activities, not musical ones. The musical experience is aural in nature. Students may achieve much by studying musical concepts, but the study of music loses most of its value without the musical behaviors of composing, performing, and listening. Furthermore, *music is an aesthetic experience before it is an intellectual experience*, and competent teachers never forget this when planning music lessons.

Courtesy of the Music Educators National Conference, Reston, Va.

Creativity Creativity is the ability to organize components or elements in a way in which they have not been organized before, thus enhancing the value and beauty of the new product. Musical creativity can take many forms: improvisation, movement, composition, conducting, interpretation, and experiments with sounds and instrumentation. Teachers nurture creativity in their students by helping them develop skills and abilities that enable the children to bring these components together to form a satisfying product. When students are engaged in creative musical experiences, several goals are possible:

> Increasing interest and motivation in music.
> Developing musical imagination.

Experimenting, developing, and testing musical ideas.

Creating new musical sounds, forms, and interpretations.

Employing analytical thought processes to musical forms.

Creativity is not the same as general intelligence. It depends on many factors, including personality traits (e.g. self-confidence), the willingness to take risks, and spontaneity. Creative-exploratory objectives should encourage students to find new ways to experience music. (For numerous examples of such experiences see the material in this text on Dalcroze, Orff, and the Manhattanville Music Curriculum Project.)

In a creative-exploratory approach, students often begin with music familiar to them. Questions that cause them to analyze and explore the structure of known music provoke similar questions about new types of music as well. Questions such as the following might be directed to individuals:

What would these songs sound like if there were no sharps or flats? Let's try them and find out.

Try a new way to notate this song.

How are songs composed? Tell us how you do it.

How does notation control sound? How accurately do you think notation does this?

What would happen to this song if you kept the same pitches, but changed its rhythms?

These questions call for answers that learners discover rather than memorize. Students explore their own ideas by using a variety of musical media and instructional materials, and as they seek answers they make additional musical discoveries. Such involvement promotes the desire to learn form, style, and notation, to listen analytically, and to understand how music is constructed, rather than to simply identify isolated aspects of music. It leads to a positive attitude toward music. In such an approach, facts and skills are not neglected but are taught as tools of learning so that students progress to a stage where they can direct their own learning.

Assessment of musical creativity relies on the teacher's examination of the product (e.g., a graphic score or a taped performance), and observation of the children while they are engaged in the creative process. Neither of these evaluative efforts is as precise as a test score, but they are better suited to creative process, and they provide valuable information about the creative effort.

Summary   When complete, the curriculum consists of five major components: (1) musical content (information, concepts, generalizations), (2) cognitive process skills, (3) psychomotor skills, (4) attitudes, and (5) creative skills. When long-term goals and instructional objectives are clearly delineated, they implement learning in all these areas, and an effective and sequentially developed program results.

Motivation and Learning　Many psychologists have studied motivation, and as a result, varied approaches to motivation have been developed. These psychologists have identified several factors that play critical roles in motivation and cannot be ignored if students are to be correctly motivated in the classroom. For example, all human beings need to experience success, and they tend to avoid situations in which they are likely to fail. Music programs, therefore, need to be organized in such a way that the students recognize they are likely to succeed. A second important principle pertains to the content of the music program. If students are to be motivated, the curriculum needs to be built around materials that they find important or desirable, or at the very least, materials that seem to have the potential to be valuable in the future. These are two critical principles of motivation: First, there needs to be a clear possibility of achieving success in the class, and second, the student must want to succeed in mastering the material.

Teachers can obviously arrange the learning environment so that students can succeed. This is done by selecting materials of appropriate difficulty, breaking musical tasks down into units of manageable size, and organizing and presenting the materials so that the students possess the requisite skills to begin each task. Much of a good teacher's curricular planning is based on these critical factors.

If the student has no interest in succeeding, even when it is clearly possible to succeed, the teacher may employ two kinds of motivation, *intrinsic* and *extrinsic*. In intrinsic motivation the student finds value or delight in the activity itself. It is something he or she wants to do. Remarks such as "Gee, Ms. Jones, that was fun," or "When can we do that again?" indicate that the students like what they are doing. The activity has intrinsic worth. The students do it because they like to do it. The key to such intrinsic motivation lies in the nature of the activity. Some activities are of recognizable quality, designed by a teacher with the skill to present something of worth. Other activities show little imagination, little effort, little thought. They are recognized as drudgery. To capitalize on the powerful effects of intrinsic motivation the teacher must constantly strive to develop activities of genuine value. When that is accomplished, many motivational problems will never occur. The students will be too busy doing the activity and enjoying it.

But even with the best of efforts, some students may not find the activity rewarding. At least, it does not seem as rewarding as a number of other things they could do. In such cases the teacher must resort to extrinsic motivation, connecting the activity with something the students do want. Many extrinsic motivators are available, such as good grades, privileges, follow-up activities of a desirable nature, some kind of tangible reward for good work, and not to be overlooked, trust in the teacher that staying with the task will indeed bring appropriate rewards later. These extrinsic motivators are used by successful teachers repeatedly.

The ultimate goal is, of course, to bring all students to the point that intrinsic motivation dominates everything they do. That goal is unlikely to be achieved. Many students continue to rely on extrinsic rewards throughout their schooling. But in good music programs they find intrinsic value in an increasing number of their activities, and discover new abilities as a result.

Questions: A Strategy for Learning

The term *question* can be used to describe any intellectual stimulus that calls for a response. Questions have always had a prominent place in pedagogy, ranging from the solicitation of simple factual answers to responses that involve sophisticated types of thinking such as analysis, synthesis, or extrapolation. Research substantiates the fact that the type of questions employed in any learning situation by either the teacher or the students affects the student's ability to think. In preparing questions for use in the classroom, the teacher should focus on a variety of question types designed to involve different cognitive processes. (See "Cognitive Process Skills," earlier in this chapter.) In any classroom, questions form some of the most important stimuli that motivate learning. Students need repeated practice in developing the skills of asking and responding appropriately to the varied types of questions that stimulate independent inquiry.

Different kinds of questions can be useful with very young children, slow learners, and average and gifted learners. Teachers should not assume that special learners should be asked only simple data-level questions and that advanced students be asked only high-level process questions.

Teachers need to construct key questions and sequence them prior to use with a lesson or an activity. An attempt should be made to attain a proper balance of questions relating to Bloom's various levels of cognition even though none of the levels is completely independent of the others.

When asking questions, the teacher needs to be alert to the following issues:

1. The type of thinking the question stimulates shapes the type of response the teacher gets. Some students may respond to a simple data question with high-level thought processes, giving an answer that was not anticipated.
2. Virtually all types of questions can be useful at all stages of mental maturity. The more mature and gifted students can respond to questions requiring a greater measure of abstract thinking.
3. Questions must be planned and written out in advance so the teacher can involve each student at his or her operational level of thinking.
4. Adequate time is necessary for students to answer questions that call for interpretation, analysis, and application. Higher level thinking requires time, and if insufficient time is provided, students can become frustrated. The teacher's silence is a powerful motivator for thought when used with discretion and at the appropriate time.
5. If the student was not paying attention when the question was asked, or does not understand it, the question should be repeated without calling attention to the student. It may be helpful to alter the question so the student's chances of answering correctly are increased.

Some General Principles of Learning

Any discussion of the teaching of music requires attention to contemporary theories of learning. Today's teachers need appropriate principles for guiding their students' intellectual development. These principles should not attempt to involve students in learning for which they have insufficient background, nor should learning be delayed past the optimum time for students to master it. An understanding of the principles of learning is invaluable when used as criteria for forming a personal philosophy, identifying goals and objectives, selecting types and levels of difficulty in materials of instruction, planning programs, lessons, and activities, selecting teaching strategies, and choosing means of evaluation. Each of these aspects should be constantly examined, and made compatible with the following principles:

1. *Following correct procedures for course preparation and curriculum development.*

Students understand in advance what is to be learned, how it is to be learned, and how the learning will be evaluated.

Teachers develop attainable goals for their students.

Teachers plan for conceptual learning through the use of high-level thought processes.

Teachers prepare materials so that student learning progresses from the concrete to the abstract.

Musical concepts are presented in a rational sequence.

2. *Promoting student motivation.*

Students find satisfaction and relevance in what they are doing, and are therefore intrinsically motivated.

Students are personally involved in what is to be learned, discovering functional applications for the newly learned knowledge, skills, and procedures.

Students have musical experiences in which they are regularly successful.

3. *Determining appropriate levels of instruction.*

Musical activities are selected based on the students' physical, intellectual, and social maturity.

There is a planned sequential, but flexible program of music instruction from level to level.

4. *Maintaining a threat-free atmosphere.*

Teachers have obvious confidence in the students' abilities to learn music, and convey that attitude to all students.

Learners are free to explore, discover, question, and profit from making mistakes.

Students experience wholesome social and emotional relationships with their peers and with their teachers.

Teachers do not connect musical activities with threats or punishment.

Teachers encourage students to explore and experiment on their own, and know when to intercede and facilitate learning.

5. *Using approaches with sufficient variety.*

Teachers employ a variety of activities and materials for individual, small-group, and large-group activities.

Classroom environments are flexible and varied.

Students experience music through a combination of senses: hearing, seeing, touching, and using body muscles for musical activities.

Students learn about music through discovery and exploration more frequently than through rote learning.

6. *Functioning as a facilitator of learning.*

Teachers arrange for musical problems to be solved by the students.

Teachers present new situations and stimuli, encouraging students to apply skills acquired earlier under different circumstances.

Teachers plan activities in which children can be successful, in which they are interested, and through which they can progress in reaching musical goals.

Students are assisted in discovering what they already know about music, and in associating these concepts with new ones.

Teachers use feedback and positive reinforcement to verify progress and correct errors.

Students have good models with which to identify, whether other children, parents, teachers, or other adults.

Teachers keep talking to a minimum, music making to a maximum.

7. *Accommodating different learning styles.*

Teacher planning takes into account that students have different abilities, learn in different ways, and are at different stages of mental growth. These different aptitudes, learning styles, and levels of proficiency are recognized and accommodated.

Students work in both structured and open, creative classroom environments.

Democratic and autocratic teaching methods are used at times appropriate to what is being taught.

Students' growing skills for learning music make possible their becoming independent learners.

Child Development and Music

Understanding how children develop is one key to becoming a competent teacher. Children learn as complete personalities. They are the product of everything that has happened to them in the past and of everything that is presently happening to them. When teachers understand how children grow and learn, they find ways to span the gap between the learner and the subject matter of music. The problem of the teacher's knowing the subject but failing to know the child is a very old one. It has affected all levels of learning. A persistent problem for teachers and curriculum planners is how to plan instruction based on both knowledge of subject matter *and* on knowledge of how children learn.

Cognitive-Interactionist Theory

Developmental psychologists state that children's behavior changes and develops as they interact with their environments. The study of such interactions has grown into a field of study known as cognitive-interactionist psychology. Adults can serve as facilitators, guides, questioners, observers, and planners—in other words, interacting with children. The learner is viewed as being dependent on both external and internal stimulation for learning.

Early research by Arnold L. Gesell identified developmental characteristics by age level. J. McVickar Hunt described the developmental process in somewhat different terms. Research by Jean Piaget described stages or levels of human development that have been widely accepted by teachers who want to understand more fully children's varied learning capacities. Jerome Bruner conducted in-depth research on cognitive processes. Most of his theories also suggest stages of development, each carrying with it embryonic elements of the succeeding stage.

J. McVickar Hunt*

J. McVickar Hunt wrote in *Intelligence and Experience* in 1961, "It is no longer unreasonable to consider that it might be feasible to discover ways to govern encounters that children have with their environments, especially during the early years of their development, to achieve a substantially faster rate of intellectual development and a substantially higher adult level of intellectual capacity." Implications from Hunt's studies are impressive:

1. Because the most rapid growth of intellectual development takes place before age 8, both enriched home environments and earlier schooling should be considered.
2. Intelligence is not fixed. Although heredity sets limits, the environment governs to what extent those limits are reached.
3. Children whose environment is lacking in various enrichments may be handicapped throughout life; children whose home enrichment is intellectually stimulating are very likely to do well in the classroom.
4. The greatest need for an enriched environment, including good nutrition, is during the early years of rapid growth.

Hunt's well-known *problem of the match* poses a task for teachers in which they are to diagnose the child's level of performance, then plan and present challenging new experiences only slightly more difficult than had been accommodated at that performance level. This is the "match." By relating these new experiences to earlier ones, and continuing the process of the match, children advance in their learning as they make new generalizations, and build concepts that incorporate both the old and the new information.

*The discussions on J. McVickar Hunt and Jerome Bruner are drawn from Vernice Trousdale Nye, *Music for Young Children*, 3rd ed. 1975, 1979, 1983 Wm. C. Brown Publishers, Dubuque, Iowa. All rights reserved. Reprinted by permission.

Jean Piaget   Jean Piaget (1895–1980), a Swiss-born biologist, has emerged as a dominant figure in today's early childhood education. He was a leading advocate of the cognitive-development theory. According to Piaget, intelligence has a biological base, in that all organisms respond and adjust in relation to environmental stimuli. This interaction with the environment takes place on both physical and mental levels. In common with other cognitive psychologists, Piaget believed that humans are endowed with an intuitive urge to learn. His theories center primarily on the nature and development of cognition, a process in which an individual cannot be given knowledge, but must obtain it through personal discovery. This discovery occurs best in an environment rich in appropriate encounters where learning is not rushed or forced.

Piaget engaged in extensive observation of very young children, following their development from birth through early adulthood. From these observations his stages of intellectual development evolved.

Piaget's Stages of Cognitive Development   The following stages are an outgrowth of Piaget's cognitive development theory, in which he emphasized that all organisms adjust and respond in relation to environmental stimuli. This interaction with the environment influences both physical and mental development.

Sensorimotor or Preverbal Stage—Birth to Age 2. This period is marked by major developments in the use of the perceptual senses and motor activities involving many body parts. During this span of time children engage in numerous interactions with objects, situations, and people in their immediate environment through use of the senses: They listen, look, smell, taste, touch, grasp, pound, manipulate, suck, and experiment with objects. Thus their evolving mental structures are altered to accommodate the new data. At this stage, infants' thinking centers around their sensory and psychomotor behaviors. They are usually unable to use representational thought processes, and of necessity must act out what is contained in their minds. The sensorimotor stage occurs prior to use of formalized language development.

Preoperational Stage—Approximately Ages 2 to 7. In this period of development the child is rapidly acquiring powers of speech, important both for communication and for the formulation of concepts, many of which are at first faulty. The child does not yet have the ability to use language for other than simple mental operations. During the preoperational years the child must span the gap between the sensorimotor activities of the infant and the internal mental activities of the school-aged child. Increasingly refined language and mental images are gradually substituted for the sensorimotor activities of infancy. For example, instead of simply reaching, things are requested. The mother is thought of even though she is not visible. Make-believe play and dramatic movement are very important because through them children are assimilating symbolically the experiences, roles, and ideas of their immediate environment. Through imitation young children are able to accommodate different experiences, thus expanding their understanding.

This phase of development is designated as preoperational because most children are unable to engage in abstract mental operations. Characteristic of most children at this level is their inability to combine parts into a whole, to arrange parts in different ways, and to reverse operations or processes. Some children can begin to classify objects with obviously common attributes. They also begin to place things in a series. Mental pictures or symbolic representations are being formed. Children usually function intuitively, not logically, based on their immediate experience and perception. Symbols are used to represent objects, and labels and names are acquired for experiences, a type of concept formation.

Concrete Operations Stage—Approximately Ages 7 to 11. The term *concrete operations* means that children can now think about objects or their representations. At the beginning of this stage the child is able to perform mental operations as long as they are limited to concrete or tangible aspects of life. Most children can extend, subdivide, differentiate, serialize, or combine existing structures. They have the ability, for example, to work with rhythms in a meter when they are presented on a graph, chart, or other visual aid. Children will not, however, have the ability to discuss rhythms and meters in the abstract.

As children acquire new knowledge, and then accommodate or adjust their mental structures to the new knowledge, thinking processes are altered. Even though most children at this stage of cognition can usually employ logic, their thinking has its basis in the concrete rather than the abstract. The mental ability necessary for the combining of various elements is developed usually toward the end of this stage. Learners discover that they can combine parts of a whole in many different ways and still not alter the total. They learn to classify, order, number, use concepts of space and time, conservation, and reversibility, and discriminate in increasing degrees of exactness.

Formal Operations Stage—Approximately Ages 11 to 15. In this last of Piaget's developmental stages the child acquires the ability for abstract reasoning. This ability usually appears in early adolescence. Children can now reason on the basis of hypotheses and other abstractions, not just on the basis of tangible objects or the concrete. For example, such activities as deductive reasoning and extrapolation are possible. Children construct new mental operations, attain new mental structures, and develop relationships between and among ideas. In other words, learners are engaged in operations, which means they are capable of thinking about and analyzing the thoughts of others, and they can identify variables in problems and analyze them critically. This is the highest level of intellectual thought.

Piaget states that the principal goal of education is to help people become capable of doing new things—to become creative and inventive. His second goal of education is to help people develop minds that examine things critically, verify information and conclusions, and do not accept things without question. This mental independence is a badly needed ability in today's society, especially with its slogans, sound bite, and commercial promotions of virtually all aspects of human endeavor.

Jerome Bruner　　Like Piaget, Bruner (b. 1915) theorizes that children have an innate urge to learn and that learning can be its own reward. He stresses the power of spontaneous learning that supplies reinforcement in its own activities. The goal of teaching is to promote the general understanding of a subject matter. Bruner would have the child comprehend the structure (conceptual organization) of music in order to relate its parts to the whole and to each other, because learning based on structure has meaning and therefore is remembered. In other words, the student must understand the subject of music, including all of the related parts that comprise its structure.

Structure consists of organized concepts and generalizations that collectively define a subject area. The structure of music as a subject of study may be organized several ways, but it is often organized around the elements that comprise music: dynamics, duration (rhythm), pitch (melody, harmony, polyphony), and tone quality (timbre). If these concepts are selected for the organizational basis of the class, research indicates that the teacher needs to organize a logical sequence of experiences for mastering them.

A program organized in a logical, sequential format provides continuity of experiences. In pre-primary and primary grades the music program is often a random assortment of unrelated activities. Even though students are exposed to a variety of experiences in this type of situation, they may not perceive the structure of music or its methods of inquiry. In a sequentially developed program, students should explore data and develop concepts commensurate with their operational levels and learning styles. When students learn the component parts of music in relation to a meaningful structure, musical content is more readily understood and its details remembered for longer periods of time. As students perceive structure, it becomes possible for them to conserve and transfer knowledge from one learning experience to another.

Bruner formulated a theory of instruction that has become popular with many music educators. His theory consists of four parts adapted here to relate to music.

1. *Motivation.* Motivation originates from within the individual and nurtures the urge to learn. It is composed of the desire for proficiency as well as the need to associate with others.

    Children's interest in music is enhanced when they are aware of the class goals and are involved in relevant musical experiences.
2. *Structure.* Musical concepts can be introduced to the child at the child's cognitive level. The structure of the body of musical knowledge can also be learned by young children when adapted to their level of cognitive development. Bruner presents three levels of development.

    a. *Enactive representation level.* The young child learns music best through action and the senses—touching and manipulating, visually examining, counting, playing musical instruments, using the body and its muscles in rhythmic interpretations, chanting and singing, and creating music.
    b. *Iconic representation level.* Young children conceptualize at the iconic (image) level. They learn music from imitating sounds, moods, movements of animals, people, machines, and plants. Simple graphic icons may be used to represent the order and nature of musical sounds.

c. *Symbolic representation level.* The child at this stage is able to use language to explain experiences. Words can be used to represent songs, rhymes, poems, and to describe musical experiences. Children can use simple standard notational symbols at this stage.

3. *Sequence.* Musical percepts, concepts, and skills should be taught in sequence. Bruner suggests that teachers begin with enactive representation if possible and move progressively up to the symbolic. Children would first be actively involved in music making prior to the use of words to explain the learning experience.

4. *Reinforcement.* Teachers must encourage and reinforce children's musical efforts. Children need to know of their progress in order to advance to increasingly higher levels of performance. Feedback should be precise and timely. If feedback is given prematurely it hampers learning; if too late, its power is lost.

Bruner's major point of emphasis is on discovery learning. Most young children come to school with an interest in music. They want to become actively involved in experimenting with musical concepts and skills. Children's spontaneous, original, and creative activity is directed from within and holds relevance and purpose for them as learners. Concepts experienced for themselves in a discovery-exploratory environment are readily retained and used to learn higher level concepts than those learned through rote learning. Although the discovery method is not the only instructional method, the teacher can use discovery skills to create an exciting and interesting environment for learning music.

According to Bruner, language is a major factor in young children's cognitive development. Research indicates that children's cognitive understandings are significantly improved when correct labels are supplied to objects and activities at the appropriate time by the teacher. Children can sort instruments by size, color, and shape, such as triangle, round, and rectangle. As they listen to musical recordings or sing songs, they need to be involved in follow-up discussions about how the music made them want to move; how different sounds can be made on instruments; or how one instrument, one song, or one recording can be compared with another, noting likenesses and differences.

Children need guidance in using words in different contexts and for various purposes. That language usage correlates highly with children's maturational levels is a widely accepted fact. It is also believed that the stimulation supplied by home, school, peers, and community increases the quantity and quality of language and music. A summary of these principles should include the following points.

1. Children's behaviors change and develop as they interact freely with their environments.
2. The role of the teacher/adult is that of a facilitator, guide, questioner, observer, analyzer, and environment planner.
3. Children possess an intuitive urge to learn and are responsive to external stimulation.
4. Children learn best through personal discovery and process learning.
5. Conceptual learning is basic to the development of intellectual thought.
6. Learning should not be rushed or forced.

Many psychologists, educators, and scientists are pursuing research associated
with the functions and operations of the brain. Much interest has been shown in
the hypothesis that the two hemispheres of the brain perform unique functions.
Data concerning ways in which the brain processes perceptual information and
how the brain controls and affects memory and motivation have stimulated increased interest in the biological and neurological structure of the brain and the
entire neurological system.

Early research caused some to conclude that the right hemisphere of the
brain controlled creativity and that rationality was dominated by the left hemisphere. This differentiation was later found to be incorrect. More recently re-
searchers report that while the two hemispheres have different perceptual
functions, both are engaged in learning music and art. Both are involved in
thinking and organized reasoning. It is clear that there are individual variances
in the way students use the brain, thus implying different learning styles. Ultimately, an individual's highest achievements result from using the complete
powers of both hemispheres. This promising field of research is in its infancy,
but it will assist educators to better understand the mental processes of learners.

In other fields of psychological research the child's mental development is
attributed to a combination of genetic endowment, cultural influences, and life-
style, especially that of the family. Today's psychologists contend that development is not as fixed or orderly as presumed in the past. The concept that the
pace of child development varies is extremely important to teachers. Children
may learn at different rates and use different styles of learning for many reasons. First, they inherit different physiological characteristics. Second, children
develop different styles of learning. In fact, as many as seven characteristics of
learning style have been identified (Letteri, 1985). Furthermore, attitudes
toward learning, and the amount learned are related to the physical, intellectual,
and social stimulation in the child's life. Finally, learning is influenced by the
amount of positive emotional support a child receives as well as the amount of
threat and alienation experienced (Calabrese, 1987).

Learning is viewed as a long, cumulative process, not a response to a small
number of learning encounters. The brain is perceived as a growing and developing organ that is influenced by both environmental experiences and heredity.
This research is bringing to light data that are expanding present-day knowledge
about the unique functioning of the brain. Benjamin Bloom emphasizes the importance of building programs and using teaching methods that stress individual
learning styles, giving more emphasis to school organizational practices that
provide for these styles. As we showed earlier, both Piaget and Bruner, along
with many other authorities, believe that students learn in different ways at different stages. For example, Erik Erikson (1963) established his well-known
Eight Ages of Man, in which eight identity crises must be resolved correctly for
a healthy personality to develop.

Other psychological studies have included another interesting line of investigation. Howard Gardner (1983) presents strong arguments for defining intelligence as a number of independent, and only somewhat related, abilities. He
presents interesting evidence that the traditional IQ score ignores several criti-

cal human capacities and focuses unduly on a cognitive variable of rather narrow scope. He then postulates a number of these independent intelligences, including linguistic, musical, logical-mathematical, spatial, bodily kinesthetic, and personal. Mary Louise Serafine (1988) takes this concept a step further. She develops a case for a variety of cognitive processes that are unique to music: some generic to all musical styles and others specific to one or another musical style. Her discussion identifies ways humans think in musical sounds, and how they process musical information without having to rely on any kind of verbal discourse.

Developmental Characteristics of Children

Developmental charts, despite their lack of universality, are useful as guides for teachers. By knowing general norms, a teacher can judge whether or not a child of a certain age is performing to the norm, or if he or she is performing higher or lower than the norm would indicate. Child development consists of mental, social, emotional, and physical growth. Any child can be above or below the norm for any one of these characteristics. Knowing this, teachers can plan for children's education on an appropriate level.

The general norms stated here are descriptions of human development. They are not limitations or prescriptions, and may be expanded or altered. They may serve as a basis for analyzing a child's level of growth and maturity and as one guide for diagnosing and organizing music curricula and daily lesson plans.

Ages 3 to 5 (Early Childhood).   Children are constantly physically active; their large muscles are better developed than their small muscles. Right- or left-handedness becomes apparent. Speech skills are little developed, although both language and speech are improving rapidly; soft palates make pronunciation and enunciation difficult for most. Teeth and bony structures grow and change. Vigorous action results in fatigue.

Most children are affectionate, and sometimes aggressive. Attention spans are relatively short. Some youngsters are shy and limited in expressing their ideas and feelings. This age group is usually very individualistic and self-centered. Emotions are intense, with brief extremes of happiness and anger. Little understanding of ownership is exhibited. Repetitious activity affords security. Children desire to be accepted by adults, from whom they seek warmth, security, and individual attention. At the same time they are beginning to develop initial independence from adults.

Cooperative play takes place in small groups. Most learning is nonverbal. Children are very inquisitive about surroundings, eager to learn, and alert. Their learning takes place primarily through sensorimotor experiences and role playing. They are interested in the "here and now," and "what for," and in realizing immediate goals. Their world is one of make-believe and imitation. Creativity, spontaneity, and naturalness are observable behaviors.

Voices are small. Rhythmic response is primary. The sense of musical pitch is often undeveloped. The harmonic sense is nearly nonexistent.

Ages 6 to 8 (Grades 1–3, Primary Level).   At age 6, eye-hand coordination is often poorly synchronized. Large muscles are still more developed than small muscles. Children tend to move with the entire body as a unit. At age 7

Photo by Juretta Nidever.

the heart grows rapidly, though muscular development is uneven; motor skills are steadily improving. Eye-hand coordination improves as attention span increases. Six-year-olds are extremely active, and they become easily fatigued. Children may alternate between very active and quiet behavior. Eyes of 6-year-olds are not ready for long periods of close work. Eyes of 7-year-olds are better developed. Missing front teeth make perfect pronunciation and diction difficult.

Students are eager to learn. They acquire a rudimentary understanding of time, space, and money values. Their learning takes place through the use of concrete materials and through psychomotor activity, especially with adult supervision. Their perception of the abstract is limited. The concepts of right and wrong ways of doing things increase in importance. They are highly imaginative and imitative. Curiosity about their environment is characteristic—they enjoy sounds and sound effects.

Youngsters of this age may be highly competitive, and sometimes aggressive, egotistical, or uncooperative. They need encouragement, acceptance, and praise from adults. Group activities increase in popularity. Interests of boys and girls may diverge.

Some children are still unable to sing in tune; most voices are light in quality, with a variety of ranges. The overlapping ranges permit five or six consecutive pitches to be sung by the large majority of students in unison singing (middle C to G or A above). Rhythmic response becomes more involved as simultaneous movements are possible. Harmonic awareness begins to develop in 8-year-olds.

Ages 9 to 11 (Grades 4–6; Intermediate/Preadolescence). As slow steady growth occurs, coordination improves with better control of small muscles of the body, hands, feet, and eyes. Because of rapid growth, students may appear listless at times, but are generally active. They express more interest than before in detailed, intricate work. Girls are more mature than boys. Posture needs attention.

Students are interested in anything new to them, including imaginary adventure. They enjoy humor and may be silly, giggling spontaneously. As their attention spans extend, they are eager to expand their knowledge, and are inquisitive about scientific facts and theories, including time and number concepts. Skills of communication and reading develop, along with an expanded vocabulary. An increasing number of individual differences and abilities appear; a wide range of reading abilities is evident. Increased awareness of a larger world and the contributions of past and present-day cultures affect perceptions. Students are increasingly conscious of what is right and what is wrong. They want to do things correctly, and seek help on specific skills and on mastering information. Their learning continues through use of varied and concrete materials and through active participation under supervision. Students develop independence and improved work-study habits as interest in activities that hold meaning and purpose becomes more intense. The desire to follow leadership of others is also present.

Children need encouragement, acceptance, and positive reinforcement from both peers and teachers. They desire the approval and understanding of adults even though they are attempting to become more independent of them. Awareness of adult role models develops, as students are attracted to those who possess humor, understanding, and warmth. At the same time individuals seek to conform to the standards of peers who are becoming increasingly important. Improved cooperation takes place in groups. This is a time for close friendships and group activities. Along with peer identification, preadolescents begin to develop a sense of self-importance and identity. They may become critical, unpredictable, and defiant. Their sense of self may lead to a need for more privacy. Teasing and hostility sometimes exist between boys and girls. Adultlike behavior may be mixed with childlike behavior. Youngsters begin to display characteristics that will continue into adulthood.

Vocal cords and lungs are developing rapidly. More control of voice and of breathing is possible. The singing voice gradually improves in quality, range, and dependability. Some sixth grade boys may experience the initial stage of voice change. Improved coordination makes more complex rhythmic responses and body movements such as folk dancing possible. It is now appropriate to begin instruction on a musical instrument because of better control of small muscles and muscular dexterity. The harmonic sense is not well developed, but improves rapidly during this period.

The following MENC chart (1986) identifies appropriate musical activities for each of the age groups previously described. It was designed to assist in identifying appropriate musical activities for each grade. It is not intended to be all-inclusive or prescriptive in nature, but rather to provide suggestions for appropriate musical experiences for children in elementary schools.

Music Experiences for Four- and Five-Year-Old Children

Four- and five-year-old children are becoming socially conscious. Appropriate music-making experiences include group activities such as singing and playing song games and playing classroom instruments. Many opportunities for individual exploration of voice, body, nature, and instrument sounds should also be included. Movement is the most effective means for children of this age to describe their musical experiences. They enjoy playing with ideas, movements, language, and sounds. Music activities that allow opportunities for free exploration provide the most positive foundation for creative musical growth later.

Ages 4–5. By the completion of kindergarten children are able to:

Performing/Reading

Utilize the singing voice, as distinct from the speaking voice

Match pitches and sing in tune within their own ranges most of the time

Show an awareness of beat, tempo (e.g., fast-slow), dynamics (e.g., loud-soft), pitch (e.g., high-low), and similar and different phrases through movement and through playing classroom instruments

Enjoy singing nonsense songs, folk songs, and song games

Utilize pictures, geometric shapes, and other symbols to represent pitch, durational patterns, and simple forms

Creating

Explore sound patterns on classroom instruments

Improvise songs spontaneously during many classroom and playtime activities

Complete "answers" to unfinished melodic phrases by singing or playing instruments

Express ideas or moods using instruments and environmental or body sounds

Valuing

By the completion of kindergarten, children:

Demonstrate an awareness of music as a part of everyday life

Enjoy singing, moving to music, and playing instruments alone and with others

Respect music and musicians

Listening/Describing

Give attention to short musical selections

Listen attentively to an expanded repertoire of music

Respond to musical elements (e.g., pitch, duration, loudness) and musical styles (e.g., march, lullaby) through movement or through playing classroom instruments

Describe with movement or language similarities and differences in music such as loud-soft, fast-slow, up-down-same, smooth-jumpy, short-long, and similar-contrasting

Classify classroom instruments and some traditional instruments by shape, size, pitch, and tone quality

Use a simple vocabulary of music terms to describe sounds

Subject Matter Achievements for Grades 1–3

The primary school years are a time of growth, wonder, excitement, exploration, and discovery. These years are crucial as the child develops a concept of music, gains fundamental skills, and acquires a sensitivity to musical sounds and their beauty. All children need to have regular and continuing musical experiences that lead to satisfaction through success in producing musical sounds, using them enjoyably, and responding to them with pleasure.

Grades 1–3. By the completion of the third grade, students are able to:

Performing/Reading

Sing in tune alone or with a group using a clear, free tone

Sing from memory a repertoire of folk and composed songs

Sing with appropriate musical expression

Respond to the beat in music by clapping, walking, running, or skipping

Play simple pitch patterns on melodic instruments such as bells or xylophones

Play simple rhythmic patterns on classroom percussion instruments to accompany songs and rhythm activities

Sing a simple ostinato with a familiar song

Sing a part in a round while maintaining a steady tempo

Interpret the basic notational symbols for rhythm patterns, including quarter, eighth, and half notes and rests, by engaging in appropriate movement, such as clapping or walking, playing on classroom instruments, or chanting

Recognize the basic features (e.g., form, melodic contour, expressive qualities) of unfamiliar songs by studying their notation

Use correct notational symbols for pitch and expression

Use a system (e.g., syllables, numbers, letters) for reading notation

Creating

Create "answers" to unfinished melodic phrases by singing or playing on classroom instruments

Create short melodic patterns on classroom instruments or by singing

Improvise songs and accompaniments to physical movement using classroom instruments

Create short pieces consisting of nontraditional sounds available in the classroom or with the body (e.g., snapping fingers, rubbing fingers on a table top)

Create, in class, new stanzas to familiar melodies

Dramatize songs and stories

Valuing

By the completion of grade 3, students:

Realize that music is an important part of everyday life

Feel a sense of respect for music and its performance and creation

Display a sense of enjoyment when participating in music

Use music as a means of personal expression

Listening/Describing

Recognize aurally the difference between long and short sounds, repeated and contrasting phrases, slow and fast tempos, duple and triple meters, major and minor modes, and other contrasting sound patterns

Indicate aural recognition of high and low pitches by making directional hand movements that follow the pitch of a melodic line

Recognize aurally the timbre of basic wind, string, and percussion instruments

Describe in simple terms the stylistic characteristics of some of the music they listen to

Use musical terms and concepts to express thoughts about music (e.g., loud, short, high, melody, rhythm)

Use hand motions and other body movements or graphic designs to indicate how portions of a musical work sound

Identify the patterns of simple forms (e.g., AB, ABA)

Subject Matter Achievements for Grades 4–6

Students in grades 4–6 continue to develop many of the skills, understandings, and values that were introduced in the earlier grades while adding many more. It may appear that there are similarities between the objectives of music instruction in grades 1–3 and grades 4–6. There are, however, sizable differences in the nature and quality of the learning. The main difference lies in the greater accuracy, facility, clarity, and ease of learning that should be evident in grades 4–6.

Grades 4–6. By the completion of the grade 6, students are able to:

Performing/Reading

Sing songs accurately and independently, reflecting an understanding of tonal and rhythmic elements

Control their voices in order to produce the desired musical quality to communicate expressive intent

Perform basic tonal patterns, rhythm patterns, and simple songs on recorder, keyboard, electronic synthesizer, and other classroom instruments

Provide choral accompaniments with instruments such as guitar and Autoharp-type instruments

Conduct songs in 2-, 3-, and 4-beat meter

Sing one part alone or in a small group while others sing contrasting parts

Sing harmonizing parts in thirds and sixths

Perform simple accompaniments by ear

Recognize tonal and rhythm patterns and musical forms from examining the notation

Continue the use of a systematic approach to music reading

Demonstrate growth in the ability to sing or play music from notation

Creating

Make thoughtful alterations and variations in existing songs

Improvise simple ostinato-like accompaniments on pitched instruments

Improvise rhythmic accompaniments for songs

Create simple descants, introductions, and codas

Experiment with variations in tempo, timbre, dynamics, and phrasing for expressive purposes

Utilize diverse sound sources, including electronic, when improvising or composing

Valuing

By the completion of grade 6, students:

Demonstrate an increased awareness of music as an important part of everyday life

Participate in music through singing and playing instruments

Enjoy listening to most types of music

Discuss personal responses to works of art

Describe the musical phenomena on which their observations are based

Listening/Describing

Listen to and demonstrate an understanding of rhythm by responding physically or with the use of instruments

Notate correctly simple pitch and rhythm patterns presented aurally

Identify by listening a basic repertoire of standard orchestral and vocal compositions

Use correct terminology to discuss the characteristics of a work, including melody, rhythm, meter, key, form, expressive qualities, and style

Discuss in their own words the qualities of a work of music

Identify by listening: most orchestral instruments and classifications of voices; formal patterns such as AB, ABA, rondo, and theme and variations; salient musical features such as tempo, dynamic level, major and minor modes, meter, counterpoint; and types of music (e.g., electronic, folk, orchestral, jazz, choral)

Used with permission: Music Educators National Conference. Reston, VA.

EXPLORATORY ACTIVITIES

1. Observe children at various age levels to find how many have the characteristics described by the norms for those age levels.
2. Stage a mock debate in which one or more classmates defend developmental norms and an equal number claim that they have little application in teaching today's students.
3. Select one of the following psychologists for study. Try to apply to music teaching the theories of J. McVickar Hunt, Benjamin Bloom, David Krathwohl, or Jean Piaget.
4. Review the developmental stages and principles stated by Piaget. Compare the stages, and determine whether students in a given class are likely to be operating at one stage only or at more than one stage. Determine how a good teacher will respond to that situation.
5. What are the implications of the statement that most learning takes place outside of school? How should this affect the content of music lessons in school? How important do you think the home environment is in education, and what should teachers do about it?
6. Explain the sequence of mental processes from percept to concept to generalization. Relate this to helping students to comprehend music.
7. Listening is referred to as one of the basic musical activities. Discuss it as a primary source of musical percepts.
8. Select a song, identify appropriate concepts to be taught with the song, and prepare a list of different types of questions appropriate to teaching those concepts to students. Identify each of the questions according to Bloom's taxonomy, and place the questions in a logical sequence.
9. What are generally the best ways for students to be motivated to learn? How can teachers try to make them possible?
10. Explain what is meant by ''the structure of music.'' Discuss the educational value and disadvantages of teaching for structure.
11. Observe a music class at the level of your choice and answer the following questions.

   How was the class motivated to learn?

   Were the students engaged in music making, or did they talk about music most of the time?

   What kinds of questions did the teacher ask?

   Were all the students participating? Why? Why not?

   Did the students have the musical backgrounds to understand what they were to learn?

   Were the students involved in planning, suggesting, or experimenting?

   What was the possibility of continuing some of the activities at home?

   What suggestions do you have for improving the content of the lesson?

12. From the list of commonly accepted principles of learning, select three to five and explain how you would apply them when teaching music at a grade level of your choice.

References

ANDRESS, BARBARA, "Music for Every Stage," *Music Educators Journal,* October 1989, 24.

BERNSTEIN, ANNE, "My Memory/Myself," *Parents,* April 1981, 49–53.

BLOOM, BENJAMIN, *Stability and Change in Human Characteristics.* New York: John Wiley, 1964.

BONDY, ELISABETH, "Thinking About Thinking," *Childhood Education,* March/April 1984, 234–238.

BOWER, G. H. and E. R. HILGARD, *Theories of Learning,* 5th ed. Englewood Cliffs, N.J.: Prentice-Hall, 1981.

BROPHY, JERE, "Synthesis of Research on Strategies for Motivating Students to Learn," *Educational Leadership,* October 1987, 40–48.

CALABRESE, RAYMOND L., "Alienation: Its Causes and Impact on Adolescent Health," *The High School Journal,* October/November 1987, 14–18.

CLARKE-STEWART, ALLISON, SUSAN FRIEDMAN, and JOANNE KOCH, *Child Development: A Topical Approach.* New York: Wiley, 1985.

ERIKSON, ERIK, *Childhood and Society,* 2nd ed. New York: Norton, 1963.

FOWLER, CHARLES B., "Discovery: One of the Best Ways to Teach a Musical Concept," *Music Educators Journal,* September 1970, 38.

FRANKLIN, ELDA, and A. DAVID, "The Brain Research Bandwagon: Proceed with Caution." *Music Educators Journal,* February 1970, 49.

GARDNER, HOWARD, *Frames of Mind: The Theory of Multiple Intelligences.* New York Basic Books, 1983.

GOTTFRIED, ADELE ESKELES, "Intrinsic Motivation in Young Children," *Young Children,* 39/1, November 1983, 64–73.

HUNT, J. McVICKAR, *Intelligence and Experience.* New York: Ronald Press, 1961.

KRATHWOHL, DAVID R., BENJAMIN S. BLOOM, and BERTRAM B. MASIA, *Taxonomy of Educational Objectives, Handbook II: Affective Domain.* New York: McKay, 1964.

LETTERI, CHARLES A., "Teaching Students How to Learn," *Theory into Practice,* Spring 1985, 112–122.

MANNING, M. LEE, "Social Development in Early Adolescence," *Childhood Education,* February 1987, 172–176.

McDANIEL, THOMAS R., "The Ten Commandments of Motivation," *The Clearing House,* September 1985, 19–23.

Music Educators Journal, Special Issue: Creative Thinking in Music, May 1990.

Music Educators National Conference, *The School Music Program: Description and Standards,* Reston, Va.: The Conference, 1986.

Music Educators National Conference, *The Ann Arbor Symposium Session III, Motivation and Creativity,* Reston, Va.: The conference, 1983.

NYE, VERNICE TROUSDALE, *Music for Young Children,* 3rd ed. Chapter 2, "An Introduction to Learning Theory," Dubuque, Iowa: Wm. C. Brown, 1983.

O'BRIEN, JAMES P. "How Conceptual Learning Takes Place," *Music Educators Journal,* September 1971, 34.

SERAFINE, MARY LOUISE, *Music as Cognition: The Development of Thought in Sound.* New York: Columbia University Press, 1988.

TIMBERLAKE, PAT, "15 Ways to Cultivate Creativity in Your Classroom," *Childhood Education,* September/October 1982, 19–21.

ZIMMERMAN, MARILYN, P., *Musical Characteristics of Children,* Reston, Va.: Music Educators National Conference, 1971.

————.''Percept and Concept: Implications of Piaget,'' *Music Educators Journal,* February 1970, 49.

2 Planning for Teaching

Designing Instructional Programs

Philosophy, Goals, and Objectives
To be concerned with curricula once meant to be concerned almost exclusively with organizing content into a logical sequence to fit whatever time was available. The differences among individual students, and the intellectual and psychological changes they experienced as they developed toward maturity, received slight attention. Today, organizing content and teaching procedures to accommodate individual differences has become very important. It is also critical that the music curriculum focus on active learning for the students, a curriculum in which students do things rather than passively watching and listening. Curriculum development is based, in part, on knowledge about human development. In planning a music curriculum we begin with what students already know, gradually expanding and organizing music content by in-

volving students in challenging, relevant, and varied learning experiences at increasingly higher levels.

Music curricula are often developed at the district level by music specialists in the system. Curriculum guides are effective when those who use them are directly involved in developing them. Guides are unlikely to be used when they are imposed on teachers who had no part in constructing them. The major responsibility of a curriculum planning committee at the district and/or school level is to determine the overall instructional goals of the music program. The planning is done cooperatively by the music supervisor, music specialists, and classroom teachers. The first action of a music curriculum committee at the district level is to develop a statement of philosophy concerning music education from which long-term goals may be defined. Such a philosophical statement stresses the importance of music education. Two examples follow:

> The place of the arts in the lives of human beings rests on a fundamental proposition: *Living* is not the same as *existing*. Living is more than just getting through life, more than having something to eat and shelter from the rain and cold. Living is making life interesting, satisfying, and meaningful. . . . Music and the arts are one of the most significant manifestations of the ability of human beings to think and to aspire restlessly for something more than survival. (Abeles, Hoffer & Klotman, 1984, p. 54–55)

> Music is (and has been) terribly important to me. The pleasures of music are simultaneously intellectual, spiritual, sensual—complete. The fact that all cultures reinvent music proves it is a basic human need. (Jeane J. Kirkpatrick, former American ambassador to the United Nations (Potosky, 1986, p. 52).)

Such statements should give direction to music teaching in the district, in the school, and in the classroom. They enable a teacher of music to make clear the value of music in the lives of students, and to help justify the program to administrators and parents. The curriculum committee next develops *long-range goals* that relate to the stated philosophy. These goals are broadly stated and general. The Oregon Department of Education's *Music Curriculum Bulletin* (1985) lists these long-range goals:

Students will

Know the basic elements and structure of music.

Be able to use notational systems.

Be able to improvise and create music.

Demonstrate performing skills.

Know the implications of music in our society, with respect to music careers, its avocational and leisure uses and, as consumers, know about musical products.

Value ethnic music and the American musical heritage.

Value music as a tool to bridge the gaps between nations, cultures, and people, thus fostering a ''world'' as well as national music.

Value music as an avenue of communication for the exchange of feelings and emotions.

Respond overtly and covertly to the inherent aesthetic qualities of music.

Develop acute auditory discrimination.

After writing long-range goals, the curriculum committee writes *instructional objectives* based upon them. These objectives are more specific, particularly in terms of the cognitive, psychomotor, and affective domains. They are sometimes written in general behavioral terms such as, "By the end of the year the students will demonstrate comprehension of _____ by _____ ." They describe the desired outcomes of a general comprehensive music program.

The teacher works from these objectives when planning instruction, translating and rewriting them so they apply to particular classes, groups of students, or individual students. There may be subobjectives related to the major objective. A subobjective is written in the same manner as the major objective, but is more precise, and is subordinate to the major objective.

The model for developing curricular objectives shown in Figure 2.1 may assist teachers in designing district, school, or classroom music curricula for a year, a specified reporting period, a week, or for a daily lesson. Teachers use these four steps in planning any part of the music program. They study state and local curriculum guides, obtain information from the principal and fellow teachers, and study children and their records as well as other appropriate music materials. Then they formulate the major goals to be attained in the coming year. They consider local, state, and national events, seasons, holidays, and special days to determine to what extent these events can be related to the year's program. They examine all available music materials and recordings to judge their appropriateness to the curriculum. They consider the separation of church and

Figure 2.1. MODEL FOR DEVELOPING CURRICULAR OBJECTIVES

> **A statement of *Philosophy* gives focus for**
>
> ↓
>
> ***Long-Range Goals,* which are guides for writing**
>
> ↓
>
> **specific *Instructional Objectives,* from which**
>
> ↓
>
> **more precise *Subobjectives* may be derived.**

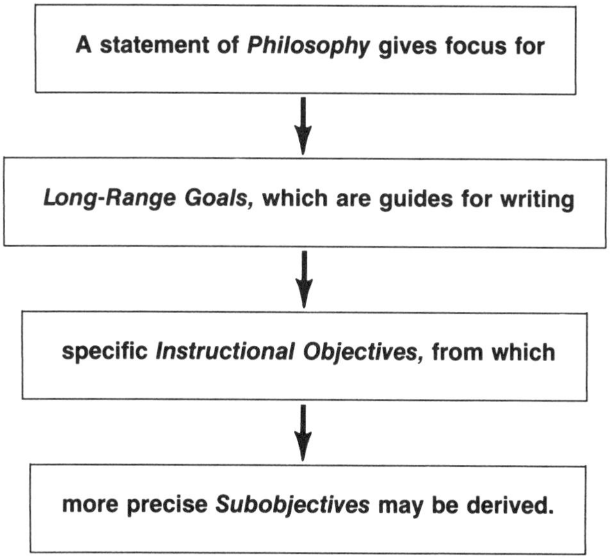

state as defined by their communities in selecting music. They incorporate flexibility into the details of planning so that students can make some decisions and choices. They realize that planning should progress from day to day and from week to week within the framework of the plan for the year.

In order to design curricular programs, it is necessary to know the amount of time allocated to teaching music. Minimum time allotments vary among states and among school districts. Obviously it is difficult to designate specific time allotments in self-contained classrooms where the teacher, in addition to scheduled time for music, integrates it when appropriate into all areas of the curriculum throughout the school day. This is especially true in nursery school, kindergarten, and first grade.

Types of plans also vary in accordance with the philosophy and objectives of the teacher and of the school, the size of the class, the number of aides, and the type of classroom organization.

Lesson plans may vary in complexity from the extremely simple to the highly intricate. However, plans that are simple in design can be intricate in their implementation. The model in Figure 2.2 proposes a simple process for diagnosing and planning for learning.

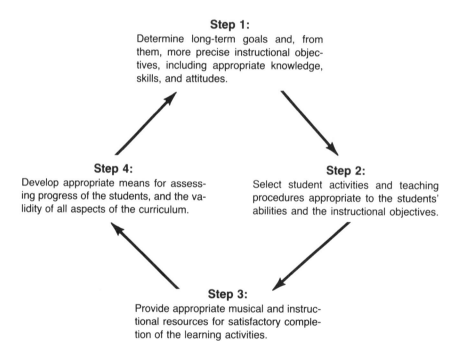

Step 1:
Determine long-term goals and, from them, more precise instructional objectives, including appropriate knowledge, skills, and attitudes.

Step 4:
Develop appropriate means for assessing progress of the students, and the validity of all aspects of the curriculum.

Step 2:
Select student activities and teaching procedures appropriate to the students' abilities and the instructional objectives.

Step 3:
Provide appropriate musical and instructional resources for satisfactory completion of the learning activities.

Figure 2.2. MODEL FOR DEVELOPING MUSIC CURRICULUM

Experienced teachers have learned that good lesson plans incorporate more than one music activity in order for students to be involved with music in different ways. They also incorporate high-level thinking skills as teachers help students develop the ability to use music in a variety of settings. As teachers gain experience, their lesson plans reflect the ability to organize more complex activities, in which several objectives and musical skills may appear.

Furthermore, when more complex and detailed plans are written, they cannot be read by the teacher during the teaching process. They are memorized in part, and the teacher follows a short list or outline of planned activities including key questions. Experienced teachers regularly use such lists, often on 3 × 5 cards. These may even be color-coded by grade level for ease of identification.

There are many different possibilities for planning, and the teacher normally chooses experiences and strategies suited both to the children and his or her personality. No teacher operates exactly like any other teacher; each is a unique personality. Thus the planning of the lesson is a reflection of the teacher who prepares it, showing how that teacher's strengths are employed and how possible weaknesses are accommodated. Such plans may be for a daily lesson, a week's work, or a more lengthy unit.

Music Content Areas In order to develop musical learning in the fullest sense, it is necessary for the teacher to select and develop objectives in four major areas:

1. Musical knowledge (factual information, concepts, and generalizations)
2. Cognitive process skills
3. Music skills
4. Musical attitudes and values

While the teacher may choose to emphasize any one of the four areas in any given daily lesson or unit plan, it is likely that elements of all four will be present in most plans. The four content areas are outlined here:

I. Musical Knowledge (factual information, concepts, generalizations)

  A. The Elements of Music

    1. Constituent elements

      a. rhythm (duration)

      b. pitch

      c. tone quality

      d. dynamics

    2. Expressive elements

      a. tempo

      b. phrasing

      c. articulation

  B. The Structure of Music (concepts, generalizations)

    1. Standard forms of musical composition (e.g., binary, ternary, rondo, variation forms)

    2. Other organizational patterns for compositions (e.g., fugue, aria, canon)

3. Structural devices within a composition

    a. motives, phrases, periods

    b. repetition and contrast

C. The Cultural Setting of Music

    1. The cultural and historical setting in which it developed

    2. The instruments in use

    3. The performance practices in effect

    4. The functions of the music

II. Cognitive Process Skills Applied to Music

    A. Comparing

    B. Classifying

    C. Collecting and Organizing

    D. Summarizing

    E. Generalizing

    F. Creative Thinking

    G. Hypothesizing

    H. Analyzing

    I. Evaluating

III. Musical Skills

    A. Listening to music

    B. Moving to music

    C. Singing

    D. Playing instruments

    E. Reading music

    F. Creating music

IV. Musical Attitudes and Values

    A. Receiving

    B. Responding

    C. Valuing

    D. Organizing of Values

    E. Generalized set

Selecting Program Content

The program content should focus on the capabilities the learners must acquire to meet the instructional objectives. It should also focus on music as a global activity that reflects both the cultural diversity and the cultural independence of the modern world. The capabilities and learning styles of each student must be considered in order to select appropriate content. In designing a course of study in music, the three categories that Jerome Bruner says comprise the structure of a discipline (data, concepts, and generalizations) are helpful.

Data refers to particulars rather than to universals. Data can be formulated as propositions or statements that refer to things in the present or the past. Some examples of musical data are

Bach died in 1750.

A sharp placed before a note raises its pitch one half step.

A quarter note has the same duration as two eighth notes.

Some teachers place major emphasis on the learning of facts as ends within themselves. As a result, they may emphasize information of only minor import. Whether or not a fact is important is usually determined by the context in which it is used. Therefore students must participate in learning experiences that help them tie together the facts they acquire to form meaningful relationships. Teachers must also help students organize facts into useful concepts and generalizations.

Concepts. Fraenkel (1973) states that concepts, unlike facts, ''are definitional in nature. They represent those characteristics that are common to a group of experiences. Concepts do not exist in reality; they represent our attempts to give order to reality—to order that information from our environment that we receive through our senses. We attempt to bring order to this sensory input by attaching symbols (word-labels) to certain similarities we perceive in our experience. . . . Notice, however, that concepts are invented rather than discovered. . . . Concepts thus are mental constructions devised by man to describe the characteristics that are common to a number of experiences,'' which include those with musical phenomena heard, seen, and felt. ''They facilitate understanding, for they make communication easier,'' thus reducing the complexity of the musical environment into manageable proportions (94).

All concepts are not realized verbally. Since concepts are inventions of the mind, they are personal creations of individuals, and may not be describable. Each learner develops his or her mental constructs, which we call concepts. These result from many experiences in which data are organized meaningfully.

Some examples of musical concepts are

the ''key'' of a musical composition

tension in a melody

melodic contour

three-part song form incorporates the establishment of, departure from, and return to a musical statement

Generalizations are statements that contain two or more concepts and show relationships among concepts. Both concepts and generalizations aid students in organizing and seeing relationships and meaning in music. Generalizations offer insights into the way music is produced and into the ways it affects human life. They not only embody facts (data) and concepts but give structure to them. Careful consideration must be given by the music teacher in the selection of valid and significant content objectives, which include the processing and mastery of relevant and worthy data, concepts, and generalizations.

Some examples of musical generalizations are the following statements:

The interaction of pitches and rhythm produces melody.

Tempo and dynamics interact to contribute to the expressive nature of music.
An ostinato may be based on rhythm, pitches, or both.

Devising Lesson Plans

The lesson plan format in Example I can accommodate all of the components of good music teaching discussed previously.

EXAMPLE I. MODEL LESSON PLAN OUTLINE

Name _____   Date _____

Grade _____ Time _____

  I. Concept(s) to be taught:

  II. Instructional objective(s):

  III. Materials and media needed:

  IV. Classroom teaching strategies and procedures:

    A. Introduction
    B. Student learning activities
    C. Conclusion
    D. Activity extension

  V. Evaluation:

    A. By teacher, to evaluate student progress in meeting stated objectives.

    B. By students, to evaluate the activities and other aspects of the lesson (not always appropriate).

    C. By teacher, to adjust the teaching of the next lesson.

Overview of Lesson Plans The value of the preceding model lies in the teacher's ability to make plans in each of the following five categories according to sound pedagogical practices.

    I. Concepts to Be Taught. In selecting the concepts, the teacher must determine the level of the students' musical understanding and proceed from that point.

II. Instructional Objective(s). The objectives state the purposes of the lesson for the students. Some may be broad in scope; others may be quite specific. *Example 1*: To expand knowledge of tonic-dominant chord changes. *Example 2*: After singing and accompanying with the autoharp several familiar songs which can be harmonized by one or two chords, the learners will identify the tonic and dominant chords in these songs when the teacher plays them. They will identify the tonic chord by raising one finger, and the dominant chord by raising five fingers.

The first objective is of a general nature, and leaves much about the lesson undefined, and perhaps undecided. More precise objectives, such as the one in the second example, call for students to behave or perform in a variety of ways, such as the following:

> *Identifying* a musical instrument, term, symbol, or aspect of notation by picking it up, pointing to it, touching it, or communicating it verbally.
>
> *Naming* an instrument, a form, term, symbol, or relationship.
>
> *Arranging* three or more phrases, terms, symbols, measures, or events in order based on a stated plan.
>
> *Describing* musical events well enough to identify a type of song, phrase, term, symbol, or relationship.
>
> *Selecting* an object, term, symbol, or phrase from two or more which might be confused.
>
> *Creating* musical compositions, accompaniments, musical instruments, drawings, or written statements about music.
>
> *Demonstrating* the sequence of operations necessary to carry out a musical procedure.
>
> *Deriving* an answer to a musical problem by employing selected behaviors from the other objectives, and organizing various types of data derived from such behaviors into a musical concept or generalization.
>
> *Performing* or *conducting* music in a manner that demonstrates comprehension of a musical concept, or acquisition of a musical skill (Nye, 1970).

III. Materials and Media Needed. In music education the term *materials* means all the musical, mechanical, and literary items needed. For example, a variety of songs and recordings of merit should be chosen. Other materials might include tape recorders, projectors, films, slides, recordings, charts, maps, books, songs, paper, and instruments. All materials should be acquired and made ready in advance of the lesson.

IV. Classroom Teaching Strategies and Procedures. To provide the core of the plan, the teacher selects the activities and determines the procedure or learning sequence that will be followed in class. These classroom activities may be of several types:

A. *Introduction.* In the first few minutes the teacher may conduct a review of a previous lesson, build readiness for the lesson of the day, establish objectives, and help the students focus on the activity to come. This introduction provides an appropriate mental and physical setting for the lesson.

B. *Student learning activities.* The teacher selects class activities to help the students reach the stated objectives. He or she also plans for a variety of activities that keep learners involved and interested. This requires that, as nearly as possible, the activities be suited to the abilities and learning styles of all students so they can experience success after due effort. As part of the preparation the teacher formulates several questions and their probable places in the lesson, using as many different types of questions as are appropriate in exploring an idea or concept—knowledge, interpretation, application, analysis, synthesis, and evaluative types of questions.

C. *Conclusion, in the form of a generalized statement.* The teacher, or a member of the class, summarizes what has been learned and brings the lesson to a close. The conclusion helps students reinforce what has been taught, and reaffirms what the teacher thinks is important.

D. *Activity extension.* Additional related activities are for students with intense interest in the subject, or for classes that move through the planned activities at an accelerated pace.

V. Evaluation. There are at least three aspects of evaluation: first, by the teacher, to evaluate student progress; second, by the students, to evaluate the activities and other aspects of the lesson; third, by the teacher, to adjust the teaching of the next lesson. (This aspect of evaluation is not appropriate in every circumstance.)

To make evaluation effective, several questions should be asked: "When can the evaluation be most effectively employed?" "How can I measure progress if there was no prelesson assessment?" "To what degree did the learners achieve the objectives?" "Were they challenged and satisfied with the experience?" "Which aspects of the plan were successful and which were not?" "Which students need more assistance?" "What are the implications for the next music lesson?"

The preceding model lesson plan will help beginning teachers become skillful in organizing a lesson. Less detailed plans are used by experienced teachers because they know many of the details and procedures and do not need to write them down. Inexperienced teachers may feel that a great many things must be packed into a lesson in order to accomplish the year's objectives, and they may err by striving to cover too much in a single lesson. The fear of omitting something of importance can become a serious burden to the lesson. Such an approach negates the idea of conceptual learning because in order for concepts to grow and generalizations to be formed, main ideas should be approached in a variety of ways. This is quite different from a random acquisition-of-information approach.

The best lesson plan is just a guide; it is not a law. Regardless of how well designed lesson plans may be, in real life they are often altered in midstream, and sometimes even abandoned. Teachers find that they must be flexible in adapting lesson plans to the interests of their students and other unplanned contemporaneous events. An unexpected event in the classroom may alter the steps planned to lead to the objective or emphasize a different concept or objective, or an occurrence outside the classroom may interrupt the sequence.

EXAMPLE II. Lesson Plan for Third grade (30 minutes)

I. Concept to be taught: The tones of melodies may stay the same, move to adjacent pitches, or move through skips.

Prior knowledge necessary:

Concepts	*Information*
high	line
low	space
skip	measure
step	
scale	
melodic line	
chord	

II. Instructional objective: The children will differentiate between melodies which move by steps, by skips, or stay the same.

III. Materials and media needed:

Chalkboard

Songs the children know. Source: Nye, Nye, et al. *Music in the Elementary School,* 6th ed. 1991 or Nye and Bergethon, *Basic Music,* 6th ed. 1987. Englewood Cliffs, N.J.: Prentice Hall, 1987.

Charts of the notation of "Kum Ba Yah," (see p. 48) and "Michael, Row the Boat Ashore," (see p. 49).

Colored art paper (one sheet per child), pastel chalk.

Recording of a simple melody.

Transparencies of "Merrily We Roll Along," "A Hunting We Will Go," "Little Tom Tinker," and "Bow, Belinda."

Log drum, guitar, xylophone.

IV. Classroom teaching strategies and procedures (expanded here for illustrative purposes):

A. INTRODUCTION (5 minutes)

Teacher: What do we remember about the song "Kum Ba Ya"?

(Teacher writes major points on chalkboard as children state them.)

Child: We sang "Kum Ba Yah" last time.

Teacher: Why did we sing it?

Child: Because we're studying music from other countries, and this one comes from Africa.

Teacher: Today we are going to do more with this song. Let's sing it again, and add the log drum. Each of you think of a way to show the high and low pitches. Try to remember how the tune goes. Can you hear it in your head without singing it?

(Children demonstrate with hands.)

Teacher: Where did you begin?

Child: Low.

(Teacher establishes the pitch and the class sings the song.)

KUM BA YAH

2. *Someone's crying, Lord, Kum ba yah!*
3. *Someone's singing, Lord, Kum ba yah!*
4. *Someone's praying, Lord, Kum ba yah!*

B. STUDENT LEARNING ACTIVITIES (20 minutes)

Teacher directs students to sing "Michael, Row the Boat Ashore" and says, "Sing it as you did last week, but this time watch me as I show you the direction of the melody." (Class sings the melody while the teacher lines the melody with hand levels.)

Teacher: Now comes the puzzle: We're going to sing the songs again while you line out the melodies. When we are through, I want you to tell me how these melodies are alike and different.(*pause*)

Sally: The tunes are different.

Brian: The rhythm is not the same.

Lisa: The way we sing "Kum Ba Ya" is a little like "Michael, Row the Boat Ashore."

Teacher: Why do you think they are alike, Lisa?

Lisa: The tune in both songs starts with the same skips.

MICHAEL ROW THE BOAT ASHORE

Traditional

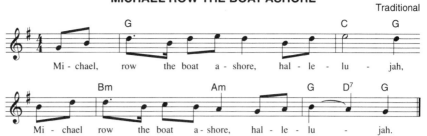

Mi - chael, row the boat a - shore, hal - le - lu - jah,

Mi - chael row the boat a - shore, hal - le - lu - jah.

The river is deep and the river is wide, hallelujah,
Milk and honey on the other side, hallelujah.
Michael row the boat ashore, hallelujah;
Michael row the boat ashore, hallelujah.

Jordan's river is chilly and cold, hallelujah;
Chills the body but warms the soul, hallelujah.
Michael row the boat ashore hallelujah;
Michael row the boat ashore; hallelujah.

(The teacher produces charts of the notation of each song and asks Lisa to explain what she means by pointing to the charts. Lisa does so.)

Teacher: Does anyone have another idea? Let's sing these songs again, watch the notes, and think how it sounds when the melody skips lines and spaces.

(The class sings the songs again.)

Teacher: Was there any part of these two songs that stayed the same?

Rob: Part of "Kum Ba Yah" doesn't skip.

Teacher: I see that you listened to the song carefully, Rob. Look at the chart and show us the part that you think doesn't skip.

(Rob points to measures 1 and 3.)

Teacher: Play those notes on the xylophone, Mark. (He does.) What did you discover?

Mark: The notes were all next to each other; there were no skips.

Teacher: Play measures 1 and 2. (He does.) What do you find there?

Mark: There is a skip in measure 2.

Teacher: Can you change the song so there isn't a skip there, Mark?

(Mark experiments to eliminate the skip. The teacher makes the changes on the chart. Mark plays measures 1 and 2 as revised.)

Teacher: Let's all sing measures 1 and 2 and see if we like them this way.

(The class sings the measures and likes the change. Mark volunteers that it is easier to play on the xylophone this way.)

Teacher: Can we analyze the melody of "Kum Ba Yah"?

(The teacher holds up the chart of "Kum Ba Yah."

Child: It's nearly all skips.

Child: There are dotted notes.

Teacher: Let's examine "Michael, Row the Boat Ashore." Can you use the chart to explain what you find?

Children: It's mostly skips and some steps; most of the skips are in the beginning of the song.

(Further discussion follows, and the teacher reinforces the learning through the following process.)

1. A familiar song is sung as the children move to show skips and steps as they hear them in the melody.
2. The class decides if skips or steps are present and states where they are found in the song.
3. The teacher shows a transparency of the notation on the screen to enable the class to verify its decision.

The children will find

"A Hunting We Will Go"	to be	all steps
"Merrily We Roll Along"	to be	all steps except one skip at the end of the first phase.
"Little Tom Tinker"	to be	all skips and repeated notes until steps in the last measure.
"Bow Belinda"	to be	a skip pattern one step lower, then one step higher, with steps in the last measure.

C. CONCLUDING THE LESSON

Teacher: Let's see if we can state in one sentence all the important things we learned about melodies today.

Children: Some melodies move in steps, some move in skips, and some tones stay the same. Some melodies use all three. (Notice how the children summarized the day's lesson by stating their findings in the form of a generalization.)

The concluding activity is listening to the recording while children draw the melodic line on the colored paper with pastels.

Evaluation: Notice that the teacher plans to work toward many more goals than stated in the focus of the lesson. Besides working toward the generalization and the stated objective, this teacher gives attention to

Tonal memory (Can you hear it in your head without singing it?)

High and low pitch

Body movement in relation to high and low in pitch

Using notation to solve musical problems

Playing an instrument (Why do you think the teacher chose Mark to play the xylophone?)

Manipulating a melody by changing it

Emphasizing listening skills

In the previous example the teacher did not develop the reference by the children to repeated notes. The class was guided in activities that emphasized skips and steps—the stated objective of the plan.

The lesson plan in Example III illustrates the use of various cognitive process skills. It is based upon the premise that students have previously mastered the concept of steady beat. Teachers should not attempt to pattern all of their lesson plans after every step listed here, for some objectives do not lend themselves to all of the processes. They should, however, include all that are applicable to the realization of the stated objectives. The plan is appropriate for 8- or 9-year-olds, depending upon their musical understanding.

EXAMPLE III. A Lesson on Cognitive Process Skills

Concepts to be taught: Beat, accent, meter signature (or time signature).

Instructional objective: The children will recognize that regular accents within pulse determine meter.

Materials: Drum, chalk and chalkboard, (specific) music book, recordings.

Classroom teaching strategies and procedures: The teacher asks the class to listen and observe. He or she then plays a drum or claps hands with steady beat, sounding no accent. "Now do it with me, stopping when I stop." The class responds.

Observing: "How would you describe what you heard?" "Could you tell what the meter (time signature) might be?" (Answer: "No.") "Why not?"

Comparing: The teacher now repeats the performance except that he or she accents every other beat. "Now you do it." The class responds. "How would you compare what you just heard with what you first heard?" (Answer: "The music moves in twos.") "What is the musical term for the stress I placed on some of the beats?" (Answer: "Accent.") "How often did I accent the beats?" (Answer: "Every other beat.")

The teacher repeats the performance, but accents every third beat. "Compare what I did this time with what you heard the other times." (Answer: "This one moves in threes.")

The teacher writes on the chalkboard what he or she did the first time. At teacher's signal, class claps what is written.

| | | | | | | | | | | | | |

A child is asked to draw a short line either above or below the note stem as the teacher plays the example again, stressing every other beat:

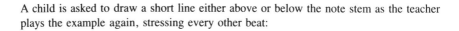

The class claps what is written. The teacher again writes the series of note stems on the chalkboard and asks another child to come forward to notate accents. He or she plays an accent on every third note.

Classifying: "How many kinds of accents do we now have?" (Answer: "Three—no accent, an accent every other beat, and an accent every third beat.") The teacher now asks a child to draw a bar line before each accented note. "What meter signatures can we place in front of these examples?" (Answer: "None for the first, 2/4—or 2/2 or 2/8—for the second, and 3/4—or 3/2 or 3/8—for the third.") "What names can we say that conform to these two-beat and three-beat meters?" (Answer: "Li-sa, Ja-son, Bry-an, Ok-la-ho-ma for two-beat meters; Me-lo-dy, Cyn-thi-a, Jon-a-than for three-beat meters.") The class repeats each name a number of times while clapping or stamping the accent. Children suggest and experiment with other names.

Collecting and organizing data: The children open their music books and search for meters with two and three beats to the measure. These are listed on the chalkboard under each category.

Summarizing statement: When a meter contains two beats, the numeral 2 appears on top in the meter signature; when a meter contains three beats, the numeral 3 appears on top in the meter signature. (An exception is fast 6/8, which will be dealt with later.)

Recognizing assumptions: The teacher says, "Some people say that most music moves in twos or threes. How can this be when some of the meter signatures you saw in your books were 4/4 and 6/8 and perhaps others?" At this point, the books are opened again, and the children are helped to find that 4/4 can be considered to be 2 plus 2, and 6/8 to be 3 plus 3. The latter meter should be closely examined in the music, for 6/8 meter is almost always written in such a manner that the measure can be divided to illustrate that 3-plus-3 characteristic (rather than a mathematically possible 2 plus 2 plus 2). Meters such as 5/4 and 7/8 should probably be reserved for study at a future date when this information becomes necessary.

Creative thinking: The teacher suggests that the class invent meters up to six beats in a measure. The class invents and labels a number of meters by placing regular accents at different intervals by clapping, stamping, or using percussion instruments.

Inferring from the data: In response to the teacher's prepared questions, students state in their own words, "Accent determines meter; regular accents result in meter; there are many meters."

Analyzing: The teacher plays recordings of short selections that clearly denote 2/4 and 3/4 meters. The children are asked to move to the beats and accents, and determine the meter of the selections.

Application: The children find songs they like in their books, sing them, and identify the meter; they also conduct the meters. This leads them to discover that some songs are more heavily accented than others, and that the strength of the accent is sometimes a matter of musical taste rather than a matter of musical mechanics. "Love Somebody" has a strong accent; "America" needs almost none.

Relationships of Concepts in Lesson Plans
We have focused attention on lesson plans that typically emphasize a few concepts and generalizations. These plans may appear to limit student activities to experiences with relatively few mental constructs. However, it is important to realize that concepts having to do with one aspect of music relate inevitably to numerous other musical concepts that operate on the periphery of a lesson plan and may not be mentioned in it. For example, activities designed to expand concepts of rhythm may include concepts of melody, tempo, dynamics, form, and note reading, just to name a few. These relationships are good, and many music concepts not mentioned in lesson plans may be expanded incidentally in the stated activities. The most interesting and fruitful plans contain materials and activities that touch many more music concepts than those mentioned in the plan.

There will be similar interrelationships of concepts in the chapters concerned with sound, rhythm, singing, and playing instruments. Each concept potentially relates to all of the musical elements, despite the stress on one primary element in a chapter. For example, listening, the basic music activity, pervades every chapter.

Evaluation of Lesson Plans
After teaching a lesson, the teacher evaluates the lesson by asking the following questions:

1. Are the teacher's instructional objectives clearly stated? Are they drawn from one or more of the four major curricular components: elements of music, cognitive process skills, music skills, or attitudes and values?
2. Are objectives stated in specific terms which indicate appropriate ways to evaluate the outcomes?
3. Do the teacher's plans provide challenging and interesting ways to motivate students to learn?
4. Does the teacher present a variety of activities in logical sequence that employs several appropriate senses—for example, hearing, seeing, and kinesthetic response?
5. Does the teacher accommodate individual differences including individual learning styles?
6. Does the teacher prepare varied questions in advance?
7. Does the teacher relate concepts to several different contexts?
8. Are the students kept active mentally and physically during the lesson?
9. Does the teacher select each activity to assist in the realization of a specific objective?

10. Does the teacher anticipate what needs to be done to make the lesson proceed smoothly? Distributing books, finding pages in books, getting instruments ready to play, and sounding the first pitch are some of the aspects to be anticipated. For example, if song titles and page numbers are on the chalkboard or transparency, the class can begin with greater efficiency.
11. Does the teacher list all necessary materials of instruction?

The checklist in Figure 2.3 is an instrument to evaluate an instructional plan.

Practical Applications The songs that follow are presented to illustrate their function in designing a lesson plan. Whether or not the plan should be written at this time is a matter for your instructor to decide. However, some preliminary thought about lesson plans could be of value. For example, teachers need to select songs and other materials of instruction that best lead to a realization of stated objectives.

Sample Songs for Lesson Plans

SONG	RELATED CONCEPTS AND ACTIVITIES
''Pussy Willow Song''	Melodic contour; scale tones; perform tune on bells
''Jennie Jenkins''	Tempo (fast); contour (disjunct melody line); chord roots; two-part form; improvise a chant on scale tones 5 and 6 (*sol* and *la*); questions and answers in text suggest two groups of singers or solo and chorus

Courtesy of the Music Educators National Conference, Reston, Va.

	Weak	Below Average	Average	Strong	Superior
Clarity of Instructional Objectives The objectives of the lesson are clear.					
Appropriateness of Objectives The objectives are neither too easy nor too difficult for the students.					
Organization of the Lesson The individual parts of the lesson are clearly related to each other in an appropriate way. The total organization facilitates what is to be learned.					
Selection of Content The content is appropriate for the objectives of the lesson, the level of the class, and the teaching procedures.					
Selection of Materials and Media The instructional materials and human resources used are clearly related to the content of the lesson and complement the selected method of instruction. They are complete.					
Beginning the Lesson The students come quickly to attention.					
Clarity of Presentation The content of the lesson is presented sequentially so that it is understandable to the students. Different points of view and specific illustrations are used when appropriate. Questioning is used to clarify and associate.					
Pacing of the Lesson The teacher "stays with the class" and adjusts the tempo accordingly. Adaptations are made for different learning styles. Transitions are smoothly executed.					
Student Participation and Attention The class is attentive. The students actively participate, both mentally and physically, in the lesson.					
Ending the Lesson There is a deliberate attempt to tie together the planned and chance events of the lesson and relate them to the immediate and long range goals of instruction. (Postevaluation)					
Teacher-Student Rapport The personal relationships between students and the teacher are harmonious and positive.					

Figure 2.3. CHECKLIST FOR EVALUATING A RECENTLY COMPLETED LESSON

"Mister Sun"	Form; meter; chord tones in the melody; chord roots to play or sing; tonic-dominant harmony
"This Train"	Provision for high and low voice ranges; the beat (marching); selection of appropriate percussion instruments to improvise an accompaniment; possible dramatization; syncopation; related recording for analysis
"Kum Ba Yah" (see page 48)	Familiar song performed in different meter (2/4) from previous version; part singing (in thirds); I-V$_7$-IV harmony; adding a chord root part (middle C, low F, and G)

PUSSY WILLOW SONG

Traditional

I know a lit - tle pus - sy with coat of sil - ver grey, She

lives out in the mea - dow, not so ve - ry far a - way, she'll

al - ways be a pus - sy, she'll ne - ver be a cat, for

she's a pus - sy wil - low, now what do you think of that?

Meow meow meow meow meow meow meow meow SCAT!

JENNIE JENKINS

American Folksong

Fast

F   C⁷

1. Oh, will you wear white, oh, my dear, oh my dear? Oh,
2. Oh, will you wear blue, oh my dear, oh my dear? Oh,

F

will you wear white___ Jen - nie Jen - - kins? I
will you wear blue___ Jen - nie Jen - - kins? I

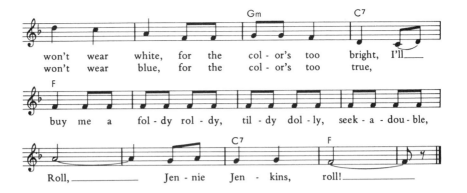

won't wear white, for the col - or's too bright, I'll___
won't wear blue, for the col - or's too true,

buy me a fol - dy rol - dy, til - dy dol - ly, seek - a - dou - ble,

Roll,_____ Jen - nie Jen - kins, roll!_____

3. *Will you wear red—I won't wear red, it's the color of my head.*
4. *Will you wear green?—I won't wear green, it's a shame to be seen.*
5. *Will you wear purple?—I won't wear purple, it's the color of a turtle.*

(More verses can be created describing different colors.)

MISTER SUN

Traditional

Oh Mis - ter Sun, Sun, Mis - ter Gol - den Sun

Please shine down on me. Oh Mis - ter Sun, Sun,

Mis - ter Gol - den Sun Hid - ing be - hind a tree.

These lit - tle chil - dren are ask - ing you, To

please come out so we can play with you. Oh Mis - ter

Sun, Sun, Mis - ter Gol - den Sun Please shine down on me.

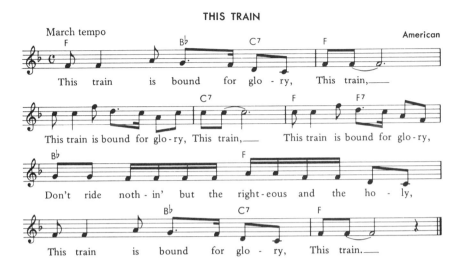

THIS TRAIN

March tempo
American

This train is bound for glo-ry, This train,___
This train is bound for glo-ry, This train,___ This train is bound for glo-ry,
Don't ride noth-in' but the right-eous and the ho-ly,
This train is bound for glo-ry, This train.___

This train is built for speed now, etc.
Fastest train you ever did see,
This train is bound for glory, this train.

This train don't carry no liars, etc.
No hypocrites and no high flyers,
This train is bound for glory, this train.

The following Conceptual Structure of Music is a highly condensed outline, and can easily be expanded. The generalizations stated in formal adult language may be used by teachers in planning programs, courses of study, instructional objectives, and lessons. They are rarely presented to students. The same concept or generalization may be sought and explored at very rudimentary levels, progressing in spiral fashion to ever higher levels as students grow in musical knowledge. Most generalizations are tentative; they will be tested and refined further. For example, young students learn that "sound and silence have duration," but this generalization will be expanded, refined, and made more specific as students have more experiences with music.

In the outline a world of music is presented in conceptual terms from which teachers can select and prepare objectives suitable for an individual, a class, a course of study, or a complete music curriculum. The Conceptual Structure of Music portrays music as a broad content area from which only a small part would be selected by the teacher for individual music lessons, a unit of study, or a year's course of study.

The complete sentences in the outline are generalizations (conclusions, principles, summarized ideas, main ideas). Following most generalizations are concepts from which they were constructed.

A Conceptual Structure of Music

Rhythm
- Rhythm in music is a grouping of sounds and silences of varying duration, usually controlled by a regular beat.

beat	dotted notes
equal divisions of the beat	rests
unequal divisions of the beat	speech-rhythm
one-to-two relation of note values	notated speech-rhythms
one-to-three relation of note values	articulations such as staccato and legato
one-to-four relation of note values	fermata
notated rhythms	

- Accent or lack of accent governs types of rhythm.

metrical rhythm	free rhythm
meter, bar line, measure, upbeat (anacrusis), downbeat, meter signature, duple meter, triple meter, primary accent, secondary accent, rhythm pattern, asymmetrical meter (5/4, 7/8, etc.)	rallentando (rall.)
	accelerando (accel.)
	rubato
	no common metrical beat (e.g., Asian and Indian music)
	"measured" rhythm with no regular recurring beat (e.g., Gregorian chant)

- Devices related to rhythm are used by composers to add interest and variety to their compositions.

rhythm patterns	canonic imitation
rhythmic ostinati	polyrhythms
augmentation	free rhythm (rit., rall., accel., rubato)
diminution	
syncopation	

- There are rhythms that are characteristic of different cultural groups.

  distinctive rhythms in national songs
  distinctive rhythms in national dances
  (e.g., minuet, waltz, polka, schottische, square dance)
  distinctive rhythms associated with ethnic groups

- Rhythm is universal, and has meanings beyond music.

the seasons	architecture
day and night	painting
life cycles of plants and animals	human movement
waves of the ocean	human speech
grain of wood	human heartbeat

Melody
- A melody is a linear succession of tones that are organized using rhythm and pitch, and are perceived by the human ear as a meaningful grouping of tones. (Children might say, "A melody is a line of tones that sounds right.")

- Melodies have direction: The successive tones of a melody may go up, go down, or remain on the same pitch.

  pitch = vibrations per second   high and low
  notation of pitch, staff, clefs, and notes   range
  numeral systems to identify pitches   contour
  syllabic systems to identify pitches

- A melody is formed by a union of pitches and rhythms.

  rhythm patterns in melodies
  pitch patterns in melodies
  sense of movement
  sense of conclusion
  relation of song melodies to word rhythms

- The tones of a melody may include conjunct tones (adjacent to each other) or disjunct tones (pitches with gaps between.)

  scales (major, minor, diatonic,   home tone
       modal, pentatonic, chromatic   key
       tone row, whole tone, devised)   key signature
  passive and active scale tones   accidentals
       (tension and release)   intervals
  tonal centers

- Melodies have form: They are usually formed of distinct parts or sections.

  phrase
  phrase relationships
       antecedent (question)
       consequent (answer)
  repetition and contrast
  sequences
  unitary, binary, and ternary song forms
  melodies and their transformations

- Melodies can be manipulated through various devices. (Children might say, "Melodies can be changed in different ways.")

  transposition   melodic variation
  diminution   rhythmic variation
  augmentation   harmonic variation
  inversion   octave displacement
  retrograde

Harmony and Texture

- Harmony pertains to the simultaneous sounding of tones, the successions of chords, and the relationships among chords. (Children might say, "Harmony means chords and their changes.")

  harmonies suggested by chord tones in melodies

- Texture, a term derived from weaving, refers to the relationships between a melody and other simultaneous musical sounds (e.g., its accompaniment). In some cases it refers to the relationships between simultaneous melodies.

Textures are sometimes described as light, heavy, thick, and thin.

- Homophonic music consists of one melody and its accompaniment.

many accompanied songs
many accompanied instrumental solos
much music of the nineteenth century

- Polyphonic music has two or more melodic lines sounding at the same time; in tonal music, these melodic lines are connected by harmonic relationships.

round, canon
counterpoint
fugue
point
imitation

- A chord is any simultaneous combination of three or more pitches; some may be more agreeable to the ear than others. (Children might say, ''A chord is three or more notes played together.'')

chord construction—usually based on thirds, but sometimes based on fourths, fifths, clusters	inversions
	triads
	major
relation to key centers	minor
cadences	consonance
full, half, plagal	dissonance
parallel chords	chord tones
relation to melody	chording
harmonizing a tune	
passing tones	
primary and secondary chords	
chords relating to no tonal center	

- Identical harmonic relationships can be sounded at different pitch levels.

transposition
key signatures

- Harmonies can be combined.

bitonality
polytonality

Tone Quality or Timbre
- Tone quality (timbre, tone color) is the distinctive sound of any instrument or voice; the difference in quality between tones of the same pitch produced by different voices and instruments.

- Some kind of sound can be produced by almost every object in the environment.

- Sounds, voices, and instruments can be classified according to tone quality, range, characteristics, and the means employed to produce them.

Conventional sound sources

voices	instruments
soprano	strings
alto	plucked
tenor	bowed
bass	strummed
	hammered
	woodwinds
	flue (open hole)
	reed
	percussion
	pitched
	unpitched
	brass
	electronic

Unconventional sound sources

- All materials found in nature

- All manufactured materials not designed to be musical instruments

- Instruments can be played in ways that produce a variety of sounds.

use of extreme ranges (high or low)	legato
glissando	vibrato
multiphonics	staccato
spiccato	muted

- Voices and instruments may be combined to produce an infinite variety of tone qualities. Composers and arrangers select different voices, instruments, and tone qualities for specific reasons.

- The differences in tone quality result primarily from the different combinations of fundamental tone and overtones produced by the various instruments.

resonance	oscilloscope
partials	overtones
harmonics	overtone series

Form
- Musical forms are in some ways similar to visual plans of construction made by architects. They may be recognized either visually or aurally.

- Melodies may be divided into parts

motive
phrase
period

- Melodies can be extended and altered

repetition	retrograde
coda	thematic development
interlude	diminution
augmentation	sequence
inversion	

- Most musical forms are based on the principle of repetition-contrast (same-different, unity-variety).

AA	rondo:
AB	ABACA; or
ABA	ABACABA, and so on.
Theme and variations	
(e.g., A1, A2, A3, A4)	

- Some forms can be classified as contrapuntal.

  round   canon   fugue

- A compound form exists when several movements are combined to form a complete musical composition.

  sonata
  suite (e.g., of dances)
  concerto
  symphony
  overture

Tempo

- Tempo (pace or speed of the music) is part of all organized music.

  presto very fast
  vivace spirited
  allegro lively
  allegretto moderately fast
  andante moderately slow
  adagio gently, leisurely
  lento slow
  largo broad and slow
  a tempo in original tempo
  accelerando gradually faster
  rallentando gradually slower
  ritardando gradually slower

Dynamics

- Dynamics (degrees of loudness and softness) add expressive qualities to a musical performance.

pianissimo	*pp*	very soft
piano	*p*	soft
mezzo piano	*mp*	medium soft

mezzo forte	*mf*	medium loud
forte	*f*	loud
fortissimo	*ff*	very loud
accent	>	more than usual stress
sforzando	*sf*	heavy accent
crescendo	*cresc.*	gradually increasing loudness
decrescendo	*decresc.*	gradually decreasing loudness
diminuendo	*dim.*	gradually decreasing loudness

Practical Applications

An example of using this Conceptual Structure of Music at elementary and middle school levels follows. Find the word ''reed'' under ''woodwinds.'' Assume the teacher has constructed the following generalization on that word. ''The family of reed instruments includes the oboe, bassoon, clarinet, and saxophone.'' In developing this generalization, concepts of each of these instruments must be formed. When considering the bassoon, for example, data such as these might be learned by the students.

Data	a long tube which doubles back on itself
	a double reed made of cane
	a conical bore
	a tone of mysterious quality
	a bass instrument
	a very wide range of pitches
Concept	the standard bassoon
Generalization (assuming concepts of the four instruments have developed)	The bassoon has some characteristics in common with other reed instruments, and is different from them in other ways.

As shown in Figure 2.4, students learn by beginning with facts, which lead to generalizations. However, when teachers plan, these steps are reversed.

Figure 2.4. THE LEARNING-PLANNING SEQUENCES

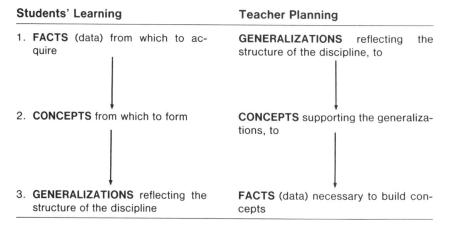

Students' Learning	Teacher Planning
1. **FACTS** (data) from which to acquire	**GENERALIZATIONS** reflecting the structure of the discipline, to
2. **CONCEPTS** from which to form	**CONCEPTS** supporting the generalizations, to
3. **GENERALIZATIONS** reflecting the structure of the discipline	**FACTS** (data) necessary to build concepts

This process in student learning requires *associative-process thinking,* in that the images and data are retrieved from mental storage, reexamined, explored, and organized so that concepts may be formed from them. Then *generalizations* are formed, based on experience with concepts. These generalizations are applied in new situations to test, change, and refine them.

This generalization about reeds may later be refined and expanded if the teacher chooses. For example, the discovery of the metal reed could be planned as a *discrepant event* which would bring the attention of students to the function of reeds in the accordion, harmonica, and reed organ. Then the concept of the ''family of reed instruments'' will expand and the concept of ''reed'' will grow. Students can discover that each metal reed is constructed to produce a definite pitch; each cane reed must in some way accommodate difference in pitch. Thus discovery grows out of discovery as the teacher guides the process in a helpful but unobtrusive way. Students are guided to discuss their findings and problems as they work with the tone qualities, range, appearance, and mechanical features of reed instruments. Such study as this is ordinarily only a part of a lesson plan which includes a variety of musical activities.

In developing concepts, students may listen to music, perform music, compose it, write it, analyze it, and discuss it. The aim is to clarify the mental image of the aspect of music under study.

Summary   Teachers of music who are competent in designing and implementing a comprehensive curriculum for students must

1. Possess a rationale or philosophy which incorporates the following questions: Why teach music? How should music be taught? When should it be taught and under what conditions? What can music do for students that no other subject can do as well?
2. Understand how students develop physically, emotionally, aesthetically, socially, and cognitively (intellectually).
3. Understand how students learn, and how teachers diagnose their musical capabilities, learning styles, and individual interests.
4. Understand some accepted learning theories and be able to apply them in program construction and lesson planning.
5. Be knowledgeable of what should be taught: data, concepts, and generalizations, process skills, music skills, and attitudes.
6. Be able to write appropriate and clearly stated long-term goals and instructional objectives for the teaching of the major components in a curriculum.
7. Select, sequence, and use a variety of appropriate learning experiences and materials to realize stated objectives.
8. Use questions that engage different levels of thought.
9. Develop appropriate teaching strategies for directing the learning activities of individuals and the class.
10. Evaluate the success of the music program for individuals, the class, the school, and the community.
11. Possess enthusiasm, a positive outlook, and faith in students' abilities to learn.
12. Continue to seek, study, and analyze current trends, materials, media, and equipment.

13. Work cooperatively with other classroom and music teachers, specialists, and consultants in revising and keeping music programs updated.
14. Voluntarily attend workshops, conferences, and conventions to observe the performance of competent teachers of music, and to obtain knowledge of how to better organize and implement a music program.

EXPLORATORY ACTIVITIES

1. Define the terms *goals* and *instructional objectives*. Explain the relationship between them and the use of each in planning instructional programs and lessons.
2. What musical behaviors form the core of the elementary music program?
3. Identify and present in class several long-term musical goals to be furthered in a comprehensive elementary music program.
4. Make a list of musical goals to be realized in a year's program. Write them in the form of instructional objectives.
5. Explain the advantages and disadvantages of long-term planned programs or curriculum guides.
6. Evaluate this statement: "We have a wonderful music teaching guide in our school. It tells the teacher exactly what to do each day."
7. Suppose that there is a state curriculum in music. What might its advantages and disadvantages be?
8. Give reasons why a sequence of music study that is well organized in terms of subject matter might fail to be sequential for a learner.
9. Illustrate the difference between a fact, a concept, and a generalization in music.
10. Design a year-long plan for music at a grade level of your choice.
11. Plan what you believe to be an appropriate music program for ages 5 through 8 (primary grades). Consider all the elements of music. Discuss your formulated program with others.
12. Examine the music curriculum guides used in a school system near you and appraise the suggested music outcomes for each age and performance level. What musical content, facts, concepts, and generalizations are suggested? Do you find serious omissions? If so, what are they? What suggestions are made for the spiral development of concepts and generalizations? Are student objectives stated in specific terms? What teaching procedures, types of questions, and methods of inquiry are listed? What musical attitudes, appreciations, habits, and values are encouraged? Then compare these suggested outcomes with those in a guide from another source.
13. Compare the curricular organization presented in *The Study of Music in the Elementary School: A Conceptual Approach* (MENC, 1967) or some other national publication with the Conceptual Structure of Music outline in this chapter.
14. Analyze the Conceptual Structure of Music outline and revise it to suit your purposes. Add or delete generalizations, instructional objectives, and concepts, or reword them. Determine how you will use your revised structure in teaching the elements of music.
15. From one of the current music series textbooks select two good musical ideas and develop your own music lesson. Follow the lesson plan outline presented in this chapter.

REFERENCES

ABELES, HAROLD F., CHARLES R. HOFFER and ROBERT H. KLOTMAN, *Foundations of Music Education*. New York: Schirmer Books, 1984.

ARNOLD, VANESSA DEAN, "Planning for Effective Instruction," *The Teacher Educator, 24*, Winter 1988–89, 10–12.

BOARDMAN, EUNICE (ed.), *Dimensions of Musical Thinking*. Reston, Va.: Music Educators National Conference, 1989.

BRUNER, JEROME, *Toward a Theory of Instruction*. New York: Norton, 1966. Discusses the spiral curriculum and discovery learning.

CATON, J. J., "Developing and Managing Effective Instructional Plans," *Business Education Forum, 40*, April/May 1986, 12–14.

Dimensions of Thinking: A Framework for Curriculum and Instruction. Reston, Va.: Music Educators National Conference et al., 1989.

FRAENKEL, JACK R., *Helping Students Think and Value*. Englewood Cliffs, N. J.: Prentice Hall, 1973.

GRONLUND, NORMAN E., *Stating Objectives for Classroom Instruction*. New York: Macmillan, 1985.

HENAK, RICHARD M., *Lesson Planning for Meaningful Variety in Teaching*, 2nd ed. Washington, D.C.: National Education Association, 1984.

HOLT, DENNIS M., "Competency Based Music Teacher Education: Is Systematic Accountability Worth the Effort?" *Council for Research in Music Education*. Bulletin No. 40 (Winter 1974), 1–6.

Music Curriculum Bulletin. Salem, Oreg.: Oregon Department of Education, 1985.

NEELY, ANN M., "Planning and Problem Solving in Teacher Education," *Journal of Teacher Education, 37*/3, May–June 1986, 29–33.

NYE, ROBERT E. and VERNICE T. NYE, *Music in the Elementary School,* 3rd ed. Englewood Cliffs, N.J.: Prentice Hall, 1970.

POTOSKY, ALICE, ed., *Testimony to Music*. Reston, Va: Music Educators National Conference, 1986.

SLAVIN, ROBERT, and MADELINE HUNTER, "The Hunterization of America's Schools," *Instructor*, April 1987, 56–58.

WERNER, LAVERNE, and KEN CRAYCRAFT, "Writing Lesson Plans for Active Learning," *Childhood Education, 61*/1, Sept./Oct. 1984, 13–17.

YARBROUGH, CORNELIA, and HARRY E. PRICE, "Sequential Patterns of Instruction in Music," *Journal of Research in Music Education, 37*/3, Fall 1989, 179–87.

3 The Delivery of Instruction

The Learning Environment

One critical aspect of the learning process is the quality of the music environment. Each teacher must pause to ask, "What factors must I consider as I design a climate in which each student learns?" To address this pertinent question, constant attention must be directed to the interaction among such factors as physical environment, school organizational plans, teaching staffs, classroom organization, and management for instruction.

The Physical Environment Pure air, comfortable temperatures, and proper lighting contribute substantially to good learning. The busy teacher who is in the classroom all day may fail to notice insufficient ventilation, unhealthy temperatures, and faulty lighting. Attention to these details is of primary importance in creating a positive learning environment.

The arrangement of the furniture reflects the type of learning that can take place. Primary grades will frequently engage in musical activities in open floor space. Seating on a carpeted floor is best for some activities. In upper elementary instruction, seating should be arranged to facilitate individual and group work, and to provide opportunity for effective listening. Chairs, desks, or risers should be selected for the varying sizes of students so that all can be comfortably seated.

The varied activities in music make open space and movable furniture necessary. Seating will be changed at times for singing in large or small groups, playing instruments, creative interpretations, rhythmic responses, individualized instruction, and dance. Special seating may be needed for students who have difficulty hearing or seeing. The manner in which students move from one activity to another must be established in advance by clear instruction from the teacher. Ways of leaving and entering a music room, going to and from a music or assembly room, and moving books, instruments, and other materials are additional aspects of classroom routine that need to be established.

Visual aids may include a drawing of the keyboard, pictures of instruments and musicians, charts of hand signals, rhythm syllables, note values, and texts of songs posted on big sheets of butcher paper. Cue cards for listening experiences can also be useful visual aids.

Photo by Juretta Nidever.

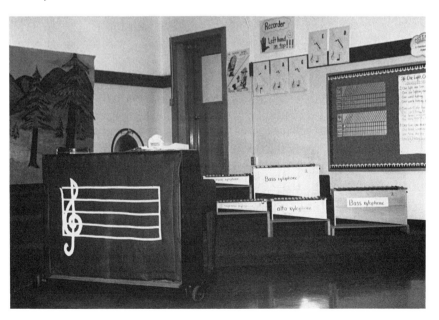

When instruments and equipment are selected, the teacher chooses those that produce excellent tone quality, are durable, attractive, and easy to store, and are suitable for the students. Every school should provide each student over age 7 with a copy of a music textbook (basal series) and access to a variety of supplementary music books and materials. Currently published music series include the following:

Music. Holt, Rinehart and Winston, Inc.,
301 Commerce Street, Suite 3700
Fort Worth, TX 76102

Music and You. The Macmillan Publishing
Co., Inc., 866 3rd Avenue, New York, NY, 10022.

The World of Music. Silver Burdett & Ginn,
250 James Street, Morristown, NJ 07960.

Recordings and teachers' books accompanying the textbooks are also recommended. When series books are selected, the selection committee should base its decision on the following criteria:

1. Philosophical basis for the series
2. Sequence of concepts, lessons, and materials
3. Quality of musical materials
4. Variety of musical materials
5. Appeal of content to designated age groups
6. Durability of cover and contents
7. Quality and usefulness of recordings (e.g., availability of accompaniment-only music on dual track, availability of CD recordings)
8. Size of print
9. Clarity of musical notation
10. Quality of paper (e.g., free from eye-straining gloss)
11. Ease of handling by students (e.g., page numbers on every page)
12. Use of color
13. Nature of illustrations (e.g., photographs of children preferred)
14. Use of nonsexist language and role models
15. Absence of visual clutter
16. Usefulness of indices (e.g., well organized, comprehensive, and accessible)
17. Simplicity and musicality of accompaniments (e.g., verses included directly under the music, spiral binding)

Each school building should contain a learning resource center that provides not only books about music but recordings, videotape equipment, computers, films, filmstrips, transparencies, projectors, and programmed and self-instructional materials. The following instruments are expected to be in each musically equipped classroom: drums of high and low pitches, thirty pairs of rhythm sticks, sandblocks, woodblocks, temple blocks, maracas, claves, cymbals, finger cymbals, tambourines, triangles, cowbell, jingle bells, gong, thirty-plus soprano recorders, assorted Orff-type instruments (pitched mallet and percussion instruments), fifteen autoharps, or omnichords, one guitar, a synthesizer, and a computer. There should be easy access to an overhead projector, screen, film projector, record and tape player, two tape recorders, television set, and a metronome.

Computer materials have value for all students in reinforcing the learning of both skills and concepts. The crucial issue is how well these materials assist in the realization of the identified objectives.

A music learning center may be located in a part of the room which is relatively secluded, yet accessible. This center serves as a resource primarily for gifted students, special projects, and other enrichment activities. It may be in a booth off the main classroom or it may consist of one large table or several smaller ones with materials and interesting directions or challenging suggestions as to what to do with them. The center could contain bulletin boards with information about community musical events, composers, recommended radio and television programs, musical achievements of students, jackets from books about music and from recordings, newspaper and magazine clippings, notation of unnamed familiar songs (which can be identified by studying this notation), favorite songs, and pictures relating to musical subjects. However, the bulletin board must be arranged attractively and changed frequently if it is to accomplish its mission of attracting maximum interest. Record players and computers with headsets can eliminate or reduce interference with other activities in the room.

The music classroom today often reflects the cultural resources in the community. This expansion of the learning environment requires the teacher to become familiar with facilities in the community that might be useful for music instruction. Students can contribute to the community by sharing their music and dance skills with senior citizens and other adults. In turn, community resources may bring special strengths to the music curriculum.

Systems for distributing and collecting material should be implemented by the students, who have been taught where and how to store them. If plastic recorders are provided, they can be sterilized between classes in the school dishwasher. Alternatively, each child might provide his or her own recorder. For sanitary reasons, instruments should not be exchanged.

Criteria must be established for proper use of the room in viewing films and television, and using the computer. A classified card file or computer index of recordings, films, and computer software should be part of the teacher's equipment.

School Organizational Plans

The educational philosophy of the administration and the school faculty (especially that of the classroom teacher and music specialist) will guide the designing of the instructional plans. These plans may differ from school to school because each plan is based upon a specific philosophy which is derived from the educational climate of that school. Therefore, no single plan can suffice for all schools. Teachers should be prepared to work in several types of school organizations, including the expedient "plan" of fitting X number of students into the space available in the existing school plant. Several plans are widely accepted. One is the 6-3-3 plan—elementary school, junior high school, and senior high school. Another plan, one that has grown in popularity, is the 4-4-4 organization—primary school, middle school, and high school. A recent effort to more clearly establish the identity of the middle school has resulted in the K–5, 3, 4 plan. This plan came about in part because the junior high school became more of an imitation of senior high school than an institution that clearly served its age group. The three-year middle school (grades 6 through 8) places fewer demands related to high school life on this age group, and through the use of longer homeroom periods, helps students acquire a greater sense of belonging.

Alternative schools are organized to meet the special interests of different segments of the community. By means of these schools, special needs are met, and the educational program is assumed to be more relevant to its learners. Such schools range from traditional schools in which the basics are emphasized to language immersion and magnet arts schools of many types. Alternative programs can include an entire school, some age levels within the school, or only one group of students.

The *self-contained classroom* is a type of curricular organization in which a group of students is in contact with one teacher for a major portion of the school day. It is in contrast to the *departmental* organization which divides the day into as many time periods as there are subjects, with each subject taught by a different specialist. Historically, there are three different types of self-contained classrooms: (1) all subjects taught by one teacher (with occasional assistance), (2) all subjects except music, art, and physical education taught by one teacher, and (3) all subjects in the primary school taught by one teacher, with varying degrees of departmentalization in the upper elementary school. Historically, art, music, and physical education were introduced into the curriculum as special subjects, taught by specialists. Even so, some schools assign responsibility for music teaching to classroom teachers through the fifth or sixth grade.

The organizational plan of the school will affect many aspects of its operation. It may affect the amount of time allocated to music teaching, although the philosophy of the administration and faculty is perhaps even more important. Many elementary schools still justify having music instruction to facilitate back-to-back reading programs. Students in the early grades are grouped by reading abilities and are combined in larger classes for music or physical education, while the classroom teacher takes from this larger class smaller reading groups for more intensive work. The organization of the school also has some influence on the music teacher's contact time with students (varying from twenty to forty-five minutes, one to five times a week), the space allocated for music instruction, and the learning materials and equipment available.

In order for students to become most effectively involved in the process of learning, they need a variety of learning environments that make possible different kinds of learning activities.

The Teaching Staff   The best musical environment for students is one in which both the classroom teacher and music specialist are involved in music teaching. Even if there is a music room to which students go to receive instruction from a specialist, students need the stimulation for music in their lives from the homeroom teacher.

The roles of the music specialist and classroom teacher are different in that the specialist is acknowledged to be the primary musical resource, the leading planner, the writer of long-term objectives and, above all, one who helps the classroom teacher in his or her efforts to teach music. The classroom teacher has the marked advantage of being with the students nearly all of the time, knowing them well, and thus being the major influence in the total education of the students. For this reason the music specialist and the classroom teacher work closely together for a balanced program of music instruction for all students. The classroom teacher may integrate music in such subjects as social studies and history, or for physiologically and psychologically necessary changes in routine. Music can improve the possibilities for general learning in any classroom. Many music specialists are not given sufficient time with students and thus have difficulty in achieving objectives without assistance from the classroom teacher. The ideal music program needs an additional staff of aides and other types of assistants, including parent volunteers.

In some situations there are no specialists, and the entire music program is the responsibility of classroom teachers. There may be one teacher who is accepted as a leader in working to establish music objectives, order materials, and act as chairperson of music for that building. In such situations there is increased dependence on the music series books as a dependable source for a minimal music program. They provide a sequential plan, songs and other materials, simple accompaniments, questions to ask, use of classroom instruments, pronunciation guides for foreign language songs, excellent recordings of singing and of instrumental music for listening, some Orff and Kodály methodology, related art and other enrichments, suggestions for teaching special learners, other individualized instruction, and special units of work called ''satellites'' or ''modules.''

Technically, a *music supervisor* has authority over a music program and its teachers, and can be very helpful in establishing and coordinating a quality program. Unfortunately, many school districts do not provide such music supervision. Many classroom teachers have expressed preference for a *music consultant* who acts as helper and resource person when called upon by teachers. In practice, classroom teachers who are competent in music teaching request the most assistance; those neglecting music or preferring not to teach it fail to contact the consultant. The authority over a music program is sometimes obscure, thereby resting with the principal by default. The environment for music learning may be inadequate unless the principal acts to ensure a good program.

Four Approaches to Learning and Their Classroom Settings

Successful learning occurs more predictably in environments that promote active student participation and provide stimuli for musical involvement. Those environments include both the approach used by the teacher and the physical setting for the class. The four types of learning we discuss have considerable overlap, even though their emphases differ. Teachers may employ any combination of the following approaches, depending on their teaching situation and immediate goals for their students.

Photo by Juretta Nidever.

1. The Conceptual Approach to Learning. Students in this environment are freely engaged in attempting to solve musical problems by exploring, discussing, performing, interpreting, analyzing, synthesizing, and evaluating. In a musical environment that is conducive to the development of these skills, students are guided in focusing their attention upon problems that have no single solution.

The comments of both students and teachers are accepted because of their pertinence to the solution of the problem being investigated. Both students and teachers have the freedom to engage in these processes.

The teacher stimulates students to explore and discuss musical problems among themselves and with the teacher, and asks questions that challenge the learners to seek appropriate answers. Students freely discuss alternate solutions to musical problems and formulate concepts or hypotheses which give the discussion focus. The teacher's statement of the problem outlines the general direction of investigation, and may imply the types of thinking and questioning needed to develop appropriate musical outcomes.

Good questions in music classes are directed toward the musical concepts being learned, and precede as well as follow the activity. They stimulate better listening, rhythmic responses, singing, playing of instruments, use of notation, understanding of musical concepts, and more creativity.

When students are involved in a conceptual approach, they need an environment constructed as a laboratory which contains music materials and media of varied types and levels of difficulty. Freedom of movement and opportunity to work cooperatively within that environment are necessities. For a more detailed description of cognitive-process thinking see Chapter 2.

2. The Creative-Exploratory Approach. If students' learning, including sensitivity to aesthetic experience, is to be fully developed, there must be time for exploring such learning in a relaxed, encouraging, and enjoyable environment. For creative involvement to occur, teachers must plan for it. The teacher's responsibility is to nurture and encourage creative spontaneity in every student. This creative-exploratory setting frees all students to explore, observe, and test their ideas. Learners can pursue problems of their choice in depth, unhampered by traditional subject barriers. Some group instruction takes place, but the focus is on the individual learner and freedom to learn.

The content of the curriculum is strongly affected by student interests. There are fewer restrictions on use of time and space, and students are free to interact with each other in order to learn from peers. The teacher's role is more that of resource person, diagnostician, and designer of the environment. Open-ended questions dominate the teacher's queries, and he or she intervenes at appropriate times to assist learning with questions and other stimuli. Evaluation emphasizes the process of learning rather than the final product of the experiences.

3. The Direct Instruction Approach. In this approach teachers are dominant figures who determine instructional goals and objectives, select and present most of the course content, and make most decisions. Interaction between teacher and students may be limited because the teacher does most of the talking and demonstrating. A more formal environment results. The teacher decides what types of behaviors are acceptable for the class and usually enforces them. Students speak, sing, and otherwise perform in ways the teacher indicates, although there may be some interaction.

The teaching may be centered on textbooks, workbooks, and a music series book. Large-group instruction is emphasized; there is ordinarily an absence of small-group and individual teaching. The expectations of the teacher are focused on the average learner. If discipline problems arise, they are found more frequently among the gifted, who are bored, and the slow learners, who are frustrated. Such a style may be found in general music classes as well as bands, orchestras, and choruses.

This direct instruction approach can be a well-planned, highly structured procedure emphasizing worthwhile educational objectives. It can involve the identification of important musical topics or skills, and the development of objectives that test learners' abilities with these topics or skills. If this process includes a mastery test, a series of lessons that teach the material assessed in the mastery test, and a series of diagnostic instruments to be administered at frequent intervals while instruction proceeds, the process is often called *mastery learning*. The diagnostic tests are vital to the process, since they provide teachers with the feedback required for them to determine the success of the instruction. As a result of the tests, students are moved to corrective work if they have not mastered the material or skill, or to extension activities if they have.

Direct instruction can provide through its diagnostic-corrective activities precise feedback on individual progress. Because it is based upon group instruction, it is easier for the average teacher to manage than some of the individualized classroom procedures. In direct instruction much class time may be devoted to textbook teaching and simple student recall of information. Current critics of public education claim that teachers should develop more student activities that involve conceptual thinking skills.

The effectiveness of direct instruction relates to the students' learning styles. Students who are less able to control their own thinking do best with this approach, but the more individualistic, creative thinkers do less well. Similarly, high-ability students have been found to do better in small groups than in large groups. Low-ability students usually need the greater direction and help provided by the teacher in the direct instruction method.

If teachers want to teach inquiry skills, they should seldom use direct instruction. If, on the other hand, teachers want to teach basic music skills, direct instruction is an appropriate method. Effective teaching involves the selection of a teaching approach that is appropriate to a specified educational outcome with a particular type of learner.

4. Social and Affective Learning. There is no single approach to social and affective learning. Any of the three approaches we just described may incorporate elements of it. Proponents of social and affective learning believe that knowledge alone is insufficient as a goal of any form of education. Without constructive attitudes, knowledge loses its practical value. Music experiences should provide aesthetic qualities as an integral part of each encounter. Many people believe these qualities relate to the human condition, and are therefore socially desirable. In any case, since social acceptance, attitudes, and feelings are related, the affective atmosphere of the classroom must be one that furthers positive emotional and social growth.

When the learning environment frustrates students by failing to meet social and emotional needs, it contributes little to the development of positive attitudes and values toward music.

It is generally agreed that feelings and emotions cannot be taught directly. The beauty of a musical selection is not taught by a teacher telling students how beautiful it is, or by the students merely verbalizing about it. Students must experience the music directly, and find in it beauty to such an extent that their responses to it and their understanding of it are positively affected.

Attitudes, emotions, and values, whether good or bad, will be developed in the classroom. It is the teacher's responsibility to promote the development of constructive attitudes. Raths, Harmin, and Simon (Raths et al., 1966) suggest that teachers plan for this by using the following steps in teaching valuing processes:

1. Encourage children to make choices and to make them freely.
2. Help them discover and examine available alternatives when faced with choices.
3. Help children weigh alternatives thoughtfully, reflecting on the consequences of each.

4. Encourage children to consider what it is they prize and cherish.
5. Give them opportunities to make public affirmations of their choices.
6. Encourage them to act, behave, and live in accordance with their choices.
7. Help them to examine repeated behaviors or patterns in their lives.

Students' attitudes and values regarding music are often close to the centers of their personal identities and the identities of their peer groups. Since students' musical backgrounds and experiences differ, teachers should not expect all children to acquire the same musical values.

The positive attitudes of teachers are important to the instructional process. The chance remark of a teacher might have a lasting influence on a student. The teacher's attitude toward music usually affects children's attitudes.

Different types of music affect people differently. Therefore, the teacher should work toward a classroom environment in which the varied opinions of students toward music are listened to with interest and respect, and given appropriate attention in the class. Such an environment permits personal differences while allowing discussion in support of positions taken. Healthy musical values take shape in a classroom in which there is neither hostility nor aggression. An intellectually sound position for a music teacher is one that attempts to judge music in accordance with how well it performs its function, the feeling qualities it evokes, and the connection it makes with a culture. In this atmosphere every facet of music from Renaissance motets to jazz to electronic music has a place, and their musical values are explored by students in the classroom.

Organizing for Instruction

In an effort to make instruction in all areas of music more effective and to provide opportunities for students to learn in a variety of ways, the teacher chooses an appropriate organizational plan which may be large-group, small-group, or individualized instruction, or some combination of the same.

Large Groups Some aspects of a lesson or activity can be accomplished more effectively in a large group. The following activities work well in a large-group setting:

Introducing a music concept or skill to be learned.

Introducing one or more problems related to the concept or skill.

Reviewing a musical skill.

Rehearsing vocal or instrumental ensembles of a wide variety.

Clarifying and planning with the students the activities to be pursued in small groups.

The large group provides an excellent setting for sharing musical ideas, projects, and performances of small groups and individuals. Large musical group performances which involve the combined efforts of smaller groups and individuals can be particularly satisfying. They can also provide powerful motivation for further musical learning. In-school class performances and musical stage productions are examples.

The Orff-Schulwerk process emphasizes that students can develop the total personality by actively sharing musical experiences within a large group through cooperation rather than competition. According to Orff, the student can act as an individual within the social context of a group. As an individual, the learner can speak, conduct, improvise, suggest arrangements of voices and instruments, propose new approaches and activities, play, dance, or sing a solo part. As a member of a small or large group the student can speak, sing, play, or respond with movement or dance, all as a cooperating member of the group. Thus the Schulwerk claims to operate in a manner in which the social values of large-group contacts are not lost. The teacher serves as guide, facilitator, stimulator, and co-worker. Music thus becomes a tightly organized social activity in which performance is shared with others.

Small Groups Teachers employ small groups in an effort to make provisions for different learning styles, varied stages of development, and special interests of students. Such groups operate in designated areas within the room, or in the library, conference room, music laboratory, or other nearby places. Activities for small groups may include solving musical problems, practicing musical skills, composing music within stated limits, planning accompaniments, learning to play an instrument, analyzing a recorded musical selection, or planning a musical performance. While small groups can be used at any level, they may be more effective with the later grades. When students have not participated in small-group work, the teacher should begin by organizing one group while the remainder of the students work as a class or as individuals. The teacher then gradually organizes additional groups until the time when most or all of the class can be involved in this manner.

There are strengths as well as weaknesses in small-group work that teachers should recognize. First, small-group work should be limited to some purpose that members of the group can share. Second, groups should be limited to activities in which the students possess the skills needed to develop the activities. Third, groups should be limited to activities in which cooperative action is required to achieve stated purposes. If an activity can be completed by an individual or by several individuals working independently, there is no need to organize a group. Fourth, groups should be limited to activities in which effective working relationships can be maintained. If interpersonal differences cannot be reconciled, progress cannot be made by forcing individuals to work in a group.

In small groups, students may

Adhere to a list of expected objectives.

Decide upon a tentative plan.

Identify the responsibilities of each individual.

Complete assigned musical activities.

Evaluate and make value judgments.

Decide how they will share their ideas, skills, or performance with the larger class.

In the larger class, the members of small groups may

Report to or perform for the class.

Answer questions asked by classmates.

Receive suggestions from peers and teachers as to ways to improve.

Evaluate works in terms of the class objectives.

During small-group instruction the teacher circulates among the groups, giving assistance. Close supervision may be necessary for productive learning to take place. Some groups need only a minimal amount of supervision, whereas others need considerable guidance. The teacher's role is to offer suggestions, ask questions, commend students for good work, and be a resource person when needed. If the teacher finds that some students lack skills to complete a task, skills groups may be organized to help them master these skills before they return to the original small group.

*Individualized Instruction** Another organizational plan is individualized instruction. In this plan teachers provide experiences for students working individually, sometimes without direct teacher supervision. In recent years computer-assisted instruction (CAI) has played an important role in individual instruction. In all cases it is an attempt to accept students ''where they are'' in musical responsiveness and to help them to progress as far as they are capable. In such a program there are both teacher-directed and student-selected activities.

Individualized instruction allows great freedom to plan a program based on an individual's learning style, developmental level, cultural background, and past achievements. To initiate such a program the teacher needs to prepare the principal, the faculty, and the parents for the experience with discussions and carefully prepared materials. There should be an open invitation to these people to visit the program in operation. Their support is necessary for its success. As is true in all valid instruction, the musical needs of each student are met in individualized instruction when (1) musical experiences begin where the student presently is, (2) the curriculum is diversified through a wide variety of learning alternatives that are offered concurrently rather than consecutively, (3) planning is made for continual progress by each individual, and (4) continuous assessment and feedback are given.

The physical environments conducive to individualized instruction may vary widely. Students may work at their desks, at tables, on the floor, at wall dis-

*We are indebted to Dr. Sylvia Cary for points of discussion of individualized instruction. The information was adapted from her unpublished dissertation, ''Individualized Music Instruction—Traditional Music Instruction: Relationships of Music Achievement, Music Performance, Music Attitude, Music Aptitude, and Reading in Classes of Fifth Grade Students,'' doctoral dissertation, University of Oregon, 1981, Dissertation Abstracts International, 1981, Vol. 42, Number 10 (Order Number DA8201812), Copyright 1981 by Sylvia Estes Cary.

plays, at chalkboards and charts, and at learning stations. These learning stations may be arranged around the periphery while chairs or desks remain in the center of the room to facilitate large-group instruction. Hallways, closets, booths, and alcoves may be used to provide space for many types of activities. There is a variety of inexpensive and free materials with which to experiment. The usual music equipment is present: melody instruments, music books and books related to music, percussion instruments, chording instruments, recordings, pictures, puzzles, games, and flash cards. The sound center recommended by the Manhattanville Music Curriculum Program should be included, and a computer laboratory is often available as well. There might be a science-of-sound center, a multimedia center, or an instrument construction center. Care must be taken, however, that students are not confused by an overly rich environment. Teachers need to arrange one that challenges and interests, but does not overwhelm.

During most of the school day or in music periods on successive days, individuals and small groups move from station to station. Many directions for each activity are in written and printed form. Some directions are on tapes or recordings; some are given directly by the teacher. The activities are created by imaginative and resourceful teachers to match the maturity, learning style, needs, and interests of each learner. Students are free to study all areas of the music curriculum. An elementary classroom may have as few as one or two music stations: a music room could have thirty. Individualized instruction may function within an elementary program that also includes more traditional large-group instruction if the stations are arranged around the outer portions of the room. Individualized instruction does not dictate a particular school or method of instruction. The techniques can operate along a continuum of choices from behavioristic to humanistic, conservative to radical, and strictly structured to loosely structured.

In addition to the usual equipment for music study, the music stations require teacher preparation of various types of meaningful materials in the form of direction sheet, booklet, learning packet, chart, manipulative instrument, or object.

Flexibility of the environment, sound and sight control, and careful storage planning are essential if the needs of individualized instruction are to be met. The entire area demands acoustical study to balance and soften the many sounds that characterize individual and small-group instruction. Sounds that seem cacophonous can in reality be harmonious if the students are intensely involved in what they are doing.

Sight barriers are important psychologically, especially at the beginning of new individualized experiences. Many students are more distracted by what they see than by what they hear. Not only do sight barriers aid in concentration, the dividers also mark off perimeters of learning stations. These boundaries, in terms of classroom control, help to avoid disputes that arise when one person interferes with another. Later in the experience, often just the hint of a sight barrier is enough to keep order.

Individualized instruction places heavy responsibility on the teacher to do each of the following:

1. Diagnose each student's musical capabilities and interests.
2. Determine the performance objectives for each station.
3. Prepare a matrix matching the musical objectives with the stations.
4. Prepare a learning sequence on Job Cards.
5. Determine an appropriate system of student rotation between stations.
6. Provide the necessary instructional resources at each station.

Figure 3.1 illustrates one possible arrangement for a music room in which individualized instruction takes place. At each of the stations Job Cards will instruct the students on the sequence of activities that are to be completed there. We recommend that the Job Cards be color-coded to indicate varied levels of difficulty. The music teacher determines where the Job Cards are to be kept, and how they will be distributed to students. Several sample Job Cards follow.

Figure 3.1. MUSIC ROOM PLAN

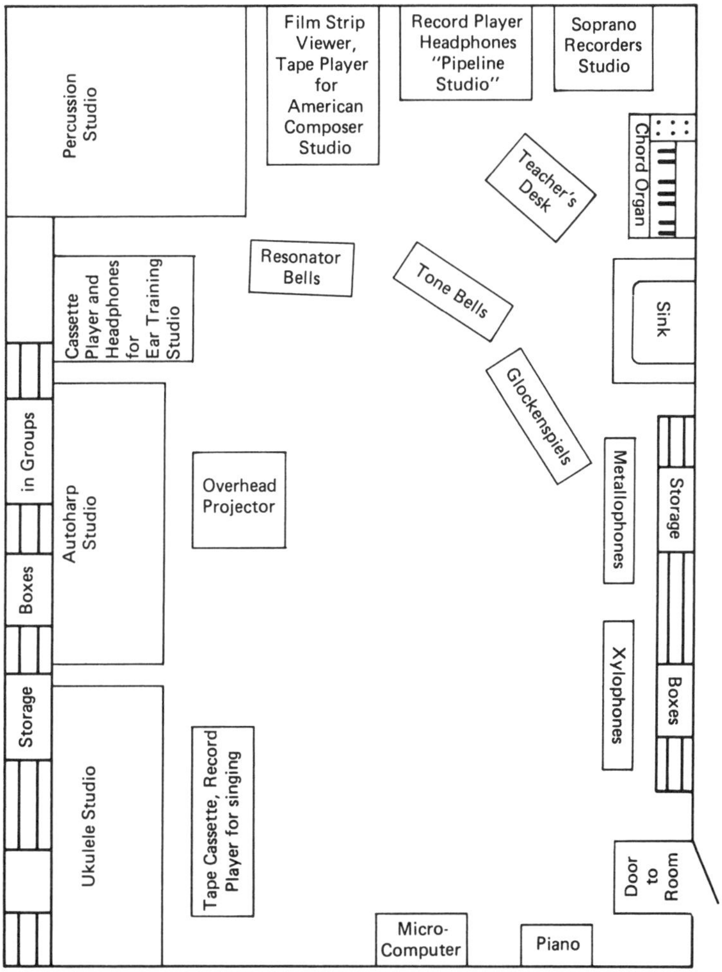

Sample Job Card 1 (Simple)

STATION A: MUSICOLOGY

"Musicology" means finding out interesting things to know about music, musical instruments, or people who make music. A musicologist is like a detective who finds new clues about music from books.

You have a choice. You may choose one of the books at this station or you may go to the library for **one book** about music that you have not read.

Ask the librarian to check it out to the music room. Bring it back to read, and at the end of class, add it to the music books already at this station. You may sit in the rocking chair.

Suggestion: If you have time, you may write a letter to a friend to tell about your favorite book.

Sample Job Card 2 (Simple)

STATION P: DRUM MESSAGES

This is a partner station. You will work with the person at Station Q. At this station you will find two drums. One of you will play a pattern of beats and pitches on the drum at the station, while the other person listens. Then the listener will try to repeat the pattern exactly as the player played it the first time. Then switch tasks and let the listener "*send the message*." Continue like this, taking turns being the listener and the player. Be as creative as you can! But, limit your number of beats to six so that the patterns don't get too hard to repeat. If you are a **Whiz Kid**, see if you can write down in **Ta** and **Tee** the pattern the other person is playing on the drum. Use the paper at this station to do this.

Example:

Have fun!

Sample Job Card 3 (Advanced)

STATION X: HARMONY WITH BELLS

You are going to learn how to build I, IV, V *CHORDS*. At Station X you will find a case of resonator bells, songsheets, and mallets. Move them to a desk.

Take out the FAC bells. Play them together. You have just built an F chord. It started with F, the first tone of the F scale, and so we will call it I. This is what it looks like on the staff:

I = FAC or *F Chord*

Now build another chord which starts on C. For this you will take out the CEG bells. C is the fifth tone of the F scale, so we will call it V. It looks like this on the staff:

V = CEG or *C Chord*

Now build a chord which starts on B♭. This is a black bell. With it you will need the D F bells. B♭ is the fourth tone of the F scale so we will call it IV. It looks like this on the staff:

IV = B♭ D F or *B♭ Chord*

Now that you have built these three chords, practice playing them. First play I, then IV and V.

Now you are ready to try to play these **chords** to a song. To play a chord, use two mallets in one hand, and one mallet in the other. Strike the three bells at the same time. You are making **HARMONY**

Congratulations!

STATION K: HIGH ROLLERS

You are going to play **HIGH ROLLERS**. Take from the bag **two dice**, **music paper**, and a **pencil**. Notice the dice are not alike—one has numbers like fractions and one has notes.[*]

Put your name at the top of a piece of music paper. Next, draw a bar line to connect five lines, and draw a **TREBLE CLEF SIGN** 𝄞.

Throw the die with the numbers on it. Write the fraction on the music paper after the **TREBLE CLEF SIGN** 𝄞. It is called a

TIME SIGNATURE

The **top number** tells you **how many beats you can have in each measure**. The **bottom number** tells you **what kind of note gets 1 count**.

Now throw the die with the notes on it **twelve times**. After each throw, write on your music paper the note that is on the top of the die.

Now you are ready to put in the bar lines.

Remember that in 4/4 meter:

𝅝   gets 4 counts
𝅗𝅥   gets 2 counts
𝅘𝅥   gets 1 count
𝅘𝅥𝅮𝅘𝅥𝅮   get 1 count (2 halfcounts)

Look at the fraction TIME SIGNATURE that you put near the **TREBLE CLEF SIGN** 𝄞. The top number tells you how many beats to include in each measure before you draw a bar line, separating notes. See if you can make measures of all the twelve notes you threw on the dice. When you finish, show Mrs. V.

If you have the right number of counts in each measure, you are a

HIGH ROLLER
Congratulations!

At pack-up time, please return everything to the bag, put your music paper in the basket on the top of the piano.

There are many types of stations teachers can create for learning. They may be given letters of the alphabet, numbers, or descriptive titles. The Job Cards for each station are named according to the musical objectives to be studied: Rhythm, Melody, Harmony, Form, Tone Qualities, Dynamics, Tempo, and sometimes Music Fundamentals or Theory. Others may be Guitar, Autoharp, Keyboards, Electronic Lab, or Filmstrip. Many teachers invent titles that amuse

[*]Teachers may prepare dice for this activity, cutting polyfoam into two oversized dice. On the faces of one die are glued different time signatures. On the faces of the other die are glued different musical notes.

learners, such as Make and Play, Drums Away, Fun and Games, Keyboard Capers, Read All About It, Play That Tune, Listen!, Composer's Corner, and Make a Tone Row.

Computer-Assisted Instruction

Undoubtedly the fastest growing area of individualized instruction today is computer-assisted instruction (CAI). As the microcomputer becomes a common instructional tool in the elementary school, musical software is being written for a wide variety of musical purposes. At present, good computer programs exist for pitch matching, rhythmic discrimination, beginning music theory, music notation, music composition, MIDI connections with electronic keyboards, and numerous other musical activities. Such electronic instruction in music works well as one or more stations in a program of individualized instruction, or as an enrichment center at the back of the room.

There is a surprisingly wide variety of instructional programs in music on the market at present. Care must therefore be taken to preview and select programs that are both educationally sound and appropriate to the content of the teacher's curriculum. Additional criteria for the selection of programs are the use of interesting graphics, a high quality of sound, an appropriate pace for students, the immediacy of feedback, the inclusion of positive reinforcement, and simplicity of operation. Because of the constantly changing market for such programs of instruction no recommendations are given here. The *Music Educators Journal* carries a regular column titled "Floppy Discography," in which new software is reviewed. Numerous computer journals review such programs regularly as well.

Individualized instruction may present a variety of opportunities, but without workable techniques of classroom management it can become chaotic. A common misconception among music teachers is that an individualized classroom is one in which all the students are quietly plugged into headphones, listening to music and perhaps writing. A few students may be doing this, but most of these learning alternatives are sound-filled interactions between the student and music.

In establishing ground rules for discipline, students should have both the freedom and the responsibility to operate within defined parameters. A simple set of necessary and clearly stated ground rules makes a program manageable, and if students have input in determining them, the students are usually more cooperative. Nonverbal signals are useful because of the level of sound that can exist and because students are working in different areas of the room. A most effective signal is the flicking of the lights for instant quiet. The teacher or student manager can then proceed with announcements.

Students can make large charts listing rules as they become necessary. For example: "Work within your studio area." "Raise your hand when you need assistance." "Do not keep anyone else from learning." "At the signal for pack-up, return all your equipment to your station."

Individualized music instruction has some specific issues for the teacher to address:

1. Analyze quickly which sounds at the stations are productive and which are not. Then intervene in a positive way with those that are not.
2. Group students carefully. Be aware of people who behave negatively when put in close proximity.
3. Calmly accept some confusion and messiness. A certain amount of it is inevitable.
4. Be aware of students needing help and guidance, and step in before they become frustrated and become disruptive.
5. Establish the idea that the students are becoming more independent and will not be constantly watched. At the same time, however, state that it is easy to notice those who are preventing others from learning and that they will be disciplined.

Learning stations, classroom management, materials, and student progress should be constantly evaluated. Teacher aides or classroom helpers are often useful in tracking individual students. Teachers must develop record keeping that is appropriate for evaluating students in each situation.

Special Learners   The joy of music knows no handicaps.

- Raini, a cerebral palsied student in a wheelchair, plays an Orff instrument with the mallet held in her mouth.
- Julie, deaf, echoes a song by lipreading.
- Malinda plays the temple blocks, though Down syndrome limits some musical tasks she can accomplish.
- Todd, hearing impaired and legally blind, responds in rhythm with creative movements.
- Aimee, also hearing and speech impaired, is learning to play the violin in a beginning strings class through the help of a music practicum student.

Today's elementary music classes include children of varying abilities. For the music specialist who has had limited contacts with exceptional children, the experience may be frustrating and discouraging. For others, it offers an exciting charge: Design a program to challenge each child to the limits of his or her ability.

When today's teachers examine the makeup of school classes, they may find exceptional children in class as a result of Public Law 94-142, which made mandatory the mainstreaming of many students with special problems. They may also find gifted students, another category of learners with special needs. Thus today's teachers view the classroom quite differently from their predecessors. Students are helped to regard themselves as unique persons who need not necessarily conform to the developmental levels of other students. However, in the process of analyzing and diagnosing students, teachers must plan so that each student will progress as far as he or she is capable. Extensive planning and meticulous record-keeping are required in programs for the exceptional child. Public Law 94-142 demands that a personal program (Individualized Education Program, or IEP) be planned for each mainstreamer and that records be kept.

Several common categories of exceptionality have been established, and are referred to with the following abbreviations:

EMR: Educable Mentally Retarded

NE: Neurologically Dysfunctioning

VI: Visually Impaired

HI: Hearing Impaired

PH: Physically Handicapped

MH: Mentally Handicapped

PSA: Personal and Social Adjustment problems

LD: Learning Disabled

Children in all of the categories are sometimes referred to as "special" or "exceptional" students.

Some students classified as special learners may function normally in most music activities; others require special consideration. Some receive additional resource room instruction to better assist their areas of deficiency and are in regular classrooms the remainder of the day. Still others have part-time special class instruction. Thus there are three general settings for special learners: (1) those in regular classes without support services, (2) those in regular classes with supplementary resource services, and (3) those in special classes part time. A mainstreamed class would ideally have no more than fifteen students.

Because music teachers may not be routinely notified about the intent to mainstream a specific child, the music teacher must assume responsibility for acquiring both the name and background information for such students. The goals of music instruction are the same as for the regular student, but methods of instruction and pace may differ.

An anciliary staff helps mainstreaming succeed. Such a staff may include some or all of the following: special education teacher or consultant, hearing clinician, speech clinician, school nurse, school psychologist, school social worker, principal, counselor, and perhaps others. The school media specialist can assist with construction of uncomplicated charts, music notation, and drawings that can be clearly comprehended by all special learners. With the assistance of appropriate staff, teachers should be able to

1. Plan course content, teaching strategies, class procedures, and evaluation methods.
2. Recognize sociological and psychological characteristics of mildly disabled students.
3. Design and implement a curriculum for the special learner.
4. Create means of evaluation appropriate to measure both classroom progress and student achievement.

The purpose of mainstreaming is to provide the exceptional child with a normal classroom experience. Integration of the exceptional child into the general music class tests every management skill of the music specialist. Subtlety is necessary to preserve an atmosphere of normalcy among advantaged and disadvantaged youngsters. The quality of curriculum and the enjoyment of music should not be diminished due to the blending of mainstreamed youth into an otherwise average setting. We urge the specialist to assess continually the social interactions occurring among all students. Manipulation of external factors such as placement of the exceptional student in relation to others will affect student motivation and hence the success of participation.

The goals of music instruction for exceptional children are the same as those for the normal child. These may be divided into three categories: (1) competencies and skills, (2) learnings and understandings, and (3) attitudes and appreciations. The experiences should be varied and include listening to music, moving bodily to music, singing, playing instruments, creating music, and eventually learning to read and write music notation.

Underestimating the capacity for musical responsiveness among exceptional children may be avoided by careful observation. Each child is unique, and while some limitations are obvious, subtle problems of perception, attention span, eye-hand coordination, and memory should be detected. Children with different dysfunctions may share similar learning patterns. For example, hearing-impaired students are often language-impaired, as are a majority of the trainable mentally retarded and cerebral palsied children. Learning specialists are eager to provide information about individual students. Classroom teachers, school nurses, and parents also contribute. Assimilating a background about each exceptional child will enable the music specialist to devise forms of musical expression adapted to the student's limited physical or mental capacity.

When placed in the regular classroom, the exceptional student may first want to observe others, a normal reaction for anyone in a new environment. Should the special student fail to respond, opportunity to experiment with or play an instrument will usually result in participation. The teacher should do nothing for a student that he or she can do without assistance because special students are independent and want to participate without help unless absolutely necessary.

There are students who are unable to follow teachers' directions which contain several different commands, such as, "Listen to the recording, find the beat, and show me with your body that you feel the tempo." The teacher may need to demonstrate the activity, specify the part of the body that is to react to it, or actively help the student find the beat. Peer tutors are often useful assistants with such activities. They may help by depressing autoharp chord bars, steadying mallets, or supporting musical instruments for the motor-impaired students. The teacher's task is to make possible some kind of success despite difficulties. Materials may have to be adapted in some way in order for individual students to find success. The more recent music series offer suggestions which may be suitable for the special learner in the mainstreamed classroom. For example, Silver Burdett's series, *World of Music* (1991) provides a separate resource book titled "Classroom Management/Special Learners." Macmillan's *Music and You* series (1991) offers mainstreaming suggestions in a colored band at the bottom of each lesson. Holt, Rinehart and Winston's *Music* (1988) provides a separate resource booklet on mainstreaming activities for each grade level.

The cooperation of parents is helpful to the mainstreamed class. Many parents of special learners are concerned about their children's acceptance by teachers and other students, and they may fear the comparison of their child to the other students. They often have pressing concerns of their own in relation to their exceptional children, and teachers may find a need for telephone calls, conferences, and support groups. The teacher must be prepared to talk with parents about the goals for the class and about short-term objectives for each student. Parents should be assisted in helping their children with music at home, and instruments, tapes, recordings, learning packages, and other materials should be available for home use. The teacher and parent need to know that each can be helpful to the other in assisting the special learner. Parents can help at times in the music class; they should be encouraged to visit the class and become involved when appropriate.

The Orthopedically Handicapped or Spastic.   One aim of the teacher is to develop the physical responses of these students to the limits of their capabilities. They normally demonstrate less fear about the outcome of their participation than do normal students. Their eagerness to try can be a good example for others. Substitute motions are required in many instances, such as hands in the air for walking, and tapping a resonant part of a wheelchair in time with the movements of others. Children wearing braces or using crutches should be encouraged to participate along with the class in all activities. Bodily movement and dances are adaptable, with head bobs and bows substituted for steps. Percussion instruments can be strapped to a hand or foot when necessary. Orff mallet instruments can be played with the mallet held in the mouth and a peer tutor assisting each strike on the bar, or holding the drum. Autoharp chord bars can be depressed by a solid wooden dowel (flat end) held in the student's mouth. The teacher or a peer helper may steady the dowel. A pentatonic scale is useful when the student is improvising. The teacher removes unnecessary bars to minimize discordant tones. These students need ample time in which to perform physically. Therefore, the teacher needs to have patience, and assist only when necessary. Furthermore, exceptional children should not be expected to play with the same precision as physically normal students.

Singing can help spastic students relax their throat muscles, thus making singing a more flowing response than speaking. Singing in a chorus can be enjoyed from a musical standpoint and result in the satisfaction of being a full participant in a large group.

The Visually Impaired.   Blind and near-blind students are capable of participating in virtually all musical activities. The National Library Service for the Blind and Physically Handicapped, Library of Congress, provides songs for the blind in braille notation, and publishes *A Dictionary of Braille Music Signs.*

The teacher should see that the partially sighted are placed close to the front of the class. Texts of songs may be displayed in oversized words written with felt pen on large sheets of butcher paper. Melodies may be taught by rote, large print, or braille notation. Autoharp bars may be marked with textured dots. Teachers should use songs that employ no more than three chords clustered near each other.

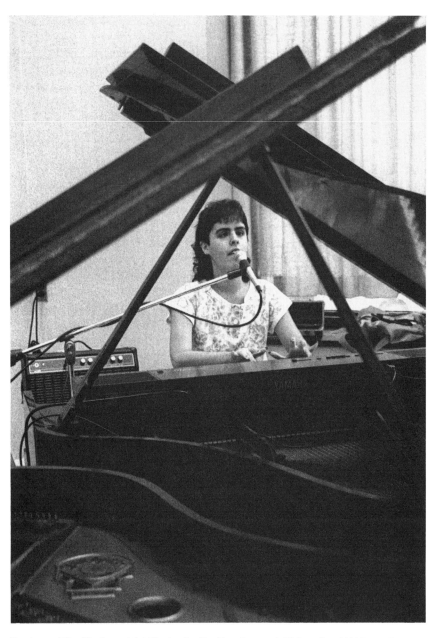

Courtesy of the Music and Art Center for the Handicapped, University of Bridgeport.

The Hearing Impaired.   Both profoundly deaf and hearing-impaired students may be found in music classes. The profoundly deaf are those whose hearing is nonfunctional for the ordinary purposes of living. The hearing impaired are those whose defective hearing is functional with or without a hearing aid. Deaf students often suffer from muscular tension, speech disorders, and language deficiencies. However, pitched vibrations can be felt through the skin, muscles, and head bones. Through feeling vibrations these students are able to perceive rhythmic sound, thus wooden floors that vibrate serve to bring them into contact with music. When partially deaf students have some ability to hear, they can learn to match tones, reproduce scales, and listen to music. Their speech tends to improve because accents and syllabic durations can be explained in musical sound and rhythm patterns. Some songs and chants provide rhythmic bases for speech improvement.

Courtesy of the Music and Art Center for the Handicapped, University of Bridgeport.

Many hearing-impaired students learn to read lips; thus they should be no farther from the teacher than 6 or 8 feet and placed at an angle from which they can easily see the teacher's lip and tongue movements. These students' learning styles are primarily visual and tactile, so demonstrations are helpful. Tapping the beat or pattern on the shoulder and placing the hard-of-hearing between good singers are also of aid to these special learners. Color-coding keys on bell sets and tone bars and on autoharp chord bars may be helpful. Recent research indicates that there are a variety of hearing impairments. Students may therefore hear some registers and timbres better than others.

The Educable Retarded.   Retarded or brain-damaged children will have limited academic success but can enjoy musical involvement, which contributes significantly to feelings of self-esteem. Most of these students operate at Piaget's earlier stages of learning, and may not be able to conceptualize or generalize at higher levels of thought. Teachers may expect shorter attention spans, difficulty in using abstractions, failure in comprehending similarities and differences, poor verbal communication, emotional overreactions to confusing situations, and limited memory. A slower pace for learning is necessary, with more structure, routine, and direction, combined with frequent changes of activity. Sequences of learning in small steps are important to the success of these students. However, the teacher should avoid excessive repetition as a method of teaching musical skills. The retarded are drilled by repetition in other academic areas, and they enjoy learning through varied approaches in the music class.

Courtesy of the Music and Art Center for the Handicapped, University of Bridgeport.

Concrete stimuli are needed. Hand puppets, visual aids, words of songs, and body movements can improve vocabulary and communication skills. Opportunities for creative sound exploration should be provided on a wide variety of instruments. Single mallet playing is recommended where hand coordination is poor. Simple repetitive ostinati on Orff instruments can be accomplished by removal of dissonant bars. Two students, one exceptional and the other normal, can cooperatively play instruments such as the log drum and the temple blocks.

Singing activities are equally important for the educable retarded. Teachers may encourage tone matching through chanting on single pitches and singing. Since many retarded students sing in monotones, class activities demonstrating the concepts of high and low tones are worthwhile. Retarded children may be interspersed among in-tune singers. They enjoy rhythmic songs, especially when accompanied by body movements, as well as songs that relate to their daily activities. Tape recorders and other simple equipment may be operated by them.

The Learning Disabled or Perceptually Handicapped. There are students who appear to be normal except for a malfunction or immaturity of the central nervous system. These children suffer various cognitive inabilities such as incapacity to organize, classify, assimilate, perceive, and to transmit information. The implications to the teacher include simple repetition of enjoyable music activities; varied approaches to learning that require more than one sense; use of short, repetitious, interesting songs, recordings, and instrumental pieces; simple imitations, such as echo-songs and echo-clapping; and body responses with both large and small muscles. The teacher's directions should be brief and explicit. Finger plays, action songs, simple games, and songs that state directions within lyrics are good for those whose minds do not process details well. Calming music is used with hyperactive children, and stimulating music for lethargic ones. Rhythmic rhymes and words can assist those who have difficulty remembering words.

The Emotionally Disturbed. Interpersonal problems which handicap these students are subtle, varied, and complex. Unacceptable behavior is symptomatic of the stress they feel. Each child needs individual consideration as well as a variety of approaches to promote self-expression in music.

Students must be taught to listen and to interpret what is heard. A calm, nonthreatening environment can be reassuring that music is a positive experience. The room should be arranged simply to avoid distracting visual clutter. Free, expressive movements can relieve the tension felt by most disturbed students. Flexible pacing of activities will accommodate the short attention span of some. Alternating music participation with listening helps to keep them at task.

Stress may produce harsh, raspy singing voices. Teachers need to encourage a free tone, matched with exercises on Orff instruments. These activities help the student focus on things other than his or her own problems. Initially, these students may lack sufficient confidence to sing with others, but as confidence develops, making opportunities for group singing is important.

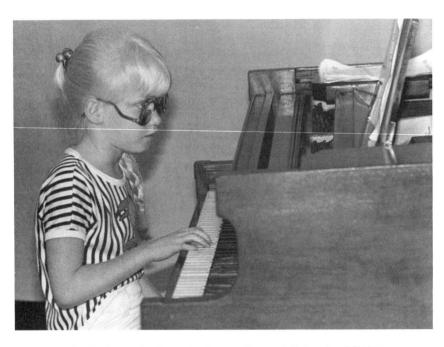

Courtesy of the Music and Art Center for the Handicapped, University of Bridgeport.

Students need opportunities for sound exploration and creative self-expression on Orff instruments. A simple, consistent procedure for the care and use of instruments is advised. Positive reinforcement of good efforts will offset the reprimands that may be received elsewhere. It is important to balance praise with reasonable expectations for continued musical growth.

The Gifted. Gifted students have many talents that may contribute positively to society. Giftedness has been unduly equated with high intelligence, but it is now known that talents are independent abilities, not necessarily related to intelligence. For example, a person can be extremely talented musically while being rather average in other respects, and other talents may be similarly isolated. Errors have been made in assuming that a high IQ student who is "good at everything" in school will be an excellent musician. In dealing with the gifted, the search should be for those of outstanding talent in a subject area or skill as well as selecting those of high intelligence.

Gifted students need a balanced program of cognitive, affective, and psychomotor education, but with additional work in creativity and in the area of their special talent. As in any individual's education, the teacher identifies the student's talent, interests, persistence, and limitations, and designs a learning environment for that student's optimum growth. Interest and persistence are vital; there are numerous examples of extremely talented students who lack the interest and persistence necessary to develop their talents. Gifted students are usually in the regular classroom for most of the day in order to continue to develop normal social relationships.

With gifted learners the teacher emphasizes problems that stimulate creative thinking and process learning. Many opportunities should be provided to exercise initiative, to develop the skills of working independently while at the same time to be accepted by peers, and to become emotionally secure and socially adept. The teacher provides enrichment activities and experiences, special materials, and sources of information. There will be higher level performing on instruments or voice, composing music, and devising dance movements. The music specialist, classroom teacher, and parent will find it necessary to work together for the gifted just as they do for other exceptional learners.

In summary, for each of the types of special learners just discussed, some suggestions for teachers follow. These recommendations were developed through observations of teachers experienced in working with exceptional children.

TIPS FOR MAINSTREAMING

Orthopedically Handicapped or Spastic

- Integrate students in braces, on crutches, and in wheelchairs into the physical milieu of the class.
- Attach a tray to the wheelchair to support instruments.
- Substitute head bobs and bows for steps.
- Allow extra time for physical movements.
- Assist only when absolutely necessary.
- Encourage the quadraplegic to manipulate a mallet or dowel in the mouth for playing Orff instruments, an autoharp, or resonator bells (a peer helper may be necessary).
- Remove unnecessary bars from Orff instruments to minimize discordant tones.
- Encourage singing to loosen tight throat muscles.

The Visually Impaired

- Position student close to the front of the class.
- Display texts of songs with oversized words on butcher paper.
- Present melodies by rote, large print, or braille notation.
- Use eurhythmic activities to develop good posture.
- Provide frequent hands-on experience with a variety of instruments.
- Have students verbalize timbral differences and clearly name each instrument when it is played.
- Mark autoharp chord bars with different textured dots.
- Choose songs that use no more than three chords clustered near each other on the autoharp.
- Play listening examples by blind musicians and composers.
- Encourage private study on the piano or another instrument.

- Acquaint young blind musicians with the resources available in braille from the National Library Service.

The Hearing Impaired

- Place student with his or her back to the window.
- Position yourself at a 45-degree angle in the student's vision no farther than 6 to 8 feet away. This enhances tongue observation.
- Stand still when speaking or singing.
- Speak in a natural, unexaggerated manner.
- Write new vocabulary or musical terms on the board.
- Do not speak when your back is turned.
- When not understood, rephrase rather than shouting.
- Explain texts of all songs sung by the class.
- Demonstrate melodic lines and pitches visually, using hand levels and instruments.
- Tap a steady beat on the student's shoulders.
- Encourage in-tune singing by placing the student between two pitch-accurate singers.
- Have students use a Kazoo to sense head vibrations of pitched tones.
- Make sure each student is *attending,* when you teach or demonstrate.
- Reduce noise level of the classroom from time to time.
- Check manual adjustment of hearing aids as you introduce new timbres (especially percussion instruments and strings).
- Choose instruments whose vibrations can be seen and felt as well as heard.
- When using recordings, determine the best volume level. Set it at the beginning of the selection, and do not change it during the piece.

The Educable Retarded

- Introduce partner games and dances.
- Use mirroring in rhythmic activities.
- Demand attentive on-task behavior.
- Vary pacing of class activities to allow slow learners occasional opportunities to function on par with classmates.
- Ascertain periodically each student's understanding of instructions and information.
- Avoid excessive repetition—be inventive in finding new ways to reinforce musical concepts.
- Provide opportunities for creative sound exploration on a wide variety of instruments.
- Offer a single mallet for playing instruments where hand coordination is poor.
- Remove dissonant bars for simple, repetitive ostinatos on Orff instruments.
- Encourage tone matching by interspersing these students among in-tune singers.
- Demonstrate the concept of high and low tones through a variety of ways.

The Learning Disabled or Perceptually Handicapped

- Consult with the classroom teacher and a learning specialist regarding the child's specific learning or perceptual problems.
- Teach music concepts with varied approaches (kinesthetic, psychomotor, aural, visual) in order to reach the child through a mode by which learning can best take place.
- Check frequently with the student to discern whether he or she is attending and understanding the musical concepts being presented.
- Encourage both rhythmic patterning and free movement activities with music to help the student cope with the frustrations of a learning disability.
- Encourage singing in a natural tone, free from tension.
- Emphasize the student's learning abilities for making music, and minimize his or her limitations.
- Suggest that the student learn to play an instrument suited to his or her learning abilities.
- Pair the student with another for assistance with musical tasks that would otherwise be difficult.
- Reassure often and give specific praise when deserved.
- Find alternate ways to test for musical learning.

The Emotionally Disturbed

- Provide a calm, nonthreatening environment for music instruction and activities.
- Reassure the student that music is a positive experience and is to be enjoyed.
- Teach the student to listen and to interpret what is heard.
- Arrange the classroom to avoid distracting visual clutter.
- Use free, expressive movement to relieve tension.
- Allow flexible pacing of activities to accommodate short attention spans.
- Alternate music participation with listening.
- Encourage a free tone in singing with exercises on Orff instruments.
- Provide many opportunities for group singing, and reward effort.
- Encourage sound exploration and creative self-expression on Orff and other instruments.
- Clearly prescribe the proper use and care of the instruments.
- Balance praise with reasonable expectations for musical growth.

The Gifted

- Consider Gardner's theory of multiple intelligences in discerning a child's specific gifted traits.
- Refrain from labeling the child as gifted in his or her presence. It could contribute to problems in adjustment and socialization.
- Encourage the child to participate with others in most class musical activities for socialization along with musical growth.

- Propose activity extensions to the student that relate to the music concepts being presented to the whole class. These extensions can take place when the student finishes a musical task early, or clearly seems ready for additional challenge.
- Appeal often to the gifted child's creativity through improvisation, composition, and performance.
- Provide challenge through computerized music programs at a learning center in the classroom.
- Communicate with parents about the value of taking the student to concerts of live music and providing music lessons.
- Encourage the student to join a beginning chorus, strings class, or band.
- Give the gifted child an opportunity to be a peer tutor to another child learning to play an instrument, or to assist a mainstreamed exceptional child.
- Provide additional listening opportunities to the student by loaning him or her tapes and records to take home.
- Take the student to both school and public libraries, and together locate sections of books about musical subjects.

Classroom Management

Social Conditions Affecting Behavior

Today's teachers face far more complex problems in classroom management than those of their predecessors, resulting from pronounced sociological and educational changes. In the past, students were in the classroom because they and their parents wanted them to be there. Today's compulsory attendance laws force them there. In former years, students were apt to be culturally more similar, while today's students represent more varied national and world cultures.

Nationally, close to one half of the students do not live with their natural parents; there are now several million single-parent families. More than 65 percent of mothers of students work outside the home, making the school a substitute parent, at least in part. Despite all this, it is heartening to find that most students want to do well, to be accepted, and to obey rules. They will normally respond reasonably to competent teachers.

Acceptable classroom conduct has to be promoted over extended periods of time with understanding and patience. Discipline problems are too often approached with immediate and forced correction rather than seeking the causes of disruptive behavior and finding ways to prevent it.

Many suburban schools have become increasingly culturally and racially diverse, including black, Hispanic, Vietnamese, and other ethnic groups. Using public schools as agencies of social change has placed students in unfamiliar social relationships charged with anxiety and concern. Uneasiness and apprehension can often be observed. Uncertain human relationships and the lack of flexible space in which to expand instructional programs have combined to result in major behavioral problems. Furthermore, parental resentment of other cultural and ethnic students can aggravate problems.

Occasionally teachers have preconceived negative ideas about some students that result in adverse relations between student and teacher. A good exercise is to draw up a list of questions to assess the effect the teacher has on students. The following list may be revised and expanded:

1. Do I place derogatory labels on students?
2. Do I use body language that communicates negative reactions?
3. Do I use descriptive words and stereotyped comments that show nonacceptance?
4. Do I allow students to become isolated or ignored in class?
5. Do I correct some students too often or in improper ways?
6. Do I select relevant and significant content when studying music of different ethnic groups?
7. Do I give all learners an equal chance to participate at their levels of ability?
8. Do I give minorities and special learners appropriate time to ask questions and to reply to questions?

Encouraging Self-Control   Classroom management is a complicated process involving the interactions of different personalities. There are no specific solutions that apply in all difficult situations. Every teacher is different, and each must determine what techniques function best in terms of his or her personality and those of the students. It is clear, however, that in order for learning to take place there must be reasonable order. The nature of the activity determines to some extent the type of order. Positive behavior is furthered in classrooms in which students assume responsibility for their own behavior. The feeling is developed that the classroom is the students' classroom and that each student has a definite responsibility in helping establish and maintain the standards by which it functions. In such a classroom the teacher helps develop the importance of the individual, a sense of respect for others, and self-control. Since self-control develops slowly, it will take time for an appropriate atmosphere to develop. After standards are well established and incorporated into the behavior of most students, teachers work with individuals having difficulty, analyzing behavior and planning ways of modifying it. Good instruction helps to alleviate behavior problems by providing a variety of activities suited to each student's interest and ability.

Other Factors Affecting Behavior   There are many factors that influence students' behavior. Much misbehavior is the direct result of conditions in the learning environment and might have been prevented had the teacher given proper consideration to the following:

Organization and Proper Routine.   Teachers who are well prepared, and who have made provision for proper directions and routine, usually project a feeling of confidence and security that is reflected in the behavior of students. Students sense insecurity in teachers and are disturbed by it. Therefore, teachers must make careful plans for learning activities, and assemble all materials needed in developing them. They must also give attention to such details as how to begin and conclude the lesson, how to keep it progressing steadily toward realization of the intended purposes, how to seat or group students for specific activities, how to distribute and collect materials, how and when to change activities, and how to evaluate and summarize with students the accomplishments of the day.

There is no substitute for clearly defined and enforced policies of performance and behavior. Ordinarily classroom rules should be clearly stated in the first class, posted somewhere in the classroom, reviewed often, and revised when necessary. When students have a part in making logical rules of class management and conduct, they understand them and are much more apt to observe them.

Challenging Every Child.   Students who are engaged in activities that are interesting and worthwhile are normally well behaved. Those who fail to find interest and purpose in what they are asked to do become bored and often disturb others. The selection of interesting activities that are at an appropriate developmental level for all the children is thus of primary importance.

Physical Comfort.   Children who are too cold, too warm, too crowded, who must breathe stale air, who cannot see or hear what is going on, who are not comfortably seated, have been seated or physically inactive for too long, often misbehave. Student seating should be arranged to facilitate their participation in, and concentration on, the activity at hand.

The Teacher.   Teachers know that students reflect their enthusiasm, interest, and confidence. Teachers should be happy and well adjusted. They should truly want to teach.

When faced with behavior problems, teachers should become active listeners, both in class and with individual students. As they understand the problem they will be able to assist students in correcting their own behavior. When unable to do this in specific cases, it is appropriate to seek assistance. Teachers know that repeatedly sending students to the principal has limited effectiveness, and should do this only as a last resort.

Good teachers' behavior is consistent, understanding, firm, and reflective of a sincere interest in every student. Teachers see humor in many situations, and know that humor, when properly used, can help in the solution of behavior problems. They refrain from using ridicule and sarcasm and are mature in their behavior. As adults, they are objective, not overly friendly or emotionally attached to children, and if they are in error, or do not know answers to problems, they admit it. Teachers retain self-control and are dependable adults in whom students can have confidence and faith. As much as possible, individual students' behavior problems are solved privately, since this is usually more effective and less disturbing to both the student in question and the class. The class is not made to suffer for what one or two students may do. Teachers are generous with positive reinforcement whenever it is deserved. Their speaking voices are pleasant and vary in pitch and intensity. They know that a tense voice disturbs students. Their singing voices are natural, sincere, and pleasing. Teachers approach difficult situations calmly. In order to accomplish these things they tend to their own physical and mental health. Their personal appearance is such that it increases the students' respect and serves to remind them to be neat, clean, and orderly.

Teachers always need to know students' names, and each student should be addressed by name for both positive and negative communication. Teachers learn to anticipate a variety of possible problems, and plan ways to offset them. They intersperse appropriate music throughout the day or period to relieve tensions and unify the group. Through thoughtful selection of music a teacher can calm or stimulate the students as desired. Small difficulties can be avoided by simple actions. For example, if a teacher sees a student about to distract someone else, or otherwise misbehave, he or she can ask the student a direct question that will bring the student back into the group activity at once. The teacher keeps eye contact with the class at all times, constantly glancing at individual students. Attention cannot be focused on notation in a music book or on piano accompaniments so exclusively that the class cannot be seen; this necessitates complete familiarity with the song being taught and its accompaniment. The division of the class at times into several groups, one singing, one accompanying, and the third evaluating the musical performance of others, is conducive to class control because it gives every student something specific to do. Other purposeful ways to involve students include tending the record player, pressing the chord bars of an autoharp, playing the bells, conducting, or interpreting music creatively through body movement or dramatization. The teacher usually refuses to talk when students are talking, and when he or she begins to speak, does so in a calm, but distinct voice.

All behavior is goal-centered and has specific causes. Teachers must continually collect information about students in order to understand the motives for their behavior and to attempt to deal with the causes of it. When a student must be corrected, this should be done with due consideration for cultural and family background and motives. Because every student is different, the manner of rebuke appropriate for one may not be appropriate for another.

When the teacher shows consistently over time that each student possesses dignity and personal worth, many will be motivated to perform school tasks that far exceed normal expectations. Effective teachers will by their actions consistently convince students that each one has something unique to offer. The teacher should make a constant effort to note every favorable aspect of a student, recognizing it and reinforcing it, thus giving that student a feeling of success and accomplishment. The ultimate goal of the teacher is to assist the student in developing the ability and desire to assume responsibility for his or her own behavior.

At times a student's behavior may originate in situations beyond the control of the music teacher, as implied in the following questions:

Did the student encounter an unpleasant situation in the previous class?

Do the student's parents exhibit serious conflicts, disagreements, and arguments in the home?

Has one of the parents left the home?

Does the student feel unaccepted and unwanted at home?

Has someone close to the student suffered a serious accident, illness, or death?

Is the safety or health of the student in jeopardy?

Has the student recently lost the attention and support of a friend?

Did the student come to school hungry or tired?

Teachers who care about each student seek an understanding of the abilities, family, special interests, and special problems of that student. They demonstrate this caring in many tangible ways. As a result they have the ingredients of a well-disciplined classroom, one where learning can take place in a friendly and accepting atmosphere. Success should be planned for each student because nothing is more basic to psychological health than finding some kinds of competence in one's life.

It is true that some students function best in a setting where interaction with peers is limited. The teacher may need to isolate a student in a part of the classroom until he or she feels able to become positively involved in the class.

Students need to know the purpose of assigned tasks and the boundaries of permissible behavior. Madsen and Madsen (1981) offer the following guidelines for establishing classroom rules:

1. Involve the students in developing the rules.
2. Keep rules brief and to the point.
3. Phrase rules, when possible, in a positive way (e.g., "Sit quietly while I work with the clarinets," instead of "Don't talk, band.")
4. Remind the class of rules at times *other* than when someone has misbehaved.
5. Post rules and review them regularly.

Some additional suggestions for managing student behavior follow:

1. Consider student reactions to your facial expressions, body language, and movements. Be sure that they reflect sincerity, personal warmth, and lack of prejudice.
2. Conduct student-teacher conferences to explore reasons for misbehavior and to determine what student and teacher can do to correct it.
3. Disassociate the misbehavior from the offender, showing that while you may dislike the behavior, you continue to respect and like the student.
4. Use visual aids to help students know what is expected of them. For example, print the order of activities and page numbers on the chalkboard or show it on an overhead projector so all students know the sequence of planned events.
5. Minimize nonmusical tasks; emphasize the musical ones.
6. Prior to the arrival of students at the music room, arrange the room and have all materials ready and easily available.
7. Anticipate arrival of students in the music room. Have a smile and greeting by name ready, conveying that you are happy to see them.
8. Always begin class promptly so that students will know that this is the established pattern in your room.
9. Be certain that every student, including the less capable and the gifted, is actively involved. Remember that students are naturally active, and unless they are active in ways you have planned, they will be active in unpredictable ways. So, keep them busy!
10. Be imaginative and operate the class in a way that, although all understand the established procedures, you manage to vary activities enough to "keep them guessing." Add interesting chords or rhythm patterns to drills. Plan a surprise dramatization. Change the furniture, wall charts, or bulletin boards. Make your room and class an interesting and challenging experience.
11. Make your enthusiasm contagious. Show it in your movements, animated facial expressions, and voice.

12. When speaking, use proper diction, appropriate volume, and good voice projection. Speak in short sentences. Speaking too fast can disrupt communication and cause misunderstandings that create discipline problems. From time to time, tape your voice in class and study how you might make it more effective.
13. Avoid competing with extraneous noise.
14. Do your best to eliminate interruptions.
15. Capitalize on student interest and enthusiasm.
16. Unchallenged learners tend to develop discipline problems, so be sure that your lesson is stimulating to every student at his or her individual performance and interest level.
17. Avoid talking too much; make music instead.
18. Let the class assume some of the responsibility for certain aspects of the lesson.
19. Give students an opportunity to discuss and share musical discoveries, questions, and performances with peers.
20. Close each lesson on a challenging, positive, and pleasant note.

Systems of Classroom Management

Over the years classroom management has remained a primary concern of new teachers, and when mastered, it contributes to the satisfaction and pride of successful teachers. Several defined approaches to classroom management have enjoyed success in recent years. Among the best known are the behavioral approach, the Dreikursian approach, and assertive discipline. To become effective in implementing any of these approaches in the classroom, thorough study of the system and personal experience with the system's tenets are essential.

In the *behavioral approach* the teacher assumes that students are basically neutral and passive, acquiring behaviors and habits from their experiences. Their behavior can be modified by the teacher through a four-step process. First, both positive and negative behaviors are pinpointed; second, the frequency of negative behaviors is noted; third, appropriate reinforcers are applied; and fourth, the results evaluated.

The *Dreikursian approach* is well known, and has enjoyed considerable success in recent years. Rudolf Dreikurs uses a democratic approach to discipline in which students participate in the setting of classroom rules and goals. He confronts mistaken goals with students, and assumes that all students want recognition. The purpose of discipline is to reach agreement on obtainable goals, and then give the students the recognition they have earned when these goals are realized.

Assertive discipline is a take-charge approach in which clear limits to behavior are established, and the teacher makes sure that consistent enforcement of those limits occurs. Both the teacher's rights and the students' rights are respected in the classroom. Assertive responses by the teacher prevent disruptions that would interrupt teaching or learning. One of the main proponents of this system is Lee Canter.

Designing a Personal Plan for a Music Classroom

As a new teacher or a teacher who is new to a school district, the first step is to inquire about the existence of an established school or district discipline policy. Such a policy will form the basis for the teacher's own discipline in the classroom, and promote consistency with other teachers and administrators on how discipline is maintained. However, the atmosphere of the music classroom differs in some important ways from the atmosphere of regular classrooms. An autocratic environment stifles creative responses and inhibits musical performance, whereas too much freedom destroys effective classroom instruction. A successful music teacher strikes an appropriate balance between control and the freedom for creative expression.

Another important aspect of a plan for discipline is the recognition of the teacher's own personality. Some procedures for discipline may work better for some individuals than others. They seem to fit naturally into a person's teaching style. This does not mean that new procedures cannot be acquired, or work successfully, but a good match between the teacher's personality and the chosen system of discipline is essential.

Successful systems of discipline often evolve throughout one's teaching career. However, it is imperative that new teachers have in mind a carefully planned approach to discipline that will be followed with consistency. When a discipline problem arises an immediate response is most effective, and such responses need to come from the carefully developed plans of the teacher rather than be improvised on the spot.

EXPLORATORY ACTIVITIES

1. Observe school classes at a level of your choice to look for evidence of mainstreaming. To what extent is it taking place? Identify problems; observe how problems are solved.
2. Review several issues of the *Music Educators Journal*. Discuss the many ways the Music Educators National Conference assists those who teach music.
3. What are some common arguments in favor of having music specialists teach all the music in a school? What are the disadvantages of such an arrangement?
4. What are some common arguments for having classroom teachers responsible for all music teaching in a school? What are the disadvantages of such an arrangement?
5. What can be said in favor of plans in which specialists and classroom teachers share responsibility for teaching music? What are the disadvantages of such an arrangement?
6. In how many ways might a music series assist teachers of music? What are series books unable to provide?
7. Design a music center for your ideal classroom. Detail your expectations or standards for students who are to work in the center.
8. Interview a local classroom teacher or a music specialist. Ask that person to identify strengths and weaknesses of music instruction in his or her school.
9. Observe a school music class to find out how behavior problems are handled. If you find few such problems, account for that situation. In your observation, did you find the physical arrangement of the classroom appropriate for the activities? What organizational plans were employed, and were they best for the tasks involved? Discuss the kinds of instruction you observed.

References and Materials

ATTERBURY, BETTY W., *Mainstreaming Exceptional Learners in Music*. Englewood Cliffs, N.J.: Prentice Hall, 1990.

_____ , "Success Strategies for Learning-Disabled Students." *Music Educators Journal,* April 1983, 29–31.

BONNER, PAUL, "Toward a More Thoughtful Use of Computers in Education," *Personal Computing,* February 1984, 153–161.

BOWMAN, RICHARD, "Effective Classroom Management: A Primer for Practicing Professionals," *The Clearing House,* November 1983, 116–118.

BROPHY, JERE, "Classroom Management as Instruction: Socializing Self-Guidance in Students," *Theory into Practice,* Fall 1985, 233–240.

CORNELL, NANCY, "Encouraging Responsibility: A Discipline Plan That Works," *Learning,* September 1986, 47–49.

CHADWICK, D. M., and C. A. CLARK, "Adapting Music Instruments for the Physically Handicapped," *Music Educators Journal,* November 1980, 56–59.

CRUICKSHANK, DONALD R., "Profile of an Effective Teacher," *Educational Horizons,* Winter 1986, 90–92.

GEERDES, ARNOLD P., *Planning and Equipping Educational Music Facilities.* Reston, Va.: Music Educators National Conference, 1975.

The Gifted and the Talented: Their Education and Development, National Society for the Study of Education, 78th Yearbook, Part One. Chicago: University of Chicago Press, 1979.

GILBERT, JANET P., "Mainstreaming in Your Classroom: What to Expect," *Music Educators Journal,* February 1977, 64–68.

JOHNSON, DAVID W., and ROGER T. JOHNSON, "Computer-Assisted Cooperative Learning," *Educational Technology,* January 1986, 12–18.

KNIGHT, CAROL J., REECE PETERSON, and BRENDA McGUIRE, "Cooperative Learning: A New Approach to an Old Idea," *Teaching Exceptional Children,* May 1982, 233–238.

MADSEN, CHARLES H., and CLIFFORD K. MADSEN, *Teaching/Discipline: A Positive Approach for Educational Development,* 2nd ed. Boston: Allyn & Bacon, 1981.

MESKE, EUNICE B., and CARROLL RINEHART, *Individualized Instruction in Music.* Reston, Va.: Music Educators National Conference, 1975.

Music Educators Journal, Special Issue: Teaching Special Students, April 1982.

Music Educators Journal, Special Issue: Mainstreaming, April 1990.

National Library Service for the Blind and Physically Handicapped, The Library of Congress, Washington, DC 20542.

RATHS, LOUIS E., et al., *Values and Teaching: Working with Values in the Classroom.* Columbus, Ohio: Charles E. Merrill Books, Inc., 1966.

SALEND, SPENCER J., "Factors Contributing to the Development of Successful Mainstreaming Programs," *Exceptional Children,* February 1984, 409–416.

SCHMIDT, CHARLES P., "Cognitive Styles Research: Implications for Music Teaching and Learning," *Update,* Spring 1984, 18–21.

SLAVIN, ROBERT E., "Cooperative Learning and the Cooperative School," *Educational Leadership,* November 1987, 7–13.

4 Evaluation

Purposes of Evaluation

It is critical to the success of any music program that evaluation be incorporated from the initial stages of planning. Evaluation is a process of assessing the degree to which objectives and goals are appropriate and have been attained. Specific and immediate student objectives, teacher instructional objectives, and long-term program goals serve as criteria that guide evaluation at all levels of teaching. Evaluation in music consists of assembling, interpreting, and using data to measure three primary aspects of the curriculum: student achievement, program adequacy, and teaching success. Accurate assessment depends on the selection of evaluative techniques which will provide the desired kinds of information. When course purposes are clearly stated, the means of evaluation are easier to determine. When they are vague, evaluation becomes equally imprecise.

Evaluation is not an end within itself; it is a continuous process that is a useful tool in adjusting learning objectives and experiences. It is not presented here as an activity to be employed exclusively at the conclusion of a program or any aspect of a program, but as an integral part of teaching.

The approach to evaluation differs depending on whether the student, the program, or the teacher is to be evaluated. However, techniques for all three need to be understood clearly, and employed for the specific purposes intended.

Student Evaluation

Three factors merit consideration when evaluating students. First, the student's own progress in music is to be taken into account. Second, the student's standing in the class or some other larger group is also important. There is no established formula for the relative importance of these two factors. Indeed, their relative importance may change from student to student. In many instances the first factor is primary with younger students, and the second factor becomes more important during the later years of schooling. A third factor is *preassessment,* meaning some kind of evaluation before instruction begins. Its purposes may include finding out what students have already learned, what new learnings they are ready to acquire, and what goals and objectives need to be set for the learning period. Preassessment also establishes the basis for postassessment— evaluation after instruction is complete.

Traditional written tests can be used to evaluate student progress with factual information related to music. Observations of individual performances will shed much light on the student's acquisition of musical performance skills. Student's listening skills may be assessed through checklists, written responses of various kinds, and observed responses. The assessment of learning in the affective domain can be difficult, but procedures have been developed that are useful to the teacher for this kind of evaluation as well. On occasion, one of the standardized music tests may be useful in comparing the students in a classroom or school to a national norm.

Students require feedback in order to understand how well they are mastering the content of the course. Teachers should provide realistic and unbiased feedback to learners on a regular basis. This process helps learners assess their efforts to learn. If they do not have this feedback they will not understand how to improve their learning.

Relating Evaluation to Course Objectives

Evaluation should be made in terms of established objectives. Some examples related to student evaluation follow.

Class Objective	*Evaluative Technique*
The student demonstrates understanding of the relationship between melodic and harmonic tones by successfully identifying where the tonic and dominant chords should support a familiar melody.	The teacher observes the student's performance on the autoharp and determines whether tonic and dominant chord changes are made in the appropriate places. The number of correct responses are tabulated.

The student indicates an understanding of the major scale by performing major scales on a pitched percussion instrument.	The teacher determines in advance how to score the performance, and whether such things as tempo will be part of the evaluation. The teacher then observes the performance and records the information.
The student demonstrates knowledge of the fingerings of the notes of the C major scale for the soprano recorder.	As part of a written test, and with printed diagrams of a recorder, the student fills in the appropriate fingering holes for each note of the scale.

Test Item Types   Many different types of evaluation are used. If learning in the three domains—cognitive, affective, and psychomotor—is to be assessed, the appropriate evaluative techniques must be employed. Some possible means of evaluation follow:

Observation	Samples of creativity
Case studies	Musical performance
Checklists	Videotape recordings
Logs	Teacher-made tests
Diaries	Standardized tests
Cumulative records	Group-made tests
Questionnaires	Anecdotal records
Attitude scales	

Teachers decide what combinations of measurement devices they need to use in accordance with the types of evidence desired. In order to measure accurately, tests should have the following characteristics:

Validity: Measure what they profess to measure.

Reliability: Measure accurately and consistently, and can be used by different persons or at different times with consistent results.

Appropriateness: Designed in accordance with the type of learning and the capabilities of the individual or group to which they will be applied.

Usefulness: Reveal data that can be easily used by the teacher, and are not unduly costly in terms of time or money.

Children practice self-evaluation by means of group discussions, folders containing samples of work such as compositions, tapes made of performances, verbal feedback from teachers and peers, criteria decided upon by the group, checklists, diaries, and more recently, selected computer programs.

When preparing written tests, the age of the student must be taken into account and an appropriate marking system selected. If the student is quite young, the teacher should provide a simple way for the student to respond to the auditory or written questions. If the test includes listening to music, the pupils should concentrate on the music, unhindered by possible struggles with writing at the same time. If writing is to be done, it should occur after the listening experience is concluded (see Figure 4.1).

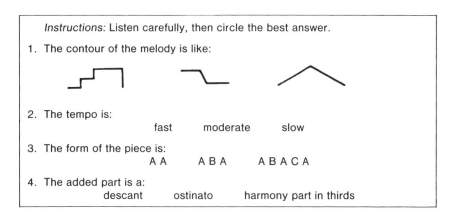

Instructions: Listen carefully, then circle the best answer.

1. The contour of the melody is like:

2. The tempo is:
   fast   moderate   slow

3. The form of the piece is:
   A A   A B A   A B A C A

4. The added part is a:
   descant   ostinato   harmony part in thirds

Figure 4.1. SAMPLE WRITTEN TEST

Simple written tests can be used before young children understand the staff. For example, if teachers' purposes include concepts about pitches moving in scale-line patterns, they can use the first three notes of "Three Blind Mice" and similar repeated patterns in songs the children have come to know well. Written correctly, this particular pattern could be drawn as follows:

On the test paper, it might appear with one misplaced note, and the children would be asked to find and circle the error:

Several other examples of test items for young children can be found in Edwin Gordon's *Primacy Measures of Music Audiation.* The marking system of circling two faces that are alike or different (smiling, frowning) is appropriate for children who are not yet readers.

If students have adequate facility with reading and writing, more traditional test items may be employed, including true-false, multiple choice, fill-in-the-blanks, matching, and essay types. Each of these has particular strengths and weaknesses.

True-False Items: This very popular type of question has several flaws. Perhaps the most serious one is the fact that students have a 50 percent chance of guessing the right answer. Another common flaw is the use of such words as "always" to make the item false.

Flawed Example:

When students play the recorder, the mouthpiece should always be inserted one-half inch into the mouth.

Another common flaw with true-false items is the inclusion of more than one idea in a single question. One of the stated ideas may be true, and the other idea false.

Flawed Example:

J.S. Bach was a famous composer and violinist.

In spite of its drawbacks, true-false questions continue to be used, perhaps because they are easily written and scored. A few examples of better true-false questions follow.

Better Example:

1. J.S. Bach was a famous violin player.
2. Bach and Beethoven lived at the same time.
3. The treble clef is sometimes called the G clef.
4. A triad consists of four notes.
5. The clarinet belongs to the percussion family.

Multiple Choice Items: This type of question is most respected by experienced educators. When well written, it can demand high-level cognitive processes, and be an accurate measure of student understanding. One primary flaw occurs when more than one of the alternatives can be true. A second flaw has to do with an intended correct answer that has both correct and incorrect components. Finally, the name *specific determiner* has been given to the correct answer when it is more precise, and longer, than any of the incorrect alternatives. Students tend to guess it is the right answer because of its precision, thereby weakening the question's power. In the following example, answer ''C'' is a specific determiner.

Flawed Example:

The ''key'' of a song refers to
a. its range.
b. its topic.
c. the tendency of its tones to pull toward a home tone.
d. its tempo.
e. its highness or lowness.

A better test question has several incorrect answers that are known as *plausible alternatives*. They are incorrect, but make the student pause and reflect to determine why they are wrong.

Better Example:

The key of a song refers to
a. the distance between its highest and lowest pitches.

b. the number of beats in each measure, and the kind of a note constituting each beat.

c. the tendency of its tones to pull toward a home tone.

d. the relative speed of the song.

Fill-in-the-Blanks Items: Many people consider this test item type to be as weak as the true-false items. One of the main flaws occurs when the teacher gives too few clues as to what is expected, or conversely deals with the completely obvious.

Flawed Example:

Chords are called _____ when the notes are all _____ .

Flawed Example:

The home tone of the C major scale is _____ .

In spite of these problems, it is possible to write better fill-in-the-blank items.

Better Example:

The four traditional families of instruments represented in the orchestra are _____ , _____ , _____ , and _____ .

Matching items: This type of test item has many strengths as long as notable weaknesses are avoided. First, the student should never be presented with a list of more than approximately ten items in each column to match. Second, the items in either column must be of the same classification or type to avoid revealing the answer by the process of elimination. Third, the instructions in the stem of the question must tell the student how to record the correct answer (e.g., "by writing the appropriate letter in each blank"). Matching questions can also be strengthened by including a larger number of answers in column B than in column A.

Flawed Example:

Match the items in the two columns.

Column A	Column B
1. D major scale	A. Romantic music
2. treble clef sign	B. two counts
3. changing from one key to another	C. two sharps
	D. two flats
4. violin	E. G clef sign
5. B flat major scale	F. modulation
6. Ludwig van Beethoven	G. stringed instrument
7. quarter note	

Better Example:

Match the items in the two columns below by recording the letter from column B in the appropriate blank in column A.

Column A

_____ 1. modulation

_____ 2. ritard

_____ 3. fermata

_____ 4. crescendo

_____ 5. accelerando

Column B

A. a sign that instructs the player to hold a note longer than its regular duration.

B. to speed up the tempo.

C. to slow down the tempo.

D. to change keys.

E. to increase the loudness of the music

F. to change keys or tonal centers

G. to raise a pitch by one half step

Essay Test Items: Because of the immaturity of elementary school children, essay questions should be quite specific, and require only short written responses. One of the strengths of essay questions is that they require students to use higher level thought processes and appropriate written communication skills. These skills are as vital in music as they are in any other academic area.

Two serious flaws in essay questions are the time it takes to grade them, and the wide variability among scores due to teacher fatigue and boredom. Both problems can be reduced by having an outline of the concepts expected in the answer, and the number of points assigned to each. The teacher then looks for each of the desired concepts and awards points as they are found. We favor the awarding of a few additional points if the answer has strengths in organization or reasoning.

Music series publishers offer assistance to teachers in evaluation. For example, Holt, Rinehart and Winston provides "Student Progress Reports" and includes Evaluation Resource Binders that provide student evaluation forms for each grade level. Silver Burdett has "Competency Tests" for grades 1 through 6, and "What Do You Hear?" answer sheets for use when students listen to recordings.

Assessment of Attitudes

Although the teacher may not want to have the assessment of attitudes reflected in grades, such assessment is important to the program in other ways. Much research indicates that student attitude is closely related to motivation as well as school performance. Observations are to be made discreetly, and students may not even know the document exists. Such an Attitude/Response Indicator serves a dual purpose. First, it can be a valuable aid in helping to assess the degree to which each student values music. Second, the picture that emerges from a composite of all the forms gives the teacher valuable information for program assessment (see next section). Figure 4.2 is an example of a document to be used by the teacher early in the school year and again in the spring.

ATTITUDE/RESPONSE INDICATOR*

Name _____   Year _____ Grade _____

Indicate appropriate number rating.
1 — never
2 — occasionally
3 — often

To what extent does the student

	Observations		Loss	Gain
	1st October	2nd April		
1. participate willingly/enthusiastically in musical activities?				
2. volunteer to perform (sing, play, conduct) for peers?				
3. influence peers in a positive way about musical activities?				
4. display unique/creative ideas in musical activities?				
5. exhibit a sense of responsibility in use of musical equipment and materials?				
6. suggest music that is a particular favorite to be used in class?				
7. appreciate the ideas and musical contributions of others?				
8. choose to attend musical performances, rehearsals, or other musical events?				

Figure 4.2

Evaluation of the Music Program

The purpose of program evaluation is to discover what aspects of the program need revision and refinement. Because of their close relationship, realistic evaluation of student achievement can lay the foundation for evaluating the music program. This aspect of evaluation is frequently neglected because of constraints of time, energy, and other program responsibilities. When program evaluation is neglected, instruction tends to wander into activities that are fun, but are often only marginally related to long-term goals. For this reason program evaluation must be carefully built into every aspect of curriculum development, including day-to-day lesson plans. Good program evaluation provides continuous data about the viability of general music in the elementary school

*Data to be taken in October and April. Students should <u>not</u> be told the performance criteria for these objectives. Marks are not intended for grading purposes. They pertain to the valuing of music. The specialist should choose items relevant to the individual student being assessed.

curriculum, and about the success of the music program being evaluated. It might, for example, disclose the need to address individual differences in musical ability or learning style.

A receptive environment facilitates learning. Bringing about such an environment requires a basic point of view or philosophy, the establishment of objectives and ways to realize them, and the use of diverse techniques to appraise the degree to which the objectives have been attained. Teachers have the leading role, serving as guides and facilitators in this process. Questions the teachers might ask include: Do the learners understand the objectives? Are they of personal importance to individual learners? What procedures can I use to help students become conscious of the steps needed to reach the objectives? How can I assist them to discover other meanings and possibilities related to the problem?

Students learn best when they are given opportunities to identify what they need to learn, have some choice in what they are to learn, plan how they are going to learn it, and appraise how well they have done so. As a result of each bit of evaluative data collected, the student should become more secure and certain of what next steps should be taken.

Program evaluation must likewise be based upon established objectives. Everyone concerned with learning in the music program should be involved in its evaluation. School administrators, music coordinators, members of the staff, parents, and students can all contribute to the continual evaluation of the music program.

Much program evaluation occurs on an informal basis through professional interchange between teachers, students, administrators and parents. Such informal evaluation is highly desirable, particularly for individual programs. However, to enhance its value the teacher must provide documentation of the information as it is received.

One of the many devices used in evaluation is the checklist. The 1986 MENC publication, *The School Music Program: Description and Standards* includes lists of general standards, such as "Each elementary school provides two current basal series for each classroom." Such checklists can be very useful in determining whether or not a school music program adheres to the stated standards. For example, an elementary music checklist drawn from those standards may have columns for responses of **no, partially,** and **yes** opposite the standard. A final column titled **plans for improvement** completes the checklist (see Figure 4.3). A checklist that appraises programs in detail can be constructed using MENC's major headings, "Standards for Curriculum," "Standards for Staff," "Standards for Scheduling," "Standards for Physical Facilities," and "Standards for Materials and Equipment."

Information thus gathered is useful for teacher-administrator conferences and planning. In addition to such review is the formal, periodic evaluation of entire schools and programs. The school district or the state department often provides instruments for evaluation (e.g., Oregon State Department of Education. *Self-Evaluation Checklist for School Music Programs: Elementary grades 1–6.* Salem, Oregon: Oregon Department of Education, 1978.) Organizations

	yes	partially	no	plans for improvement
The elementary music program				
has a sequentially organized program				
has a well-qualified staff				
has adequate materials of instruction				

Figure 4.3. PROGRAM EVALUATION

such as the National Study of School Evaluation provide sophisticated means for both school and program evaluation (e.g., *Elementary School Evaluative Criteria*. Falls Church, Virginia, 1987.)

These examples of program evaluation are of value only when they serve as feedback about the strengths and weaknesses of the music program, as well as its general adequacy. Those who formulate the program must use the evaluative evidence to change the program when necessary, and to preserve the integrity of the program when success is demonstrated.

Teacher Self-Evaluation

Teacher self-evaluation is important because teacher improvement rarely occurs by chance. When improvement comes about it is because the teacher recognizes a teaching weakness or an inadequate musical skill, and sets out to improve. Much of the time this process is completely informal. However, most teachers can improve more systematically when the self-evaluation is formal.

The list of competencies needed by a good teacher is very long. This third aspect of evaluation calls for the teacher to have some systematic way to diagnose his or her effectiveness with students. This will involve, for example, consideration of the teacher's musicianship, knowledge of child development, ability to utilize equipment, interpersonal relationships, and both verbal and body language.

One of the best ways for a teacher to evaluate his or her classroom performance is to tape-record or videotape an entire music period. During playback of the tape, the teacher can make judgments about the effectiveness of the teaching. That teacher may discover both positive and negative actions, and thus make more informed decisions for improvement. If a videotape is used, the viewer can judge general appearance, including body language, expressions used, movements of self and students, language, student involvement, missed teaching opportunities, misbehavior of students, and lesson content. Such information makes it easier to determine if the teacher taught effectively, or if modification is necessary.

Music teachers must strive to provide the most effective program possible under existing conditions, and evaluation should help to attain this goal. *Existing conditions* refer to space, scheduling, equipment and supplies, budget, number of students, and contact hours. These are also in need of appraisal, revision, and improvement as they relate to the learning process.

EXPLORATORY ACTIVITIES

1. Examine courses of study in music published by city, county, and state education departments to learn what evaluation procedures are suggested and to what extent evaluations are made in terms of purposes and needs.
2. Indicate practical ways in which each of the evaluative criteria in this chapter may be used in music teaching. Which ones do you believe should receive more attention? Which do you think are the most difficult to employ?
3. Arrange to observe a music class and discuss with the teacher the evaluative techniques used. Share this with your college class.
4. Examine a cumulative record form used in a local school system. What music data are recorded? What additional entries, if any, are needed? Why?
5. Prepare a sample checklist, a guide for an observation, a questionnaire, and a chart that can be used in a music unit you plan to teach.
6. How can you use discussion as an evaluative technique in a unit or lesson you are teaching? Anecdotal records? Tape recordings? Open-ended questions? Musical performance? Logs and diaries? Tests? Discuss these techniques critically with other students and with your instructor.
7. Formulate a lesson plan on the basis of pertinent objectives. Then devise ways to evaluate the success of the plan in terms of achieving these objectives.

References and Materials

General

BOYLE, J. DAVID, "Perspective on Evaluation," *Music Educators Journal,* December 1989, 22–25.

COLWELL, RICHARD, "Musical Achievement: Difficulties and Directions in Evaluation." *Music Educators Journal,* April 1971, 41–43, 79–83.

DUBERT, LEE ANN, "Two Ideas for Grading Simulations and Higher Level Thinking Activities," *The Clearing House,* February 1987, 266–269.

HOFFER, CHARLES, R., "Critical Issues in Music Education," *Music Educators Journal,* September 1988, 18–21.

LAI, MORRIS K., and JUDY SHISHIDO, "A Model for Evaluating Art Education Programs." Paper presented at the annual meeting of the American Educational Research Association. (Washington, D.C., April 20–24, 1987). ERIC document.

LEHMAN, PAUL R., "Assessing Your Program's Effectiveness," *Music Educators Journal,* December 1989, 26–29.

National Study of School Evaluation. *Elementary School Evaluative Criteria,* 2nd ed. Falls Church, Va.: 1987.

Oregon Department of Education. *Self-Evaluation Checklist for School Music Programs: Elementary General Music, Grades 1–6.* Salem, Oreg., 1978.

POPHAM, W. JAMES, "Educational Measurement for the Improvement of Instruction," *Phi Delta Kappan,* April 1980, 531–534.

RODACY, RUDOLPH E., "Evaluating Student Achievement," *Music Educators Journal,* December 1989, 30–33.

SHEPARD, LORRIE, "Norm-Referenced vs. Criterion-Referenced Tests," *Educational Horizons, 58*/1, Fall 1979, 26–35.

The School Music Program: Descriptions and Standards. Reston, Va.: Music Educators National Conference, 1986.

Tests

BENTLEY, ARNOLD, *Measures of Musical Abilities.* London: Harrap, 1966.

COLWELL, RICHARD, *Music Achievement Tests.* Urbana, Ill.: School of Music, University of Illinois, 1970.

GORDON, EDWIN, *Iowa Tests of Music Literacy.* Iowa City, Ia: Bureau of Educational Research and Service, University of Iowa, 1971.

————, *Musical Aptitude Profile.* Boston: Houghton Mifflin, 1965.

————, *Primary Measures of Music Audiation.* Chicago: G.I.A. Publications, 1979.

PART II

5 Teaching Children Rhythm and Dynamics

Tempo and Dynamics
The Beat and Its Subdivisions
    Word-Rhythms
    Echo-Clapping
    Teaching the Concept of *Rest*
    Divisions of the Beat
    Dotted Notes
    Articulation
Accent, Meter, and Rhythmic Patterns
    Rhythmic Exercises
    Rhythmic Development
    Conducting
    Exploring Common Meters
    Exploring Less Common Meters
    Rhythm Patterns in Songs
Expanding the Concept of Rhythm
    Rhythm-Related Compositional Devices
Activities for Teaching Rhythm
    Individual Differences
Normal Expectations
    Levels 1 and 2
    Levels 3 and 4
    Levels 5 and 6
Selected Songs for Experimentation
Additional Activities and Suggestions for Lesson Plans
    Tempo
    Dynamics
    Rhythm
    Accent and Meter
    Form
References and Materials

The study of rhythm should be integrated with other musical activities, and seldom taught as an isolated element. Any number of activities could be featured in the instruction, such as movement, singing, playing of instruments, improvisation, and composition. Listening is also an essential part of the teaching of rhythm.

At the beginning of music instruction, teachers have numerous rhythmic concepts in mind for children to explore. Among them are the following:

Duration	*Tempo*	*Dynamics*
Beat	Fast, moderate, slow	Loud, soft
Accent	Accelerando	Accent
Divisions of the beat	Ritard or Ritardando	Crescendo
Meter		Decrescendo
Rhythm patterns		
Rests		
Word-rhythms		
Articulation		
staccato (detached)		
legato (connected)		

Tempo and Dynamics

Tempo and dynamics differ from rhythm and melody. Fast-slow and loud-soft are among the first music-related concepts young children learn, but the first one deals with tempo, and the second deals with dynamics. In order to avoid confusion, they should be introduced separately. The teacher can help children discover their own natural tempo by playing a drum or the piano to their steps as they walk across the room, perhaps as part of a game. After the relation between their steps and the sound the teacher makes has been realized, the children will be able to govern their steps in accordance with the tempo the teacher plays, and can walk slower or faster. For young children this can be a challenging game. The difference between slow and fast music can be examined by comparing two songs, one of them slow and the other fast. Characteristics of slow and fast music should be discovered through and reinforced by physical responses to music, and these responses may include aspects of dramatization, often of animal movements. Body movement, percussion instruments, and hand clapping may be used to develop the concepts of *accelerando* (gradually faster) and *rallentando, ritardando,* and *ritard* (gradually slower). These can be felt and seen when children move to the tempo of the music.

Loud and soft are easily understood concepts, and from them children gradually learn the relative degrees of each. Then they are ready to learn the concepts of *crescendo* (gradually louder) and *decrescendo* (gradually softer). Through echo-clapping some teachers teach *crescendo* by having children imitate them as they clap hands or sound an instrument softly when held low, near the floor, then gradually increasing the volume as the hands move higher. The process is reversed to teach *decrescendo*. These aspects of musical expression should be related to familiar songs and recordings. *Accent* is a quality of dynamics easily taught in relation to loud-soft. *Adventures in Music* (AM) recordings which can help teach this concept include *Petite Ballerina* by Shostakovich, *Can Can* by Rossini, *Departure* by Prokofiev (all from grade 2): *Dagger Dance* by Herbert and *Tarantella* by Rossini (from grade 3). From the third grade up, recordings such as *Pacific 321* by Honegger, and *Fêtes* by Debussy can be useful in studying tempo and dynamics on an expansive scale.

Songs should be selected which exemplify the use of *crescendo* and *decrescendo* as well. Indexes of music song series should be helpful in locating these. The teacher can draw attention to tempo and dynamics by well-planned questions: ''Would this song be better if it were sung slower, faster, softer, or louder?'' ''Let us try it a different way.'' ''Which did you prefer?'' ''Can you think of other ways we might try it?'' ''Let's find the very best way to sing the song expressively.''

Musicians use Italian terms to describe tempo. English terms are ordinarily learned in the primary grades and their Italian counterparts introduced in the intermediate grades. Some of the terms in more common use are listed in the Conceptual Structure of Music outline, Chapter 2. Such a vocabulary should be a useful one—not one to be learned because a book lists terms. The terms should be used by teacher and children to describe the tempo of any given piece of music, to explain how fast or slow the children's own compositions should be performed, and to be able to discuss music intelligently. Memorization is usually boring and self-defeating, but practical use of these terms makes good sense. In the intermediate grades a glossary of musical terms should be made available to the children to help them solve their musical problems and to enable them to answer their own questions. Some music books have such glossaries.

Some teachers and children have made imaginative posters illustrating musical terminology. For example, *adagio* might be illustrated by the turtle, *allegro* by a swift-flying bird, *accelerando* by a rocket taking off, and *grandioso* by a regal king.

As work on tempo and dynamics continues through the years, relationships between these and the other elements of music are discovered, and appreciation of them grows. There are relationships between tempo and dynamics, and between them and melody, harmony, form, and texture. These are waiting to be explored through experiences planned by teachers.

The Beat and Its Subdivisions

Adults are apt to overlook or underestimate the need children have to experience the regular and continuous beat that is characteristic of most music. To the adult, this regular beat seems to be too simple for much consideration, and some teachers tend to give it too little attention. The results become obvious later when children have difficulty understanding division of the beat and meter, and when a large number of adults cannot march, keep in step, or clap in a natural, rhythmic manner. All children need extensive metric experience, and they need teachers who realize how important this concept is to musical growth, as well as to physical and mental development.

Beat and *pulse* are terms most people use interchangeably. We use the term *beat,* in the sense that in moderate tempo, 4/4 meter has four beats.

The ear, the eye, and the body are employed in building the concept of the beat. Children listen to the teacher's playing on a drum, the piano, or clapping hands. They also listen to selected recordings which stress the beat. They see the teacher play on a drum or clap hands and try to imitate those motions, and by so doing, learn little by little to respond "in time" with the motions. Children explore and analyze the beat for themselves through their body responses and by experimenting with various percussion instruments. They also see the beat pictured in simple notation:

The body is employed in a number of ways. One aim of the teacher is to have all children feel the beat together. The children feel the beat with their whole body by walking, marching, swaying, hopping, or by clapping, slapping thighs (*patschen*), and making other hand-arm movements. They can also respond with words that reflect the beat and its subdivisions which are repeated over and over, such as:

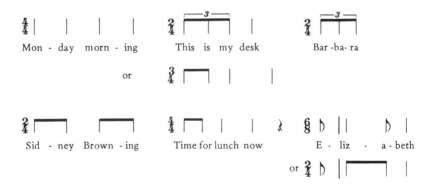

When a rest falls on any beat of the measure (see the 4/4 example) a pulsed gesture opposite to clapping is employed.

From street calls and jingles most children have experienced the beat and many of its divisions. For example:

> *One potato, two potato, three potato, four;*
> *Five potato, six potato, seven potato, more.*

Teachers should bring catchy commercials and jingles into the classroom and make use of them. (See Table 5.1 for examples of jingles to be used in this way.)

Table 5.1. Word Patterns*

Chant	Play Instruments	
Chant in a deliberate manner, emphasizing the last word in each line of the following:	*Six children, each with a different instrument, play in turn the underlying beat, while the class chants.*	
Bonefish, bluebird, black sheep, CROW	Triangle	
Chickadee, doodlebug, robins in a ROW	Tambourine	
Banty rooster, peep squirrel, caterpillar, FLEA	Sticks	
Muley on the mountain and a BIG BUMBLE BEE	Drum	
Fly in the cream jar, frog in the POOL	Finger cymbals	
Clap for all the children here at SCHOOL	Maracas	

*From *This Is Music,* Book One, by Adeline McCall. Copyright © 1965 by Allyn and Bacon, Inc. Used by permission.

The quarter rest can be introduced by challenging the children to invent motions to do with beat patterns such as the following one:

│	│	│	│
│	│	│	
│	│	│	│
│	│	│	

After involving the children this way, and deciding on a motion, the symbol for the quarter rest ( ) is written in.

Music series books for the kindergarten and first grade provide easy piano pieces which encourage responses to the beat, and their publishers provide recordings of marches, marchlike songs, and dances which do the same for all grade levels. Other commonly used recordings include the *Adventures in Music* (AM) albums (RCA), and the *Bowmar Orchestral Library,* particularly BOL 54 (marches).* The teacher should seek out these collections, study the suggestions provided for teachers, and select the music appropriate for the class. Hap Palmer's albums, *Mod Marches* and *The Feel of Music,* provide useful recordings as well.

Word-Rhythms The use of word-rhythms is a natural way to introduce rhythmic response. There is rhythm to be discovered in the spoken word, and children use and enjoy this rhythm in their play. The sounds of words attract children in the early primary grades, and people of all ages react to them, as demonstrated by rhythmic cheers at athletic events. The rhythms of both simple and complex note values can be assimilated with ease when teachers relate these to familiar words or names.

Examples:

*These recording collections are referred to throughout the text as ''AM'' and ''BOL'' respectively.

123 TEACHING CHILDREN RHYTHM AND DYNAMICS

Percussion instruments, clapping, and stamping can be added to enhance rhythm and add to the interest. Most of these word-rhythms can be altered in different ways by accenting words. For example, "Lemon cream pie" might be

Several rhythms may be correct for one word. Rhythms of some radio and television commercials are interesting to work with, and they have the advantage of being familiar to children.

Echo-Clapping Echo-clapping, a favorite Orff activity, is one appropriate introduction to rhythmic instruction because most children of school age have the physical coordination to do it. If children can imitate the teacher's clapping perfectly, the teacher knows that they are comprehending the rhythms and that they possess the physical coordination to respond. Children of all ages are interested when the teacher suddenly says, "Listen to what I clap; then you clap it."

Soon children will be able to clap improvised patterns to be echoed by the class.

Another interesting type of echo-clapping is the *question-and-answer,* in which the teacher or a child claps a rhythmic question to be answered creatively, such as

This activity leads to discovering and creating questions and answers in melody, and to increasing comprehension of the nature of the phrase. Later on, echo-clapping in canon form can develop rhythmic memory. In this activity the class echoes perhaps one measure behind the leader and in so doing must (1) remember what was clapped and repeat it later while at the same time (2) hear and remember what the leader is doing at the moment. For example,

Children can take the part of the leader, and percussion instruments can be used instead of the clapping.

Children may also be taught to associate the different note values with specific hand or foot movements, or spoken sounds. Table 5.2 gives examples of such systems of association. After children have learned to respond to note values in these ways, they can analyze the notation of simple songs by clapping, speaking, and stepping. Songs such as "Hot Cross Buns" can be explored in this way by young children.

Table 5.2. Some Possible Responses Relating to Note Values

Note	Clapping	Speaking	Stepping
Whole	clap-squeeze-squeeze-squeeze	who-o-ole note ta-a-a-a du-u-u-u	step-point-point-point
Dotted Half	clap-squeeze-squeeze	half-note-dot ta-a-a du-u-u	step-point-point
Half	clap-squeeze	half-note ta-a du-u	step-bend
Quarter	clap	quart-er ta du	walk
Eighth ♫	clap-clap	eighth-eighth ti-ti du-de	run-run
♩ ♪	clap-clap	skip-ty ta-ti du-di	skip-ping
♫♩	clap-clap-clap	tri-o-la tri-ple-ti du-da-di	ŕun-run-run
♬♬	clap-clap-clap-clap	ti-ri-ti-ri du-ta-de-ta	ŕun-run-run-run

walk   walk   step-bend   walk   walk   step-bend

run-run run-run run-run run-run   walk walk step-bend

Notation is often associated with specific body movements, and certain rhythm syllables have been invented or adapted by many teachers to be used with the different note values. Table 5.3 shows body movements, systems of notation, and the rhythm syllables of Kodály and Gordon as they are associated with movement and notation.

Table 5.3. Body Movements, Rhythm Syllables, and Notation

Movement	Line Notation	Rhythm Syllables	Music Notation	Meter
walking thigh slapping hopping clapping	— — — —	ta ta ta ta du du du du	| | | |	$\frac{2}{4}$ or $\frac{4}{4}$
running clapping tapping	- - - - - - - -	ti-ti ti-ti ti-ti ti-ti du-de du-de du-de du-de	⊓ ⊓ ⊓ ⊓	$\frac{2}{4}$ or $\frac{4}{4}$
skipping, galloping	— — — - — - —	ta-ti ta-ti ta-ti ta-ti du-di du-di du-di du-di tim-ri tim-ri tim-ri du-ta du-ta du-ta du-ta	♩ ♩♪ ♩♪ ♩♪ ♪	$\frac{6}{8}$ $\frac{2}{4}$ or $\frac{4}{4}$
swaying sliding skating rocking swinging	——	ta-a-a du-u-u	♩.	$\frac{3}{4}$
step-bend jumping	— —	ta-a ta-a du-u du-u	♩ ♩	$\frac{2}{4}$ or $\frac{4}{4}$

Some teachers make charts such as the following for children to study.

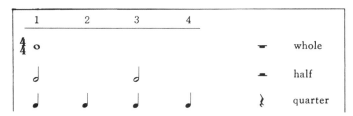

Teaching the Concept of Rest

At the time the song "Bingo" is learned, the beat and the rhythm of the melody can be experienced by marching to the song and clapping. The repeated pattern "long long short-short long" can be sung as *ta ta ti-ti ta*. Clapping softly with the fingers, not the palms, the class sings the song as written, then on its repeat, omits singing *B* and squeezes hands instead of clapping on that beat. On the next repeat, the letters *B* and *i* are not sung, the hands clenched on those beats. This is continued until silently clenched hands are squeezing the complete pattern. The name *rest* can be attached to the short and long silences the children have felt.

BINGO

American Folksong

There was a farm-er had a dog, And Bin-go was his name-O,
B - I - N-G-O, B - I - N-G-O,
B - I - N-G-O, and Bin-go was his name - O.

Divisions of the Beat

The necessity for divisions of the beat appears very soon after learning the concept of the steady beat. The initial division of the beat is into two equal parts. Words such as "Rain, rain, go a-way" provide learners with examples in which the short-short sound is equal to one long sound. Another way of illustrating beat division is with short and long lines: ____ ____ __ __ ____ . In a third method the quarter note beat is spoken with the syllable *ta* (tah) and eighth notes with *ti* (tee). Thus the above-mentioned rhythm pattern would be *ta ta ti-ti ta*. The Gordon syllables would be *du du du-de du*. Young children can easily read and write this introductory form of notation. Later on they can add note heads. The triplet was once regarded as a complexity to be taught in intermediate grades, but today young children can easily identify it as *tri-o-la, tri-pl-et*, or *du-da-di* and understand that in this division of the beat there are three notes to one beat. The Gordon rhythm syllables have the advantage of *du* being always on the beat point. They also avoid the sometimes negative response to *ti-ti's* by older children.

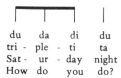

du   da   di   du
tri - ple - ti   ta
Sat - ur -   day   night
How   do   you   do?

From this beginning the 7-year-old can eventually understand the concept of four-to-one and its variants:

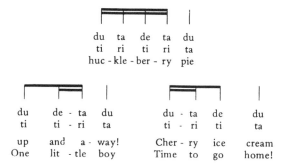

du   ta   de   ta   du
ti   ri   ti   ri   ta
huc - kle - ber - ry   pie

du   de - ta   du   du - ta   de   du
ti   ti - ri   ta   ti - ri   ti   ta

up   and   a - way!   Cher - ry   ice   cream
One   lit - tle boy   Time   to   go   home!

Divisions of the beat should be studied in relation to words, body movement, songs, and improvised percussion patterns. For example, children are guided to observe the *short-short long* and *long short-short* patterns in the melody of "Jennie Jenkins." Later they can find that "Ten Little Indians" is constructed from the same rhythm pattern used in a different way, with part of it repeated many times.

Dotted Notes   While the rhythm of the dotted quarter note may have been practiced by imitation, emphasis on this concept is usually in third and fourth grades. By notating a familiar song such as "America," the value of the dot being worth half again the value of the note it follows is evident. The class should also be guided to discover where the second beat-point falls within a dotted quarter note (Answer: on the dot).

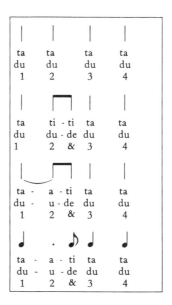

All uses for the dot should be explored in the notation of songs. The fact that the dot adds half again the original value of the note it follows should be reviewed as frequently as is needed to understand the music being performed or composed by the children.

When this relationship of dots and beats has been established, it is not difficult to apply it to such patterns as the dotted-eighth-and-sixteenth note pattern.

"Kum ba yah" is one of many songs that employ dotted rhythms. Children should have numerous experiences with such melodies, singing and clapping them and listening to recorded versions. They might experiment by changing the rhythm, singing it in even eighth notes, then discussing whether this is preferred to the uneven rhythm of the written song. They should examine the notation carefully. After comparing the even eighth notes with the dotted-eighth-sixteenth notes, the following teacher-made chart might be studied:

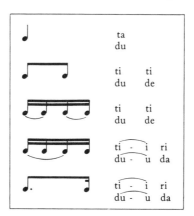

By means of the chart the children should be able to analyze the divisions of the beat by dividing it into halves (eighth notes) and then into quarters (sixteenth notes) to understand arithmetically the dotted note rhythm they have used in listening, clapping, and singing.

Such activities also enable children to discover beat units written in different note values and different divisions of the beat. They can find them in the melodies of songs by singing, clapping, and playing on percussion instruments. By looking at notation of music they have worked with and know, they will find that beat units can be written in different note values:

They will discover equal divisions of the beat:

and unequal divisions of the beat:

They will also find that three notes of equal value can occupy a beat unit normally divided in twos:

Competent teachers know that it is important for learners to experience all these aspects of rhythm in a variety of contexts.

Articulation   Such musical terms as *staccato* and *legato* can be included in the study of rhythm because they affect the duration of sounds. They are means of musical *articulation;* for example, staccato, indicating disconnected tones and legato, indicating connected tones. ''Skinnamarink'' can be sung in either staccato or legato style; the children can evaluate each of these kinds of articulation in this and other songs and instrumental pieces.

SKINNAMARINK

Traditional

Among the many recordings that illustrate musical articulation are the following:

LEGATO

Stravinsky, ''Berceuse'' from *Firebird Suite. Adventures in Music* (AM), grade 1, vol. 1

Fauré, ''Berceuse'' from *Dolly.* AM, grade 2, vol. 1

Bizet, ''Cradle Song'' from *Children's Games.* AM, grade 1, vol. 1

Offenbach, ''Barcarolle'' from *Tales of Hoffman.* AM, grade 3, vol. 1

STACCATO

Mussorgsky, ''Ballet of the Unhatched Chicks'' from *Pictures at an Exhibition.* AM, grade 1, vol. 1

Kodály, ''Viennese Musical Clock'' from *Háry János Suite.* AM, grade 2, vol. 1

Stravinsky, ''Dance Infernale'' from *Firebird Suite.* BOL 69; Keyboard Junior Recordings

Vaughan-Williams, ''March Past of the Kitchen Utensils'' from *The Wasps.* AM, grade 3, vol. 1

von Suppé, *Light Cavalry Overture*

Another aspect affecting duration of sound is the *fermata,* or hold (⌒). This is found in some familiar songs such as ''Erie Canal'' and ''We Three Kings of Orient Are.'' It can be identified in recorded compositions when the regular beat stops for a time and one tone or chord is sustained before the beat and the melody continue.

Accent, Meter, and Rhythmic Patterns

Rhythmic Exercises Beginning with very easy movements, teachers help children feel basic rhythms by having them patsch, snap fingers, tap desks, and stamp heels, first as exercises, then with verse, songs, and recordings. A major purpose is to build concepts of metrical rhythm. The long-term objective has three stages. The first stage begins with symmetrical meters—those divisible by two or three—because they are easiest and therefore the logical starting point. These include the familiar 2/4, 3/4, 4/4, and 6/8. The second stage introduces children to alternations of meters—2/4-3/4-2/4. The third stage features asymmetrical meters such as 5/4, 7/8, and others not divisible by two or three, which have irregular accents. Ten- and 11-year olds will discern that these are formed from the familiar two- and three-beat groups they know from their study of the more conventional meters, but now arranged in a different, less regular order. Movements, spoken words, or phrases can be found or invented to help the children learn to feel these meters, just as appropriate movements and words helped them with the common ones. Such meters are commonly used in the music of Africa and Asia, and they comprise an important element of Western music being written today. Thus, school music has been freed from the metrical straitjacket of earlier years and is ready to undergo an exciting expansion in rhythm. Some examples of Orff-type rhythmic exercises follow.

March rhythms such as "This Old Man," "Pop! Goes the Weasel," "Clap Your Hands," "Four in a Boat," and "Shoo Fly" can be felt by movements such as those that follow:

Waltz rhythms such as "Ach du lieber Augustin" ("The More We Get Together") can also be experienced by movement:

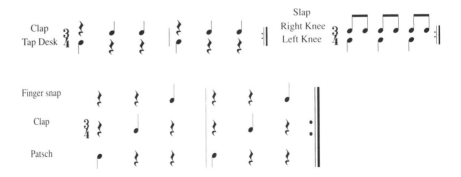

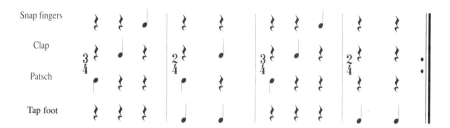

Percussion instruments (pitched and unpitched) can be used instead of body movements to produce the sound in such exercises. While the class does one pattern softly in unison, one child can improvise rhythmically by clapping or by playing a percussion instrument. If the basic beat is felt and understood, children should be able to recognize many of their patterns in notation. They should be guided to discover that the natural accent determines where the bar lines are placed.

Rhythmic Development

The approach of Carl Orff includes percussive body sounds such as stamping feet, patschen, clapping hands, and snapping fingers. These sounds have four levels of pitches from low to high: stamp, patsch, clap, and snap. They not only help children feel the beat and rhythm patterns, but the physical action adds to their pleasure.

Courtesy of the Music Educators National Conference, Reston, Va.

Example of percussive body sounds:

patsch   clap   *patsch snap-snap*   *patsch*   *clap*   *patsch snap-snap*
Hickory   dickory   dock (tick-tock);   the   mouse   ran   up   the   clock   (tick-tock).

　　　patsch   *clap*   *patsch*   *clap*   *patsch*   *clap*   *patsch snap-snap*
The   clock   struck   one,   the   mouse   ran   down;   hickory   dickory   dock   (tick-tock).

After this pattern has been mastered, some of the class can add the percussion instruments suggested by the song.

A new melody for the song can be improvised on a small keyboard instrument on the pitches of the C pentatonic scale: C-D-E-G-A. In this learning sequence the student progresses creatively from speech sounds and word rhythms to body percussion, then to percussion instruments, and finally to a melody.

For generations this Mother Goose song has been accompanied by children playing rhythm sticks slowly, two beats to the measure, in imitation of the clock which is a big old grandfather's clock that really ticks and tocks. In addition, one child is the mouse, who plays *glissandos* on the bells—going up in pitch when the mouse runs up, and down in pitch when the mouse runs down. The tick-tock indicated during the rests can be performed by a child playing on two tone blocks, one higher than the other in pitch. Children may decide to play a different instrument on the accent.

HICKORY, DICKORY, DOCK

Words from Mother Goose

Music by J. W. Elliot

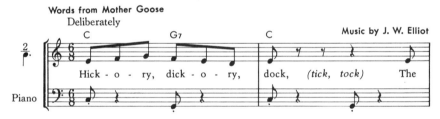

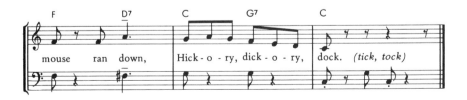

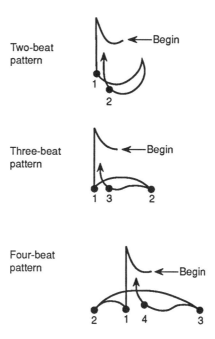

Two-beat pattern

Three-beat pattern

Four-beat pattern

Figure 5.1. CONDUCTING PATTERNS

Conducting   Conductors' beat patterns are another way of responding to meter rhythmically, usually in the intermediate grades. After the patterns have been learned they can be used by the children to match meters they hear in recordings. The primary (heavy) accent of each measure is indicated by a downbeat, as illustrated in Figure 5.1. A drum played on the downbeat helps the children hear the accent. In 4/4 and slow 6/8 meters a secondary accent occurs on beats 3 and 4, respectively.

Exploring   When short word rhythms are repeated and when longer groups of rhythmic
Common Meters words are spoken, there is a natural tendency to group the beats by accenting some of them. In their most common usage these accents are spaced regularly, at intervals of two or three beats. If children clap hands loudly on the accented beats and clap softly on the unaccented beats, they can determine whether the beats are grouped in twos or threes. Songs and recorded music useful for exploring common meters are very easily found in the elementary school literature.

Number of Beats	*Duple Meter*	*Triple Meter*
1		3/8, 3/4 (tempo di valse)
2	2/4, 2/2	6/8, 6/4
3		3/8, 3/4, 9/8
4	4/8, 4/4, 4/2	12/8

Meter signatures indicate how many of a certain kind of note or its equivalents can be found in one measure. The upper figure generally tells us the number of beats in a measure, and the lower figure generally indicates the kind of note that receives one beat. If the meter signature is 3/4, there are three quarter notes or their equivalent value in the measure.

The most commonly found meters are 2/4, 3/3, 4/4, and 6/8. *Alla breve* meter (¢) is really 2/2 meter, and is quite common. The meter 3/2 is not uncommon; songs such as "Kum Ba Ya" may be written in that meter, and 9/8 is the meter for "Down in the Valley." Familiar songs can and do change meter, as in "We Three Kings of Orient Are."

There is a possibility that in stressing meter teachers limit the capacity of children to think beyond its regularity. Many songs demand that meter be deemphasized in performance. The song "America" is a good example. When performed with a strong first beat, "America" takes on the characteristics of a waltz. When performed without metric accent it becomes a solemn and dignified melody.

An examination of gregorian chant reveals no regular recurring beat or accent. Like some other kinds of music it is usually based on speech rhythms. Music of India, and Asia may also have no regular metrical beat. Syncopation also upsets the normal meter and accent by deviating from the regular recurrent accent; it shifts accents to normally weak beats. The familiar "Hokey Pokey" and "Dry Bones" are among the many songs from which children can learn about syncopation. Again, the teacher should examine the indexes of music books for the heading "syncopation." When possible, rhythmic notation should be written on the chalkboard to help children analyze syncopation. The beat points—the place or note in the measure where the metric beat falls—should be indicated, and the accents clearly marked. Latin American music is a useful source in studying syncopation, and some spirituals are excellent as well. When learning to perform syncopated music, children should relax. The more they tense themselves and "try very hard," the less success they are apt to have.

Figure 5.2. CHART OF METERS

	Simple				Compound				Composite		
2	2/2	2/4	2/8	6	6/4	6/8	6/16	5	5/4	5/8	5/16
3	3/2	3/4	3/8	9	9/4	9/8	9/16	7	7/4	7/8	7/16
4	4/2	4/4	4/8	12	12/4	12/8	12/16	11	11/4	11/8	11/16

Exploring Less Common Meters

Music of today often reflects a desire for some contrast to commonplace meters and rhythms. Thus there is continuing emphasis on less familiar meters once the common ones have been mastered. Here are some examples:

Meter	Title	Composer/Performer
5/4 (3 + 2)	"Second Movement," *Sixth Symphony*	Tchaikovsky
5/4, 7/8	"Fourth Movement," *Trio*	Ravel
5/4, 6/4	"Promenade," *Pictures at an Exhibition*	Mussorgsky
5/4	*Take Five*	Dave Brubeck

MENC audiocassettes in the series *Sounds of the World* feature rhythmic recordings of many cultures. Some record jackets of Asian Indian music explain the metrical organization of that music, and the indexes of the music textbooks guide the reader to songs and recordings having composite meters.

Older students enjoy experimenting with less common meters. They may listen to popular examples or compose percussion pieces and songs that have such beat groupings. Composite meters are normally combinations of 2 and 3 beat groups. The meter 5/4 is either 3 + 2 or 2 + 3; 7/8 either 2 + 2 + 3, 2 + 3 + 2, or 3 + 2 + 2.

"Gerakina" is an example of 7/8 meter in the configuration of 3 + 2 + 2. The tempo of this song is rather fast; counts 1, 4, and 6 mark the beat points. The class might choose different instruments to depict Gerakina's jingling bracelets.

The original Greek song ends less happily. Gerakina (pronounced "Yehr-ah-kee-nah") went to the well to bring fresh water, with her bracelets jingling. When she fell, shouting, into the open well, young and old ran to the rescue. The singer felt miserable because he was in love with her and she had ignored him. He ran with the others to help her, but never succeeded in rescuing her.

GERAKINA

Words adapted by H. V. N.

1. Ger - a - ki - na, one fine day,____ Took a walk just to dis -
2. Ger - a - ki - na did not look,____ Took a step and fell ker -

play her brace - lets fine, Jing - jang - ling on her way,____
floop! down in the well, Jing - jang - ling on her way,____

Then, as she went a - long, she gai - ly sang a song to brigh - ten the
And, as she fell down in the well, she sang a song to brigh - ten her

day,   gai - ly   sang   a   song   to   brigh - ten   the   day.____
stay,   gai - ly   sang   a   song   to   brigh - ten   her   stay.____

From *Toward World Understanding With Song.* Reproduced by permission. Copyright 1967 by Vernice T. Nye, Robert E. Nye, and H. Virginia Nye.

> 3. *Gerakina gave a shout, Soon a young lad pulled her out for all to greet, Jing-jangling on her way.*
> *Then, as she thanked the lad, she gaily sang a song to brighten his day, gaily sang a song to brighten his day.*
> 4. *Gerakina took a look, Looked and felt her heart go floop! then very soon, Jing-jangling, they were wed,*
> *So, all through life, they say, they gaily sang a song to brighten each day, gaily sang a song to brighten each day.*

An interesting challenge for a class is to devise a logical conductor's beat for 7-beat and other less standard beat groups. An assignment for individuals and small groups could be structured as shown in the blank score to be filled in by students, and then performed (Figure 5.3). The first experiment should be very simple, using only two or three instruments for four measures. By means of an overhead projector the entire class might study, read, perform, and evaluate such scores.

Figure 5.3. PERCUSSION SCORE IN 5/4 METER

	1 2 3 4 5	*1 2 3 4 5*	*1 2 3 4 5 etc.*
Triangle			
Tambourine			
Wood block			
Bongo drums (or small drum)			
Conga drum (or large drum)			

Rhythm Patterns in Songs One of the ways students become conscious of definite rhythm patterns is by echo-clapping, described earlier. Teachers help children to recognize the patterns found in selected songs. For example, they can discover the syncopated pattern of the "Ch, ch, ch" in "Brush Your Teeth" by echo-clapping, and then, if advanced enough, work on its notation.

All of "Ten Little Indians" except the concluding two measures consists of the pattern:

 - three times

With the exception of the final three measures, "I Love the Mountains" is constructed on two rhythm patterns:

 - two times

- four times

Younger children can identify patterns, and teachers can write them on the chalkboard if the children are unable to notate the rhythms of what they hear. Older children can look for these repeated patterns in notation, as well as identifying them when listening to songs and recordings.

Many songs do not contain such distinct patterns. Teachers must seek songs and recorded music which are best suited to build specific musical concepts. Words of songs can be helpful when children are performing rhythm patterns. A simple example is the song "Sally Go Round the Sun," in which young children may choose to use the rhythm of the first four notes as an ostinato played by sticks throughout the song.

The children can remember the rhythm of the pattern by repeating silently the words: "Sally Go Round."

They might decide to have a woodblock play the repeated rhythm of the last two measures while the sticks play the original one. The new rhythm pattern could be remembered by the rhythm of the words "Sunday afternoon."

Some of the numerous songs usable for the study of rhythm patterns are "Jingle Bells," "Over the River and Through the Woods," "Hanukkah," and "Skip to My Lou." Examples of the many recordings which serve the same purpose are *Country Gardens,* arranged by Grainger, RCA Rhythm Album 6; *The Little White Donkey,* Ibert, AM, grade 2, vol. 1; "Habañera" from *Carmen,* Bizet, BOL 56; and *Variations on The Theme "Pop! Goes the Weasel,"* Cailliet, AM, grade 4, vol. 1.

Expanding the Concept of Rhythm

Besides expanding their concept of rhythm in music, children should be helped to find rhythm in other areas of life. Rhythm exists all about us—in the human heartbeat, ocean waves, day and night, life cycles of plants and animals, the rhythmic sounds of machinery, poetry, speech, and dance. The teacher might ask questions such as "How did Debussy compose music that reflects the rhythm of the ocean in *La Mer?*" or "How do composers of art songs manage the rhythm of the poems they set to music?" Other good questions might include "Do the beat and its divisions have anything in common with certain examples of architecture?" "Is there evidence of unity, balance, and contrast in rhythm?"

Rhythm-Related Compositional Devices

As children compose, they may have an interest in some of the devices used by the adult composer. The terminology may seem complex at first, but it is rather simple when explained, as illustrated by the terms *augmentation* and *diminution.* To augment something, make it larger; to diminish something, make it smaller. This is what happens in rhythm. If young composers are writing a score for percussion instruments based on the pattern

they may follow a process such as the following:

1. Apply diminution by reducing each note in the pattern to one half its original value:

2. Extend the original pattern by repeating it once to add to a feeling of tension.
3. Augment the pattern by making each note of the original twice as long.
4. Combine these patterns to construct a four-measure composition in 4/4 meter, which builds up to a climax followed by a feeling of release.

To continue the process the children might then take the following steps:

5. Use this pattern as a rhythmic ostinato, assigned to a woodblock player.
6. Add a continuous eighth-note pattern played by maracas for stability to unify the piece.
7. Experiment with polymetrics by adding a hand drum playing quarter-note beats in 3/4 meter.

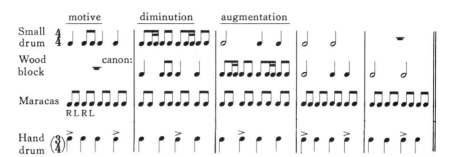

The above 3/4 part is written in 4/4 meter by using the bar lines of the other parts. The accent dicates the true meter.

8. Record the composition as a class. Play it back and evaluate it as a group, considering what might be done differently another time.

In such an exercise the children have done what many adult composers do—used diminution, augmentation, ostinato, and polymetrics. They have also composed, performed, and evaluated original music.

Activities for Teaching Rhythm

Individual Differences Since children differ in levels of ability, development, and skill, teachers can expect an easy rhythmic response for one child to be a difficult one for another. To assist children who find rhythm difficult, teachers guide them to success either with the same rhythm at a slower tempo, or with a simpler rhythm to which they can respond at their own tempo. It helps some children to produce the sounds of the rhythm by clapping, singing, speaking, chanting, or making up sounds; their sounds and actions are then more easily synchronized with each other, and a habit of physical response to movement begins to develop.

Sometimes 6-year-olds do not understand the desired relationship between sounds they hear and corresponding movements. Teachers should remember that when children are asked to move in time with music, they are expected to (1) control a specific movement, (2) listen to the music, and (3) synchronize the two. It is natural that some children find the teacher's request confusing, and the teacher must help children learn the movement well before asking them to add the other two aspects. Sometimes the use of a paper streamer or a scarf helps children perform a fluid motion that is difficult with the arm alone.

Some children cannot clap their hands in time with music, but they might succeed by patsching, or by reducing the complexity of the desired response. For all children, regardless of their coordination, the teacher at times encourages responses of a creative nature. Body movements and percussion instruments can provide means for successful participation other than singing.

Normal Expectations

Rhythmic activities for young children are free and informal; they emphasize use of the big muscles in large, free motions. Children learn through imaginative and creative play, imitating people, animals, and things. They respond to simple patterns played on the drum, piano, tone block, or record player with actions such as walking, marching, running, jumping, hopping, skipping, galloping, and tiptoeing. Concepts of high-low, heavy-light, long-short, and soft-loud can be acquired. Simple directed action songs and singing games are played, such as "Skinnamarink," "Eensy Weensy Spider," and "Hokey Pokey." Such songs are found in quantity in nursery and kindergarten series books. Dramatizations, finger plays, and hand movements contribute to rhythmic development. Children learn to play percussion instruments in time with music, and to use them for sound effects that add interest and variety to musical experiences.

Photo by Juretta Nidever.

Levels 1 and 2:

- Ability to respond with large free motions: walking, running, jumping, hopping, skipping, and combinations of these.
- Performance and enjoyment of action songs such as "If You're Happy" and "Thumbkin," as well as singing game songs such as "Bluebird," "My Pretty Little Miss," "Looby Lou," and "Clapping Land."
- Ability to respond to rhythm creatively with movements such as swinging, bending, twisting, swaying, stretching, pushing, pulling.
- Rhythmic dramatization.
- Ability to do simple dance steps and formations including galloping, sliding, skipping, bowing, and circling with or without a partner.
- Ability to understand the relationship between rhythmic movements and quarter, eighth, and half notes.
- Ability to play rhythms on percussion instruments.
- Ability to devise suitable percussion accompaniments for live or recorded music.
- Ability to perceive whether music "moves" in twos or threes (duple or triple meter).
- Awareness of repeated rhythm patterns and repeated and contrasting phrases or sections of music in level 2.

Levels 3 and 4:

- Experience with many action songs, singing games, and dances.
- Ability to create and notate simple percussion scores.
- The transfer of rhythmic understanding gained from body responses to note and rest values, including the dotted note.
- Increased understanding of beat, rhythm patterns, accent, meter, and form as reflected through body responses.
- Increased awareness of differences between different kinds of music through creative rhythmic dramatization.
- Knowledge of conductor's patterns for 2-, 3-, and 4-beat meters.
- Ability to perform combined movements of walk-step, step-hop, skip-hop, step-slide, slide-hop, and to use these movements in dances and dramatizations.
- Ability to march to duple and quadruple meters, accenting the first beat of each measure.
- Identification of 2-, 3-, and 4-beat meters in live and recorded music.
- Ability to move to the rhythm of selected familiar songs.
- Ability to write notation for simple rhythm patterns played by the teacher.
- Depiction of musical phrases through the body movement.
- Ability to create and notate percussion scores to songs and recordings.
- Ability to interpret songs and recordings with rhythmic movement.
- Ability to use percussion instruments to play both metric and melody rhythms.

- Ability to dramatize work songs, ballads, and other kinds of music.
- Ability to notate more complex musical patterns.
- Knowledge of meter, notation, and melody in relation to the beat.
- Creative interpretation of music's expressive qualities through movement.
- Ability to use conductor's beat patterns for all common meters.
- Ability to create more complex percussion scores and to use percussion instruments for sound effects with music.
- Depiction of the concept of syncopation through movement and the use of percussion instruments.
- Increased skill in moving to more complex musical patterns.
- Increased experience with asymmetrical meters.
- Acquisition of a repertoire of songs and folk dances representative of the United States and the rest of the world; an understanding of their place in musical cultures.
- Ability to play and enjoy percussion instruments of other cultures (e.g., Africa, Latin America).

Selected Songs for Experimentation

IF YOU'RE HAPPY

Traditional

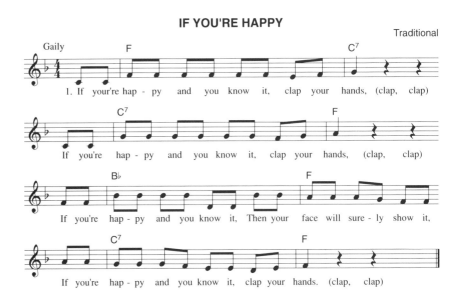

2. ...tap your toe, (tap, tap)
3. ...nod your head, (nod, nod)
4. ...do all three, (together)

SOME SUGGESTED RHYTHMIC ACTIVITIES

Students suggest action words for more verses.

One student plays the first note of each measure on an alto xylophone as the class sings the song.

Different students conduct verses of the song.

Students suggest motions for the rests.

DOWN BY THE STATION

Traditional School Song
For ages 5—7

Down by the sta - tion ear - ly in the morn - ing

See the lit - tle puf - fer - bil - lies all in a row.

See the en - gine driv - er pull the lit - tle han - dle.

Choo! Choo! Toot! Toot! Off they go!

SOME SUGGESTED RHYTHMIC ACTIVITIES

Children clap the meter, four beats to the measure, and chant ''Chug, chug, puff, puff.''

Define the word ''puffer-billies,'' and have the children clap and chant it.

Children clap the word-rhythms as the teacher says the words.

Children learn to select appropriate percussion instruments for these rhythms.

Select a rhythm pattern from the song (e.g., the rhythm of ''Down by the Station''). A child plays it as an ostinato on a percussion instrument while others sing.

Older children may sing this song as a round.

The children step the note values, first of selected measures, then of phrases, and finally of the entire song.

Advanced children identify each rhythm pattern, step it, and notate it in stem notation.

SAILING

Italian Melody
for Grades Two and Three

Leisurely

Come, sail - ing with me; _____ Let's

float on the sea. O - ver the waves with the
spray fly - ing high, Come sail - ing with me.

SOME SUGGESTED RHYTHMIC ACTIVITIES

Children sway in time with the music.

One group of children claps hands or uses percussion instruments on the first beat of each measure while another group claps the meter.

Draw attention to the song's phrase structure by helping the children mark the ends of each of the four phrases with movements or percussive sounds.

The class conducts 3/4 meter.

Teach a simple waltz step. Example:

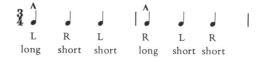

L R L R L R
long short short long short short

OLD MACDONALD

American Song

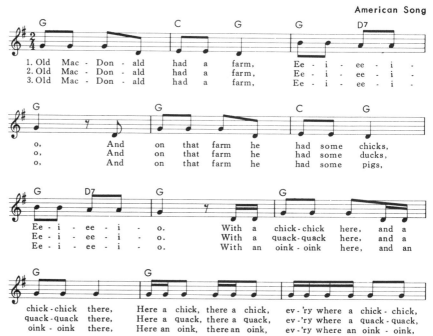

1. Old Mac - Don - ald had a farm, Ee - i - ee - i -
2. Old Mac - Don - ald had a farm, Ee - i - ee - i -
3. Old Mac - Don - ald had a farm, Ee - i - ee - i -

o, And on that farm he had some chicks,
o, And on that farm he had some ducks,
o, And on that farm he had some pigs,

Ee - i - ee - i - o. With a chick - chick here, and a
Ee - i - ee - i - o. With a quack - quack here, and a
Ee - i - ee - i - o. With an oink - oink here, and an

chick - chick there, Here a chick, there a chick, ev - 'ry where a chick - chick,
quack - quack there, Here a quack, there a quack, ev - 'ry where a quack - quack,
oink - oink there, Here an oink, there an oink, ev - 'ry where an oink - oink,

Old Mac - Don - ald   had   a   farm   Ee - i - ee - i - o.
Old Mac - Don - ald   had   a   farm   Ee - i - ee - i - o.
Old Mac - Don - ald   had   a   farm   Ee - i - ee - i - o.

SOME SUGGESTED RHYTHMIC ACTIVITIES

Children sing the song, discuss aspects of it that may suggest a percussion accompaniment, then create a percussion score and notate it graphically.

Children invent actions for each repetition of ''Ee-i-ee-i-o.'' They may dramatize the song.

The class conducts the song in 2/4 meter.

Treat the following song as a pentatonic melody. Children may add bordurs and ostinati. They may also improvise a simple dance.

FIVE LITTLE SKELETONS

Walter Bates

Verse 1

Five lit - tle skel - e - tons dan - cing through the door.

One tripped and fell, now there's on - ly four!

Verse 2:

Four little skeletons
Happy as can be.
One fell apart __
Now there's only three!

Verse 3:

Three little skeletons
Stirring up some stew.
One fell in __
Now there's only two!

Verse 4:

Two little skeletons
Looking for some fun
One got bored __
Now there's only one!

Verse 5

One lit - tle skel - e - ton noth - ing left to do, but it's

Hal - lo - ween and he's com - ing for you! Boo!

SOME SUGGESTED RHYTHMIC ACTIVITIES

Children create a dance-dramatization of the song.

Use the song to teach the relation of word-rhythms to note values.

Use the word-rhythms of the verses to suggest simple ostinati.

Children devise a percussion score.

RIG - A - JIG - JIG

SOME SUGGESTED RHYTHMIC ACTIVITIES

Children create a dance and compare 2/4 and fast 6/8 meters in the process.

With percussion instruments, reinforce the walking effect of the verse and the skipping effect of the refrain.

R.E.N.

TO PUERTO RICO

With languor

Song for Grades Five and Six

SOME SUGGESTED RHYTHMIC ACTIVITIES

Assist students in devising and notating a Latin American percussion score.

Possibilities include

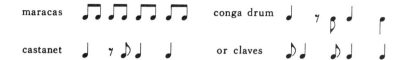

maracas   conga drum

castanet   or claves

Explore the concept of syncopation as employed in this song.

For part singing, students may improvise a new part a third higher than the melody.

THE COUNT

Brazilian Song for Grades Five and Six

1. He wrote me a let-ter, ca-ram-ba! It asked for my
2. This he told my fa-ther, ca-ram-ba! Fa-ther shook with

hand.   I wrote him my an-swer, ca-ram-ba!
wrath.   He broke ev-'ry pot in the kich-en;

Said, "No wed-ding band."   I ran down the path!

SOME SUGGESTED RHYTHMIC ACTIVITIES

Assist students in devising a Latin American percussion score.

Teach the rhythm pattern through use of the word *caramba* which children enjoy emphasizing in the song.

Teach ♩ ♩ ♩ ♩ ♩ by comparing it with ♪♩ ♪♩ ♩ "To Puerto Rico"; it is the same rhythm twice as fast. The generalization is that the same pattern can occur in lesser or greater note values (diminution or augmentation).

Additional Activities and Suggestions For Lesson Plans

The two-record album, *Shakin' Loose with Mother Goose* (Kids Matter, P. O. Box 3460, Ashland, OR 97520) is a rich collection of traditional Mother Goose rhymes set in contemporary American and Baltic styles. Its poetry and songs can provide material for chants, sing-alongs, and percussion ostinati.

There are many things learners can do to become more rhythmically aware. As examples, they may imitate, identify, contrast, differentiate, classify, or invent rhythms. They may utilize one or more of the following activities to do these things: singing, playing instruments, moving, creating, reading notation, improvising, and composing. Children need an opportunity to listen before they attempt to respond with movement or with voices. Teachers should avoid presenting too much material in one lesson.

An appropriate introduction to rhythmic activities may help children experience the beat of the music. This may happen physically or aurally through body percussion, such as hand clapping, through counting, or through the playing of an introduction on an autoharp or percussion instrument.

Prospective teachers need not feel responsible for all of the activities listed in the following pages; the activities are presented as a list from which to choose. Some of them require teaching experience to do well. Therefore, those activities and suggestions can be dealt with in part in the college class, in part during student teaching, and in part during later years of professional teaching. They combine both American and European teaching strategies and are listed in order of increasing difficulty.

Tempo A DEVELOPMENTAL PLAN

OBJECTIVE: The children reveal their understanding of concepts relating to tempo by body movement or verbal identification.

Children discover their natural tempos.	The teacher adapts drum or piano accompaniment to the natural walking tempos of individual learners.
The children recognize fast and slow tempos in songs, drum beats, and recorded music.	The teacher provides the opportunity for the children to compare two songs, one fast and one slow, and two recordings, one fast and one slow.
The children discover tempos appropriate for imitating movements of animals or depicting activities.	The teacher uses songs and recordings that suggest the movements of animals and humans. The teacher shows pictures of objects that illustrate tempo markings: a marching band—*marcato*; a turtle—*adagio*; a sleeping baby—*largo*; a jet liner—*presto*; a windup toy slowing down—*ritardando*; a rocket taking off—*accelerando*
The children recognize various tempos in contrasting activities.	After children have learned to maintain a steady beat, they are asked to dramatize an activity that is done to a steady beat, such as jumping on a trampoline, hammering, sawing, or rowing. They do different dramatizations in appropriately different tempos, adding to their concepts of fast and slow.
The children recognize tempo designations in musical scores.	The teacher selects music that includes tempo markings and has the children locate and define them.
The children are able to provide appropriate tempo terms for music sung and heard.	"What would happen if we sang the song more slowly?" "Do you like it better?" "Can you think of other ways to vary the tempo that might improve this song?" "What words can you use to describe the changes in tempo?"

Dynamics   A DEVELOPMENTAL PLAN

OBJECTIVE: The children reveal their understanding of concepts of dynamics by body movement or verbal identification.

piano (p)—soft
forte (f)—loud
The children begin to understand the differences between soft and loud, and degrees of softer and louder.

The teacher plans experiences in which children use these terms. Songs and recorded music offer experiences which increase comprehension of the variations in dynamics. Children are able to express variations in creative body movement and visual drawings.

Larger musical vocabulary becomes useful to learners in their own performances and compositions.

Accent, crescendo (cresc.), decrescendo (decresc.), mezzo piano (mp), pianissimo (pp), mezzo forte (mf), fortissimo (ff).

The children demonstrate increased understanding of music with respect to dynamics.

The children suggest dynamics for their musical interpretations, and they experiment with dynamic levels for the purpose of communicating ideas by means of music. They listen to several selected recordings and compare the use of dynamics heard in them.

Crescendo and decrescendo are identified.

The teacher selects recorded music that clearly illustrates these dynamics, such as "Bydlo" from *Pictures at an Exhibition*, Mussorgsky, Adventures in Music, grade 2, vol. 1. Have the students choose body movements to illustrate the music.

Rhythm   A DEVELOPMENTAL PLAN

OBJECTIVE: The children reveal their understanding of concepts relating to rhythm by body movement or verbal identification.

The children reflect a steady beat by movement.

The teacher adapts patschen, clapping, a drum beat, or piano improvisation to the natural rhythm of the learner's walk.

The children reflect various tempos of beat through movement.

Children dramatize the beat by walking. "How many different ways can you walk?" (tired, slow, lightly, fast, heavily, like a marcher in a parade, like a rag doll.)

The children realize their own pulse.

The teacher assists children in finding, feeling, and imitating their pulses. The children determine when the pulse quickens or slows down.

The children notate the beat.

After young children have learned to walk in time with the beat, they are asked to draw illustrations of the beat.

The children recognize the rhythm of speech.	Children use rhythmic speech with rhymes such as "Hickory Dickory Dock" and "Brush Your Teeth," speaking the words and clapping or walking to the beat on word syllable accents.
The children reflect eighth notes through rapid movement.	Children dramatize running. "How many ways can you run?" (rapidly, as if in a race; slowly, as if you are tired; quietly, so no one will hear you).
The children accent specific syllables of speech.	The teacher selects children's names that have different numbers of syllables, and has the children speak the names while drumming or clapping on each first syllable:

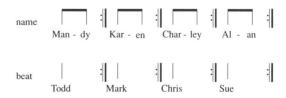

The children reflect word-rhythms and rests through movement.	Children chant, step, or devise motions for rhythmic verses such as "Brush Your Teeth," "Hickory Dickory Dock," "If You're Happy and You Know It," and "Pease Porridge Hot." (They invent a motion at the end of appropriate phrases for the rest.)
The children realize rhythmic patterns in names.	Children play their names on a drum as they speak them. Other children answer, speaking and playing their own names. The experience is heightened by using two drums, one of high pitch and the other of low pitch available to each child as he or she speaks and plays. Example:

high drum
low drum
John - ny   John - son

After this experience, the children can begin to use drum talk to say things such as the following:

I   live   in   Chi - ca - go,   Chi - ca - go,   Ill - in - ois.

Two such statements can be combined as an experiment in sound.

The children demonstrate various locomotor motions.	The teacher improvises with drum or piano; the children respond with appropriate motions such as walking, run-

ning, skipping, galloping, hopping, swaying, or rowing. When the piano is used, black keys provide an easy way for any child to improvise acceptably.

The children realize rhythmic notation through movement.

The teacher writes a simple quarter-note or quarter-and-eighth-note pattern. Children devise physical gestures appropriate to the note durations. They then write the rhythmic figure in graphic symbols such as large and small circles or notation:

ta ta ti - ti ta
du du du-de du

The children recognize divisions of the beat.

A beat is established by everyone patching and clapping a steady duple tempo. The teacher then introduces the following rhyme in a call-and-response format:

Round in a circle;

Round in a game.

When we come to you

Say your name.

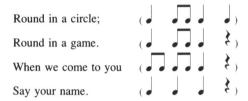

One at a time individual students then respond with:

My name is Sheri.

—followed by the classes' response:

Her name is Sheri.

After four individual students have responded, the class chants in unison:

And the beat goes on.

The teacher then resumes the call and response from the beginning, and four more students chant their names individually. Later on, names can be written in stem notation, and still later, in traditional notation without the staff. The rhythm of the names can be related to movement and eventually to notation.

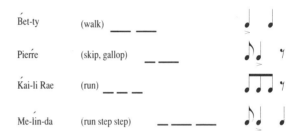

Bet-ty   (walk)   __ __

Pierre   (skip, gallop)   __ __

Kai-li Rae   (run)   __ __ __

Me-lin-da   (run step step)   __ __ __

The children realize rhythmic patterns of their names through notation.

The class beats a slow, steady beat with clapping, pounding lightly on desks, or with percussion instruments while each child says his or her name twice in time with the beat. Next, the class translates the rhythm of some of the names into rhythmic syllables. The teacher selects some of these to be written in quarter- and eighth-note stem notation. (This last step requires that names be screened by the teacher because some demand a complexity beyond the present ability of the children to notate them. The class could chant the complex names but not notate them at this time.)

The children improvise rhythmic patterns with divided beats.

Teacher and children can make up patterns for the class to read with rhythmic syllables and with percussion instruments. Example:

Many interesting words can be written to match this simple notation.

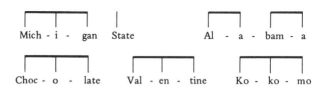

Mich - i - gan   State   Al - a - bam - a

Choc - o - late   Val - en - tine   Ko - ko - mo

The children visualize divisions of the beat.

Students may experiment with the use of paper cutouts for note values.

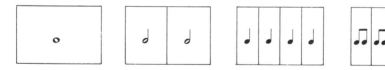

then 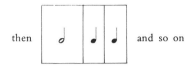 and so on

Children play games by arranging these note values and performing them. However, the note groupings cannot be larger than the whole sheet, which represents the whole note.

Divisions of the beat, continued.

Students can manipulate colored Cuisinaire rods in sizes to represent the relative values of whole, half, quarter, and eighth notes. Students arrange the rods in various combinations with the stipulation that no combination can be of larger size than the largest rod. Students can place these on the desk or the overhead projector and clap, walk, or step them as they count the beats of the measure. More advanced students can chart short songs in this manner.

The children visualize the concept of rests.

The concept of a rest can be taught by the use of sheets of colored paper.

The children devise a percussion score using word-rhythms.

Young children can invent percussion scores through use of word-rhythms such as

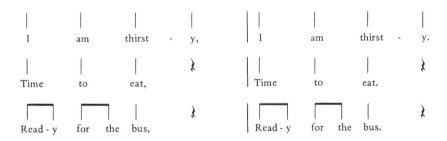

Contrasting rhythm patterns are created by students.

Rhythmic patterns can be performed on percussion instruments, and by hand clapping, patschen, or snapping. One child creates a rhythm pattern within limits set by the teacher, such as using only *ta* and *ti-ti*. A second child creates a different pattern that fits with the first one. The two patterns may be written on the chalkboard; the class plays or claps them in sequence, then in combination. Percussion instruments of contrasting tone qualities may be added.

The children memorize rhythmic patterns.	The teacher may use flash cards with simple rhythm patterns, showing a card, concealing it, and having the class clap it.
The children express rhythm patterns while maintaining a steady beat.	As an extension of the previous activity, students may clap rhythm patterns while maintaining the beat with heel taps. Ultimately the students can sight-read rhythm patterns from flash cards while maintaining the steady beat.
The children improvise rhythm patterns.	Several students choose percussion instruments. One establishes an ostinato to be performed throughout an original percussion composition; others enter and depart at different times to add interest and variety to the piece.
Game for improvising patterns	The teacher selects six to eight participants, and then establishes a steady beat in a specific meter. One at a time, each of the six children claps a pattern which fits with the beat. Every pattern must be different. The children continue clapping their patterns until all six have been added. Then the game begins again with a different group of children. The teacher may want the class to notate some of the improvised patterns, which can then be performed on percussion instruments.
The children recognize rhythmic patterns by hearing.	"Which one did I play?" The children select the rhythmic pattern clapped by the teacher from six different flash cards at their desks or from six charted patterns on the blackboard. The patterns may be written in stem or traditional notation.

Accent and Meter   A DEVELOPMENTAL PLAN

OBJECTIVE: The children reveal their understanding of concepts relating to tempo by body movement or verbal identification.

The children visualize the concept of accent.	The concept of an accent can be taught by the use of two shades of any one color. It may reflect any meter the teacher chooses.

The children reflect the accents of syllables by clapping.

The children seek words with different accents. They then recite and clap them with appropriate emphases. Examples: mu-sic, a-rith-me-tic, math-e-ma-tics, ge-og-raphy.

Children recognize duple and triple meters.

Regular accents result in meters. Children accent beats grouped in twos and threes, producing duple and triple meters. Once the meters are established, they are related to familiar songs.

The children combine word accents and meters.

The accented word patterns in the following illustration can introduce children to the concept that in normally accented music, the bar line is placed before the heavily accented beat. Variety in rhythm can be achieved in any meter by changing the accents.

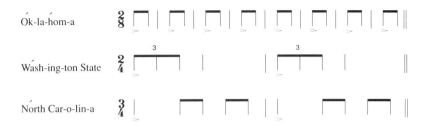

Students experiment with varied meters.

Students may invent meters by placing regular accents at different intervals while clapping, stamping, or using percussion instruments.

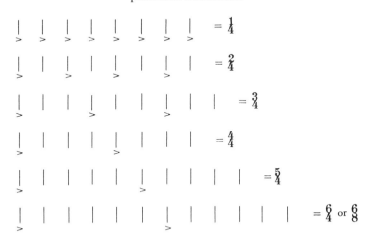

Children reflect various meters with movement.

Children choose movements to respond to the beats and accents of various meters. Examples:

2/4: patsch, clap
3/4: patsch, clap, snap
4/4: patsch, clap, snap right, snap left

Younger children may push both hands high into the air for the first beat and rest on the other beats.

The children compose with changing meters.

When working with advanced students, the teacher may assign children the task of composing a percussion score with an unusual metric pattern such as one measure each of 3/4 and 4/4 in succession. Other metric combinations may be explored as well.

The children experiment with syncopation.

Syncopation can be introduced by using a song such as "To Puerto Rico" (p. 148). The teacher guides the students to discover that while the beats of the meter are regular, some accents fall on a part of the measure not usually accented. There are several kinds of syncopation with which students can experiment:

Writing accent marks on beats not normally accented.

Beginning a measure in 4/4 meter with an eighth note followed by a quarter note to place syncopation between beats:

Using a tie to connect a weak beat with a strong one:

The students compose with polymeters.

Polymeters result from unlike meters sounding at the same time. They can be introduced by word-rhythms.

Students can write simple polymetric scores to play, tape, and evaluate in class.

The students create dances.

Students can create dances based on accents, meters, and rhythm patterns. The rhythm patterns of traditional dances can be noted and related to body movements.

Form   A DEVELOPMENTAL PLAN

OBJECTIVE: The children reveal their understanding of concepts relating to musical form by body movement or verbal identification.

Students indicate phrases through movement.	Students select a destination in the room to move to during a musical phrase. They listen to the phrase, and choose locomotor movements suggested by the music. As the phrase is sounded again, the students travel to their selected places with appropriate movements, arriving there at the end of the phrase.
The students indicate cadences through movement.	The students decide upon movements or body position to reflect each of the following:

—a complete cadence, which culminates on the tonic (I, or home) chord, and evokes feelings of finality or rest.

—an incomplete cadence, which usually culminates on some chord other than the tonic, such as the dominant (V, V_7) or the subdominant (IV) and evokes feelings of expectation or temporary rest.

Musical phrases are acted out, with different movements depicting different cadences. When a new phrase begins, either body movements or direction may change.

The students create a rondo.	The class or group agrees upon a rhythmic pattern to be used as a basis for a rondo. This pattern is designated A, and performed with body percussion. Then a child creates a new rhythmic pattern called B. After its performance, A is performed again by the group. Part C is created by another child. Thus the composition develops into A B A C A B A.

Next, the body percussion patterns can be transferred to percussion instruments appropriate to the pattern. Variations: One or two rhythm patterns could be combined with A. Crescendo could be incorporated into A. Parts B and C could include recorder or pitched percussion improvisations. The resulting piece could be tape-recorded, listened to, and discussed. A dance could be created to reflect the patterns and their sounds. Other versions of the rondo (*ABACA, ABACADAEA*) could also be explored.

References and Materials

General   ANDRESS, BARBARA, *Musical Experiences in Early Childhood.* New York: Holt, 1980.

FAULMAN, JO, "Montessori and Music in Early Childhood," *Music Educators Journal,* May 1980, 41–43.

Music Educators Journal, Special Issue: Early Childhood, March 1974.

POND, DONALD, "The Young Child's Playful World of Sound," *Music Educators Journal,* March 1980, 39–41.

REGELSKI, THOMAS A., *Teaching General Music: Action Learning for Middle and Secondary School,* New York: Schirmer, 1981. Based on the Manhattanville approach.

RICHARDS, MARY HELEN, *Aesthetic Foundations for Thinking,* Richards Institute for Music Education and Research, 1977.

TAIT, MALCOLM J., "Whispers, Growls, Screams, and Puffs . . . Lead to Composition," *Music Educators Journal,* February 1977, 33–34.

WEBSTER, PETER R. (ed.), "Creative Thinking in Music", *Music Educators Journal* (May 1990), 21–52. A series of seven articles on the topic.

Movement, Games, and Dance

ATHNEY, MARGARET, and GWEN HOTCHKISS, *A Galaxy of Games for the Music Class.* West Nyack, N. Y.: Parker, 1975.

CARLSON, DEBORAH LYNN, "Movement as a Channel to Understanding Music," *Music Educators Journal,* September 1980, 52–56. Includes bibliography.

CHASE, RICHARD, *Singing Games and Play Party Games.* New York: Dover, 1967.

CHERRY, CLAIRE, *Creative Movement for the Developing Child.* Belmont, Calif.: Fearon, 1971.

DOLL, EDNA, and MARY J. NELSON, *Rhythms Today.* Morristown, N.J.: Silver Burdett, 1965.

Handy Play Party Book. Order from World Around Songs, Route 5, Burnsville, NC 28714.

HSUS, GRACE, "Movement and Dance Are Children's Play," *Music Educators Journal,* May 1981, 42–43.

JONES, BESSIE, and BESS LOMAX HAWES, *Step-it-Down.* New York: Harper & Row, 1972. Games, plays, songs, and stories from the Afro-American heritage.

KENNEY, MAUREEN, *Circle Around the Zero* (1974). Play chants and singing games of city children. Order from 63 E. Clinton St., New Bedford, MA 02740.

Methodist Church Publishing House, *World of Fun Folk Dances* and *New World of Fun,* 407 Church Street, Nashville, TN 37219.

PALMER, HAP, *Hap Palmer Favorites.* Sherman Oaks, Calif.: Alfred. Songs for early children learning through music and movement.

STECHER, MIRIAM B., HUGH McEKHENY, and MARION GREENWOOD, *Music and Movement Improvisations,* Threshold Early Learning Library, vol. 4. New York: Macmillan, 1972.

WUYTACK, JOS, and TOSSI AARON, *Play Sing Dance.* Paris: Alphonse Leduc, 1972. American play parties for voices, recorders, Orff instruments, with dance instructions.

For Hawaiian dances, refer to *Comprehensive Musicianship* textbook Zone 111-A.

Helpful recordings include RCA's *Festival of Folk Dance* and *The World of Folk Dance,* Bowmar's *Folk Dances* and *Singing Square Dances,* and Folkways Records' *American Square Dance Music.* Good marches include "March from *King David,*" Vanguard VR 6–1090; "Stars and Stripes Forever," BOL 54; AM, grade 4, vol. 2; "March from *Aida,*" BOL 61; and "March from *The Love for Three Oranges,*" BOL 54.

Reading Music

CURATILO, JOSEPH S., RICHARD C. BERG, and MARJORIE FARMER, *The Sight and Sound of Music.* Delaware Water Gap, Penn.: Shawnee Press. A program to develop sight-reading skills beginning in grades 2–4. Includes books, cassette tapes, transparencies, and spirit masters.

DANIEL, KATINKA, *The Kodály Approach: Book 3*. Belmont, Calif.: Fearon-Pitman, 1973.

ELLIOTT, CHARLES A., ''The Music-Reading Dilemma,'' *Music Educators Journal,* February 1982, 33–34, 59.

Music Educators Journal, ''Sound Before Sight: Strategies for Teaching Music Reading,'' April 1980, 53–55, 65–67.

RICHARDS, MARY HELEN, *Threshold to Music:* Experience charts for the first year. Teachers text/manual *The First Three Years.* Belmont, Calif.: Fearon, 1964. Also see revised edition by Eleanor Kidd (1974).

Temporal Acuity Products, Inc., Bellevue, Wash. *TapMaster Rhythmic Sight Reading System.* Elementary Series K–4; Intermediate Series 4 through college. Cassette tapes and book.

Sources of Materials

Bowmar Records, Belwin Mills Corp., Melville, NY 11747. See catalog of recordings for rhythmic responses, singing games, folk and ethnic dances. Also march and dance music in the *Bowmar Orchestral Library (BOL).*

Capitol Records, 1750 N. Vine St., Hollywood, CA 90028. See the Capitol and Angel Records Educational Catalog.

Children's Book & Music Center, 2500 Santa Monica Blvd., Santa Monica, CA 90404. See the helpful catalog of tested materials.

Children's Record Guild and Young People's Records, Franson Corporation, Distributors, 225 Park Ave. South, New York, NY 10003. Recordings for children ages 2–10.

Educational Activities, Inc., 1937 Grand Ave., Baldwin, NY 11510. Catalog available.

Elephant Records. 514 Carlingview Drive, Rexdale, Ontario, Canada M9W5R3.

Folkways Records, 43 W. 61st St., New York, NY 10023. Rhythmic recordings including those of Ella Jenkins. Also a source of ethnic recordings; see catalog.

Lyons, 530 Riverview Ave., Industrial Park, Elkhart, IN 46514. A comprehensive catalog. Distributor of *Listen, Move, Dance,* Vols. 1, 2, for movement and electronic sounds.

Machlis, Joseph. Recordings for *The Enjoyment of Music.* W. W. Norton and Co., Inc., 4500 Fifth Avenue, New York, NY 10036.

MENC. *Sounds of the World* audio cassettes. 1902 Association Drive, Reston, VA 22091.

Methodist Church Publishing House, 407 Church St., Nashville, TN. Source of *World of Fun Folk Dances* and *New World of Fun.* 37219.

Multi-cultural Perspectives in Music Education. Reston, Va.: Music Educators National Conference, 1989.

RCA Victor *Dance-A-Story* Records (storybook-record), Ginn and Company, Boston, MA. 02117; Ginn and Company, 35 Mobile Drive, Toronto, Canada.

RCA Music Service, Education Dept. A., 1133 Ave. of the Americas, New York, NY 10036.

Temporal Acuity Products, Inc., 1535 121st Ave. S.E., Bellevue, WA 98005. *TAPMaster Rhythmic Sight Reading System* with integrated hardware and software. Elementary through professional levels.

Creative Audio-Visuals, 12000 Edgewater Drive, Cleveland, OH 44107. Filmstrips, cassette tapes, self-correcting sheets, and books.

Dance Your Own Way, UCLA Educational Film Sales Department; also from Dance Films, Inc.

Discovering Rhythm, United World Films, Universal Education and Visual Arts, 221 Park Ave. South, New York, NY 10003. Concepts in rhythm for children from preschool to seven years.

Hello, I'm Music.: EMC Corporation, 180 E. 6th St., St. Paul, MN 55101. Six color filmstrips, six records or three cassettes, 240 worksheets, and a teacher's guide. Melody, rhythm, harmony, form, and tone color are presented to children.

Let's Begin with the Beat, EMC Corporation, St. Paul, MN 55106. A sound-filmstrip.

Looking for Rhythm, Universal Education and Visual Arts.

Pantomimes, Brandon Films, New York, NY 10019. How the body communicates ideas.

Reading Music.: No. 2 Finding the Rhythm, Coronet Films, 65 E. S. Water Street, Chicago, IL 60601.

Rhythm Around You, Encyclopedia Britannica Educational Association.

Rhythm, Rhythm Everywhere, Coronet Films.

What Is Rhythm? and *Discovering Dynamics in Music,* BFA Educational Media, 2211 Michigan Avenue, Santa Monica, CA 90404.

The American Music Conference, 1000 Skokie Blvd., Wilmette, IL 60091, publishes a list of recommended films.

**Recordings for
Specific
Concepts**

TEMPO, FAST

Corelli, "Badinerie" from *Suite for Strings,* BOL 63

Kabalevsky, "Intermezzo" from *The Comedians,* BOL 53

Rossini-Respighi, "Tarantella" from *The Fantastic Toy Shop,* AM, grade 3, vol. 2

TEMPO, SLOW

Ravel, "Pavane of the Sleeping Beauty" from *Mother Goose* Suite, BOL 57

Corelli, "Sarabande" from *Suite for Strings,* BOL 63

FAST AND SLOW

Slow Joe, Franson YPR 9003 (ages 6–10)

ACCELERANDO

Grieg, "In the Hall of the Mountain King" from *Peer Gynt* Suite, AM, grade 3, vol. 2; BOL 59

ACCENT

Prokofiev, "Departure from *Winter Holiday*", AM, grade 2, vol. 1

Rossini-Respighi, "Can Can" from *The Fantastic Toyshop,* AM, grade 2, vol. 1

Herbert, "Dagger Dance" from *Natoma,* AM, grade 3, vol. 1

PERCUSSION

Strike Up the Band, Franson CRG 5027 (ages 5–8). Children can play a game to identify percussion instruments. The order on the recording is drum, cymbal, woodblock, jingle bells, sticks, triangle, tambourine.

BEAT (PULSE)

Gounod, "Waltz" from *Faust Ballet* Suite, AM, grade 3, vol. 1

Herbert, "Dagger Dance" from *Natoma*, AM, grade 3, vol. 1

Dvořák, *Slavonic Dance No. 7*, AM, grade 4, vol. 2 and various marches

FERMATA, RITARD, ACCELERANDO

Brahms, *Hungarian Dance No. 5* BOL 55

Shostakovich, "Petite Ballerina" from *Ballet Suite No. 1*, AM, grade 2, vol. 1

METER

Sousa, *Stars and Stripes Forever*, AM, grade 4, vol. 2 (2/4 meter)

Bach, "Gigue" from *Suite No. 4*, AM, grade 1, vol. 1 (two beats, 6/8 meter)

Delibes, "Waltz of the Doll" from *Coppelia*, AM, grade 1, vol. 1 (3/4 meter)

Ippolitov-Ivanov, "Cortege of the Sardar" from *Caucasian Sketches*, BOL 54 (four beats, 4/4 meter)

Offenbach, "Barcarolle" from *Tales of Hoffman* AM, grade 3, vol. 2 (6/8 meter)

CHANGES IN METER

Cailliet, *Pop Goes the Weasel* (variations), AM, grade 4, vol. 2 (6/8, 3/4, 4/8, 3/4, 2/4 meters)

Copland, "Street in a Frontier Town" from *Billy the Kid*, AM, grade 6, vol. 1

Piston, "Tango of the Merchant's Daughter" from *The Incredible Flutist* (5/8 meter), Mercury 90423

LESS COMMON METERS

Ginastera, "Wheat Dance" from *Estancia*, AM, grade 4, vol. 2

Copland, "Hoe-Down" from *Rodeo*, AM, grade 5, vol. 2

Guarnieri, *Brazilian Dance*, AM, grade 6, vol. 2

Brubeck, *Time Out*, Columbia CL 1397

Brubeck, *Time Farther Out*, Columbia CL 1690 (7/8 meter)

POLYRHYTHMS

Copland, "Street in a Frontier Town" from *Billy the Kid*, AM, grade 6, vol. 1

The Study of Music in the Elementary School: A Conceptual Approach, Charles L. Gary, ed. (Music Educators National Conference, Washington, D.C., 1967), 47–50

Source Book of African and Afro-American Materials for Music Educators (Music Educators National Conference, Washington, D.C., 1972); for two beats against three, p. 34.

RHYTHM PATTERNS

Bartók, "Bear Dance" from *Hungarian Sketches*, AM, grade 3, vol. 2

Tchaikovsky, "Fourth Movement" from *Symphony No. 4*, AM, grade 6, vol. 2

Beethoven, "Second Movement" from *Symphony No. 8*, AM, grade 6, vol. 1

Ibert, "The Little White Donkey" from *Histories No. 2*, AM, grade 2, vol. 1

Bizet, "Habañera" from *Carmen*, BOL 56

Milhaud, "Copacabana" from *Saudades do Brazil*, AM, grade 4, vol. 2

Gottschalk, ''Grand Walkaround'' from *Cakewalk,* AM, grade 5, vol. 1

Benjamin, *Jamaican Rhumba,* BOL 56

SYNCOPATION

Gottschalk, ''Grand Walkaround'' from *Cakewalk,* AM, grade 5, vol. 1

Debussy, ''Golliwog's Cakewalk'' from *Children's Corner* Suite, BOL 63

Copland, ''Hoe-Down'' from *Rodeo,* AM, grade 5, vol. 2; BOL 55

Chabrier, *España*, AM, grade 5, vol. 1 (also for study of the beat)

6 Teaching Children About Tone Quality

Sound and Tone Quality

Many substances can vibrate to produce sounds. Because substances vibrate differently, the sounds they produce are also different. The way a substance vibrates causes a pattern of overtones that is unique to it, and is described as its *tone quality*.

The terms *tone quality, tone color* and *timbre* (TAM-br) may be used interchangeably. In music they identify the differences in sound between tones of the same pitch when produced by different instruments or voices. For example, the same pitch played on a violin, a trumpet, or a flute is audibly different, and the differences are due to the tone qualities of the instruments.

Research has shown that very young children can learn to identify different tone qualities. This ability should be nurtured, not only by learning to identify differences in tone quality, but in learning what physical properties in a given instrument produce its particular tone quality. Children might also consider how the player of an instrument can affect its tone quality by his or her manner of playing; why particular tone qualities are selected by composers for their melodies and harmonies; and how tone quality interrelates with melody, harmony, texture, and form in a composition.

Children should study the ways different instruments produce musical sounds. In some woodwind instruments—the flute and piccolo—the sound is produced by a vibrating column of air; in others—the clarinet, oboe, and bassoon—the sound is initiated by a vibrating reed. By taking a bottle and blowing across its open top, a sound can be made that comes from a vibrating column of air. By pouring water into the bottle, children can discover that the longer the vibrating air column, the lower the pitch, and the shorter the vibrating air column, the higher the pitch. To imitate the vibrations of the double reed of the oboe and bassoon they can flatten one end of a soft drink straw, cut off the corners, and practice blowing into the straw through this flattened end. When brass instruments sound, the player's lips are the vibrating agent. Some children will be able to make a circular cup "mouthpiece" with their thumb and index finger, put their lips together on it, and blow into it to produce a sound with their vibrating lips. They can watch large drumheads to see that striking them causes vibrations. They can examine a piano to discover that hammers strike the strings and cause them to vibrate. By plucking the lowest string on a guitar, children can see the string vibrating to produce sound. Stringed instruments are made to vibrate by striking the strings with a mallet or hammer, plucking the strings, or bowing them.

Environmental sounds appeal to the natural curiosity of children, and a study of their tone qualities may lead to the study of formal instruments. Recordings by Paul Winter frequently incorporate the natural sounds of animals, which are followed by melodic interpretations of those sounds on traditional instruments. A unit on tone quality might also explore the qualities of various materials, and how those qualities enhance or inhibit sound production.

Other topics of interest include the *vibrato* as it is used by instrumentalists and singers, the overtone series and its relation to tone quality, and the historical development of modern instruments; these can be investigated by older children. Some may be interested in the similarities and differences between the clavichord, harpsichord, and piano, in the relationship between viols and the modern string family, and in the evolution of valved instruments.

Children may be encouraged to create new sounds with familiar instruments, such as placing materials of different types (pieces of metal, paper, felt pads) on piano and autoharp wires, and combining these experimental tone qualities with other instruments to create a background for a poem or story. Some teachers challenge children to create new tone qualities by taking sounds from their environment, taping them, and organizing them in some way. An example might be outdoor sounds, in which a short piece might utilize the sound of feet walking, cars passing, talking, or a dog barking, and so forth. These could be varied by playing the tape at different speeds and retaping them. Other ideas for environmental sounds could include sounds of a shopping trip, sounds of the city, sounds of the country, and sounds of various kinds of machinery.

Such an approach is used to involve children in the sounds of experimental composition. Electronic sounds are included, often using the assistance of tape recorders and synthesizers, which provide many of the types of tone qualities composers use today.

Sound Sources

Nonpitched Percussion Instruments
One primary source of nonpitched percussive sounds is the human body. Among the many possibilities are hand clapping of various kinds (flat-palmed, cup-palmed, and fingers only), stamping feet, tapping toes, patsching, snapping fingers, and various sounds with the mouth. All of these contribute sounds which can be organized with a beat and with accents to form rhythmic ostinati. These body sounds are limited in tone quality, and should lead to the exploration of many percussion instruments. The teacher can assist this exploration by asking, "How many ways can you play this instrument?" and "How many different sounds can you make with it?"

There is a greater variety of instruments in the percussion family than in any other group of instruments. The teacher needs to know the tone qualities that can be produced by each percussion instrument, and how to play each of them. In general, commercially made instruments are superior to those made by teachers and children, although some of the latter can be quite effective, and a few can be of permanent value.

Percussion Instrument Sound Chart

Membranes	*Woods*	*Metals*	*Special Effects Instruments*
Congas	Xylophone	Metallophone	Vibraslap
Bongos	Rhythm sticks	Triangle	Slap stick
Hand drum	Claves	Finger cymbals	Chimes
Tambourine with head	Maracas	Cabasa	Chinese bell tree
	Sandblocks	Cow Bell	Flexitone
	Woodblock	Agogo bells	
	Tone block	Tambourine without head	
	Castanets	Shaker	
	Guiro	Metal chocallo	
	Temple blocks	Jingle bells	
	Wood kameso		

Drums There are many kinds and sizes of drums, manufactured and teacher-made. Some have one head, others two. They come singly or in various combinations. For different effects they can be struck off-center or in the center, with the fingertips, the heel of the hand, or with various types of beaters or mallets. There should be several drums in every classroom; both pitched and unpitched. The many types of commercial drums include the tom-tom, tunable drums, bongo, and conga drums. Homemade drums of varying quality may be devised from cans, ice cream cartons, flowerpots, shortening canisters, and wastebaskets. The covering membrane can be made of soaked parchment, rubber (inner tubes) and plastic. These membranes are attached by wrapping with string, laced, or thumbtacked. Old drumheads can be used, salvaged from stores or from the high school bandroom. Color is an important element in constructing any of the instruments because it makes them more attractive to children.

Drum beaters can be purchased or constructed. They can be made from sticks of doweling of sufficient diameter cut to proper length, with yarn or soft rubber balls added. Various sizes and kinds of wooden spoons make good beaters as well.

The *conga drum* is a large, long Cuban drum played with the palms of the hands, usually with the heel of the left hand striking the edge of the head and the fingers of the right hand striking the center of the head.

The *bongo drum*, another Latin American instrument, is a double drum; one is larger than the other. Held between the knees with the small drum on the right, it is generally played with the tips of the fingers and the thumbs.

The commercially produced *tambourine with head* is an especially useful instrument in elementary music. It is held at the place on the instrument where there are no metal jingles. To play it, the head is struck against the heel of the hand, or it is shaken. The instrument strikes the hand; the hand does not strike the instrument. Experimental effects can be produced by tapping it on the knee, tapping it with fingers, and using a rubbing motion with the thumb followed by striking, tapping, or shaking. The head is coated with shellac and powdered rosin when professional drummers use the thumb roll. Tambourines lend atmosphere to gypsy, Hebrew, Spanish, and Italian songs.

Wooden Instruments

Rhythm sticks can be made from hard wood dowels purchased from lumberyards. They range in diameter from 3/8 to 5/8 inches in diameter, and are usually cut in 12-inch lengths. Ends can be smoothed with sandpaper. Children hold one in each hand and strike them together. They should explore differences in pitch and sound by tapping different places on the sticks, by scraping the sticks together, and by tapping the sticks on suitable objects such as the floor and desk.

Claves are paired resonant sticks about an inch in diameter. They can be made from 6-inch lengths of a broomstick or from doweling that is an inch in diameter. The professional method of playing is to hold one clave loosely in the partly closed left hand, resting on the heel of the hand with the other end resting on the fingernails and on the thumb and index finger. This clave is struck with the other clave held sticklike in the right hand. An example of claves rhythm is

Shave, hair___ cut,   six bits!
(or ten bucks!)

A more intricate claves rhythm is played in 4/4 meter on the underlined numbers, which represent eighth notes:

<u>1</u> 2 3 <u>4</u> 5 6 <u>7</u> 8 <u>1</u> 2 3 <u>4</u> 5 6 <u>7</u> 8.

Maracas can be purchased, or made from a pair of gourds in which a suitable number of dry seeds, pebbles, or bird shot is placed. They accompany many Latin American dance songs. Maracas are held either by handles or by the neck of an elongated gourd, with the player's forefinger extended toward the head, and are usually shaken in a steady eighth-note rhythm. The arms move back and forth; the wrists are stiff. For a soft effect they can be tapped by the fingers rather than shaken. A single maraca on a long handle is used as an American Indian rattle. It can be decorated with feathers and furs.

Sandblocks, used largely in primary grades, can be made from any soft wood from 3/4-inch to 1-inch thick and approximately 3-inch by 3-inch square. Handles can be made by attaching door or drawer pulls, spools, leather, or small pieces of wood. The handles are fastened with screws, and 80-grit sandpaper or emery cloth is placed on the rubbing side of the block, and secured with thumbtacks along the edges. One block is held in each hand, and their rough surfaces are rubbed together.

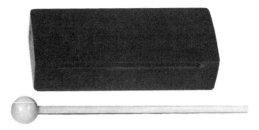

Woodblocks are best obtained from commercial sources. They are struck lightly with a hard rubber, plastic, or wooden mallet at the hollow side near the edge over the slot. They can be held in the hand or placed on a desk while being played. Children should experiment by striking them at other places, and with different beaters.

The *tone block* is produced commercially. The instrument is held upright in the left hand with the cut side toward the player, and is struck lightly with a stick, above the cut opening. Different sizes have different pitches, which can be useful in song accompaniments.

Of Spanish origin, *castanets* are made of a pair of cupped pieces of resonant hardwood, usually chestnut, attached by a cord. The adult Spanish dancer holds a pair of unmounted castanets, one set in each hand. The skilled dancer-player produces a variety of exciting effects from a sharp click to a sustained muffled rattle. There are two types of castanets manufactured today, one in which the two parts are held together by a cord, and one which is mounted on a spring base. The latter kind is easier for children to play. A recording of Chabrier's *España* illustrates its use in the orchestra.

The *guiro* a Latin American instrument, is a large gourd with ridges cut along its side. It is played with a small stick or a wire scratcher scraped back and forth across the ridges. Besides the scratching sound it can be made to produce a tap-scrape-tap rhythm.

The *triangle* comes in several sizes, and is suspended by a cord or a wide rubber band. It is struck lightly by a metal rod on the inside corner of the instrument. The tone can be continued by moving the beater back and forth rapidly on the inside edges of two sides.

Finger cymbals are small replicas of the larger cymbal, and come in several sizes. One cymbal is usually held stationary, and the other cymbal is moved past the first, striking its edge. The pair may be struck together lightly like crash cymbals for a different effect.

Crash cymbals are held one in each hand and struck together in a glancing blow with hands moving up and down in contrary directions. Other effects can be found by striking the cymbal on its edge with different beaters or sticks. The standard wire brush also creates an interesting effect.

Jingle bells are played by shaking them vigorously. Some are mounted on sticks; others are worn around the wrist or ankle. A small tinkling sound can be produced by holding them in one hand, and moving them back and forth with a gentle motion of the wrist.

The major use of *jingle clogs* is in the primary grades. They are held in one hand and tapped against the palm of the other hand in a manner that leaves the jingles free to sound.

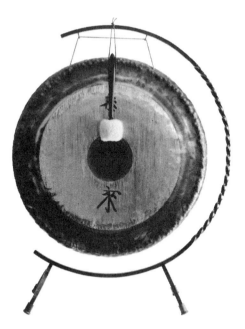

The true *gong* is relatively expensive. A large one could be borrowed from the high school band. Although the gong is not a regular classroom instrument its tone quality adds a special dimension to some musical numbers. Its use is especially appropriate in some types of multicultural music.

Other classroom instruments useful in providing contrasts in tone quality include the *cowbell, Agogo bells, tambourine without head, metal chocallo, wood kameso,* and the *cabasa* which was originally a large gourd with small beads strung loosely around it.

Special Effects Instruments There are a number of percussion instruments used in bands and orchestras which can contribute special effects to music in the elementary school, and play central roles in sound stories. Among these instruments are the *Vibraslap, slap stick, chimes, Chinese bell tree,* and the *Flexitone.*

Summary In introducing the many nonpitched percussion instruments, children need hands-on experience with them, followed by specifically chosen listening examples that illustrate their use. Some of the many possible songs for use with percussion instruments are the familiar "Hickory, Dickory, Dock," "Jingle Bells," "Ten Little Indians," "This Old Man," "When the Saints Go Marching In," "Mister Sun," "Down by the Bay," "Sandy Land," and "Tinga Layo."

Recordings of twentieth-century pieces that emphasize percussion instruments can be useful in giving students ideas about composing their own percussion music. The following three pieces are illustrative:

Toccata for Percussion, Carlos Chavez, Columbia CMS 6447; HBR 21003, 2 discs

Concerto for Percussion and Small Orchestra, Darius Milhaud, Capitol HBR 21003, 2 discs

Ionization, Edgar Varèse, Columbia MS 6146, also on Folkways's *Sounds of New Music,* FX 6160, and Machlis's *The Enjoyment of Music Series.*

Group improvisation can provide an opportunity for exploring rhythm patterns and contrast in dynamic levels. For example, a class may be asked to improvise a percussion accompaniment for a parade march such as "Parada" from *Divertissement,* AM, grade 1, vol. 1. As an introduction, the teacher may discuss the drum and other percussion instruments, rhythm patterns, dynamic levels, and crescendo and decrescendo. After the improvisation, the class may be asked to evaluate the performance and make changes as agreed upon. When satisfied with the sound, class members might notate some of the rhythm patterns used.

Concepts of the phrase, repetition, and contrast can be enhanced by creating percussion scores which reflect these aspects of form. Feelings for mood can be reflected in the choice of and the manner of playing the instruments. Graphic and standard notation can be employed in composing percussion scores. Every concept of rhythm may be strengthened by the use of these instruments. The following is a list of addresses of companies that sell percussion instruments:

ABA Music For Children, 217 Madrona S. E., Salem, OR 97312

Magnamusic-Baton, Inc., 10370 Page Industrial Blvd., St. Louis, MO 63132

Music Is Elementary, P. O. Box 24263, Cleveland, OH 44124

Oscar Schmidt International, 230 Lexington Drive, Buffalo Grove, IL 60089

Peripole, Inc., P. O. Box 146, Lewiston Rd., Browns Mills, NJ 08015

Rhythm Band, Inc., P. O. Box 126, Fort Worth, TX 76101

Sonar Primary Line (instruments available through local music companies)

Studio 49 (instruments available through local music companies)

Suzuki Musical Instrument Corporation, P. O. Box 261030, San Diego, CA 92126

Pitched Instruments and Voices

Voices   Children notice that their voices are higher or lower in pitch than others, and that some are clearer in tone quality. They can generalize that all persons have different, and perhaps unique, qualities in their voices. While the voices of children are traditionally identified in terms of high, medium, and low ranges, the terms for adult voices—soprano and alto for women; tenor, baritone, and bass for men—can be introduced in the upper grades. Suitable recordings may be used to compare the qualities of each. If possible, the children should hear a soprano and an alto sing the same song in person, then discuss the difference in tone quality. The same can be done with a tenor and a bass. A man and a woman might sing the same song an octave apart, with the students describing those differences as well. Each voice type has a characteristic tone quality. (More detailed information about the child's voice can be found in Chapter 8: Teaching Children to Sing.)

Recordings to illustrate voices are usually not found in the educational collections. Middle school students may enjoy classifying the voice qualities of popular singers, folk singers from different cultures, and classical or operatic singers. The comparison of these various styles can be of interest.

Pitched Percussion Instruments   One of the areas of greatest improvement in elementary music of recent decades has been the introduction of premier quality pitched percussion instruments. In addition to a variety of instruments such as temple blocks, there are three main categories of pitched percussion: xylophones, metallophones, and glockenspiels. Because of the dominant role Carl Orff played in constructing these instruments for children's use, they are often referred to as *Orff-type instruments*. (See Figure 6.1.) Orff originally intended these instruments for use by adults in physical education classes, but they are now used widely in classes for children.

A introduction to pitched percussion instruments is available through the album *Percussion* from the Standard School Broadcast, ''Music Makers'' series, Standard Oil Company, 225 Bush Street, San Francisco, CA 94104. As is typical for all recordings in this series, it features both interviews of performers and examples of their playing.

Additional examples of percussion instrument tone qualities include the following:

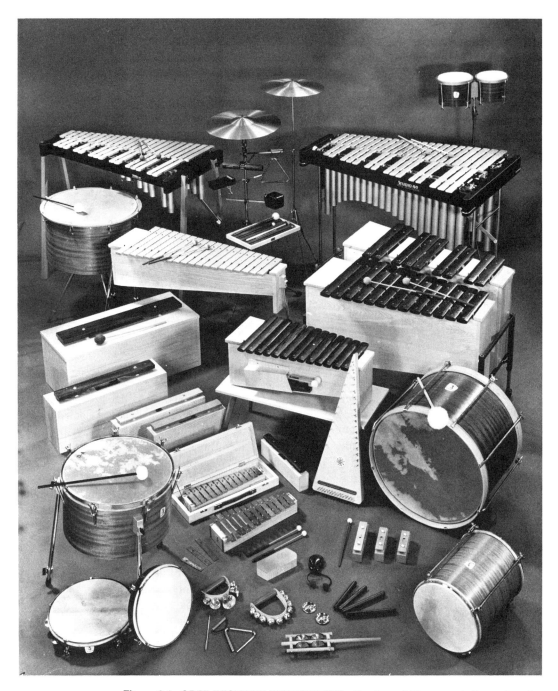

Figure 6.1. ORFF-DESIGNED INSTRUMENTS. Courtesy of Magnamusic Baton, Inc., St. Louis, Missouri 63132.

CYMBALS, DRUMS	Saint-Saëns, *Danse Macabre*
	Herbert, "Dagger Dance," *Natoma,* AM, grade 3, vol. 1
	Sousa, *Semper Fidelis,* AM, grade 3, vol. 2
TIMPANI:	Grieg, "In The Hall of the Mountain King," *Peer Gynt Suite,* AM, grade 3, vol. 2; BOL 59
XYLOPHONE:	Thomson, *The Alligator and the Coon,* AM, grade 3, vol. 2
PIANO, HARPSICHORD:	*Said the Piano to the Harpsichord,* Young People's Record 411

The following selected recordings feature percussion:

Cage, Cowell, et al., *Concert Percussion for Orchestra*
Music of Bali, Period SPL 1613

Films can also be useful in teaching percussion:

Percussion Group. Encyclopedia Britannica, Educational Corp., 310 S. Michigan Ave., Chicago, IL 60604

Percussion, Pulse of Music, Indiana University, Audio-Visual Center, Bloomington, IN 47401

Percussion Sounds, Churchill Films, 12210 Nebraska Ave., Los Angeles, CA 90025

Stringed Instruments

Stringed instruments exist in a wide variety. Some of the most popular string instruments in the world are not part of the symphony orchestra, including the guitar, banjo, ukulele, mandolin, lyre, zither, and autoharp. These should be explored to identify their tone qualities. There is excellent guitar literature for most age levels. Children should become familiar with the names of performers who play these instruments.

The orchestral string family is made up of the violin, viola, violoncello, and double bass (string bass, bass viol). These instruments are approximately the same shape, with the violin the smallest, the viola somewhat larger, the cello, large enough that the player must sit in a chair and rest the instrument on the floor, and the double bass so large that the player ordinarily stands up to play it. These instruments are called "the first family of the orchestra." Listening to symphonic music reveals that the strings are truly the backbone of the orchestra, with the brass, woodwind, and percussion sections assisting by adding many contrasting tone qualities.

Figure 6.2 shows the seating position of the various instruments in the orchestra.

Stringed instruments produce a variety of tone qualities, which can be further altered by the player. Many use *vibrato,* a slight varying of pitch produced by rapid movement of the left hand and forearm while pressing down on a string. The term *consordino* means with a mute; when the mute is attached, the tone becomes smaller and more nasal. These instruments produce *harmonics,*

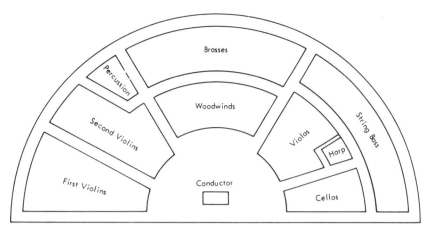

Figure 6.2. THE ORCHESTRA

higher pitches of reduced resonance that occur when the player touches, but does not press down on a string, and bows or plucks very lightly on that string.

When bowed instruments are played by plucking strings, it is called *pizzicato,* still another tone quality. A short, fast stroke played in the middle of the bow with a slight bounce from the string is *spiccato* bowing. Double stops, the playing and bowing of two strings at once, gives a third effect. The *tremulo* produces a rather tense sound; it is executed by moving the bow back and forth a short distance at an extremely fast rate. The *glissando* is produced by sliding a finger of the left hand up or down the string to change the pitch in a sliding effect.

Children, older students, and adults should be asked to demonstrate these instruments in class. While films and recordings are helpful, nothing takes the place of a well-qualified performer.

The harp is another stringed instrument frequently associated with the orchestra. It can be compared to the piano in some ways; it has a range of six octaves and a fifth. There are seven foot pedals, each of which can be pressed down two notches, each notch representing one half step. Because the player plucks the instrument, the harp's sound is unlike any other sound in the orchestra. Although it is not timbral in nature, one of the harp's special effects is the *glissando* which is produced by sliding the fingers rapidly over all of the strings. Harmonics are sounded by placing the palm of the hand in the middle of the strings; this places the pitch one octave higher than normal, producing a mysterious quality. A different tone quality is made by plucking strings close to the sounding board.

Keyboard instruments are part of the string family, and include the piano, harpsichord, and celesta. In the piano, felt hammers strike the strings. The tone qualities of the piano should be thoroughly explored; special effects can be made by preparing the strings of the piano with felt or rubber wedges, wax paper, tin foil, or even hanging paper clips from the strings. Sound is produced by reaching inside the piano to pluck, strum, strike, or scrape the strings. These alterations, known as "prepared piano," can be heard in Henry Cowell's composition, *The Banshee*. The harpsichord strings are made to vibrate by means of a plucking mechanism. The harpsichord—older than the piano—was the favorite keyboard instrument at the time of Bach and Handel. Its tone quality is considerably lighter than the piano, and it has less expressive capability. The Young People's Record 411, *Said the Piano to the Harpsichord,* is informative, and it communicates to children. The celesta is basically a percussion instrument. Its keyboard causes hammers to strike the steel bars, producing a tone quality resembling the glockenspiel. The tone is of unusually light quality. A familiar celesta piece is "Dance of the Sugar Plum Fairy" from the *Nutcracker Suite* by Tchaikovsky.

Examples of recordings portraying tone qualities of stringed instruments include

violin cadenzas	*Scheherazade* Suite, Rimsky-Korsakov
violin	*Flight of the Bumblebee,* Rimsky-Korsakov, BOL 53
strings	*Eine kleine Nachtmusik,* Mozart, AM, grade 4, vol. 1
	"Strings," from the Standard School Broadcast, "Music Makers" series, Standard Oil Company, 225 Bush Street, San Francisco, CA 94104
viola (second theme)	*Danse Macabre*, Saint-Saëns, BOL 59
violoncello	"The Swan," *Carnival of the Animals,* Saint-Saëns, BOL 59, and AM, grade 3, vol. 2
double bass	"Elephants," *Carnival of the Animals,* Saint-Saëns, RCA, VCS-7095 Stereo, "Great Children's Favorites"
	"Jimbo's Lullaby," *Children's Corner Suite*, Debussy, BOL 63
	Theme from the movie score of *Jaws,* by John Williams, MCA Records, MCA-2087
guitar	"Guitar," from the Standard School Broadcast, "Music Makers" series, Standard Oil Company, 225 Bush Street, San Francisco, CA 94104
keyboard	"Keyboard," from the Standard School Broadcast, "Music Makers" series, Standard Oil Company, 225 Bush Street, San Francisco, CA 94104

Suggested films include.

Percussion Sounds, Churchill Films
String Sounds, Churchill Films

Listening to Good Music: The String Quartet, Encyclopedia Britannica Films

The String Choir, Encyclopedia Britannica Films

The String Trio, Coronet Instructional Films

The Trio, World Artists, Inc.

Woodwind Instruments

Woodwind instruments are widely used as solo instruments, in chamber ensembles, and in the orchestra. In the orchestra they enrich the sounds of the strings by adding a variety of tone qualities and dynamic capabilities. As the orchestra developed over the centuries there have been increasing numbers of woodwind instruments added to it.

Because there are no strings in the concert band, the woodwinds have been used in their place. For example, a clarinet choir is used instead of the violin section.

The modern flute is a descendant of the recorder. It is a *transverse* flute, which means that the player holds it at right angles to the mouth and blows across a hole in its side. The recorder is an end-blown flute. While it is said that the best recorders are made of wood, the modern flute is generally made of silver. Its tone quality varies with the range. Low pitches are relatively big and somewhat breathy; higher tones become increasingly bright and penetrating. A flute solo can be found at the beginning of Debussy's *Afternoon of a Faun.* The solo is followed by colorful effects on a harp. In the title of this composition, the *faun* is a creature from rural Roman mythology, principally human, but with a goat's tail, pointed ears, short horns, and sometimes cloven feet. Another composition featuring flutes is Tchaikovsky's ''Dance of the Toy Flutes,'' from the *Nutcracker* Suite, Bol 58.

The piccolo is a small flute, half as long, and pitched one octave higher. It plays the highest pitches of any instrument in the woodwind family, and its tone quality is exceedingly brilliant and penetrating. A favorite piccolo solo is in Sousa's *Stars and Stripes Forever,* Bol 54. Other piccolo passages are found in the ''Chinese Dance'' from Tchaikovsky's *Nutcracker* Suite, Bol 59, and ''Entrance of the Little Fauns'' by Pierné, BOL 54.

Clarinets are made of wood, ebonite, and occasionally of metal. Although several other sizes exist, the most commonly used clarinet is in B^b. Some of the children who are studying this single reed instrument can demonstrate it for the class. In the family of clarinets, the instrument in E^b is smaller and higher in pitch, and the alto and bass are both lower. There are other less common clarinets, including the clarinet in A and the double bass in B^b, the latter being an octave lower than the bass clarinet. The B^b clarinet has three registers, each with a different tone quality. The lowest is rich and full-bodied, though its upper part is sometimes breathy. The middle register is known as the clarion register, from which the instrument derives its name. The highest register is brilliant and can be shrill. This variety of tone qualities gives the clarinet breadth of expression. It is prominently featured in Prokofiev's *Peter and the Wolf,* Saint-Saëns's ''*Cuckoo in the Deep Woods,*'' from *Carnival of the Animals,* RCA, VCS 7095 Stereo, and the second movement of Rimsky-Korsakov's *Scheherazade* Suite.

The tone quality of the saxophone is considered by many to be much like the human voice. It is seldom found in orchestras, but it is widely used in bands and dance bands. There is a family of saxophones, including soprano, alto, tenor, baritone, and bass. They are most commonly seen in the following order: alto, tenor, and baritone. Although they have cane reeds like clarinets, they are made of metal. The tone quality of the instrument can be changed markedly by the player; it can be sweet, raucous, or brusque as desired in certain types of jazz, rock, and occasionally classical music.

Two families of instruments use double reeds: the oboe and the bassoon. The oboe is about the same size as the B^b clarinet. The English horn is an alto oboe. Other sizes and types of oboe exist, but are less common. The oboe tone quality is often described as nasal, pastoral, Oriental, or plaintive. Prokofiev's *Peter and the Wolf* demonstrates the oboe tone quality, as does the second movement of Tchaikovsky's *Symphony No. 4* and his "Puss in Boots and the White Cat," from the *Sleeping Beauty*. AM, grade 3, vol. 1. The English horn has a pear-shaped bell which is one source of its melancholy tone quality. Examples of its sound appear in the "Largo" of Dvorak's *New World Symphony,* Sibelius's *Swan of Tuonela,* and "Puss in Boots and the White Cat," mentioned earlier.

The bassoon is unique in that the instrument's length is folded back on itself. Children should discover how the bassoon is built, since the design permits it to have a great length of tube, projecting above the other seated players of the orchestra. It serves most often as a bass instrument, and on occasion plays solo passages. While its tone quality can be rather even except at extreme high and low ranges, it has a versatility which enables it to project plaintive, gruff, and humorous impressions. The contrabassoon is the lowest instrument of the orchestra, playing an octave lower than the bassoon. If its length were fully extended, the contrabassoon would be over 16 feet long.

Examples of music in which the bassoon is featured are "In the Hall of the Mountain King," from *Peer Gynt* Suite, by Grieg, AM, grade 3, vol. 2 and BOL 59; "Berceuse" from Stravinsky's *Firebird* Suite; the second movement of Tchaikovsky's *Symphony No. 4* and *Rondo for Bassoon and Orchestra,* Children's Record Guild 1009. The grandfather theme in *Peter and the Wolf* is played by a contrabassoon.

The film *Introducing the Woodwinds,* Indiana University, introduces the instruments of the woodwind quintet to children. These are flute (and piccolo), clarinet, oboe, bassoon, and French horn—the brass instrument that possesses a tone quality which blends with both the woodwinds and the brasses. *Wind Sounds,* Churchill Films, presents woodwinds as well as brasses. "Woodwinds and Reeds," from the Standard School Broadcast, "Music Makers" series, Standard Oil Company, 225 Bush Street, San Francisco, CA 94104 presents examples of woodwind music as well as interviews with musicians.

Brass Instruments

Children can quickly find a major difference between a bugle and a trumpet, or cornet, in that the bugle lacks valves. They can then discern why the bugle can play only bugle calls whereas the trumpets and cornets can play both bugle calls and melodies. They should study the valve and its length of tubing to find out how valves alter pitch. They will see that the cornet is shorter than the trumpet, and they will hear that its tone quality is less brilliant. The player has a great deal to do with the tone qualities of these instruments, producing tones of varying quality at will. An instrument that has grown in popularity in recent years is the flügelhorn, which has the appearance of an oversized cornet. The baritone is a larger instrument found in bands; the mellophone is an instrument about the size of a French horn but which lacks its tone quality. It is used in marching bands and by students who may later progress to the more difficult French horn. The tubing of the French horn should be examined to try to determine how long the instrument would be if it were a straight horn like the alphorn, a folk instrument from the Alps. In the French horn both tone quality and pitch are influenced by a practice called *stopping,* which is the insertion of the hand into the bell. Mutes made of metal, wood, plastic, or fiberboard are used to change the tone qualities of most brass instruments. Both school band and dance band players can demonstrate several types of mutes in the classroom. While the cornet and trumpet have the most commanding tones, the French horn has the tone that blends with other instruments very well.

Four sizes of trombones are used in the symphony orchestra, the most common being the tenor. This instrument and an occasional bass trombone are seen in school bands. The trombone and baritone have larger mouthpieces than those of the cornet, trumpet, and French horn, resulting in a tone quality of less brilliance. Children will be interested in how the trombone's slide shortens or lengthens the air column. Because of the slide, trombones can produce a *portamento,* which is a sliding tone through a selected span of pitches.

The lowest pitched instruments of the brass family are the tubas and sousaphones. The tuba is found in the band and occasionally in the orchestra. The sousaphone is the instrument carried on the shoulders of its players in marching bands. As expected, these bass instruments have the largest mouthpieces. As told in the children's recording, *Tubby the Tuba,* Decca Records, the tuba seldom plays melodies. Instead, it normally supports the band as the primary low bass instrument, and it assists the double basses of the orchestra. Its tone is deep. Its huge shiny bell makes an impressive appearance. New plastic materials are being used today in place of metal in sousaphones, in order to reduce the weight the player must carry.

Examples of brass instrument tone qualities include:

Trumpet:	Rossini, "Finale," *William Tell* Overture, AM, grade 3, vol. 1 BOL 76
	Bizet, "Changing of the Guard," *Carmen* Suite, AM, grade 3, vol. 2
	The King's Trumpet, Children's Record Guild 5040
French horn:	Prokofiev, *Peter and the Wolf*
	Mendelssohn, "Nocturne," *Midsummer Night's Dream*
	Brahms, *Symphony No. 3* "Third movement"

Trombone:	Wagner, "Prelude to Act 3," *Lohengrin*
	Sousa, *Stars and Stripes Forever*, Am, grade 4, vol. 2 BOL 54
Tuba:	Mussorgsky, "Bydlo," *Pictures at an Exhibition,* AM, grade 2, vol. 1; BOL 82
	Prokofiev, "Departure," *Winter Holiday,* AM, grade 2, vol. 1
Brasses:	"Brasses" from the Standard School Broadcast, "Music Makers" series, Standard Oil Company, 225 Bush Street, San Francisco, CA 94104

Synthesizers and Computers

There is increasing acceptance of synthesizers and computers as tools to help children learn and reinforce music concepts. Many students in the elementary grades find these instruments to be of tremendous interest; accordingly, they are attracted to electronic stations where they can experiment with sounds, learn about music, and compose or arrange music to their liking. The teacher should have sufficient expertise with these machines to use them effectively as part of the instructional program. Strange and new sounds are likely to attract children's interest and since the synthesizer can produce a rich variety of sounds, the instrument possesses a natural attraction. The oscilloscope should at times be a companion to the synthesizer because it gives a visual representation of the sound-wave form of every sound analyzed. The device can be involved in experiments such as the effect of attack, decay, harmonics, vibrato, and tremulo on tone quality.

Synthesizers are available today in many degrees of complexity, from sophisticated models suitable for a professional electronic laboratory to simple models that are relatively inexpensive. The latter are easily portable, and are sometimes carried from school to school, permitting one to be shared by many children. Aebischer, Nickerson, and Bruya (Fall 1989, pp. 8–11) have developed a list of electronic media recommended for the elementary classroom, and organized the list for a three-year period of acquisition. Prices listed are approximate.

Year 1

1. Electronic keyboards (several units)
   Cost: $150 to $250 per unit
2. T.A.P. computers for rhythm and pitch
   Cost: $875 (T.A.P. Rhythm Master unit and tapes)
   $1,080 (T.A.P. Pitch Master unit and tapes)
3. Macintosh Classic computer with Microsoft Works
   Cost: $999 for Macintosh Classic computer
   $200 for Microsoft Works
4. Selected student software

Level:	Title/Publisher/Description:	Price
Primary	Magic Musical Balloon—MML (melody-visual & aural)	$ 25
Primary	Toney Listen to Music—MML (melody-aural)	90
Elementary	Note reading-Wenger (treble and bass clef)	69
Elementary	Music Fundamentals, I, II & III—Silver Burdett	125
Elementary	Music Tool Box—Wenger (notes, symbols, etc)	119
Elementary	Cat Steps—Wenger (intervals on treble & bass clef)	59
Intermediate	Major/Minor Scale Tutor—Wenger	69
Elem/Jr/Sr	Keyboard Note Reading—Wenger	69
Elem/Jr/Sr	Instrumental Tutors—MML (brass note reading)	70
Inter/Jr/Sr	Do, Re, Mi—MML (melodic dictation)	75

Year 2

Synthesizer (e.g., Roland U-20) and sequencing program for the Macintosh Classic computer.

> Cost: $500 for Roland U-20 synthesizer
> $180 for Delux Music Recorder (sequencing program)
> $500 for Performer (sequencing program)

Year 3

Music notation program

> Cost: $750 for Finale
> $400 for ProComposer by Mark of Unicorn
> $250 for MusicProse
> $ 70 for NoteWriter
> $ 85 for Deluxe Music Construction Set

An electronic station may be located in part of a room, in an unused office or practice room, or in an otherwise vacant area. When this equipment is of marked value, special security is necessary to prevent theft or damage. There must be electric outlets and a table on which to place equipment. A bulletin board is necessary not only to schedule use of the equipment and to post assignments and directions for individuals and small groups. No chalk should be used in the area because the dust can accumulate on sensitive equipment. To eliminate chalk dust, use pins to attach notices to bulletin boards or dust-free plastic boards that employ wax crayons. It is also important to keep the area free of all kinds of food and liquid.

Multiple-track tape recorders are part of most laboratories because they increase the possible uses of the synthesizer. Since most synthesizers include no speaker system, they must be attached to an appropriate amplifier. A good quality four-channel stereo recorder-player is considered basic, although some teachers have done well with more limited equipment. Recording tape, a tape splicer, and a roll of leader tape are likewise useful. Teachers and students who use the laboratory need to know the techniques of editing tapes and the ways to manipulate them, such as playing and recording at various speeds to gain certain effects, creating tape loops, recording backward, and using time delay, which is possible only on certain machines.

Computers may be used in conjunction with synthesizers for composing in the classroom, but their primary function lies elsewhere. They can serve teachers in the following ways: drill and practice, testing, and teaching, usually individualized or in small groups, or record keeping (such as grades). Once students have been introduced to a musical subject such as key signature, the computer can provide drill and exercises on that subject. If the topic is aural, such as hearing phrases, the computer can sound music to provide practice in phrase identification. Furthermore, the device can give immediate feedback and can store information regarding how well the learner did, so that the teacher can inspect the results. Students can, by themselves, go through a module that presents information, provides drill and practice, and tests them. New software is being developed regularly, and the teacher needs to identify several sources that review current offerings. The *Music Educators Journal* carries a regular column titled "Technology for Teaching" that presents current information on computers, synthesizers, and other electronic technology. On occasion it includes reviews of recently released music software. In some cases the teacher may have the ability to create computer programs to satisfy specific needs. Because of numerous significant computer developments, computers seem to have a secure future in the classroom. Every teacher needs to know and understand the machine, its functions and capabilities.

Synthesizers have been built into some microcomputers. If not, synthesizers can be added to them through MIDI technology. With the synthesizer keyboard, music can be played and stored for later reproduction.

When selecting a computer for purchase, the teacher needs to keep in mind that software is designed for a specific type of computer, and the industry is not sufficiently standardized to permit the same software to be used on all machines.

An example of computer software is Atarimusic I, which explains lines and spaces, sharps and flats, and whole steps and half steps. It also includes games for drill, and can be obtained from Atari, P. O. Box 427, Sunnyvale, CA 94086. A free catalog of music software may be obtained from Musitronic, P. O. Box 441, Owatonna, MN. 55060. The programs in this catalog include learning music theory, composition, and synthesis. The Silver Burdett Music Series, 1984 Centennial Edition, contains references to music fundamentals software for use on Apple II Computers or on Atari 800 and Atari 1200 XL.

The following is a list of sources for electronic and computer-related materials:

Computer Applications Tomorrow, P. O. Box 605, Birmingham, MI 48012

Control Data Corporation, 8100 34th Ave. South, Minneapolis, MN 55440

Educational Audio Visual, Inc., Pleasantville, NY 10570

Electronic Courseware Systems, P. O. Box 2374, Station A, Champaign, IL 61820

MicroMusic and Temporal Acuity Products, 1535 121st Ave. S. E., Bellevue, WA 98005

Notable Software, P. O. Box 1556-ME, Philadelphia, PA 19105

Tutor Company, P. O. Box 41092, San Jose, CA 95160

Video Teaching Aids, P. O. Box 1104, Statesville, NC 28677

Experimenting with Sound and Tone Qualities

The Early Years   Children in nursery school, kindergarten, and first grade need to experiment with the sounds made by miscellaneous objects of wood, paper, metal, glass, and stone when they are tapped, shaken, and struck. (see Table 6.1). When working to establish the concepts of high and low, the teacher might group a variety of sound producers accordingly at either end of a table, for children to

Table 6.1 Unconventional Sound Sources

Paper	Rubber	Wood	Metal	Outdoor Materials
construction paper	bands	ruler	sheet metal	dirt
wax paper	balloons	spatula	saws	pebbles
tissue paper	hose horn	yardstick	tools	stones
newspaper	balls	bowls	can tops	leaves
lightweight cardboard	inner tubes	bamboo sticks	pie plates	grass
brown, bag paper	tires	tongue depressors	oven shelves	snow
white stationery paper	toys	pencils	wire	rain
sandpaper		blocks	cans	twigs
cardboard strips	**Glass**	whistles	pails	branches
napkins		toys	baking pans	pine cones
magazines	soda bottles	tables	cookie sheets	eucalyptus pods
cardboard dividers	jugs	chairs	pipes	water
foils		clothespins	strips	
cardboard boxes	**Plastic**	poles	whistles	**Other**
paper balls	funnel (horns)	popsicle sticks	toys	string
old books	ruler	broom handles	tables	rope
egg crates	straws	kitchen utensils	chairs	twine
cardboard cylinders	food containers	containers	washtub	flowerpots
toilet tissue cylinders	bottles	strips	nails	calfskin
paper towel cylinders	sprayers		screws	chamois
carpet cylinders	toys	**Food**	washers	
material cylinders	brushes		bottle caps	
corrugated cardboard	buttons	condiments	paper clips	
fruit crates	combs	seeds	funnels	
straws	old records	kernels	scissors	
milk containers	plastic strips	rice	bolts	
papier-mâché	boxes	coffee	foils	
toys	tools	sugar	kitchen utensils	
paint buckets	cups	corn flakes	waste basket	
ice cream containers		bread crumbs	springs	
cigar boxes		grains	machines	
cups		macaroni		
		coconut shells		

Source: MMCP Interaction

sort according to high and low pitches. Other comparisons of tone quality could be made with instruments that ring, scratch, rattle, or jingle. After handling, sounding, and naming all these sound producers, the children may turn away from the table, and identify and describe the unseen sounds that the teacher makes.

A first grade teacher made these comments concerning activities that culminated from experimenting with these objects:

> The children are given many opportunities to initiate their own rhythmic activities. Duration, volume, accent, tempo, and moods are felt with hands, fingers, feet, and moving bodies. Percussion instruments are but extensions of tapping feet and clapping hands. Thus the children gradually use drums, bells, woodblocks and sticks to accompany or to create rhythm patterns. Be careful listening children find one drum lower or higher in pitch than another. They discover differences in quality as well as in pitch by tapping different places on their instruments. They suggest that part of a song reminds them of a bell or a gong. Tambourines and other instruments can be used for spontaneous self-expression and interpretation during story time.

In this first grade class the teacher engaged the children in "drum talk"— beating out the rhythms of words in drum language; they had walked, run, or tapped instruments as they spoke their names in rhythm; they had used scarves, streamers, and balloons to help them to feel and see other rhythms. Instruments were introduced slowly over several weeks, one at a time. Clapping generally preceded playing. Early playing was informal; each child played each instrument at one time or another. Songs were used in which the light-sounding instruments played first, then the heavier-sounding instruments took their turn, and the two were combined in the concluding climax. As the children experimented with concepts of meter, those with wooden instruments played on the primary accents, and those with metal instruments played on the other beats.

Children need opportunities to explore unusual ways to use percussion instruments. For example these instruments may be used to imitate walking, marching, and skipping. They may find that chopsticks can make a sound suggestive of rain falling on a roof, that sandblocks can imitate a train, that rattles and drums contribute to the quality of some American Indian songs, and that words of songs sometimes suggest certain accompanying instruments or percussive sound effects. They may find that instruments can be played to produce accents which will eventually outline the meter, and that instruments can reproduce the rhythm of the melody—usually the rhythm of the words. As they grow older, by keeping their toes on the floor they can make the *heel-clap* sound for two-beat meters, the heels sounding the downbeat and the hands clapping the upbeat. They may discover that dances are sometimes accompanied in this way. Graphic notation may be introduced after children have heard and felt the rhythmic patterns.

In the early years the instruments are introduced individually as sound exploration, for rhythmic exercises, or as accompaniment for songs. Music series books contain songs and exercises with which to introduce instruments. Since an emphasis today is upon children's creativity and musical discrimination, graphic notation is more appropriate at first than traditional scores.

The mass rhythm band activity for kindergarten and first grade, while still found, has never been appropriate. Children at this age level are more individualistic rather than fully cooperating members of a larger group.

Later Years   By the third grade, children can create their own percussion scores for small and large ensembles, based on their growing understanding of rhythm, playing instruments, the tone qualities of instruments, notation, and form. To add instruments to recorded music, the children first listen carefully, discuss what they have heard, consider appropriate tone qualities and dynamics, experiment with the instruments, and finally, devise the score. Certain criteria should be used, such as

Is the effect musical?

Can the recorded music be clearly heard when the instruments play?

Are there musical reasons for the selection of the instruments?

Is the form of the music reflected in the choice and use of the instruments—when they play and when they are silent?

How does the choice of instruments determine the music's texture?

There is opportunity in this activity to use rhythmic music of all types, from classical to ethnic, jazz, and rock.

Using percussion instruments to contribute to the interpretation of songs continues through the elementary school into middle school. Children at all levels enjoy the challenge of creating descriptive sound effects to enhance or embellish the music. One or two drums can add immeasurably to an American Indian song: a tambourine or two can lend atmosphere to an Israeli song and dance; a combination of tambourine, drums, claves, and maracas can contribute to a Latin American song. Percussion accompaniments may be constructed from part of the rhythm of the song, its meter, or a traditional pattern. Contrasting rhythms can be played on two or more different instruments or groups of instruments, and the combinations of two or more patterns with the rhythm of the meter can be challenging, as well as a test of rhythmic growth.

With only minor modifications, some activities are appropriate for all elementary school children. For example when composers select certain instruments or voices for a composition, one of the reasons may be to imitate a sound of nature. Children may discover why the clarinet, flute, and piccolo are often chosen to imitate a bird, by comparing the tone qualities of these instruments with others. Children should be able to describe why a composer would choose the tympani rather than a tambourine to imitate a clap of thunder. Other sounds of nature that have been depicted through music include the rustling of leaves, shimmering water, the wind, trains, and many more. However, there is a vast amount of music that has no such associative meaning, and teachers should not try to impose associations on all music.

While listening to music children discover why composers select certain instruments to perform certain melodies, why these instruments are more suitable than others, and how poorly some would sound if assigned the same melodies. Of course teachers know that once in a while children may disagree with composers, and when the children have logical reasons for their point of view, their judgment is to be respected. The Leonard Bernstein film, *What Does Orchestration Mean?* (McGraw-Hill Films, 1 hour, grades 5 and up) deals with choosing "the right instruments at the right time in the right combination." Every student should acquire some appreciation for the great contribution tone qualities make to contrast and variety in music.

Sound Sources and Qualities   Children need many opportunities to explore and experiment with sounds. The Manhattanville Music Curriculum Program (MMCP) uses both conventional and unconventional sound sources to help children discover the many properties of sound and its organization as music.

Prior to MMCP, Maria Montessori planned exploratory experiences in the following order for young children: finding sound sources that produced the same sound, finding sound sources that produced contrasting sounds, and finding scale-line pitch arrangements by ordering a series of bells of identical appearance. Montessori's procedure can be of use to teachers when they assess the level of musical development of young children. MMCP recommends a classroom arrangement that includes a sound materials center for individual and small group use. Equipment in the center should include a tape recorder, a record player, a cassette player, a CD player, a synthesizer, and a variety of other instruments and unconventional sound sources (see Table 6.1 on p. 187).

There is an order to experiences with sound that is helpful to teachers. The first phase is exploratory, in which children discover types of sounds made by voices and objects. The second phase is associative, in which musical sounds are related to various human experiences and feelings. The association of these musical sounds with the variety of human experiences produces sound imagery. The third phase involves the musical elements of duration, dynamics, pitch, and tone quality, often in improvisatory ways. This phase differs from the previous ones in that comprehension of the elements of sound become more specific and definable. Identifying *same* and *different* can lead to discovery of the phrase and other components of musical form. The fourth phase involves the composing of music, and recording it, if it is to be preserved for later use (Tait, 1977).

Improvising and composing are important developments in the teaching of music. They move the curriculum away from the practice of relying primarily on singing songs from books and some listening experiences. It was found that as children grew, they resented this simplistic approach and that many teachers and children became bored and frustrated. Proponents of change claimed that children learn about music best by behaving like musicians in the following activities:

discovering musical sounds and how they are produced
improvising and composing music

using their voices, bodies, and instruments to perform music they create

interpreting and evaluating what they create

notating what they create

More precisely, they should learn music by acting out the roles of the musician—singing, playing, improvising, composing, listening, conducting, interpreting, and evaluating. Those who promote this approach believe that learners must produce music as well as respond to music of others. The learners then come to realize that music is a continuously evolving art, and that they may be actively involved with contemporary music as well as with the art, ethnic, and folk music of the past. These learners become explorers and innovators in music, free to take risks in their creative endeavors.

Early promulgators of these ideas were the American composers Henry Brandt and Lionel Nowak. Following their pioneering efforts, the Contemporary Music Project (CMP), an outgrowth of a young-composers-in-residence program that began in 1958, was in operation from 1963 to 1969, financed by the Ford Foundation. This project included seminars and workshops for music educators, and pilot programs in elementary and secondary schools to study methods of presenting contemporary music and to learn about music through creative experiences. The results of three pilot programs appeared in *Experiments in Musical Creativity,* a 1966 publication of the CMP and MENC. One conclusion made by the San Diego pilot program was, ''Activities related to contemporary music, such as composition for percussion instruments, synthetic scales, and new sound sources provide a unique medium for creativity. The student with little or no background. . .can 'create' with enthusiasm and success, thus gain a first-hand contact with music that he might otherwise miss'' (p.61). CMP did much to make these ideas known, but the most powerful thrust toward new methods of instruction was made from 1965 to 1970 by the Manhattanville Music Curriculum Program (MMCP).

In most classes the activities just described will be an important part of a well-rounded music program. A music textbook series that exemplifies this is *Comprehensive Musicianship Through Classroom Music,* published in 1972 by Addison-Wesley. This series resulted from the Hawaii Music Program, a state-financed project. Each elementary level teacher's book contains a Scope and Sequence Chart that includes the concepts to be learned, the songs and recordings that may assist this learning, and the musicianly roles to be assumed by the students. The teacher can quickly discern how improvisation and composition are integrated with the other activities that comprise a balanced program of music instruction. Recent editions of other music series books incorporate this approach.

Manhattanville Music Curriculum Program

The Manhattanville Music Curriculum Program can be adapted to any age group. Like all methods, it requires some years to develop its full potential. Aspects of the program should be introduced in college methods classes in order that the college student may understand its special emphasis on musical involvement. A complete explanation of this approach to music teaching of young children aged 3 through 8 can be found in *MMCP Interaction: Early Childhood Music Curriculum*. The following is a list of concepts that children from the ages of 3 to 8 acquire through the learning experiences described.

Sounds are everywhere. While in the classroom or on a short field trip children listen to and describe sounds of the environment. "Are they high, low, soft, loud, dull, short, steady, rumbling. . .?" Vocabulary is developed with which to discuss sound and tone qualities.

Sounds have pitch. Children search the classroom for objects that can produce sounds, and classify them as producers of definite and indefinite pitch.

Our bodies can be used to make sounds. Children explore the varied sounds that can be made with the body. These include clapping hands, patsching, snapping fingers, stamping feet, clicking tongue, hissing, "shh," and others. Several of these can be organized into a short composition, and recorded and played for the children's evaluation.

We can imitate the sounds we hear. Children can imitate sounds better than many adults. They may imitate sounds from their environment such as sirens, birds, and jet planes.

Objects can produce different kinds of sounds or tone qualities. In order to increase sensitivity to tone qualities, young children may be asked to identify sources of sounds in listening games. The teacher might use a cardboard screen to hide the sound source. Suggestions of such sources might include an egg beater, air escaping from a balloon, pouring water, crinkling paper, as well as more conventional sounds.

Sound has vibration. Children might be asked to explore different ways in which sound vibration can be seen or felt. Some experiments include feeling vibrations of drumheads, cymbals, and other instruments through the sense of touch, or seeing the effects of sound vibration by submerging a large tuning fork in water, or watching the blur of a bass string vibrating on a guitar. Children may also discover that some percussion instruments need to be held in a way in which they freely vibrate.

We can analyze instrument sounds. With young children the teacher may select an instrument such as a tambourine and make sounds with it. Questions may be asked such as "Can it sing a song?" (no) "Can it play softly?" (yes) "Can it play loudly?" (yes) "Does it make jingling sounds?" "Can it make a short sound?" "Can it make a long sound?" After this, children find uses for the tambourine in a song or as a sound effect in a story.

Percussion instruments can be classified in many ways. Young children can classify percussion instruments according to the type of sound. Which instruments click, ring, jingle, swish, rattle, or boom? Which instruments have sounds that are light, heavy, and medium in quality? Older children might use more comprehensive classifications and decide to group percussion instruments under headings such as membranes, wooden instruments, metal instruments, and special effect instruments.

Sounds can be the same or different. The teacher prepares a number of sound producers in pairs to assist young children to recognize similarities and differences in sounds. There may be identical jars or cans or plastic containers with the same and different numbers of peas, beans, marbles or beads in them. The children's task is to shake them, listen to them, and classify the pairs that sound alike.

Tone qualities relate to sound effects. Young children can decide on the suitability of specific instruments or other sound sources for sound effects. They can select them to correspond with characters in stories about the "The Three Bears," "The Muppets" or Sesame Street characters. Older children can create stories in sound such as "My Day," "A Storm in the Mountains," "A Haunted House," "Halloween Night," and "A Space Journey."

Every voice sounds different. With closed eyes, young children listen to different speaking voices in the class and identify them. Such listening games emphasize the uniqueness of the voice of each person. Children then classify the speaking voices in terms of low, medium, and high.

MMCP Interaction. The following material explains in brief the strategies involved in the Manhattanville Music Curriculum Program for children aged 3 through 8.

Music consists of sounds and silences presented in some organized manner.
There are many kinds of sounds. Sounds can be classified.

The free exploration of sound sources (paper, metal, body, rubber, plastic, glass, and materials from nature) is recommended. This comprises the first of a series of steps that lead to experiences with every component of music. Step 2 is *guided exploration,* in which the teacher encourages the children to find additional sounds, to find more ways to produce sounds (this involves skills), to label new sounds (this involves vocabulary), to classify new sounds in various ways, to listen and react to sounds produced by other children and by the teacher, and to learn to respect the efforts of others. The purpose of evaluation is not to point out failure, but to clarify and extend children's ideas and judgments. The teacher assists the children's learning by such actions as presenting clues and examples, presenting words, asking questions, showing pictures and other types of illustrative material, and presenting musical examples. Contrasting words (walking-running, crawling-skipping) suggest different movements in time; those such as whispering and shouting suggest different dynamic levels and different ways of producing sounds.

Sounds can be organized and related.
Two or three people may produce more varied music than only one person.
We can compose music as individuals or in small groups.

Step 3 is *exploratory improvisation*. The child is encouraged to repeat sounds he or she enjoys and to relate them to other sounds. This relationship might be contrasting sounds, through which the child may learn that contrast can heighten the expressive implications of sounds, or it might be that by combining two or more sounds a new and different effect can be achieved.

Step 4 is *planned improvisation*. In this phase children gain performance and memory skills necessary to produce compositions that are aesthetically satisfying. They are guided by the teacher to organize groups of sounds into meaningful music ideas, to identify the ways these sounds are arranged, to criticize constructively the arrangement of the sounds, and to use this experience to suggest other ways of improvising their own music.

The teacher accepts and works with whatever the child produces, regardless of its quality, remembering that these exploratory experiences are important and real to the child, and that the type of learning is basically intrinsic, not dictated by the teacher. After a trial run of a student composition, teachers might ask questions such as "How do you know when to start and stop?" (This helps them to discover the need for a conductor if they do not have one.) "Do you have a leader?" "Did you hear a change of tempo?" "What kinds of sounds did you hear?" "Did it sound the way you wanted it to sound?" "Would you want to change this piece if you had a chance to do it over?" "Are you satisfied with it?" The composing and performing of a composition can bring into focus problems in duration, pitch, tone quality, dynamics, and tempo, and teach compositional techniques such as the *ostinato,* a repeated rhythm or tonal pattern, in a practical setting that is honest and logical to the child.

Step 5 is *reapplication*. As children continue to compose their own music, they discover a need for all the component elements of music as well as skills in musical notation. First they find a need to save their compositions, and invent notation for this purpose. Eventually standard notation is necessary for them to do what they want to do with their musical ideas. When children are trying to invent their own notation, teachers ask questions such as "What if you wanted to show a thin texture in your music?" (Use a thin symbol.) "What if you wanted to show a thick texture?" (Use a thick symbol.) "What if you wanted to show low?" (Use the bottom of the page.) "High?" (Use the top of the page.) "Short?" (Use a short symbol.) "Long?" (Use a long symbol.) "Rising pitch?" (Use a rising symbol.) "Silence?" (Use a blank space or a circle.) "Falling pitch?" (Use a descending symbol.)

This same type of musical learning can also be used by older children. Even the middle school student may enjoy the rewards of experimenting freely with music.

There are, however, problems to be anticipated with this approach. One of these is the noise factor, termed "creative fallout" by MMCP. As group work expands, there must be space for children to work, and in many schools this is not easily found. Many teachers have discovered that children are able to work in small groups while several groups are meeting in the same classroom. The size of the group will vary in accordance with the assigned task. It can range from two to six persons, with four and five commonplace. When there is much activity in the classroom the teacher may want to use a signal for silence, such as the flicking off of the lights, as we mentioned earlier. When the lights are turned back on, sound activities may resume.

The following example is reproduced from *MMCP Interaction*.

Alternate Series: Metal Encounters

Phase I—Free Exploration

Instructional Objective: To explore a wide variety of sounds using metal sound sources.

Procedure:

1. Place a variety of metal objects, such as old kitchen utensils, large nails, horseshoes, pipes of varying sizes and lengths, metal bars, keys on a key ring, pans, pan lids, tea trays, empty coffee cans, and so on, in a place designated as the sound materials center.

2. Encourage pupils to select and explore the objects for sounds. This may be done on an individual basis during the course of the school day, or pupils may select metal objects and share sounds in groups.

3. After adequate time for initial sound explorations, the following questions may serve to stimulate discussions of the sounds:
Were any sounds alike? If so, how were they alike?
Why were some sounds different? Could the differences be described?
Pupils will identify the differences and similarities in sounds in many different ways, including the physical techniques involved in performing them, relating sounds to personal experiences, and their acoustical characteristics, that is, timbre, pitch, duration, volume.

4. Suggest that pupils find other metal objects, metal toys, pie plates, paint cans, and so on, to add to the sound materials center.

5. All new objects should be explored for the variety of sounds they can produce.

Phase II—Guided Exploration

Instructional Objective: To explore a wide variety of metallic sounds and sound-producing techniques.

Procedure:

1. Invite pupils, as a class or in small groups, to find two very different or contrasting sounds with the metal objects they have selected from the sound materials center.

2. Allow an appropriate amount of time for exploration.

3. After individual pupils perform their sounds, other group members or the entire class should attempt to imitate the two contrasting sounds on other metal objects.

4. Discussion during and after performance and imitations may deal with the following:

How was the sound made? Did the beater make a difference?

Can the sound be made in any other way? Are any imitations exactly the same?

Note: A few minutes of exploration may be desirable before volunteers are ready to imitate a performed sound.

5. Pupils should be given two or three minutes of exploration time to investigate each of the following questions posed by the teacher:

What kind of sounds can you find that remind you of a clock ticking; water dripping; a baby walking; a father's heavy footsteps; a ball bouncing; teeth clattering; a horse galloping; a snake crawling?

6. After each question and a period (two or three minuets) of pupil exploration, volunteers can be invited to perform their sounds.

7. After all sounds have been performed and taped, listen to the tape and try to identify the sounds, for example, clock ticking, snake crawling, and so on.

Phase III—Exploratory Improvisation

Instructional Objective: To explore a variety of ways of producing and combining repeated patterns.

Procedure:

1. Pupils should select three sounds which they can play over and over again in the same manner with metal objects.

2. Allow an appropriate amount of time for selection of sound sources and sounds, and for rehearsals of the desired patterns.

3. As a class, or in small groups, listen to the repeated patterns performed by individual pupils.

4. Discussion can be centered on the following: Were any of the sound patterns difficult to repeat? Why?

If some were difficult to repeat, can you suggest an easier way of playing them? Which two patterns do you think would sound well together (one after the other)?

5. Experiment with combinations of sound patterns as suggested by the pupils.

6. Tape combined performances of repeated patterns for immediate playback and discussions.

7. Play for the students some recording containing a repeated pattern of metallic sounds, such as the *Symphony of Machines—Steel Foundry* by Alexander Mosslov.

8. Discussion of the listening example can be focused with the following questions: What did you hear? Did you hear any repeated patterns?

How could we build a sound machine?

Phase IV—Planned Improvisation

Instructional Objective: To arrange repeated patterns in ways which are expressive and meaningful.

Procedure:

1. Build a sound machine. A sound machine is a game in which a number of sound patterns, organized in various sequential combinations, aurally represent the mov-

ing parts of an imaginary machine. The patterns developed in the previous encounters may be used, or new patterns may be investigated.

2. Pupils may work in groups of three, four, or five, or the teacher or volunteer pupils may construct a sound machine by conducting members of the class in a sequential performance of their patterns. Students may wish to physically display the motions of the machine as well as their sounds.

3. Tape all the performances for listening and comparison of the differences and similarities.
   Were the sound machines different? If so, how were they different? If not, what could we do to make the sound machines sound different from one another?
   Were the sound machines the same in any way? If so, how were they the same?

4. When appropriate extend the discussion with the following:
   Were the conductors satisfied with their results? Did performers do what was expected of them?
   If not, discuss how better results might be achieved. Pupils should lead these discussions as much as possible.
   Note: In order to successfully control entrances and exits of groups of performers, pupil conductors may have to develop simple gestures for starting and stopping performers.

5. The following questions posed individually during follow-up encounters may stimulate further thought and experimentation:
   What would happen if
     some patterns or sounds were played at the same time?
     all metal objects were silent some of the time?
     the sound machine slowly broke down rather than suddenly stopped?
     we had two sound machines—a big one and a little one?

The primary document of the Manhattanville Music Curriculum Program is a publication titled *MMCP Synthesis*. It consists of a spiral-type curriculum that presents the elements of music on gradually advanced levels termed "cycles," based on the elements of timbre (tone quality), dynamics (degrees of loud-soft), duration (degrees of long-short and rhythmic elements), pitch (including melody, harmony, and polyphony), and form. As in *MMCP Interaction,* composing of music on the child's level is the major activity. The students compose, conduct, perform, and evaluate music. Sample strategies are suggested for teaching music at sixteen levels (cycles). These begin with the same types of sound exploration described earlier, but move quickly into compositions that are taped in order that the composers and the class can hear them and evaluate them.

In cycle 1 the student begins with activities such as finding sounds made from objects in the classroom, performing different sounds from the same object, and experimenting with dynamics and with combinations of sounds, adding a steady beat to ordered combinations of sounds. In each of the activities, the book suggests questions to ask the students, and recordings of music of all types to stimulate interest, and furnish information needed by the student composers.

College classes may experiment with sample lessons provided in *MMCP Synthesis* in order that prospective teachers understand this approach to learning about music. The teacher functions as a guide who presents problems to be solved by the children, and serves as a resource person. The teacher stimulates rather than dominates, encourages rather than controls, and questions more than answers. The classroom is a laboratory in which children act as musicians who have a world of sound to explore.

Examples from *MMCP Synthesis* follow:

SAMPLE STRATEGY I

Cycle 1. The quality or color of sound, the timbre, is a major factor in the expressiveness of music.

Each student selects an item or object in the room with which he or she can produce a sound. Preferably, the item or object is something other than a musical instrument.

After sufficient time has been allowed for students to experiment with sounds or selected objects, each student may perform the chosen sound at the location of the item in the room.

Focus on "listening" to the distinctive qualities of sounds performed. Encourage students to explore other sound possibilities with the item of their choice.

Discuss any points of interest raised by the students. Extend the discussion by including the following questions: How many different kinds of sounds were discovered?

Could the sounds be put into categories of description, that is, shrill, dull, bright, intense, and so on.

After categories of sound have been established, experiment with combinations of sounds.

Is there any difference between sounds performed singly and sounds performed in combination?

In listening to the recorded examples focus on the use of tone qualities.

How many different kinds of sounds were used?

Could we put any of the sounds in this composition into the categories we established earlier, for example, bright, dull, shrill, and so on.

Were there any new categories of sounds?

Could we duplicate these?

ASSIGNMENT: Each student should bring one small object from home on which he can produce three distinctly different sounds. The object may be a brush, a bottle, a trinket, or anything made of wood, metal, or plastic.

Suggested Listening Examples:

Wond Steel Band, *Steel Drums;* Folk 8367.

Wuorinen, Charles, *Prelude and Fugue for Percussion;* GC 4004.

Antheil, George, *Ballet Mécanique;* Urania (5) 134.

SAMPLE STRATEGY II

Cycle 1. The pulse is the underlying beat that may help to create a feeling of motion in music.

Allow 30 seconds for each class member to think of an unusual vocal sound. The sound can be made with the throat, voice, lips, breath, or tongue.

Each student may perform his or her sound for the class. Focus "listening" on the distinctive qualities of the vocal sounds performed.

Discuss any points of interest raised by the students. Extend the discussion by including some of the following questions:

Did anyone perform his or her sound long enough to communicate a feeling of motion? How would you describe the motion?

Divide the class into groups consisting of four or five students. One person in each of the groups should be a conductor. Each group concentrates on producing individual sounds to the motion of an item of its choice or one which has been suggested by the teacher, for example, the steady motion of a carpenter hammering a nail, the steady motion of a worm crawling, the steady motion of a person jogging, the steady motion of a horse galloping, and so on.

Allow approximately 10 minutes for groups to plan and practice their improvisations. At the end of the designated time each group will perform.

Tape each improvisation for immediate playback and analysis. Discuss any comments made by the students. Extend the discussion by including the following questions:

How would you describe the motion, slow, medium, fast?

Did it have a steady beat or pulse?

Summarize the discussion by introducing tempo as the characteristic referring to the speed of music and pulse which is the underlying beat (sometimes not heard but only sensed).

In listening to the recorded examples focus attention on the use of tempo.

How would you describe the tempo—slow, medium, or fast?

Did the pulse or underlying beat change before the end of the composition? What was the effect?

Suggested Listening Examples:

Flight of the Bumblebee—Rimsky-Korsakov, Nicolai; Epic LC 3759.

String Quartets Op. 76, No. 5, No. 79—Haydn, Joseph; Turnabout TV 34012S.

Careful planning is essential when teachers utilize improvisation and composition to help students form musical concepts. This interesting way to learn has the potential for exploring every aspect of musicianship in active ways. The January 1980, issue of the *Music Educators Journal* featured improvisation and contained helpful suggestions. Basic musical concepts can be developed by creative activities from the outset of a pupil's musical experience if they are designed with care.

The tasks are given time limits. Some of those listed here can be accomplished in two or three minutes, others in five, ten, or fifteen minutes; there are others that will require two or three class periods. Some assignments can be completed by individuals working at home or at school after regular hours or after other work has been done. There must be a predetermined signal, such a switching lights on or off, at which time the class reassembles to hear the results of the individual and group work and to analyze them.

Listening to recordings becomes listening to find out how other composers solved similar problems; thus there is an active, purposeful type of listening that should encompass all musical styles. It is obviously for a different purpose than simply trying to understand a composer or becoming familiar with a certain type of music. Improvisation and composition are individual matters which can be of primary importance to students.*

Accompaniment. Provide an appropriate percussion accompaniment for selected poems and stories.

Beat and divisions of the beat. Have small groups create a piece by using rhythm patterns derived from names.

Repetition and contrast. Employing either vocal or instrumental sounds, plan a composition that begins and ends with the same sounds, but has different sounds in the middle. Invent a way to notate it. Tape the result; listen to it; and analyze the different ways in which contrast is achieved.

Beat, pitch, chant. Establish a steady drum beat over which individuals create a chant based upon *sol mi,* using G and E on pitched percussion to pitch the chant.

Word rhythms. Create new words to known songs. Example: "If You're Happy," page 144. Use words denoting action or motion with this song, and perform them.

Imitating. Listen to "Leap Frog" from *Children's Games* by Bizet, AM, grade 1, vol. 1. After acting out the music, compose a piece with similar sounds by experimenting with pitched percussion, keyboard, or autoharp.

Muscular response. Improvise a dance to a recorded composition or song that suggests dancing.

Dynamics, pitch. Improvise music with percussion instruments to demonstrate concepts such as crescendo, decrescendo, soft, loud, low pitch, high pitch.

*Some of the activities in this section are inspired by those in the *Comprehensive Musicianship* music series published by Addison-Wesley. Refer to the teachers' books of this series for a detailed, sequential treatment of the subject.

Following this, compose music, using f p, ⬅➡, and ➡⬅ to interpret the score.

Pentatonic melody, dynamics, duration. Improvise music on the black keys of the keyboard or pitched percussion instrument in which dynamics and duration (long, short) are illustrated.

Repetition, contrast, duration, dynamics, notation. Improvise vocal pieces in small groups; using different mouth, tongue, and throat sounds, demonstrate long and short sounds in this music. Devise symbols and notate the sounds. Rehearse the compositions and tape them. Listen to the taped performances and have students evaluate them. After this, perform them again, emphasizing *crescendo* and *decrescendo* to add interest to the scores.

Music can be improvised by a conductor. The teacher distributes from four to six percussion instruments having contrasting tone qualities. A student conductor establishes a steady beat, then points to those children who are to play, cuing the players in and out, having them play alone or in combination. From this experiment should come interesting sound sequences organized as a composition. This can be done with an entire class by assigning specific instruments to groups.

New or unusual sounds can be produced when tone qualities are combined. The teacher selects four sound producers, each with a distinctively different tone quality. The teacher assigns groups of children to combine them in a musical composition. It may be necessary to devise notation. The results are taped so that students may evaluate them in class discussion.

Repetition, contrast in devised notation. In groups, students compose music using nonpitched percussion instruments, inventing symbols for the instruments and ways to notate the repetition and contrast of sounds.

Tone qualities, beat, rhythm patterns. Groups improvise accompaniments to familiar songs with percussion instruments. Roles played by students include singer, instrument player, and conductor. Actors could be added for songs easily dramatized.

Beat, tone quality, dynamics, articulation. Students improvise an appropriate percussion accompaniment to a selected recording, demonstrating soft and loud, or legato and staccato.

Notation. Using line notation that suggests pitch levels and duration, each student draws a score, explains his or her notation, and interprets it vocally or conducts the class in a performance of it. The scores can be placed on transparencies for the class to view, analyze, and perform (see Figure 6.3).

Expression of human feelings through musical sounds. The class explores a variety of vocal sounds intended to evoke specific feelings. Each sound is evaluated on its appropriateness to the identified feeling. Students discuss the relationship of different dynamics, pitch levels, and durations to different feelings.

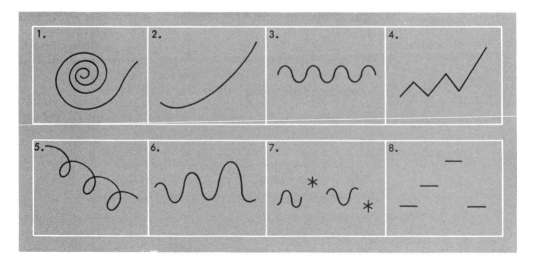

Figure 6.3. SAMPLE SCORES

Notation, pitch, tone quality, dynamics, duration. Pairs of students compose sound frames such as those in Figure 6.4, perform them vocally, tape them, and discuss how the aural reflects the visual.

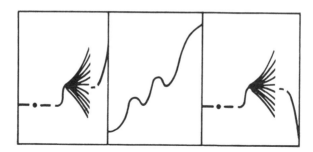

Figure 6.4. SOUND FRAMES

Ostinato. After hearing the recording *Ostinato Pianissimo* by Henry Cowell, Time Records S/8000, *Concert Percussion,* students improvise an original ostinato.

Rondo. After studying *Sleeping Beauty Waltz,* by Tchaikovsky, AM, grade 4, vol. 2, as an example of an *A B A C A B A* rondo, students will compose and notate a simple percussion rondo.

Synthesized tone qualities. Students learn to make sounds of various pitches on a synthesizer. They select several of the ones they like and tape. These taped sounds are then altered to produce an electronic composition.

The creative teacher

1. Keeps in mind that learning comes primarily from the student's interest, curiosity, and self-motivation.
2. Is satisfied with quick or brief answers, but replies with "How did you know that?" "Can you tell me why you like the musical result?" "How can you be sure?" and other statements that lead students to deeper analysis.
3. Watches and listens carefully for personal learning opportunities.
4. Does not quickly decide issues between students by telling them the correct answer.
5. Develops the ability for divergent thinking among students.
6. Develops a nonthreatening environment so learners may feel secure.
7. Considers the needs of the students rather than following precisely a certain methodology, curriculum guide, or other specific materials.

Band and Strings in the Elementary School

With the advent of the middle school, fewer elementary schools have band or string programs, although many of these instruments can be played by children in the intermediate grades. Group or individual lessons may be available on these instruments by the teacher of instrumental music. In some cases these lessons are given during the regular school day. The temporary withdrawal of some children from the general classroom may be a disruption unless the classroom teacher and the music specialist can plan cooperatively.

Teachers of general music in grades 4 and up can encourage membership in band and orchestra classes. Preliminary steps toward this end can include performances by live instrumentalists, bulletin board displays of instruments and instrumentalists, recordings, films, and filmstrips that illustrate instruments, visual mobiles of families of instruments, and children's books that include pictures of children playing instruments. The general music teacher and the specialists in instrumental music should plan times when the specialist can speak to the class and when he or she and the student players can demonstrate instruments. The sending of notices to parents and the planning for parent-teacher conferences about the selection, rental, or purchase of instruments should also be done jointly by the general teacher and the specialist. The specialist should bring instruments to the class and permit children to try them. The specialist demonstrates the importance of finger size, length, and flexibility in playing the clarinet, for example, and the importance of being able to "buzz" the lips in playing the trumpet. The importance of teeth formation should be discussed. For instance, a small overbite is preferable for small brass instruments; a large overbite is acceptable for bass and baritone. Both the general music teacher and the specialist can utilize instrumental scores in textbooks, and they can plan some of these correlated activities together. The child most likely to succeed in band and orchestra is sufficiently mature physically to play the instrument, generally musical, and reliable and persevering.

1. Students identify and compare the recorded tone qualities of the orchestra and band.
2. Students study various folk instruments and their tone qualities. (Note: Album L 24, *Folk Instruments of the World,* Follett Publishing Company, provides an explanatory folder which includes drawings of the instruments.)
3. Students compare the tone qualities and the instrumentation of various vocal and instrumental ensembles: duets, trios, quartets, quintets, and sextets.
4. Students compare the seating arrangements of a band and an orchestra, draw diagrams of them, and compare them.
5. Students research the synthesizer as a musical instrument, listen to recordings of its music, describe its tone qualities, and compare them with other instruments.
6. Students explore acoustics as related to music, including resonance, the overtone series (harmonics or partials), and attack and decay.
7. Children listen to electronic music, discuss the tone qualities they hear, and compare the sound of those of traditional instruments.
8. Students compare the tone qualities and the instrumentation of the marching band, the symphonic band, and the rock band.
9. Students work with an oscilloscope, and compare the wave forms of the flute, violin, and trumpet when they sound the same pitch.
10. Students listen to a recording of a gamelan (orchestra) from Indonesia, and devise a similar ensemble of pitched and nonpitched percussion instruments which requires a conductor to bring in sections and have other sections stop playing at times. Each section creates pentatonic ostinati or rhythm patterns, which are repeated as long as the conductor desires. The group evaluates the performance.
11. Students examine an orchestral score while the composition is played and follow a specific instrument part.
12. Students listen to a musical recording and design a record jacket that includes information about the composition, its history, and the composer.
13. Students listen to several recordings of the same composition and compare the conductors' interpretations, the performers' skills, and the general quality of the recording.
14. Students develop sound stories in which they dramatize the characters by creating masks, selecting appropriate body movements and musical tone qualities, and interpreting the story.

REFERENCES AND MATERIALS

Books and Articles

AEBISCHER, DEL, ROGER NICKERSON, and CHRIS BRUYA, "What Every Music Teacher Needs," *Oregon Music Educator, LXI/*3, Fall 1989, 8–12.

COPE, DAVID, "The Mechanics of Listening to Electronic Music," *Music Educators Journal*, October 1977, 47–51.

COPLAND, AARON, *What to Listen for in Music* (rev. ed.). New York: Mentor Books, 1964, Chapter 7.

DENNIS, BRIAN, *Experimental Music in the Schools*. London: Oxford University Press, 1970.

Friend, David, Allan R. Pearlman, and Thoman D. Piggot, *Learning Music with Synthesizers*. New York: Hal Leonard, 7777 W. Bluemound Road, P.O. Box 13819, Milwaukee, WI 53213. Copyright 1974 by ARP Instruments, Inc., Newton, Mass.

Kassner, Kirk, "Rx for Technophobia" *Music Educators Journal*, November 1988, 18–21.

Keyboard Publications, 1346 Chapel St., New Haven, CT 06511. Films, recordings, teacher guides for electronic music.

Lyons Teachers Guide. Lyons, 530 Riverview Ave., Elkhart, IN 46514. Contains components for classroom electronic music, and audiovisual materials for exploring new types of music.

Marsh, Mary Val, et al., *The Spectrum of Music with Related Arts: Electronic Music, Sounds of Singing Voices, Sources of Musical Sounds*. New York: Macmillan, 1975. Booklets with recordings.

McMahon, O., "Young Children's Perceptions of the Dimensions of Sound," *Bulletin of the Council for Research in Music Education*, No. 85, Fall 1985, 131–139.

MMCP Interaction: Early Childhood Music Curriculum 2d ed., 2101 Ontario Street, Bellingham, Wash.: Americole, 1979.

MMCP Synthesis. USOE V-008, USOE 6-1999. Media Materials, Inc., P.O. Box 553, Bardonia, NY 10954.

Palmer, Mary, *Sound Exploration and Discovery*. New York: The Center for Applied Research in Education, Inc., 521 Fifth Avenue, New York, NY 10017, 1974.

Paynter, John, and Peter Aston, *Sounds and Silences*. New York: Cambridge University Press, 1970. Thirty-six projects in creative music for intermediate grades through college.

Placek, Robert W., "MûsicShapes," *Music Educators Journal, 74/8*, April 1988, 57–60.

Schafer, R. Murray, *Creative Music Education*. New York: Schirmer, 1976.

Tait, Malcom J., "Whispers, Growls, Screams, and Puffs . . . Lead to Composition," *Music Educators Journal*, February 1977, 33–39.

Thomas, Ronald B., *MMCP Synthesis*. Elnora, N.Y.: Media, Inc., n.d.

Walton, Charles, *Teaching Guide*. Camden, N.J.: RCA-Victor (Instruments of the Orchestra recordings).

Willman, Fred, *Electronic Music for Young People*. New York: Center for Applied Research in Education, 521 Fifth Avenue, New York, NY 10017, 1974.

Pictures and Charts

Construction of the Grand Piano; Evolution of the Grand Piano, Baldwin Piano Company, Cincinnati, Ohio. Also pamphlet, *Story of the Baldwin Piano*.

Families of Instruments (posters), *World of Music* Series, Morristown, N.J.: Silver, Burdett and Ginn, 1989.

Instruments of the Orchestra Charts, J. W. Pepper and Son, 1423 Vine Street, Philadelphia, Pa. Twenty-two charts for use with RCA recordings.

Meet the Instruments, Bowmar Records, Belwin Mills, Melville, NY 11747. Twenty-five laminated posters.

Musical Instrument Pictures, C.G. Conn, Ltd., 2520 Industrial Parkway, Elkhart, IN 46516.

Musical Instruments, York Band Instrument Company, Grand Rapids, Mich.

Range Chart for Band and Orchestra Instruments, C. G. Conn, Ltd., 2520 Industrial Parkway, Elkhart, IN 46516.

Recordings *Complete Orchestra, The.* 5 records, 33 instruments featured. Music Education Record Corporation, Box 445, Englewood Cliffs, NJ.

Composer and His Orchestra, The, vol. 1. Mercury Record Corporation. Howard Hanson tells how he uses instruments.

Ensembles, Large and Small. Bowmar Orchestral Library Album 83. Includes Britten's *Young Person's Guide to the Orchestra,* a string quartet, percussion ensemble, brass ensemble, and chorale.

First Chair. ML 4629, Columbia Records, 799 Seventh Ave., New York, NY. Features bassoon, cello, clarinet, flute, French horn, oboe, trumpet, and violin.

Franson Corporation, 225 Park Avenue South, New York, NY 10003. Children's Record Guide and Young People's Records.
Drummer Boy
Hunter's Horn
King's Trumpet, The
Licorice Stick
Little Brass Band
Mr. Grump and *The Dingle School Band*
Neighbor's Band
On Lemmer Lemmer Street (violin)
Rondo for Bassoon and Orchestra
Runaway Sheep (wind instruments)
Said the Piano to the Harpsichord
Strike Up the Band
Wonderful Violin

Guitar Music from the Courts of Spain. Mercury Record Corporation. Caledonia Romera plays.

Military Band, The. COL 1056, Columbia Records, 799 Seventh Ave., New York, N.Y.

Peter and the Wolf, Tubby the Tuba, Pan the Piper. CL 671, Columbia Records, 799 Seventh Ave., New York, N.Y.

Popular Classics for Spanish Guitar. RCA Victor. Julian Bream plays.

Rusty in Orchestraville. Capitol Records.

Saint-Saëns. *Carnival of the Animals* and Britten, *Young Person's Guide to the Orchestra.* ML 5768, Columbia Records, 799 Seventh Ave., New York, NY.

Tchaikovsky, *Symphony No. 4, 3rd movement.* BOL 71. To identify classes of instruments.

ELECTRONIC MUSIC
Badings: "Ragtime" from *Evolutions.* Epic BC 1118.
Country Moog: Switched on Nashville. Gilbert Trythall. Athena 6003.
Electronic Music: Vox Productions, Inc.
Electronic Sound: George Harrison. Zapple Records ST 3358.
LeCaine: *Dripsody.* A drop of water makes music on a tape recorder. On *Electronic Music.* Folkways FM 3436.

Luening: *Gargoyles,* for violin and synthesizer. On *Columbia-Princeton Electronic Music Center,* Columbia MS 6566.

Luening and Ussachevsky: *Poem in Cycles and Bells for Tape Recorder and Orchestra.* Composers Recordings Inv. CR1 1 12.

Music for Voices, Instruments and Electronics. Kenneth Gaburo. Nonesuch Records H7199.

Silver Apples of the Moon. Morton Subotnick. Nonesuch Records H-71 174.

Varèse: *Deserts,* Angel S-36786

UNCONVENTIONAL SOUND SOURCES

Cage: Second Movement, *Amores.* Wood sounds. Time 58,000.

Cage and Harrison: *Double Music.* Eight rice bowls. Time 58,000.

Harrison: *Canticle No. 1,* on *Concert Percussion.* Time 8,000.

Oliveros: *Sound Patterns.* Mouth sounds. Odyssey 3216–0156.

Partch: *The World of Harry Partch.* Hand-made instruments; an invented tonal organization of 43 tones within the octave. Columbia MS 7207.

Sounds of New Music (Cage, Luening, Ussachevsky, Varèse). Reverberation, tape loops, music concrète. Folkways FX 6160.

PREPARED PIANO

Cage: *Amores No. 1.* Children can be guided by this recording to try for new sounds on the autoharp.

Cowell: *Banshee.* A banshee is a female ghost that warns of approaching death. Children can relate this piece to Halloween and use the autoharp to imitate the sounds made on the prepared piano. On *Sounds of New Music*, Folkways FX 6160.

Films *Bing, Bang, Boom.* National Film Board of Canada.

Discovering Electronic Music. Barr Production.

Discovering Electronic Music. Discovering Music Series: RSC-774.

Discovering String Instruments. Bailey Films Educational Association.

Introducing the Woodwinds, Music for Young People Series, NET Films Service, Indiana University, Bloomington, IN 47401.

Learning About Sound. Encyclopedia Britannica Educational Association.

Music Is Composed. National Audio-Visual Center.

Music Is Tone. National Audio-Visual Center.

Music Makers. Universal Education and Visual Arts.

New Sounds in Music. Churchill Films, 622 N. Robertson Blvd., Los Angeles, CA 90069.

Percussion, Music for Young People Series, NET Films Service, Indiana University, Bloomington, IN 47401.

Percussion Sounds. Churchill Films, 622 N. Robertson Blvd., Los Angeles, CA 90069.

Piccolo, Saxo and Company. Modern Learning Aids.

Pretty Lady and the Electronic Musicians. Xerox Films.

Pulse of Music, Music for Young People Series, NET Films Service, Indiana University, Bloomington, IN 47401.

String Sounds. Churchill Films, 622 N. Robertson Blvd., Los Angeles, CA 90069.

Symphony Orchestra, The, Encyclopedia Britannica Films, 1150 Wilmette Ave., Wilmette, IL. Traces growth of the symphony orchestra from string quartet to the modern orchestra.

Toot, Whistle, Plunk and Boom. Walt Disney Media.

What Is Music? Churchill Films, 622 N. Robertson Blvd., Los Angeles, CA 90069.

Wind Sounds. Churchill Films, 622 N. Robertson Blvd., Los Angeles, CA 90069.

Filmstrips *Creating Music Through Use of the Tape Recorder.* Keyboard Publications, 1346 Chapel St., New Haven, CT 06511. Two color sound filmstrips, one recording, eight study prints, one teacher guide.

Electronic Music. Keyboard Publications.

Instruments of the Symphony Orchestra (recordings with six filmstrips) Jam Handy, Prentice-Hall Media, 150 White Plains Rd., Tarrytown, NY 10591.

Meet the Instruments (recordings with two filmstrips) Bowmar Records, Belwin Mills, Melville, NY 11747.

Musical Books for Young People, a series of six filmstrips. Society for Visual Education, 1345 Diversey Pkway., Chicago, IL 60614. Strings, brass, woodwinds, percussion, keyboard, and folk instruments.

New Sounds of the Classics. Keyboard Publications.

7 Teaching Children Pitch, Melody, and Harmony

The Nature of Pitch

For sound to occur, something must move to vibrate. Young children can experiment with a rubber band stretched across an open-top box by plucking it, watching it vibrate at a fast rate, and listening to it produce a sound. Every time the rubber band moves back and forth, one oscillation or cycle is completed, and a sound wave is formed of molecules of air. As the rubber band is tightened, it vibrates faster, and its pitch is consequently higher. As it is loosened, the band vibrates more slowly, and the pitch becomes lower.

All sound is produced by the vibration of some object or substance: a string, a reed, a piece of wood or metal, a column of air. The pitch of any tone is directly related to the number of vibrations per second in that substance.

Scales and Melodic Movement

A melody exists when a series of different pitches are organized to develop a sense of connectedness. Many words are used to describe melodies and the ways they are organized: tonal, atonal, high, low, conjunct, disjunct, consonant, or dissonant. Sometimes all the tones in the series relate to a tonal center, and when organized consecutively from low to high or high to low, they are part of a musical scale. All cultures have musical scales, which vary substantially from one another.

What Is a Scale? The term *scale* comes from the Latin word for "ladder." It refers to an arrangement of rising or descending pitches. The earliest experiences children have with scales may be with the pentatonic scale, set up by teachers of early childhood music. The most common pentatonic scale corresponds with the black keys of the keyboard, and is known as a gapped scale because of the gap of 1½ tones between steps 3 and 4. All other tones are a whole step apart (see Figure 7.1).

Pentatonic Scale	1	2	3		5	6		8
	d	r	m		s	l		d

Figure 7.1

Pentatonic Scales. The pentatonic scale is especially useful for children's improvisations before they understand major and minor scales. Figure 7.2 shows this scale at four different pitch levels.

Older children become familiar with the major scale through experiences with scale songs and playing the C scale on step bells and the xylophone. Step bells, pitched percussion instruments, and keyboards are effective audiovisual devices for exploring the major scale, with its arrangement of whole steps between all tones except tones 3–4 and 7–8, which are half steps (see Figure 7.3).

Major Scales. The major scale can begin on any black or white key of the keyboard by preserving this pattern of whole and half steps. Although this pattern embodies an important concept, students typically do not discover it until

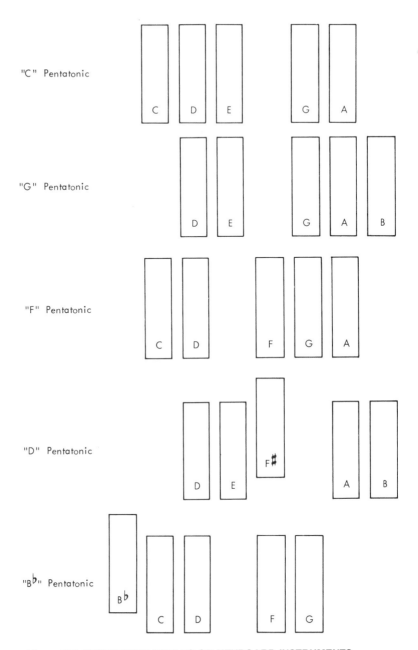

Figure 7.2 PENTATONIC SCALES ON KEYBOARD INSTRUMENTS

the intermediate grades. Some teachers use hand signs to explore the scale and its intervals. One advantage of hand signs is that they involve the children in powerful psychomotor learning that makes the understanding of scale tones less abstract.

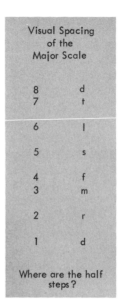

Figure 7.3

In more advanced grades the major scale can be compared with pentatonic and minor scales. In any study of scales there should be an immediate association with song materials to explore how a scale relates to the music. Because so many American songs are in major keys, this association is fairly obvious. Songs employing minor and pentatonic scales need to be studied in like fashion through songs that employ them. In working with songs built on less common scales, the students might first determine which note is the tonal center, and then try to construct the scale from that note, using the other notes from the melody. Children as young as 8 years old can begin to learn scale structures through experiences with songs.

Minor Scales.   Every major scale has a relative minor scale. Two systems are used to describe their tones. In one, the home tone of the minor scale carries the name of the sixth step (*la*) of its relative major scale. Thus, in C major, the relative minor scale (A minor) would begin on the note *la* and proceed to the next *la* above. In this system the syllables and note numbers remain the same for the major scale and its relative minor (see Figure 7.4).

Another system for describing the tones of the minor scale is to call the home tone of the minor scale *do* or step 1, as was done with the major scale. If this method is followed new syllable names must be learned for steps 3 and 6 of the scale, because they have been flatted. Most adults prefer whichever system they learned first; however, general preference is for the system using *la* as the home tone.

MAJOR			do		re		mi	fa		so		la		ti	do
PENTATONIC			do		re		mi			so		la			do
MINOR natural	la		ti	do		re		mi	fa		so		la		
MINOR harmonic	la		ti	do		re		mi	fa			si	la		

Figure 7.4. COMPARISON OF SCALES

With selected major, minor and pentatonic song materials and recordings, these scales can be studied. However, an understanding of these various patterns develops only very slowly. As part of their studies, children should be encouraged to use them in their own compositions. Among the questions for students to answer are "Which scale does this sound like?" "In which scale is *ti* closest to *do?*" and "What feelings are communicated by use of minor scales and keys in music?" In the latter question they should find that there are at least as many kinds of feeling communicated by minor keys as by major keys, and that minor is not necessarily associated with sadness.

Tonal Activity of Scale Tones

Major Scales. Students learn easily to identify scale tone 1 (the home tone) as the pitch to which all the other scale tones are related. Through experience, children begin to recognize scale tone 5 as the next most influential tone, even though tone number 7 is very active. Scale tone 4 is the third most important tone. These three tones (1, 4, 5) are the root tones for the primary chords in any major or minor key.

When students sense the tonal activity of various scale tones thoroughly, they recognize that certain tones awaken a greater sense of stability, while other tones suggest movement to an adjacent pitch above or below. Using the major scale as an example, tone number 1 of the scale is the most stable tone, evoking feelings of rest or conclusion. The most active tone is probably tone number 7 (the *leading tone*) which pulls strongly to tone number 8. The remaining tones may move up or down, depending on the context in which they are used. For example, tone number 2 may actively pull down toward tone number 1, or in other cases pull up toward tone number 3. Tone number 6 is often a passing tone, and may move either direction. These qualities of scale tones can be discerned by children. Older students feel them more strongly than young children because their harmonic sense is developing. To explore the passive and active qualities of scale tones, children may be asked to sing slowly up and down the scale, stopping at different scale tones. They may then be asked which way they feel the tone should move—up, down, or stay the same. The tendencies of a tone are strongly influenced by the context of the melody in which it is found. However, Figure 7.5 illustrates some tendencies commonly associated with the tones of the major scale.

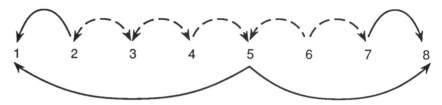

Figure 7.5

Pentatonic Scales. Songs based on the pentatonic scale are quite common. They are particularly valuable in elementary music because the movement of tones within the scale is not as rigid as with other scales. Therefore, they work very well with children's improvised melodies and accompaniments. Almost any tones of the pentatonic scale harmonize pleasantly with any part of the melody. Pentatonic scales are easily set up on pitched percussion instruments by the removal of all nonpentatonic bars prior to classroom use. Pentatonic songs are listed in classified indexes of most current music series. Examples include "Goodbye, Old Paint," "The Barnyard Song," "Leatherwing Bat," "Old Dan Tucker," "Old Texas," "The Canoe Song," "The Riddle Song," and "Night Herding Song." As stated earlier, they can be played on the black keys of the keyboard, an activity which assists the development of tonal memory.

PENTATONIC SCALES

Tonal center ↑

Key Signatures. Students who have explored scales and understand their organization have no difficulty in determining why key signatures are necessary. When they fit the major scale pattern to different places on the keyboard, the necessity for sharps and flats becomes apparent. Unless students find uses for key signatures, however, they soon forget them. One logical use is in the performance of music. In instrumental music we must use the key signature in order to know what note to play and what fingering to use. In vocal music the singer has less need for that information. Instead the teacher often has the class sing 1-3-5-3-1 (using the first, third, and fifth tones of the scale) to establish the tonality of the song, and then sings the beginning tone. With that aural information the class can begin singing. Thus in a purely vocal approach the teacher must rely on other situations in which the key signature is of use to the learner. For example, establishing the key of a song by its key signature is essential in determining the primary chords necessary for a chordal accompaniment. Another good way to teach key signatures is to have students notate their own compositions.

Movement of Tones in a Melody   The tones of melodies move in three ways: they can repeat, they can move in steps (conjunctmotion), and they can move in skips or leaps (disjunctmotion). There are, of course, limitless numbers of ways these three can be accomplished. When these concepts are being developed, the teacher selects music that most clearly reveals these tonal contours. In songs such as ''That's the Way Tunes Go'' and ''Space Ship'' the concepts of repeated tones and stepwise progression can be studied by the children in response to the teacher's question, ''In what different ways do you think this melody moves?''

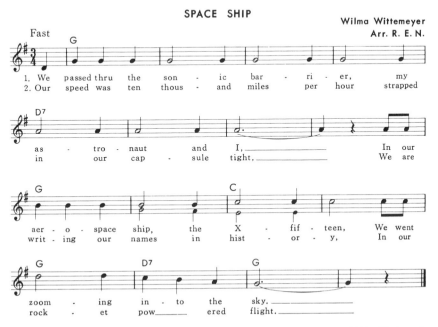

SPACE SHIP

Wilma Wittemeyer
Arr. R. E. N.

1. We passed thru the son - ic bar - ri - er, my
2. Our speed was ten thous - and miles per hour strapped

as - tro - naut and I, _____ In our
in our cap - sule tight, _____ We are

aer - o - space ship, the X - fif - teen, We went
writ - ing our names in hist - or - y, In our

zoom - ing in - to the sky. _____
rock - et pow _____ ered flight. _____

From *Exploring Music with Children* by Robert E. Nye and Vernice T. Nye. © 1966 by Wadsworth Publishing Company, Inc. Reprinted by permission of Wadsworth Publishing Company, Belmont, Calif. 94002.

''Pussywillow Song'' is another scale-line song with repeated notes; it is also useful to demonstrate the octave leap (see p. 56.)

Suggestions for use: ''Pussy Willow Song'' can be used to introduce children to the C major scale. Children find the scale easy to play on step bells, a pitched percussion instrument, or keyboard. After the song is learned, one child can sing the first measure, another the second measure, another the third and fourth measures, and so on. The teacher might also add hand signs and syllables to reinforce tonal memory.

''Sandy Land'' is a song in which some tones of the melody outline a chord (chord-line song); it also contains skips, leaps, and repeated notes. By experi-

SANDY LAND

Briskly
F

Oklahoma

C7

1. Make my liv -ing in sand - y land. Make my liv -ing in sand - y land,

Make my liv-ing in sand-y land, La-dies, fare you well.

2. *Raise potatoes in sandy land, etc.*
3. *Dig potatoes in sandy land, etc.*

menting, older children can find that F, A, C and C, E, G are notes that can be played together as chords to accompany the song, thus beginning to relate chord-line melodies with accompanying chords.

Accidentals, Chromatic Scales, and Whole-Tone Scales

Accidentals (sharps, flats, or natural signs not stipulated by the key signature) are to be found in much music. Songs such as "Down by the Bay," and "Hokey Pokey" contain accidentals. A discussion of accidentals helps children understand these notational symbols in the music, and can lead to their exploring the chromatic scale, which consists entirely of half steps.

CHROMATIC SCALE

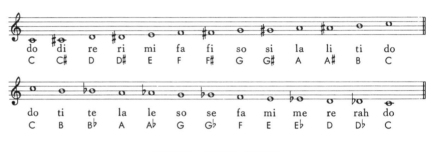

WHOLE-TONE SCALE

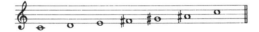

Highly chromatic scales and whole-tone scales lack the feeling of tonality characteristic of major and minor scales. The composition *La Mer* (The Sea) by Debussy (AM, grade 6, vol. 2) employs many chromatics, and illustrates this fact. When students analyze how songs based on major and minor scales establish home tones, they find that the half steps contribute to the feeling of tonal movement and tension. The chromatic scale, on the other hand, has nothing but half steps, and therefore no tendency to move toward one or another of the tones. Neither the whole-tone scale nor the pentatonic scale has half steps, and tonality is consequently weakened. Some interesting questions may come from this. For example, what kinds of feelings would a composition such as *Mists* by Howard Hanson awaken? (It is a composition utilizing the whole-tone scale.)*

*From *For the First Time*, Mercury Recording. A song constructed on the whole-tone scale is "The Cage" by Charles Ives. It appears in several of the music textbook series.

The whole-tone scale can also be compared to the common pentatonic scale, and students can discuss the differences between the two. Songs and recordings based on these scales will provide aural examples for the students to compare.

The Less Common Modes Some scales or modes were used more frequently in earlier centuries. Today both contemporary composers and folk singers have brought the early modes to a more prominent position. In the elementary classroom they can be used to compose songs and instrumental pieces with a different sound, and to represent much older historical periods. For example, a troubadour song could be written with both words and melody communicating feelings from that time in history. Indexes in many song series guide teachers to modal songs.

Another way to explore modal scales is to compare their structure to the major scale. If you employ only the white keys of the keyboard, the major scale or Ionian mode begins and ends on *do,* the Dorian mode on *re,* the Phrygian mode on *mi,* the Lydian mode on *fa,* the Mixolydian mode on *sol,* and the natural minor scale, or Aeolian mode, on *la.* Some of these less common modes are shown in Figure 7.6. Children enjoy finding and playing these scales on a keyboard instrument.

Some examples of songs written in less common modes are the folk songs "I Wonder as I Wander," "Every Night When the Sun Goes Down," "Old Joe Clark," and "Ground Hog." Religious plainchants also exemplify the use of older modes. Recorded examples of these may be interesting to young listeners.

Figure 7.6. LESS COMMON MODES

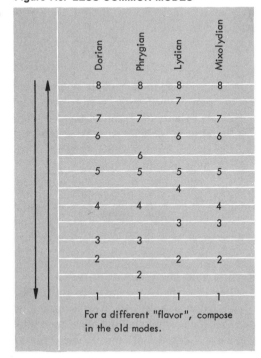

Ethnic Scales   The concept of *scale* is further expanded when ethnic scales are introduced, primarily through listening examples. There are many such scales, and music education is only beginning to explore them. They relate very well to some aspects of social studies. For example, in a unit about Japan, children can study the music of that country and its scales. One Japanese scale is the common pentatonic scale. Another is the pentatonic scale used in the song "Sakura," which is available in most music series books. Beautiful songs can be composed by using this scale:

Much of the popular music of Japan is based on this pentatonic scale:

This gypsy scale might be used for a student composition:

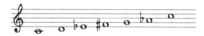

A scale of Afro-American origin is also useful:

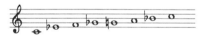

Two background sources on scales and modes of other culture are James P. O'Brien's *Non-Western Music and the Western Listener* (Dubuque, Iowa: Kendall-Hunt, 1977), and Donald J. Funes's *Musical Involvement: A Guide to Perceptive Listening* (New York: Harcourt Brace Jovanovich, 1975). The explanations on some record jackets of Asian Indian music also explain the scale structures used in the music.

Another interesting activity involves helping the children invent an original scale as a basis for their compositions. In this activity the learners devise a scale built on a regular arrangement of intervals such as a consistent alternating of whole and half steps or a consistent use of an interval such as the minor or major third.

The Tone Row   The tone row is normally based on the twelve steps of the chromatic scale. Resonator bells are uniquely suited for devising a tone row. They may be placed in an order that, when sounded, does remind the listener of any tonality. This requires moving the bars about until the new scale sounds *atonal*—that is, without any definite tonal center. The tone row originally included all twelve tones of the chromatic scale, but tone rows of shorter length are less complicated for children.

To explore tone rows, the class may develop one and then experiment with it by playing the rhythms of familiar melodies such as "Three Blind Mice" on the new scale. The result will be a familiar rhythm with a new melodic sound. The class may also use its new scale in a composition which features the succession of pitches repeated.

A reel-to-reel tape recorder and splicing tape are useful in making a tape loop of the class's tone row. The tone row is recorded one or more times; the tape is cut at the end of the recording, and spliced together. It is then played back on the recorder with the use of a pencil for tension on the tape loop. It can even be played at various speeds for different sound effects. At a later time, other tape loops of varying length can be constructed and played simultaneously on several tape recorders. Because of the different lengths of the tape loops, the interacting sounds constantly change.

With the tone row, traditional harmony is absent; a new concept of harmonization is constructed, often being built from the vertical "happenings" of multiple melodic lines instead of the chords of traditional harmony.

Intervals and Tone Patterns

Intervals When two different pitches are sung in sequence the result is a *melodic* interval. Because of the ease in singing the descending interval of a minor third, this melodic interval can be used as a beginning point in studying tone patterns.

When the descending minor third is introduced, it can be related to rhythm through a game of clapping (*sol*, scale tone 5) and patchen (*mi*, scale tone 3). After establishing the pitches, and relating them to the motions, the teacher can demonstrate them for the class, and ask the students to mirror the motions while singing the intervals in simple rhythmic patterns:

The experience with tones 5–5–3 is quickly expanded to include other pitches and intervals. The next scale tone to be introduced is usually *la* or scale tone 6. An activity with these three tones might have children sing the following words to decide where the tone is to drop from 5 (*sol*) to 3 (*mi*). They should use normal word rhythms in singing the words.

5 3 5 3
Star-light, star-bright,

5   6 6 5 5   3
First star I see to-night.

5 5 3-   5 5 3-
Wish I may, wish I might,

5   5   6 6 5 5   3-
Have the wish I wish to-night.

After singing the words using intervals, the children might clap these rhythms in unison. The teacher gradually introduces scale tones 6, 2, and 1 (*la, re, do*) and asks class members to name the new intervals they have created. Then the class composes longer tone patterns or a new melody using intervals based on all five tones. Eventually students may want to create bordurs and ostinati for the melody, using Orff instruments. If so, those intervals should be identified as well.

The use of tone patterns and intervals is an integral part of reading music. Children can comprehend tonal and rhythmic groups just as they comprehend words and phrases in English. The intervals that comprise tone patterns found in songs can be taught as parts of those songs. Some tone patterns are found in many familiar songs. Some common patterns include the following:

1. the minor third — "So Long" / "Brahms' Lullaby" / "The Blacksmith"

2. the children's chant — "The Caisson Song" / "A-Tisket, A-Tasket" / "Camptown Races"

3. — "Hot Cross Buns" / "Are You Sleeping" / "Polly Wolly Doodle" / "Golden Slippers" / "Shortnin' Bread"

4. — "Star Spangled Banner" / "Blue Danube" / "Dixie" / "Goin' to Boston" / "Bow, Belinda"

5. — "There Was a Little Woman" / "Dixie" / "The First Noël"

In learning melodic intervals, the student usually begins with the descending minor third. Next, the octave, major third, major sixth, fourth and fifth are easily heard and recognized by children. These intervals appear commonly in children's songs, and are learned through associations with those songs. The minor third is found in "The Caisson Song", and "Lightly Row"; the major third in "All Hid, Little David", and "Swing Low, Sweet Chariot"; the fourth in "Brush Your Teeth", "I've Been Working on the Railroad", and "Hark! the Herald Angels Sing"; the fifth in "Twinkle, Twinkle, Little Star", and "Baa, Baa, Black Sheep"; the sixth in "My Bonnie", "Bendemeer's Stream", and "It Came Upon the Midnight Clear"; and the octave with "Pussywillow Song", "Annie Laurie", and "Wait for the Wagon".

As an example, "Love Somebody" contains several tone patterns, and the repeated thirds form triads, which can lead to the students' discovery of their existence.

LOVE SOMEBODY

After analyzing several songs for intervals and tone patterns, a song such as "Barney's Tune" can be introduced. This song successfully alternates scale passages with intervals. As in all cases, such songs should be learned for their own musical enjoyment, and then analyzed for conceptual teaching. "Barney's Tune" can be used by the teacher, who asks students to locate scale passages and intervals, and describe or sing the differences.

Analyzing Melodies

When students analyze melodies, they should seek answers to such questions as

How do tones move? (scalewise, stepwise, repeated tones)
Where do phrases begin and end?

BARNEY'S TUNE

Hilary Smith

Verse 2:
Feelin' happy chasing butterflies,
I see you coming and I want to say "hi".
If I were a kid, I'd want to shout;
Instead something quite else comes out.
If I can't shout like you, what's a dog to do? (Bark!)

Verse 3:
I'm happy and sad and all kinds of things
It seems like the only thing to do is sing.
You might hear me, Howlin' at the moon,
And think that sure is a funny kind of tune.

How do the phrases relate to each other?

Which scale is employed? (major, minor, modal, pentatonic, tone row, ethnic scale)

What is the range?

Is there evidence of tension and release? If so, how is this achieved?

Is there evidence of a climax? If so, how is this achieved?

Does the song possess other significant features (such as rhythm patterns, tone patterns, dynamics, sequence)?

Some Activities Related to Songs

There are numerous activities possible with songs. Among them are the following:

1. Moving in time with the beat by motions such as clapping, swinging, tapping, rocking, skipping, and jumping.
2. Walking on the beat while standing in place or moving as directed.

3. While walking to the beat of the song, doing things such as slowing down, speeding up, and dramatizing loud and soft.
4. Clapping the rhythm of the melody.
5. Clapping the rhythm of the melody while walking the beat.
6. Singing phrase 1; doing ''inner hearing'' with phrase 2; singing phrase 3; doing ''inner hearing'' with phrase 4, except for singing the last pitch of the song. Repeat the exercise while walking the beat.
7. Establishing the pitch and tempo of a song. Clapping the beat, thinking the song with ''inner hearing,'' then singing only the final word.
8. The teacher or a student leader turns the singing on and off with an imaginary knob; the children try to keep the rhythm steady so that they can come in together when the song is ''turned back on.''
9. Within a circle, singing while an object is passed from hand to hand on the beat. Then the object is passed on the first word of each phrase.
10. A one-measure rhythmic pattern is selected from the song, or created. This ostinato is repeated while the children sing the song.
11. If the song is pentatonic, selecting a phrase from the song which a group can sing repeatedly while the rest of the class sings the song.
12. If the song is pentatonic, trying it as a round.
13. If any two pentatonic songs are in the same meter and have the same number of measures, singing them together as ''partner songs.''
14. Determining whether the music moves in twos or threes.
15. Having the students conduct the song by using appropriate metrical beat patterns.
16. Leveling the pitches or the melodic contour with hands and arms.
17. Having the class identify significant rhythmic and tonal patterns.

What Do Melodies Communicate?

Songs are the union of poetry and melody; their words combine with the music to express the thoughts being communicated. Students should be encouraged to discuss how well the melody reflects the message of the words. The union of poetry and melody might be discussed for a lullaby, a work song, a TV commercial, or a dance song. Appropriate questions might include ''This song is said to be a lullaby. How does the melody suggest that it is a lullaby? How well does it succeed in communicating this idea?'' A song such as ''Sleep, Baby, Sleep'' could be used as an example. When such questions are asked, the teacher helps the students see the relationship by asking questions. ''How does the melody suggest the message of the words? How well does it do it?'' The first question stimulates analysis and the second a value judgment. In the song, ''Sleep, Baby, Sleep'' students might observe its tempo, note durations, repetition, contrast, and ascending or descending patterns.

SLEEP, BABY, SLEEP

moth- er shakes the dream-land tree, And from it falls sweet dreams for thee;

Sleep, ba - by, sleep! Sleep, ba - by, sleep!

2. *Sleep, baby, sleep! The large stars are the sheep.*
   The little ones, the lambs, I guess,
   The gentle moon, the shepherdess,
   Sleep, baby, sleep! Sleep, baby, sleep!

Harmony and Texture

Relating Melody and Harmony   The introduction of harmony most often follows the introduction of rhythm and melody. Whereas Western music emphasizes harmony, music of Asia and Africa emphasizes rhythmic and melodic developments more complex than those of the West. In the music of Asia and Africa, harmony is incidental to the interrelation of rhythm and melody, although intervals of a wide variety occur.

Polyphony is another word for counterpoint. Its earliest definition had to do with point against point (note against note). For our purposes we regard it as a

Photo by Juretta Nidever.

combining of melodic lines into a unified musical texture. In traditional Western music, polyphony operates in accordance with certain harmonic principles. However, in some contemporary music it disregards traditional harmonic practices. Thus there can be said to be two general types of polyphony: harmonic and nonharmonic. In most cases harmonic polyphony tends to sound more consonant and nonharmonic polyphony tends to sound more dissonant. The music of Johann Sebastian Bach is often polyphonic; it can be described as horizontal threads of melody moving along together. At the same time, when this music is considered vertically, chords and chord changes appear throughout. A common example of this combination of the horizontal and vertical aspects of music is the round. Teachers should occasionally write a round on the chalkboard, each entry written on a staff beneath the previous entry. Students can then see, as well as hear, how the polyphony fits together harmonically.

Texture refers to the relationships between melodies and other simultaneous sounds in music. Adjectives commonly used to describe texture include heavy, light, open, thick, and thin. Texture is influenced by the number of different melodies and accompaniments employed, their ranges, and their tone qualities. A two-part round is of thin texture; three- and four-part rounds have correspondingly thicker textures. Low ranges can influence textures toward heaviness while high ranges can produce an opposite effect. The terms monophonic, homophonic, and polyphonic refer to the classification of textures.

monophony = an unaccompanied melodic line
homophony = a single melodic line with accompaniment
polyphony = two or more independent melodies occurring together.

Children are normally first exposed to monophonic texture in the simple unaccompanied songs of early childhood. Homophonic texture follows, because it is the dominant texture of simple accompanied songs of all kinds. Teachers can introduce polyphonic textures through the use of canons, rounds, chants, ostinati, and descants that children perform after they have learned to sing in tune or to play a melody instrument with a group. For most students the ability to hear and sing harmonically develops between the ages of 9 and 13. This growing harmonic sense is reflected by an emphasis on part singing for the 10- and 11-year-olds.

Learning to Hear Chord Changes   Young children like the sounds of harmony even before they can hear it analytically or perform it. On the other hand, harmony may be overused; it can confuse some children who are trying to comprehend and sing melodies. Further research is needed to determine at what levels of development harmony should be added to young children's musical experiences. It seems logical that the young child should first be helped to comprehend rhythm and melody. After that, the child should be exposed to melodies with simple harmonic accompaniments of a wide variety. A next step initiates the development of the child's ability to comprehend two or more melodic lines that occur at the same time.

Some concepts related to traditional harmony are these:

Harmony is a vertical arrangement of pitches.

Tonality results when the harmony of a piece of music indicates a tonal center to which its other tones are attracted or related.

When two tones are on adjacent lines or spaces, they form the interval of a third.

There are two kinds of intervals: harmonic and melodic.

The tones of the dominant seventh chord (V_7) resolve naturally to the tonic chord, establishing or reinforcing a tonality.

The tones of the subdominant (IV) chord frequently resolve to either the dominant seventh chord or the tonic chord.

When a feeling of partial or complete repose is suggested at the end of a phrase, the chords which communicate this feeling become a cadence.

The IV-I cadence is sometimes referred to as the "Amen" cadence.

Contemporary Harmony

One possible approach to contemporary harmony could take place after students have worked with chords in traditional harmony. The teacher might ask, "What would happen if chords were built of fourths rather than thirds?" and let the students find out by their experimenting with fourths. Then the teacher might ask the same question about fifths, sevenths, and seconds. The teacher might also ask, "What kinds of chords are needed to harmonize a composition written in the whole-tone scale? Write one and be ready to tell the class about those chords."

Music of today is in a period of unprecedented experimentation. It is described by some as involving deliberate abandonment of the traditional harmonic system. The absence of tonal centers, the use of parallel chords, chords built on fourths, and other such practices are characteristic of contemporary harmony. It is likely that such music will continue to be a part of the contemporary music scene. Music educators have the responsibility to help children think musically in both traditional and contemporary harmony.

Recordings useful in exploring contemporary harmony include the following:

Bartók, "Bear Dance" from *Hungarian Sketches* AM, grade 3, vol. 2

Bartók, *Concerto for Orchestra*. (quartal harmony—chords built in fourths)

Copland, "Circus Music" from *The Red Pony*, AM grade 3, vol. 1 (tone clusters, polytonality)

Harris, *Folk-Song Symphony*, Vanguard (contemporary harmonizations of U.S. folk songs)

Hindemith, *Mathis der Maler*, Columbia (harmony constructed of fourths and fifths)

Honneger, "March" from *King David*, Vanguard (polytonality: three keys at one time)

Ives, "Putnam's Camp" from *Three Places in New England*, BOL 75; Columbia; Mercury (bitonality; describes two bands playing in different keys). Also *Fourth of July*, Columbia MS-6889 and *Variations on America*, Columbia MS-7269 and Victor LSC-2893.

Milhaud, "Copacabana" from *Saudades do Brazil*, AM, grade 4, vol. 2 (bitonality, dissonance).

Milhaud, "Laranjeires" from *Saudades do Brazil*, AM, grade 4, vol. 2 (dissonance, bitonality)

Shoenberg, *Survivor from Warsaw* from *Recordings for The Enjoyment of Music* by Joseph Machlis.

Sounds of New Music, Folkways FX 6160 (electronic music, tone clusters. See music of Charles Ives and Henry Cowell.)

Varèse, *Ionization* from *Recordings for The Enjoyment of Music,* by Joseph Machlis.

Webern, *The Complete Music,* Columbia K4L 232 (tone row music)

Electronic music is bringing about a reexamination of current definitions for most aspects of music. In electronic music, the simultaneous sounding of two tone qualities, with or without definite pitch, is nevertheless harmony. Polyphony in electronic music may consist of simultaneous sounding of different streams or bands of sounds that produce a contrapuntal effect. Composers who have worked with electronic music include Karlheinz Stockhausen, Milton Babbitt, Mario Davidovsky, and Morton Subotnick.

Additional Suggestions for Lesson Plans

Pitch Discrimination *Pitch.* Game: Children turn their backs to the teacher, identify the sound source, and tell which of two sounded pitches is higher. Later, they are asked to match the pitches with their voices if the pitches lie in their normal singing ranges.

Vocal imitation. Children are asked to imitate by singing, whistling, or with other mouth sounds, the sounds of birds, animals, musical instruments, train whistles, auto horns, and other environmental sounds.

High, low. Game: The teacher of young children selects simple instruments or other sound sources that produce only one pitch. The children (one, two, or three at a time) experiment with them and compare their high and low sounds. Later the teacher mixes the sound sources and the children are asked to group them into those that produce high pitches and those that produce low pitches.

High, low. The children relate high and low pitches to relative high and low positions of the body. As an extension, the teacher plays selected pitches on a pitched percussion instrument while a small group of children indicate with marks on the blackboard the relative pitch levels heard. Under the teacher's guidance the children then find the various pitch levels in speaking voices, tone bars on other pitched percussion instruments, and different-sized drums. The teacher then directs the class toward such generalizations as "the larger the sound source, the lower the pitch."

High, low. Game: When the children hear the highest of three pitches (e.g., middle C, the C an octave above, and the G between), they raise their hands over their heads for the highest pitch; they stretch their hands out in front of them for the middle pitch; and place their hands on their thighs (or hips, if standing) for the lowest pitch. Having eyes closed prevents children from imitating others.

Inner hearing. The children learn the concept of inner hearing by singing the phrases of a known song loudly and softly. The soft phrases are sung ever softer, until they are silent. At that point the phrase is not audible, but is heard internally.

Improvised question-and-answer. The class learns to use tonal conversations in which the teacher sings questions, comments, or directions to which the children improvise singing replies. They may use any pitches they like. Examples:

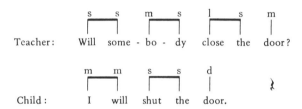

Hand signs for sol, mi. The children learn the Curwen (or Kodály) hand signs for *sol* and *mi* (see p. 351). The teacher sings various combinations of the two pitches; the children listen, then respond with singing and the appropriate body responses. Later, tonal patterns are related to rhythm syllables and to abbreviated notation:

Hand sign for la. The teacher shows the hand sign for *la* and asks the children to sing with the three familiar hand signs (*mi* and *la*). Game: The teacher makes hand signs for some sequence of the three pitches. The children watch, think silently what the pitches will sound like, then at the teacher's signal, sing the pitches the signs indicate.

Children's chant: 5–3–6–5–3. This tonal pattern can be used in various creative combinations. As the teacher introduces it, the pitch levels can be demonstrated by the teacher's hand.

```
s            l          s    s    m
Port  -    land,       O  - re - gon

s    s    s    l      s    m
Mis - si - sip - pi   Ri - ver

s    l      s    s    m    s    s    l    l    s    s    m
Rain, rain,  go  a - way,  come a - gain some o - ther day.
```

```
m    s    l    s    m    l    s    m
The  bus  is   com - ing, let's go  home.

s    s    l    s    s    m    s    s    l    s
Moth-er   is   wait-ing, and she's all  a  - lone.
```

Name songs. Using a pitched percussion instrument, the teacher isolates bars C D E G A, and has each child play a melody representing the rhythm of his or her name.

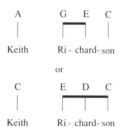

After playing the melody, the class sings the name with the words and with "sol-fa" syllables.

Improvisation on a drone. The teacher plays a repeated drone interval of a perfect fifth on the piano or low-pitched xylophone, metallophone, or cello. While listening to the drone, a child or small group experiments vocally, relating its improvised pitches to the drone.

Tonal memory, inner hearing. Words, syllables, or numbers can be used. The teacher or a child hums a familiar melody, or sings it with a neutral syllable such as *la* or *loo*. The children then try to identify the melody. After it is identified, the entire class may sing it with the leader.

Hand signs for "re" and "do". The teacher shows the hand signs for these pitches, then uses scale tones 1, 2, 3, 5, 6 for songlike drills and for the creation of melodies and songs by the children. Eventually the teacher shows the pitches on the staff and explains, "This is what the notes look like when the melody sounds that way."

Improvising endings. The teacher provides the first two measures of a four-measure phrase. Individual children improvise vocally the final two measures to complete it, and then the class echos the whole phrase. Example:

Hand sign for "fa". The hand sign for scale tone 4 (*fa*) is shown. The teacher slowly sings the pitches 1, 2, 3, 4, 5, 6 in syllables or numbers. Children make hand signs to match each pitch as it is sung. Later the teacher sings these pitches with *loo* or *la* (neutral syllables), and the children continue to identify the pitches by hand signs.

Tonality. The teacher analyzes the melodies of known songs to find and notate pitches forming the scales upon which these songs are constructed. They may be major, minor, pentatonic, or modal scales. The teacher assists the students in discovering that the final pitch of a song is a fairly reliable clue to the first step of the scale. Example: "Wayfaring Stranger" page 307. Some students may decide that the scale is D minor; others may find a pentatonic scale with D as the tonic (tonal center).

Note values and composing. Students select a simple poem of four phrases to be set to music. The teacher gives the children the first phrase with the pitches written in even note values. The words are placed under the staff, and the class changes note values to correspond to the rhythm suggested by the words. Then the teacher assigns groups to compose the melody for the other three phrases. The class evaluates the results and suggests changes if these seem necessary. When the song is completed, the class sings it.

Modulating melodies. The teacher challenges the class to learn to read examples of modulating melodies with syllables and with hand signs. Example:

d r m f   s l s   d t l t   d d   s f m r   d r d

**Scales and the
Tonal Center**

Scale. Game. The teacher writes the major scale vertically on the chalkboard in numbers or syllables. The class sings the pitches to which the teacher points, making it very easy at first, then increasing the difficulty as the children master the relation of the pitches to the scale.

Major and minor. The teacher has the class sing "Merrily We Roll Along" in a major key, with a simple chorded accompaniment. Then the teacher sings it in a minor key, again with a simple chorded accompaniment. The class is asked to describe the difference, and then to sing it with the teacher. The same activity may be done with other familiar songs.

Key signatures. The teacher explores the reasons for the use of key signatures with the class. Simple familiar songs are played with arbitrarily changed key signatures, and the results are discussed.

Pentatonic scale. Students relate the common pentatonic scale to the black keys of keyboard instruments. This scale pattern of whole steps and minor thirds is transposed to the keys of C, F, and G. Students compare the pentatonic scale pattern to the major scale pattern in those keys. Students use these scales to compose pentatonic songs and melodies. As an extension, students may listen to a recording of pentatonic music such as Bartók's *An Evening in the Village* (AM, grade 5, vol. 2).

Minor chords. Students relate major and minor scales to major and minor chords by singing and playing the first, third, and fifth steps of each scale. The teacher plays paired chords such as D major and D minor or G major and G minor, helping the students learn to hear the differences between major and minor tonalities. This exercise may need to be repeated many times.

Minor chords. The teacher plays "We Three Kings of Orient Are." Students are asked to indicate each minor chord that they hear in the harmonization by raising a hand. The same exercise can take place as students listen to Bizet's "Farandole" from *L'Arlésienne Suite No. 2* AM, grade 6, vol. 1.

Major and minor keys. The teacher has the class sing "Streets of Laredo" and has students determine when it is in a major key, when it is in a minor key, and where the change occurs.

Natural minor. The teacher assists the students in finding the natural minor scale pattern by beginning the scale on *la,* or scale tone 6 of the major scale in any given key. The class determines its pattern of whole and half steps, which the teacher draws on the board. Students compare this natural minor scale pattern with the major scale pattern, and play examples of each on a pitched percussion instrument or keyboard. As an extension, the class may compose melodies in this minor tonality.

Whole-tone scale. The teacher reviews the pattern of a whole-tone scale with the class. The class then converts "Polly Wolly Doodle" to a whole-tone scale, which the teacher writes on the board. The class then sings it from notation.

Invented scales. Students invent their own original scales, which might have as few as four steps or as many as twelve. During the activity, the teacher plays each scale to help the student determine whether any changes are desired. The class then writes simple melodies based on these scales.

EXPLORATORY ACTIVITIES

1. Make a collection of songs with limited range such as middle C to G or A above that can help the underdeveloped singer match tones, and eventually sing in tune.
2. Develop a list of songs that employ minor or pentatonic scales for future use in teaching.
3. Compose songs or melodies using major, minor, pentatonic, and whole-tone scales.
4. Select several songs and analyze them to determine which notes determine the supporting chords of their accompaniment. Rehearse those chord changes on an appropriate chordal instrument.
5. Find recorded examples of twentieth-century music in which there is no detectable key center. Develop a plan for using such music as part of the elementary music curriculum.

References

APFELSTADT, HILARY, "Melodic Perception Instruction—What Is Its Effect Upon Pitch Discrimination and Vocal Accuracy Among Kindergarten Children," *Update, 4/2,* Spring 1986, 6–8.

_____ . ''The Teaching of Pitch Perception in Elementary Vocal Music: A Survey of the Literature,'' *Update, 2*/3, Summer 1984, 3–6.

BERGER, MELVIN, *The Science of Music,* New York: Thomas Y. Crowell (Distributed by Harper & Row), 1989.

HACKETT, PATRICIA, *The Melody Book.* Englewood Cliffs, N. J.: Prentice-Hall, 1983.

JORDAN-DeCARBO, J., ''The Effect of Pretraining Conditions and Age on Pitch Discrimination Ability of Preschool Children,'' *Journal of Research in Music Education, 37*/2, Summer 1989, 132–145.

SWINDEL, WARREN E., ''The Development of Pitch and Rhythm Skills: The Research of Edwin Gordon,'' *Update, 3*/1, Fall 1984, 3–11.

Suggested Films   *Melody,* Oxford Films. (Distributed by AIMS Media, 6901 Woodley Ave., Van Nuys, CA 91406.)

Music Makers, Universal Education and Visual Arts, Universal Studios, 100 Universal City Plaza, Universal City, CA 91608.

8 Teaching Children to Sing

The Child's Voice

The child who sings naturally and in tune is musically equipped for the rest of life. Children begin to learn to sing when they first utter sounds. The cooing sounds of an infant may be described as early singing, and in human development they precede speech. Singing is initially a natural expression, preceding the cultural tendency to match pitches of other voices. In its mature form, the human voice is capable of a surprisingly wide variety of vocal feats including extreme ranges, unusual vocal techniques, varied tone quality, and a wide range of expression.

Research Studies on the way children learn to sing have led to the following conclusions:

A preliminary step to singing is the production of premusical phrases, or *subsongs,* by very young children.

Many more boys than girls experience difficulty in singing in tune.

About 18 percent of elementary school children may be undeveloped singers.

The child must learn to differentiate his or her singing voice from the speaking voice.

As an early singing skill the child must experience unison with another voice, and learn to match tones at will.

Intervals no smaller than a minor third are easiest for young children to sing.

Part of the difficulty in matching pitches comes from poor vocal control.

Out-of-tune singing may be a symptom of other learning problems.

An opinion survey which led to a publication titled *Finding and Learning to Use the Singing Voice: A Manual for Teachers* by A. Oren Gould estimates that children who teachers would classify as "nonsingers" comprise 50 percent of all first graders. The percentage of children that teachers classified as "problem singers" was 36.6 percent in the first grade with a gradual reduction to 11 percent in the sixth grade. This study claims to have established two basic principles of learning to sing: (1) the child must learn to hear his or her own voice in speaking or singing, and to control high and low pitch levels with it, and (2) the child must experience unison with another voice and learn the sound and feeling of his or her own voice as it matches the pitches heard. Both visual and tonal associations are needed to develop concepts of high and low in speaking and singing. Recommended activities include speech-to-song activities; repeated patterns in play or game songs like those found in echo-songs, songs about animals, and roll-call songs; use of humming and neutral syllables; body movements of many types which dramatize pitch and tonal direction; and mechanical devices such as pitched percussion instruments and keyboards to hear and to visualize pitch changes. The survey revealed "a certain amount of consensus" in the following:

1. All children can be helped to participate to some extent in singing activities with enjoyment and success.

2. Inability to sing a prescribed pitch does not prove that the child cannot hear pitch differences; it may mean only that he or she has not yet learned "what it feels like" to use his or her own voice in unison with another.
3. The most common vocal problem is that of the low speaking voice coupled with the child's inability to sing comfortably at the higher pitch the teacher prescribes for the class.
4. Many of the children's psychological inhibitions toward singing can be traced to attitudes and remarks of parents and teachers.
5. Remedial measures in the group are more easily employed during kindergarten through grade 3; in later grade levels more individual attention is necessary.

In a review of recent research associated with the singing of children in general music classes, Goetze, Goetze, Cooper, and Brown (1990) reported on several important findings. They discussed a number of studies related to children's singing abilities, the processes required for accurate singing, pitch discrimination, vocal range, factors that affect vocal accuracy, and other related topics. They summarized their findings with the following statements, each of which was discussed briefly:

1. A positive relationship exists between age and singing ability.
2. Additional research is needed to clarify the relationship between pitch discrimination ability and vocal accuracy.
3. The vocal range children demonstrate may be affected by the vocal register they use. Both register and range can be influenced by the presence, pitch, and quality of the vocal model.
4. Additional research is needed regarding the influence on singing of melodic direction, intervals, and the placement of intervals within patterns of singing.
5. The effects of harmonic accompaniment on children's singing are not clearly established.
6. Children appear to sing more accurately with a female model. Those learning from a male model may take longer to match pitches consistently.
7. There may be a difference in the accuracy of young children who sing alone compared with those singing with another voice. In some cases singing alone is more helpful to the development of pitch accuracy.
8. Findings are inconsistent on the question of whether it is better to learn to sing with or without a text.
9. Breath control training may be an effective way to improve singing accuracy in general music classes.
10. Reinforcement through verbal and/or visual feedback following a performance significantly improves children's singing.
11. Inaccurate singers do benefit from vocal instruction. Various techniques have been identified that appear to be especially helpful, such as "vertical keyboard activities" and "activities going from speech to song."

The study concludes with an important bibliography on children's singing.

Voice Production and Range

The child's voice is often described as being light in quality as well as soft in volume. It is also an extremely flexible mechanism, as illustrated by the strident cries of the playground. The teacher, then, is confronted by a voice that is capable of expressing many sounds in song. Since there are many moods to express, the child's voice might be soft and ethereal as it sings "Twinkle, Twinkle, Little Star" and might be momentarily rambunctious as it sings "Hokey Pokey." A logical way of deciding on the voice quality desired in any song is for the teacher and children to discuss what manner of voice should be used to express the meaning of the words properly and to evaluate this continually when they sing. Although the child voice is light in quality, it should not sound weak or overly soft.

Throughout the elementary school years, the teacher can help children learn to sing by focusing on the following suggestions:

1. Make a generally pleasing sound (simple, natural, and clear).
2. Sing in a free manner that avoids strain and tenseness.
3. Support the voice by taking natural, deep breaths.
4. Learn to sing on pitch.
5. Enunciate clearly, and sound final consonants distinctly and in unison.

Stages in Learning to Sing

First Year
>   Cooing and babbling
>   Imitating others
>   First sustained pitches intentionally produced

Second Year
>   Spontaneous vocal fragments produced
>   Intervals of seconds and thirds audible
>   Awareness of songs sung by others
>   First attempts to reproduce song fragments

Third Year
>   Spontaneous singing
>   Developing sense of rhythm in songs, especially through simple movements and finger plays
>   First efforts to reproduce short songs
>   Little sense of tonality

Fourth Year
>   Rapidly increasing verbal ability
>   Awareness of the meaning of songs
>   Increased ability to duplicate song rhythms
>   Developing awareness of melodic direction and contour
>   Little sense of tonality

Fifth Year
>   Emerging recognition of the pulse in songs
>   Ability to reflect a steady beat in singing
>   Beginning realization of tonality

Individual voices vary greatly in range, particularly in their ability to sing high pitches. Three-year-olds generally sing in a range of three to five notes:

4- and 5-year-olds sing in a range of five to six notes. Throughout the primary grades the preferred range is six notes (middle C to A above).

The range within which most songs in series books are written is the following:

The range seems to be a basic one; it suits most adult voices well, and is also the playing range of many of the small wind instruments. With good vocal instruction, the teacher can help most children in the upper elementary grades sing the following expanded range:

There should be no hesitancy on the part of teachers to vary from these ranges on occasion. It is obvious that there are different ranges for different age groups and for boys and girls at some levels. However, all children, even in kindergarten and first grade, should be encouraged to use all of their comfortable range, especially that of middle C to fourth line D.

Teachers often search for songs of limited range with which to initiate easy singing experiences. Examples follow:

3-note range:	Hot Cross Buns	Trampin' (refrain)
	Merrily We Roll Along	Fais do do (Go to Sleep)
	Good News (refrain)	(first part)
4-note range:	Sally Go Round the Sun	A-Hunting We Will Go
	Hokey Pokey	(one version)
5-note range:	Go Tell Aunt Rhody	Whistle, Daughter, Whistle
	Cradle Song (Rousseau)	Old Woman (some versions)
	Lightly Row	When the Saints Go
	Sleep, Baby, Sleep	Marching In
	Mary Had a Little Lamb	Jingle Bells (refrain)
	Oats, Peas, Beans, and Barley	Hey, Lidee
	Flowing River	Love Somebody
6-note range:	This Old Man	Caisson Song
	Baa Baa Black Sheep	Jolly Old St. Nicholas
	Old MacDonald	Up on the Housetop
	London Bridge	Au Clair de la Lune
	Lovely Evening	Susy, Little Susy

Hey, Betty Martin	The Mocking Bird
Skip to My Lou	Tom Dooley
Goodbye, My Lover, Goodbye	Twinkle, Twinkle, Little Star
O Susanna	Old Paint
Old Brass Wagon	Michael, Row the Boat Ashore
Pop! Goes the Weasel	Cindy
Hickory Dickory Dock	Kum Bah Yah
Looby Lou	Bluebird

When a textbook presents a song in a particular key, the writers have selected that key with the child's vocal range in mind. There may be considerations, however, that lead teachers to change this range. Most of the songs in recent books are pitches in an easy, fairly low range, even though the child's natural placement for singing is the head voice. The teacher has the option of (1) transposing the song to a higher key before teaching it, or (2) after a song has been learned, pitching it higher. Other songs may be printed in keys that demand a high range. Should a class be as yet unable to reach this range, the teacher may transpose these songs somewhat lower—usually not more than two whole steps.

Teachers need to be able to change the key of a song when the stage of development of the children's voice range makes this advisable. This can be done by establishing the primary chords of the new key (e.g., tonic, subdominant, and dominant) on a keyboard, guitar, or autoharp, and determining the beginning pitch of the song in this new tonality.

The matter of correct pitching of songs becomes more complex in the sixth grade, where some of the boys may be in the first stage of voice change. The full range of these voices normally drops approximately a fourth; thus a well-developed range of B^b below middle C up to top line F drops to a range of from F on the bass staff extending up to an octave above middle C.

Since the highest and lowest pitches of any range may be more difficult to sing than the middle pitches, teachers select music that does not stress these extremes. The implications are two: first, that boys cannot sing many of the melodies in sixth grade songbooks as they are written, and second, that this problem cannot be ignored by the teacher. To sustain interest in singing, the teacher plans musical numbers or vocal parts boys can sing easily in their range, and takes special care to provide for individual differences. Low harmony parts and chord root parts (parts derived from the root tones of the chords) may be helpful for some.

A successful music specialist knows that the natural range of the child's unchanged voice is fairly high when properly developed. Vocal range depends upon correct breathing, breath support, and voice production. In intermediate grade classes, exercises in breathing may be helpful. One appropriate exercise is to have the students stand "proudly" with arms hanging freely at their sides, and take deep breaths while noting that their voluntary muscles below the waist make this possible. Shoulders should remain level, and the breath should be expelled as though they were flickering the flame of a candle, but not blowing it out. This and other exercises, such as holding a small piece of paper against a wall with the breath for gradually longer periods of time, are done to develop breath control.

To extend the range further, students can vocalize up and down the first five tones of the major scale with vowels such as *ah, oh,* and *oo.* It is important that this exercise begin high enough that the children will be using the head voice. The exercise is then performed one half step lower each time, working to bring the techniques of head voice production to the lower part of the range. The jaw should be held naturally and loose. The teacher takes special care not to injure voices by vocalizing them too high or too low, and can tell by the facial expression when the children are straining to sing pitches beyond their range.

A problem of some classroom teachers is that they have not learned to use their own singing voices properly, and therefore hesitate to sing pitches they consider high. Many have used only a chest voice which they try to force upward in an attempt to sing high pitches. They need to learn to sing in their head voices in a fairly straight tone, free of vibrato.

The teacher needs a clear, natural voice. Children are attracted by singing that sounds natural and normal. The male teacher's voice is no longer as rare as it once was in elementary school music. Most children are well oriented to listening to and singing with this octave-lower voice on recordings, television, and radio as well as at home with their fathers. Once in a while a child is confused by it and tries to match its pitch. When this occurs, the male teacher should explain that his voice changed, and that he cannot sing as high as the children. He should play the song on an instrument that gives proper pitch, have a child who knows the song sing it, or sing falsetto. In instances where teachers believe they cannot sing well enough to use their singing voices in teaching music, they can employ substitutions such as recordings, musical instruments such as the soprano recorder, and children who sing well.

Some physical requirements for good singing follow:

1. *Posture.* Place feet on the floor with the weight of the body somewhat forward, not on the back of the chair. Sit up straight, but not in a stiff or tense way. If standing, place the weight of the body toward the toes, not on the heels.
2. *Breathing.* Fill the abdominal region with air first (i.e., breathe "low," not high in the chest). The goal in breathing is a supported, continuous flow of breath. A husky or breathy sound indicates wasted breath.
3. *Open Throat.* Use an open, relaxed throat. Sing with the mouth open, but not so wide that it causes tension.
4. *Good Enunciation.* Open the mouth and use lips and tongue precisely in pronouncing words. Be sure to pronounce final consonants distinctly.

Poor results often come from singing too loudly, singing too softly, opening the mouth insufficiently, a slouching posture, a stiff and tense posture, a lack of interest, an unhealthy room temperature, and failure of the teacher to have the children focus on the pitch and harmonic background of a song before asking them to sing it. For elementary school children singing should be a natural, relaxed expression. The teacher should refrain from emphasizing the physical requirements for good singing, which may cause the children to be self-conscious.

The Changing Voice While soprano voices remain in the majority at ages 11 and 12, the voices of some students become somewhat heavier in quality, reflecting the beginning of the changing voice. Some boys' voices will be breathy, with the upper range faltering while the lower range drops, although there are many variations. The teacher should take great care that music is provided to accommodate the range of every voice. Straining to reach high pitches must be avoided to prevent permanent voice damage. The teacher may need to write special parts for changing voices when printed music cannot supply the required ranges. Simple ostinati are useful.

There are few true alto voices among girls, and most music for this age group is of a range that permits every child to experience singing several parts. Parts other than the melody present the best challenge for note reading in most music. Older boys' voices could be classified as soprano, cambiata (changing), and baritone. Voice testing is best done quickly in small groups because individual testing can cause tension and embarrassment. The teacher listens for both range and quality to determine assignment of parts. Cooper and Kuersteiner (1972) present class voice testing in detail. Part of their suggested method is to have the boys sing "Jingle Bells" in D major. This results in some boys singing naturally in the upper octave, and others in the lower octave. Those who choose to sing in the lower octave are baritones. The remaining boys sing the song in A♭ major while the teacher listens to detect soprano voices. After the sopranos are determined, those remaining are the cambiata (changing voices).*

Pitch Discrimination and Learning to Sing

Some 6- and 7-year-olds confuse the terms *high* and *low* as they relate to music. Young children sometimes associate *high* with *loud* and *fast* and *low* with *soft* and *slow*. This is perhaps because the concepts of high and low in pitch are abstractions; the association of high and low pitch with high and low physical levels is artificial, however necessary for understanding. To make these experiences concrete for children, teachers often associate "high" and "low" pitches with high and low physical position both with the body and with objects, in pictures, and by relating to things in the child's world such as airplanes, trees, and stars (high), floor, rug and grass (low). Step bells and pitched percussion

*A publisher specializing in music for the changing voice is Cambiata Press, P.O. Box 1151, Conway, AR 72032.

instruments can be held on end with the large bars down to demonstrate differences in pitch. Teachers employ songs in kindergarten which children dramatize and later relate by discussion to high and low. One of them is the "Pussywillow Song."

Children are taught to play little action games in first grade by having the teacher sing the following while the children respond with appropriate actions:

The example relates high and low to widely spaced pitches illustrating these words and dramatizing them in terms of physical movement. The following example is relatively more complex:

Many simple examples of songs useful in teaching these basic concepts are to be found in series books on kindergarten and first grade levels. However, teachers can improvise their own songs for this purpose.

Acting out the melody line of songs in terms of pitch levels is a device that aids people of all ages to be more conscious of differences in pitch. The hand is used with a generous motion to move up, down, or to stay the same according to differences in pitch. When children are guided to respond in this manner, their concepts of pitch relationships often improve to a remarkable degree. In the preceding example the hand would move vertically to reflect the melodic contour:

The fact that at a certain stage of development a child does not sing in tune in no way proves lack of musicality. It is clearly possible for an out-of-tune singer to be an excellent musician. Among the reasons for people's inability to match tones with their singing voices are generally immaturity, a minimal musical environment, psychological blocks imposed by adults who tell them they cannot sing, failure to try as a result of fear, lack of sufficient energy behind the tone, and rarely, physical abnormalities requiring the attention of a physician. If the teacher establishes a favorable environment and works with the child properly, virtually every child can sing in tune. However, if the teacher does not establish the pitch, if there is a confusing accompaniment, or if the psychological situation is one where muscles become tense, the child will probably fail to match tones.

In most cases, inability to sing in tune should disappear during the elementary school years if children are given consistent help. In today's schools there are often a few students in the upper grades who cannot match tones consistently. Teachers should be ready to assist these students in singing accurately while sustaining their musical interest through a program of varied activities—rhythmic responses, playing instruments, creating music, reading about music and musicians, experimenting with musical concepts, and continuing to try to sing on pitch.

During some stages of development, children do not sense the pitch of their own voices and often sing loudly (and happily) off key. In some cases the child deliberately sings off key to hear his or her own voice. There arise the following problems: (1) how to help children to listen, (2) how to keep these voices from hindering other children who are trying to keep on pitch, (3) how to help them to make as real a contribution to the group as the children who sing well, and (4) in the upper grades, how to help them with their errors in such a way that they are encouraged to remain confident of eventual success.

For young children who have not yet learned how to sing, the chanting of rhymes such as "Humpty Dumpty", "Mary, Mary Quite Contrary" and "Rub-a-Dub-Dub, Three Men in a Tub" can be helpful. Children like the feel of rhyming or repetitious words; they enjoy saying them together. If the teacher establishes the pitch of a low note such as middle C and helps them chant the words on that pitch, a beginning can be made in singing one-pitch songs.

Many of the children who cannot match tones try to sing with the same voice they use when they speak. Therefore, it is the task of the teacher to help such children distinguish between their speaking and singing voices. This may be done in a game situation. A favorite device is to have children pretend to be the wind, a bird, or a siren. Children often sense pitch differences more keenly through actions such as the teacher's lifting a child's hand up high, or the children's starting from a squatting position (low) and moving to a standing position (high). Another popular device is to have a child pretend to call someone who is far away. When this is done, a sustained speech results—and when speech is thus sustained (vowel held) singing takes place.

When a child sings, but sings low and does not match the anticipated pitch, the teacher and class may want to try matching the child's pitch and singing the song in that key.

The term *tone-matching* is not intended to convey emphasis upon isolated drill. Echo-songs and games may help uncertain singers. Such a song or game may be sung by a class, and a child may be selected to sing a part at the correct time. The part sounds at the right time because the teacher sings with the child in case of faltering. Little or no attempt is made to correct faulty pitch while the song is being sung. Sometimes the teacher must wait weeks and months for some children to sing in tune.

A commonly used device for listening and tone-matching is the calling of children's names in song and having each child answer "here" or some other appropriate response on the same pitches. The teacher varies the pitch of these conversations-in-song, singing to each child in the range in which success will be most likely. Later, the purpose of the teacher will vary according to the progress of each child. Some successful singers may begin to improvise answers on pitches other than those the teacher sings; little question-and-answer tunes are created in this manner.

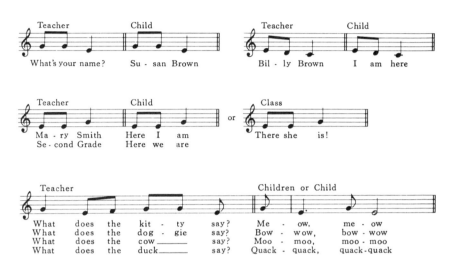

The teacher can sing questions such as, "What did you do last Sunday?" and "What did you have for breakfast?" and the child can create an answer with rhythmic and melodic variety. When a child has difficulty in matching tones with the teacher in any of these tone games, matching tones to another child's singing may solve the problem. It is not wise to remain working with any one child too long in any of these procedures. To do so would make the other children restless, and it would unduly draw the child's attention to a relative lack of success.

A further aid to listening is the suggestion that the children "tune in" their voices just as they tune in radio stations. This is a concept children can understand because they know that the dial must be in exactly the right place for the station to come in properly. Another suggestion is to sing a familiar grouping of tones (or even a single pitch) for the children while they listen. Then ask them to listen with their "inner ears" while this is repeated for them. Next, ask the children to sing it. Finally, ask them if they sang exactly what they heard. Some of the children, who cannot yet match tones will know that they have not sung what they heard. This process, when repeated over weeks and months, has notably improved the ability to listen and to match tones, especially when the teacher plans so that part of the class listens to and evaluates the singing of groups within the class, thus involving every child in the room with either singing or listening. Spontaneous tone games such as creating a "song" from children's words—for example, "Johnny has a haircut,"—and having children sing these words or additional words of their own in turn can sometimes help.

Picking out melodies or parts of melodies on pitched percussion instruments or keyboard can be of value. These instruments are used with songs containing tones or tone patterns which are both played and sung. Listening for the proper time to play the instrument and being sure the correct pitches have been sounded constitute a good listening experience in a challenging context. It may provide the background that leads to eventual singing on pitch.

There are certain tonal patterns that are particularly easy for children to sing. If the teacher selects songs that contain these tonal patterns, and if they are repeated in songs with easy singing ranges, the group singing should improve. Among these tonal groups are the following:

Number 1 is the easiest interval for children to sing; it is the descending minor third (5–3). Number 2 is an extension of number 1; it is sung by children all over the world in their natural, undirected play. Number 3, a descending series of three tones in whole-step arrangement, and number 4, the ascending fourth, are easy to sing. Number 4, is often found in 5–8 position in major scales. Number 5, a pentatonic mode, is an important aspect of music children create spontaneously; songs based on it are easy to sing because no half steps are involved. "This Old Man" emphasizes the minor third. "Three Blind Mice" and "Mary Had a Little Lamb" stress the 3–2–1 note pattern, with the ascending fourth also stressed in "Three Blind Mice." The popularity of many songs can be traced to their utilization of these easily sung tonal patterns. It follows that if simple songs are pitched in appropriate keys, they can speed the progress of children in becoming skilled in tone-matching.

At times it is impossible to prevent the voices of out-of-tuners from hindering to some extent the progress of those children who are further advanced in singing skills. However, it would be unwise to make any obvious division of a class between in-tune singers and undeveloped singers. One exception would be when the teacher works with a small selected group of undeveloped singers outside of class to address specific problems with consistent tone-matching.

Careful listening is essential, but listening and never singing does not produce singers. Undeveloped singers should have many opportunities to listen to good examples of singing. These include the use of small groups or solo singers as examples, and the inclusion of some in-tune singers mixed in with the undeveloped singers when such temporary groupings are made. When undeveloped singers respond rhythmically to music, when they play the autoharp and pitched percussion instruments, and when they offer ideas for interpretation, dramatization, and experimentation, they are making real contributions to group music even though they are not yet independent singers. The increasing informality of seating in today's classrooms tends to make any rigid seating plans for music unlikely. The arrangement should not isolate undeveloped singers, but should place them between independent singers. It should also permit the teacher to move freely among the class in order to listen to each singer.

Children who cannot sing in tune often know that they cannot. Therefore, small group work apart from the class may be desirable. The teacher may work with out-of-tuners in groups of two or four, with each child paired with another of like voice quality and range. The teacher may place each child at a far corner of the room. The activity begins with a story of children who have become separated in the woods, and who are trying to find each other. One child is then asked to sing to a partner across the room as though the partner were far away. The call may be sung in two pitches—the descending minor third pattern, and the partner is to answer on the same pitches. When this contact through tone-matching has been established, they next begin singing other information back and forth, such as "Where are you?" "I'm over here," "Are you hungry?" and so on. Most children find that they can hear the pitch given to them in this way, and that they can answer it with surprising accuracy. After this introduction comes the repetition and extension of the singing back and forth, then eventually the singing of easy songs pitched in a range comfortable to the voices.

When a problem singer can experiment over a period of time with singing into a tape recorder and playing back what was taped, the interest generated can result in ultimately singing on pitch. "The excitement from hearing one's voice on tape may lead the problem singer or reluctant singer to work diligently toward any improvement of that sound, especially if the recording is made when alone or in a corner of the room, or even at home, with no one else to criticize or laugh. The child who never sings in person may proudly present the teacher with a recording revealing success" (Meske and Rinehart, 1975).

Some boys have musical difficulties that stem from attempting to imitate the low voices of adult males, and wanting to sound like men, not like their mothers, their female teachers, or girls. This issue should not be brought up by the teacher, but if students raise it, it can be overcome by explaining to the boys that their voices ordinarily change in grades 7 through 9. In fifth and sixth grades this is important to boys, and their understanding of this may determine whether they will use their still unchanged voices naturally or whether they will attempt to sing unnaturally lower. It is best to avoid using the adult terms "soprano" and "alto" and use instead "high" and "low." In three-part singing the parts are "high, middle, and low" rather than the terms descriptive of adult voices.

Establishing Pitch for Singing   One of the most common failings of teachers is not giving the children sufficient time to hear the beginning pitch of songs a class is reviewing. Too often the teacher "hears with the inner ear" the song in its proper harmonic setting, but forgets that many of the children are not hearing it. Too often these teachers sound a pitch and start the singing before children have had time to orient themselves to this pitch, its relation to the scale in which the song is to be sung, and the harmonic setting of the first tones of the melody. This failure to help children sense the pitch in its proper context places some of them at such a disadvantage that they are out-of-tune singers when they need not be. When reviewing a song with a class, the following procedure is recommended:

1. Sound the 1–3–5 (tonic) chord built from the keynote of the song on an instrument. The class then sings 1–3–5–3–1. This establishes a feeling for the key, and for the home tone in relation to the scale.
2. Sound at some length the initial note of the song. This should be sung or sounded on an instrument such as the piano or recorder.
3. Ask the children to sing it and help them to match it.
4. Set the tempo by singing in rhythm and on the opening pitch, "One, two, ready, sing." This preparation may be varied for different meters and for songs with pickup notes.

Selecting Songs for Tone-Matching

Melodies of songs may be analyzed to determine whether or not they are useful in "listen-then-sing" activities. There are songs with easily sung repeated-note patterns and phrases, songs with parts that can be echoed, songs with limited ranges, songs with final measures that can be repeated to create codas, question-and-answer songs, and dialogue songs. These permit children to sing in turn and to listen carefully to the singing of others. Three song examples follow, the first for intermediate level and the last two for primary level. The first example, "When the Saints Go Marching In," has a tone pattern repeated twice in the original melody, and can be used in this form. However, it is printed here in a specially arranged form to repeat the pattern four times, and to add another repeated pattern near the end. It is an example of how teachers arrange songs to adapt them to tone-matching. The song has a small range, and children enjoy its rhythm and spirit.

WHEN THE SAINTS GO MARCHING IN

New Orleans Song
Arr. R. E. N.

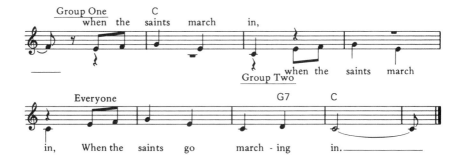

The second group must listen carefully to the first group, and is challenged to echo the tone pattern perfectly.

Examples of Other Echo-Type Songs
"Are You Sleeping?"
"By'm By"
"Barnyard Song"
"Sipping Cider Through a Straw"
"Three Blind Mice"
"Today Is Monday"
"Who Did?"
"Bill Grogan's Goat"
"Every Night When the Sun Goes In"
"How Do You Do?"
"If I Ask You"
"What Did You Do Last Summer?"
"John the Rabbit"
"Old Texas"

Examples of Other Repetitious Songs
"Good-bye, Old Paint"
"Hot Cross Buns"
"Rain, Rain, Go Away"
"Old Woman's Courtship"
"Polly Wolly Doodle"
"Tideo"
"Angel Band"
"Clickety-Clack"
"Hole in the Bucket"
"Tisket, a Tasket"
"Trampin' "
"Hush Little Baby"
"Whistle, Daughter, Whistle"

Tonal Memory   Tonal memory is necessary for the singer. Teachers can assist the development of tonal memory by activities such as the following:

1. Humming a familiar tune and asking the children to identify it; then asking children to hum it back to the teacher.
2. Arranging a signal whereby children stop singing during the performance of a familiar song, but continue to think the tune for a phrase or two. Then the teacher signals them to change from thinking the tune to singing it.
3. Playing a game in which children hum a tune for the class to identify.
4. Having the class sing songs with neutral syllables (*la, loo*) rather than the words so that the singers can concentrate on the melody.
5. Challenging the class to sing songs with numbers and/or syllables.
6. Challenging individual children to explore the black keys of the piano—to work alone to find the melodies of pentatonic tunes they know such as "*Old MacDonald,*" *All Night, All Day, Get on Board, Land of the Silver Birch, The Campbells Are Coming,* and *Swing Low, Sweet Chariot.*

Teaching Rote Songs

Selecting Songs for Rote Teaching

There are almost as many approaches to teaching rote songs as there are songs. However, the following guidelines have proved effective:

1. Choose a simple song appropriate in difficulty for the grade level.
2. Introduce the song through a visual clue or association—motivate students to want to learn the song.
3. Provide three hearings of the melody before asking students to echo its phrases:
   a. Sing it for the class at least once without accompaniment.
   b. Keep accompaniment simple and nondistracting.
   c. Give students a text feature for which to listen.
   d. Give students a musical feature for which to listen.
   e. Ask questions regarding the song's form or design, including such features as repetitions.
4. Teach the song by echo of phrases or the whole melody, giving a clear starting pitch and using hands to indicate who is singing.
5. After each of the first two phrases are echoed by the students, sing the combined phrases and have the class echo both phrases. This additive process continues until the whole song can be echoed.
6. Reinforce musical concepts within the song through repeated singing and listening.
7. Encourage students to improvise accompaniments and sound effects when appropriate.

Many short songs can be taught as complete songs rather than in sections. However, one of the easiest types to begin with is the song which calls for an answer. "John the Rabbit" is one in which children reply, singing the words "Yes, ma'am." "Old MacDonald" is another. Children want to sing "Ee-i-ee-i-o" while the teacher sings the rest of it.

OLD MACDONALD

American Song

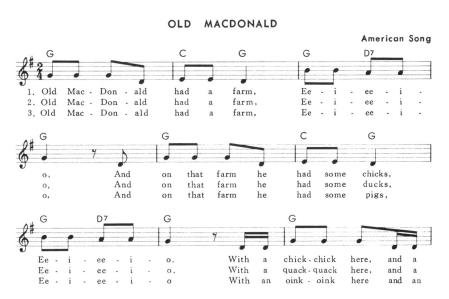

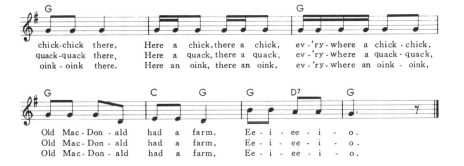

chick-chick there,   Here a chick, there a chick,   ev-'ry-where a chick-chick,
quack-quack there,   Here a quack, there a quack,   ev-'ry-where a quack-quack,
oink-oink there,   Here an oink, there an oink,   ev-'ry-where an oink-oink,

Old Mac-Don-ald had a farm,   Ee-i-ee-i-o.
Old Mac-Don-ald had a farm,   Ee-i-ee-i-o.
Old Mac-Don-ald had a farm,   Ee-i-ee-i-o.

"Old MacDonald" may be accompanied by a pentatonic ostinato and bordun.

After the children have learned to sing the three-pitch "Ee-i-ee-i-o" part, the teacher may suggest that they learn the one-pitch "Here a chick, there a chick, everywhere a chick-chick" section. Soon part of the class can sing the first two measures, "Old MacDonald had a farm," and another part can sing "Ee-i-ee-i-o"—and everyone sings "Here a chick," and so on. Soon the entire song can be sung by the class. It is always fun—and it adds variety—to have different groups sing different parts.

Young children react to rote learning in individual ways. Some may want to begin singing before they have listened to what they are to sing. There must be an understanding that they are to listen carefully before singing. The reason for their silence needs to be explained. Most of them will want to contribute actively as soon as possible; this is why songs with easy answering parts or parts suggesting simple physical responses are enjoyed and usually learned rather quickly. The logical procedure is to always work with the easiest parts first.

The echo-type song is one in which children sing parts that repeat pitch for pitch what the teacher has sung. "Are You Sleeping?" is one of this type. Every measure of this song is followed by an exact repetition. Thus the teacher presents it as a complete song first, then eventually asks the class to sing each part as an echo. Gestures are developed that indicate the teacher's turn to sing and the children's turn. "Old Texas" can be sung in the same manner; 6-year-olds who can sing on pitch perform it well. "Follow On" is an echo-song for older children. When they have learned the song, some of the children sing with the teacher, and ultimately the class can be divided into two groups, one of which sings the teacher's part.

ALL HID

Chorus   Traditional

All hid,   All hid,   All hid_____   All hid_____

Five, Ten, Fif - teen twen - ty, All___ hid, All___ hid.

Verse 1

This old man, He played one, He played Knick Knack on my thumb.

Knick Knack Pad-dy Wack, Give a dog a bone, This old man came rol-ling home.

Verse 2: *Horse and a flea and the three blind mice*
Sat on a curbstone, shootin' dice.
Horse he slipped and fell on the flea.
Whoops, said the flea, there's a horse on me!
(from: Boom, Boom, Ain't it Great to be Crazy)

CHORUS

Verse 3: *One elephant went out to play*
Upon a spider's web one day.
He had such enormous fun
That he called for another elephant to come.

Repetitious songs are easily taught by rote. "A-Tisket, A-Tasket" is a young children's song centered about the 5-3-6-5 tone pattern. Its singsong repetitiveness makes it easy for children to learn. Other songs of this type include "Tideo," "Rig-A-Jig-Jig," "Pick a Bale of Cotton," "Hole in the Bucket," and "Trampin' ".

After the teacher introduces "Trampin'" by singing it all the way through more than once, the children may begin entering on the chorus part, "Tryin' to make heaven my home." In reviewing the words and meaning of the song the teacher may ask, "What is the singer doing?" (trampin') "What is trampin'?" "Where is the singer going?" Later on, a child or group of children may sing the teacher's solo part, with everyone singing the chorus.

"Trampin'" is a call-and-response song; "Swing Low, Sweet Chariot" is another song of this type for older children. Both songs may be treated as pentatonic songs.

TRAMPIN'

Leisurely march tempo

Spiritual

I'm a - tramp - in, tramp - in, Tryin' to make heav-en my home,

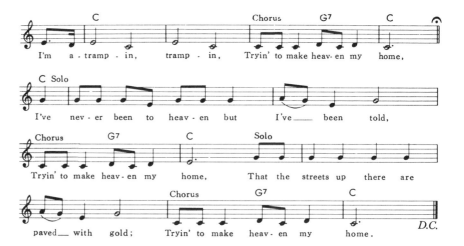

I'm a-tramp-in, tramp-in, Tryin' to make heav-en my home,

I've nev-er been to heav-en but I've____ been told,

Tryin' to make heav-en my home, That the streets up there are

paved__ with gold; Tryin' to make heav-en my home. *D.C.*

Music Concepts and Rote Teaching

While rote singing is a necessary step in musical growth, teachers who go no further than this type of teaching may promote music illiteracy. Phyllis E. Dorman (1967) writes, ''There is a certain dignity and logic in the simplest song. A song, any song, makes use of the same tools present in the most complicated of the musical classics. Every element is there: rhythm, melody, form, tonality, texture, dynamics, color, and aesthetics. Songs should be used to teach musical concepts.''

Although singing rote songs may take place at any level and with any age, more rote learning is necessary with very young children who cannot read notation. However, even rote songs contain elements the teacher can use to teach musical concepts and readiness for notation. Several examples follow:

Phrase. As the teacher sings the song, phrase order and repetition can be stressed. Young children can move in a circle while singing, changing directions for each phrase. Older students may sense the phrase order by listening and singing. Logical questions include ''How many phrases did you hear?'' ''Are there any that are the same?'' ''How many are different?''

Melodic direction and Contour. Children can level the contour of the melody with their hands as they sing.

Independent Singing. After the children have heard a song several times they should be able to sing it without the teacher's voice. The teacher can assist with high and low hand positions, joining in the singing only if absolutely necessary.

Texture. As children sing the song, different accompanying instruments may be used for varying textures.

Tone Quality. Tone qualities of voices and of accompanying instruments can be evaluated in terms of their suitability to the song.

Dynamics. The children can be encouraged to sing the song at different dynamic levels, and to determine those most suited to the song.

The teacher needs to learn the song thoroughly before attempting to teach it. In the lesson the children need to participate actively in learning the song as soon as possible. All the verses of a song do not need to be learned at first. The teacher should not plan to do too much with the song in one day. Possible activities for children to do while learning a rote song include the following:

Clapping hands (tips of fingers) without sound to the beat.

Clapping hands without sound to the rhythm of the words.

Listening for repeated rhythmic patterns.

Acting out pitch levels and melodic contours with hands and arms.

Listening for tonal patterns of notes that stay the same, move in steps, or move in skips.

Among its several purposes, teaching songs by rote can be designed to prepare students for concepts about standard notation. Some activities that build notational concepts include having older children

1. Compare the notation of two familiar songs of the same tempo, one which uses many eighth and sixteenth notes and another which has whole notes, half notes, and quarter notes.
2. Look for familiar rhythm patterns and note patterns in the notation of songs they have learned.
3. Look at the notation of phrases of familiar songs to find out that when phrases sound the same, they look the same, and when they sound different, they look different.
4. Watch the notated melody line as the song is sung, and follow it on the page with an index finger.

Recordings can be substituted for teachers' voices in teaching songs. Children learn some songs from recordings they play at home, and from radio and television programs. However, when recordings are used, many of the flexible techniques just suggested cannot be employed.

The children must sing softly in order to hear the recording. The volume of the record player can be gradually turned down as the children learn a song so that they will become increasingly independent of the recording. It is helpful to emphasize teaching the words when songs are learned by rote from recordings. They are frequently written with colored felt markers on big sheets of butcher paper and posted on the chalkboard or elsewhere.

The recordings that accompany the series books and some other songbooks can be of genuine value in teaching songs. More recent editions provide appropriate examples for children to hear and imitate. They often bring to the classroom fascinating instrumental accompaniments that could be provided in no other way. Some series books provide dual track recordings of songs, so that once a song has been learned, it may be sung with only the accompaniment track on one speaker. These recordings also assist the teacher in learning the songs correctly, both rhythmically and melodically. Beginning teachers should study the recordings that accompany the books they are to use in their classrooms before school begins in the fall. If they hear these over a period of time they will have absorbed a repertoire of songs they need to know for future lesson plans. No matter how well qualified a music specialist may be, there are times when a recording will provide an effective way to teach some songs.

The Piano and Other Voice Substitutes In addition to recordings, the recorder or a keyboard instrument may be substituted for the voice by teachers who lack confidence in their singing voices and do not have recordings of songs they need to teach. However, the teacher is encouraged to develop sufficient vocal skills for vocal modeling. Until that time the procedure for teaching songs with the assistance of recorder or keyboard follows the same guidelines outlined for rote singing. For a song of some length the phrase method may be desirable. After playing the entire song, the teacher plays the melody of the first phrase, which is echoed by the children. This can be continued throughout the remaining phrases, combining them along the way. As the song is learned, the support of the instrument is gradually withdrawn to establish the children's independence.

Although it is highly desirable to have a keyboard available, the instrument is not essential to teach or to accompany songs. In a normal situation where the teacher sings, the piano or synthesizer has its greatest use at the end of the learning process. A song may be introduced by playing it in a simple manner, for younger children find it difficult to hear a melody when an elaborate accompaniment is played. A simple accompaniment that permits the melody to predominate distinctly is the most effective style of playing. Most of the time the keyboard has little use, for three reasons: (1) when the teacher is playing it the children cannot be heard well enough to determine if each child is singing correctly, (2) the teacher is in a stationary position while playing the instrument, and is unable to move through the class to hear and to help children with their problems, (3) if it is used constantly the children cannot sing independently of it. If a guitar is used, these problems disappear. After a song has been learned, the addition of an appropriate accompaniment can be a satisfying experience, adding greatly to the musical effect of the performance.

Creating Songs

Teachers at all elementary levels should be alert to children's spontaneous creating of songs and calls. The child's earliest examples are spontaneous subsongs, which the teacher immediately sings back to reinforce what the child has sung. Other songs created by children may be notated or taped by the teacher for later use. The following song was created by a child and notated and used by the teacher:

A BEAUTIFUL DAY

First Grade, Washington School
Eugene, Oregon

Oh what a won-der-ful day,   Oh what a won-der-ful

day!   Oh   what   a   beau - ti - ful   day!

When the teacher heard the child singing this song, she asked the child to repeat it and they sang it together so they could remember it. When they returned to the classroom they shared it with the others. Another teacher of a first grade group had just concluded a reading lesson in which children had learned new words. It was shortly before lunch, and the children suddenly related the new words to their interest in food:

1. One   two   three,   come   eat   with   me.
2. Blue   and   red,   will   we   be   fed?

The classroom teacher is in the most strategic position to establish an environment in which children feel comfortable creating music. The teacher knows the interests of the children and has most to do with encouraging creative responses. Children are normally creative, and when they find they have the ability to compose simple songs or instrumental pieces, they will frequently do this at home as a play activity, bringing their compositions to school.

Creating simple songs is an ability that grows under the guidance of capable teachers. It is only a short step from spontaneous creative activity to a teacher saying of a well-known poem, "Let's sing it today instead of speaking it," and the setting of poetry to music becomes a classroom activity.

Short verse that has a clearly defined rhythm is most appropriate material for original melodies. As a background for this activity children should have chanted many short poems and simple word rhythms. In chanting, the words are spoken by the children in a regular beat pattern set by the teacher. A pentatonic scale for the melody of the poem can be used, or a diatonic scale can be used by older students. While the teacher maintains the meter, individual children are asked to sing the poem. The other children may be urged to continue to speak the words softly while they listen to the melody take shape. If the rhythm is maintained, many children will be able to create a melody as spontaneous and uninhibited as speech. It is as natural for children to have many musical ideas as it is for them to have many verbal ideas. This approach to song creation can be effective on any level.

Instruments are sometimes helpful in stimulating the creative process. In one example, a teacher used four tone bars on a pitched percussion instrument with a first grade class. The children were interested in new shoes, which several of them had worn that day. With the aid of the four tones they created a song on the subject, "New Shoes," which they also learned to play on the instrument. Its repetitious words are typical of first grade children. This song was sung throughout the term whenever one of the children came to school with new shoes.

NEW SHOES

Laboratory School
University of Wisconsin
Milwaukee

New shoes, new shoes, nice, new clean shoes.

New shoes, new shoes, nice, new shoes.

Melodies without words are created by children who have opportunities to experiment with tuned water bottles, pitched percussion instruments, keyboards, recorders, and instruments of the band and orchestra.

If a teacher has had ear training, he or she can notate the music when the children create a song. Since few classroom teachers have had this kind of training, most of them rely on other means. For example, the teacher who heard the student sing ''A Beautiful Day'' sang it with her so that when she returned to the classroom she could play its melody on an instrument. To help remember the melody, the less experienced teacher can invent pictorial ways to record melodies, for example, drawing a continuous or a broken line showing the directions of the pitches and drawing short and long dashes to represent comparative note values. Some teachers write melodies with numerals or syllables and determine the notation later. Some use tape recorders and notate it later. Others have the children help them remember the song until a special music teacher or another classroom teacher has time to help notate it. There is always a way to notate these songs, and any teacher who tries will improve with practice.

One worthwhile activity is the adding of original verses to existing songs. To do so, children feel the fundamental rhythm and accommodate new words to this rhythm. Words can be set to music so that accents used naturally in speech fall on musically accented beats. For example, ''the'' and ''a'' are normally unimportant words; they are sung on parts of the measure of little rhythmic importance—almost never on accented parts of the measure or notes of long duration, since this would give them undue emphasis.

As soon as children can use notation, the song-creating process in the classroom should include the notating of the song on music notepaper at the desk, on a portable flannelboard, on the chalkboard, or on a transparency where everyone can participate to some degree in seeing that it correctly represents what was created. When children take such songs home to play on instruments, they are learning about music notation as a by-product of their creative activity and sharing it with their parents.

When children can compose poetry and songs, the writing of simple musical stories is not beyond the possibilities of the intermediate grades. Since the form of most of the songs children compose is simple in structure, the teacher can help students write a series of songs that illustrate the story. It may also be appropriate to intersperse dialogue between the songs as part of the production.

One procedure teachers may follow when they guide students in group song writing in grades 3 and above is as follows:

1. Choose words that are simple, have steady rhythmic flow, and are understood by children.
2. Write the words on the chalkboard under the staff. Discuss the meaning of the words, seeking ideas that will influence the melody, including descending or ascending pitch.
3. Have the class read the words in unison so that a definite rhythm is established. Use clapping or stepping if necessary. The most heavily accented words or syllables can be underlined. Measure bars can be drawn to the left of these words or word syllables.
4. If this activity is comparatively new to the children, sound the tonic chord by singing 1-3-5-3-1 (*do-mi-sol-mi-do*), or by playing it on autoharp, guitar, or keyboard. If these instruments are used, it is better to play the chord sequence I-V$_7$, -I to establish a definite key feeling.
5. Ask for suggestions to start the song. There are several approaches. In the earliest stages of learning to compose, a teacher may have all or part of the first phrase written and ask the class to finish that section of the song. This can be done by the class thinking what the rest of the song might be (after singing the first part several times) and completing it, the teacher accepting the majority opinion. Soon individuals will have melodic suggestions to offer, and the process becomes one of both group and individual contribution. The composition generally proceeds phrase by

Photo by Juretta Nidever.

phrase with the group singing frequently from the beginning of the song. The teacher notates the song in some manner as it develops.

6. Have the class determine the meter signature. If the bar lines have not already been placed, they can be written before the heavily accented notes. Sometimes the song needs to be transposed to a more suitable key for the voices. The key signature is determined, as are note values. Stems, flags, beams, and dots are added wherever necessary.

7. Autoharp, guitar, or keyboard chords can be added as desired.

8. The children can now evaluate their song. Does it reflect the meaning of the words suitably? Does it communicate the mood desired? Can the song be improved? Is it notated clearly?

9. If the song is of good quality, it should be preserved on tape. If it is in a key in which children can play its melody on recorder, it may be reproduced so that the children can play the song at home for their families.

The goal of this musical activity is to develop the ability of individuals to compose music—for each child to write songs with the same ease with which children paint pictures.

When children write their own music, they are personally involved with such aspects of music as melody, form, tempo, and dynamics. They are also concerned with tension and release, repetition and contrast, range, and melodic contour. Creating songs is a superior means of acquiring music concepts. It is a genuine musical experience.

Part Singing

Part singing presents one of the most important aspects of music making to children. No musical culture is more advanced in the use of harmony than the Western world. Preparatory part singing in the primary grades includes ostinati, chants, echo-songs, simple rounds, canons, and descants. It relates to the study of harmony and polyphony. Furthermore, singers enjoy the aesthetic and social values of good part singing.

Dialogue Songs   Dialogue songs are also known as *call-and-response* songs. They involve the alternation between teacher and students, or between two groups of children on a melody. Dialogue songs are a first step toward vocal independence. The song "Follow On" is an example.

Rounds and Canons   The singing of rounds and canons is an important step toward independent part singing. There is a rich heritage of rounds and canons that are appropriate for elementary school music. Many cultures have contributed to this genre, making it an integral part of the study of the world's music.

The teaching procedure for rounds and canons may be outlined as follows:

1. The children learn the melody well.
2. The children are told how many times they are to sing the song.
3. To hear the second entrance of the round, the class sings the melody, while the

teacher comes in later, singing the same part softly. Children hear how the parts join together to create texture in music.

4. Some children join with the teacher on the new part. The children listen to both parts, while maintaining their own.
5. If the round is of more than two parts, the new parts are added in the same general manner.
6. Once the children can maintain the parts securely, the teacher works to establish balance between them.
7. Rounds can be ended in three different ways: Each part can finish separately, all parts can end on a chord together (each part stopping wherever it may be in the round), and each part can sustain the final note of that part until all parts are finished.

DOWN BY THE BAY

Traditional

*Down by the bay, where the wa-ter-mel-ons grow.

Back to my home. I dare not go.

For if I do, my moth-er will say…

Did you ev - er see a goose, kiss-ing a moose.

Down by the bay? Down by the bay?

Down by the bay, where the watermelons grow,
Back to my home, I dare not go,
For if I do, my mother will say…
Did you ever see a whale, with a polka dot tail,
Down by the bay?

Down by the bay where the watermelons grow,
Back to my home, I dare not go,
For if I do, my mother will say…
Did you ever see an octupus, dancing with a playtypus,
Down by the Bay?

Down by the bay, where the watermelons grow,
Back to my home, I dare not go,
For if I do, my mother will say…
Did you ever see a fly, wearing a tie.
Down by the bay?

* The second group ("echo" group) begins the song as the first group sings the second beat of the second measure (on the word "bay").

Pentatonic melodies can usually be sung as rounds. As the children hear a recording of the round, they can focus on both parts and how they relate to each other.

Rounds and canons are more frequently used in fourth and fifth grades than in the primary grades because most younger children are unable to sing independently. It is possible, however, for third grade children to sing canons such as "Down By the Bay."

Frequently sung rounds include "Are You Sleeping?", "Three Blind Mice," "Row Your Boat," "Scotland's Burning," "Sweetly Sings the Donkey," "Kookaburra," and "The Canoe Song." Other examples of rounds children can sing are the following:

TOOOOOH THE ZOOOOOH!

Robert de Frece
©1984

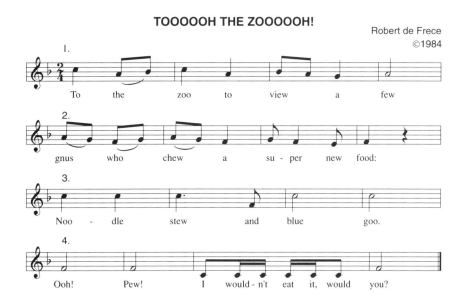

1. To the zoo to view a few
2. gnus who chew a su - per new food:
3. Noo - dle stew and blue goo.
4. Ooh! Pew! I would - n't eat it, would you?

COME, FOLLOW, FOLLOW

John Hilton
(1599-1657)

1. Come, fol - low, fol - low, fol - low, fol - low, fol - low, fol - low me.
2. Whi-ther shall I fol - low, fol - low, fol - low, Whi-ther shall I fol - low, fol - low thee?
3. To the green-wood, to the green-wood, to the green-wood, green - wood tree.

A RAINY ROUND

ML Van Rysselberghe

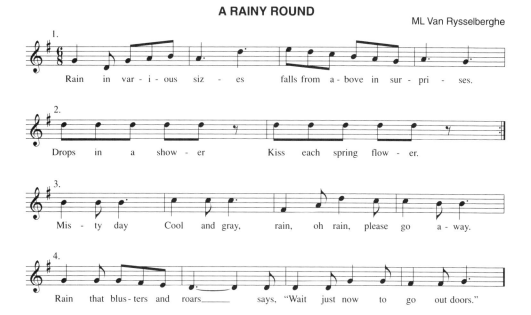

1. Rain in var - i - ous siz - es falls from a - bove in sur - pri - ses.

2. Drops in a show - er Kiss each spring flow - er.

3. Mis - ty day Cool and gray, rain, oh rain, please go a - way.

4. Rain that blus - ters and roars_____ says, "Wait just now to go out doors."

Composing Chants

Chants are recurring vocal patterns or figures. They are usually added to songs previously learned. These created parts have value in part-singing activities designed to develop independent part-singing. Chants are usually devised by the teacher for familiar songs, and taught to the children by rote. Two chants for "A Rainy Round" were created by a teacher, and are shown here:

CHANTS FOR A RAINY ROUND

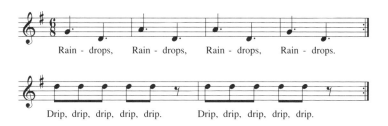

Rain - drops, Rain - drops, Rain - drops, Rain - drops.

Drip, drip, drip, drip, drip. Drip, drip, drip, drip, drip.

Initial experiences in harmonic writing of simple chants may be gained through the use of well-known songs that can be accompanied by only one chord such as "Row Your Boat" and "Are You Sleeping?" The first tone to be used would be the chord root. Using this tone, invent a rhythm pattern that contrasts with the melody. The regular recurrence of this rhythmic pattern is sung on the pitch of the chord root (i.e., the home tone, 1, or *do*). For example, in the case of "Row Your Boat" the patterns that can be composed to be sung in conjunction with the melody are myriad. A few of them are

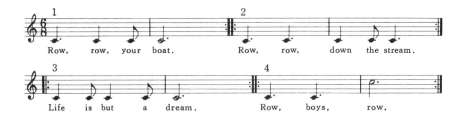

Percussion instruments are frequently used to accentuate the rhythm of a chant, and pitched instruments sometimes help children stay in tune. For dramatic effect, those children singing the chant often start about four measures before the melody begins, thus adding an introduction to the song. They also may continue for a few measures after the melody is finished, thus adding a coda. "Row Your Boat" may be sung as a melody with an added chant. When sung as a two-part round, addition of the chant results in a form of three-part singing, and when extended to be a four-part round, the chant adds a fifth part. With such simple song material, three- and four-part singing of this type can be done in intermediate grades. Furthermore, the chant itself can be extended so that still more parts result.

Thus far we have been concerned with the one-note chant. Two, three, and four-note chants are also possible. For example, "Are You Sleeping?" could have chants as follows:

Multiple chants (two or more different ones) could conceivably be employed in the same song. However, if too many different words are sung at one time, the meaning is lost and the effect ceases to be very musical. Experimenting by substituting neutral syllables or melody instruments may be worthwhile.

When chants are sung with two-chord songs, the initial experiences are usually with scale tone 5 because that tone is common to the two chords, I and V_7. It is the only common tone to the two chords.

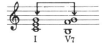

Another commonly used chant is one based on the scale tones 5 and 6. Scale tone 6 is a member of neither the I nor the V_7 chord, yet it has the unusual quality of not interfering with the harmony as long as it is placed on an unaccented part of the measure. "Looby Loo" is a song which describes the days in America before indoor plumbing. The custom was for children to take a bath in a washtub before the kitchen stove every Saturday night.

LOOBY LOO

2. left hand   3. right foot   4. left foot   5. whole self

A multitone chant for "Looby Loo" using scale tones 5 and 6 could be

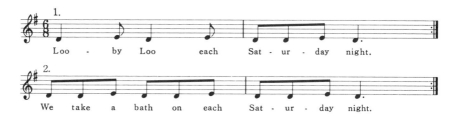

This 5-6-5 pattern works very well with songs such as "Old Texas," "Ten Little Indians" and "Skip to My Lou." Children can also invent rhythmic variants of it.

Although all good chants are essentially simple, slightly more complex chants can be written for songs such as "Looby Loo." One way to proceed with writing such a chant is to analyze the harmony of "Looby Loo" and chart it to find what this harmony demands of a 4-measure-long chant. Looking at the song, we find that it consists of four 4-measure phrases. The problem is to find what chords harmonize each of the measures, and how to write a chant that will fit this harmonic arrangement.

measure	1	2	3	4 (of each phrase)
phrase 1......	G	G	G	D₇
phrase 2......	G	G	D₇	G
phrase 3......	G	G	G	G
phrase 4......	G	G	G D₇	G

Courtesy of the Music Educators National Conference, Reston, Va.

Looking down the columns it can be seen that a chant for "Looby Loo" must be written in the following harmonic scheme: The first measure of the chant requires a pattern related to the G chord (I); the second measure requires a pattern related to the G chord; the third and fourth measures require patterns related to both G and D_7 (V_7) chords. This means that during measures 3 and 4, the chant is restricted to patterns such as those made up of scale tone 5, or scale tones 5 and 6—simple patterns that sound well with either I or V_7.

Chants may become monotonous because of their constant repetition. Therefore it is desirable that they be omitted from some sections of songs.

Countermelodies and Descants   Singing countermelodies and descants constitutes another type of part singing. A countermelody is an added melodic part, usually lower than the original melody, which often imitates it and moves in contrary motion. Ideally, a descant is a melody in its own right although written to accompany another melody. The descant is frequently, but not necessarily, subordinate to the melody. It is higher in pitch than the melody. A small group of children may sing either the descant or the countermelody while the majority of the children sing the melody. When teachers understand the relation between countermelodies or descants, the chords, and the original melodies, they can guide children to compose them.

In "Fish and Chips", a melody is supported by as many as two countermelodies.

FISH & CHIPS

Camp Song

Don't throw your junk in my back - yard, my back - yard's full.

Another example of a countermelody follows for "Down in the Valley."

DOWN IN THE VALLEY

American Folksong
Arranged by R. E. N.

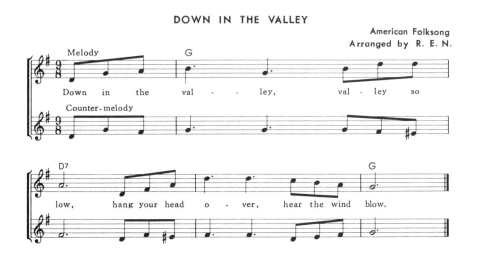

Melody

Down in the val - ley, val - ley so

Counter-melody

low, hang your head o - ver, hear the wind blow.

Sometimes descants for older children can be very sophisticated. A challenging descant for a familiar song is illustrated in "Old MacDonald."

OLD MAC DONALD

Arr Bob deFrece
©1984

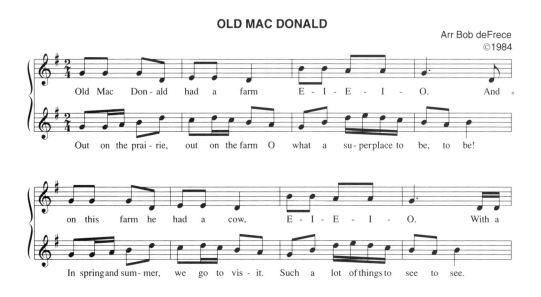

Old Mac Don - ald had a farm E - I - E - I - O. And

Out on the prai - rie, out on the farm O what a su - per place to be, to be!

on this farm he had a cow, E - I - E - I - O. With a

In spring and sum - mer, we go to vis - it. Such a lot of things to see to see.

Ideally, countermelodies and descants should be learned in relation to the original melody so students can more easily recognize the harmonic relationship of the two parts. The melody should be well learned first of all, and a feeling for the harmony may be established with guitar, autoharp, or keyboard.

The elementary school chorus may learn a descant or countermelody to be sung while the others sing a melody; and these may be combined in a musical performance. Likewise, students who are musically advanced may prepare descants out of school to be used in class with the melody sung by the others. Another use for this type of added part is with certain melody instruments—from recorders to violins and flutes.

Partner Songs   Some songs have identical harmonies, and can therefore be sung together. Partner songs have value if they are taught in the same general manner. "Three Blind Mice," "Row Your Boat," "Are You Sleeping," and "The Farmer in the Dell" can be combined with each other. Other combinations are "Bow, Belinda," "Sandy Land," "Paw Paw Patch," "Ten Little Indians," and "Skip to My Lou." The choruses of "Blue-Tail Fly" and "Shoo Fly" are compatible. "Goodnight Ladies" fits with "When the Saints Go Marching in" "Annie Laurie" and "Old Folks at Home" also can be sung together.

Students should be guided to answer the question, "Why do these songs sound acceptable when they are sung at the same time?" The answer should be found by conducting experiments. "Let's try 'America' and 'The Star-Spangled Banner' to find out how they sound together." "What happened?" "Why don't they sound well in certain places?" "Let's write those notes on the board to see what they are and how they combine." "How many different aspects of music must be the same when two songs can be combined?" "Let's try to list them." Older children may be able to make a generalization that when melodies have the same meter, tempo, and harmonic pattern, they can be combined. The following example of partner songs shows the compatibility of their harmonies.

THE LONE STAR TRAIL

(Descant: "Leavin' Old Texas") American Cowboy Songs
Arranged by R. E. N.

From *This Is Music,* Book V, by William R. Sur et. al. Copyright © 1971 by Allyn and Bacon, Inc. Used by permission.

Harmonic Endings and Freeze Tones

Harmonic endings and freeze tones, a simple and effective way to develop a feeling for harmony, may be initiated as early as third grade, where two-part harmonic endings may be used and expanded in later years to three-part endings. In *harmonic endings* the teacher adds a part to the final note or notes of a song. For example, "Three Blind Mice" ends with scale tones 3-2-1. The class would be told to sing or hum those tones softly while they listen to the teacher sing the words on scale tones 3-2-3. Next, those who believe they can sing the new part join with the teacher while the others continue singing the melody.

Two alternative harmonic endings follow:

As their name implies, harmonic endings occur at the ends of songs. *Freeze tones* are similar, but may occur at the beginnings and ends of phrases as well. For example, in "Three Blind Mice" one group of children could sustain the first tone of the song ("Three") throughout the first phrase while the rest of the children sing the regular descending pattern of the phrase. This device could be employed at the beginning of each phrase.

Harmonic endings and freeze tones can be easily arranged. The teacher must examine the beginning of phrases and the end of the song in advance to determine on which tones the harmony would naturally fall. Once these tones are determined, it is recommended that they be taught first by rote, since their purpose is to develop an awareness of harmony.

Chord Roots and Vocal Chording

Chord roots constitute one of the easiest parts to add to a song because of the harmonic strength of the root, which is the foundation tone of each chord. Although this activity is primarily for older students, it is possible for some younger ones to take part in it. The songs employed are those that are best harmonized by only two or three chords. The following example can be harmonized by the chords G and D_7 (I and V_7), thus the notes *G* and *D* are the chord roots. First, the melody is learned: then the harmony is heard by the class as the teacher chords an accompaniment. Finally, the chord roots are added instrumentally, then sung. Individual contrabass xylophone bars are excellent for illustrating root tones. Numerals, note names, or syllables may be sung on these pitches as well. Later, the words to the song may be added to the pitches of the chord roots.

Singing chord roots stresses the concept of chord change, and chord change is the essence of harmony. The singing or playing of melodies to which students "find" the roots by ear is a natural progression in harmonic development. It requires harmonic thinking without the aid of notation. Because this thin texture of melody and chord root is not always aesthetically satisfying, success with the activity quickly prompts the addition of more parts in order that a richer texture will make the harmony more complete.

To provide for individual differences and to support the new chord root part, some students can play this part on pitched percussion, keyboards, and small winds. The cello can provide the bass. To explore the concept of chord roots, the teacher might place the melody of "Hokey Pokey" on the chalkboard. The first task is to find out which chords are needed in the song, and where chord changes occur. Once the chord locations are determined, the students try out their harmony with the melody to see if it is correct.

If a student knows the chord, he or she also knows the note that is the chord root, because the chord takes its name from the root. These chord roots are placed on a staff below the other music already written.

THE HOKEY POKEY

American Folk Song

Next, they may invent rhythm patterns for the song, which they play on suitable percussion instruments. To add to this simple melody, harmony, and rhythm, students may create more parts in the form of chants and simple countermelodies. There will be continuous experimenting which involves singing and playing of parts, an understanding and use of harmony, and different ways of presenting the melody. The beginning of the score may look like this:

THE HOKEY POKEY

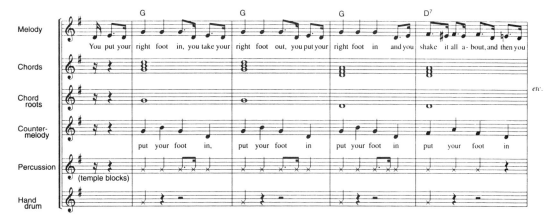

The opportunities for creative experiences are many in this approach to music. Creating and experimenting with such a score can provide a basic experience for understanding harmony. Singing chord roots contributes markedly to the further comprehension of harmony because they form the foundation tones of the harmonic structure that supports the melody. Since comprehending chord roots comes from understanding the chords, it stimulates the addition of other harmonic parts. This can lead to vocal chording, in which the class may be divided into four groups, with one assigned the melody and the other three assigned the three chord tones. This activity would logically begin with one-chord melodies and progress to three-chord melodies. It may start in a simple way in intermediate grades, and in upper elementary grades it is sometimes emphasized as an approach to three-part singing.

The ease with which students can learn to chord vocally is determined by their ability to hear harmony. Their ability to learn harmony is in turn favorably influenced by successful experiences in instrumental chording and by guided listening activities that assist the hearing of chord changes. The chords to be sung can be arranged in several positions. Although numbers or syllables may be used to introduce this work, humming or the syllable *loo* is used in performance. The following excerpt from "Silent Night" illustrates this activity:

Learning to Hear Chord Changes

The experience with chord roots encourages students to sense chord changes. Teachers may contrive situations in which the sounding chord is "wrong," and the students determine this and correct it. Wrong and right chords are played; the students choose the ones that fit the melody best. The experience commonly includes the teacher's selecting a familiar two-chord song (I and V_7 or I and IV) and playing the tonic chord all the way through or until the students show in some way that the harmonic accompaniment should be changed. Teachers let the children select the chords which sound the best to them, and continue to help them determine chord changes. After students have learned to play the chords on some instrument, they can improvise accompaniments to songs of simple harmonization, listening to find when the melody demands a chord change, and choosing the chord that sounds best. With two-chord songs the problem is a simple one of deciding which of two chords should be used. When skill in this has been developed, teachers select three-chord songs for student to harmonize. Some can become expert in chord selection when their teachers have planned experiences which help them develop this responsiveness to harmony.

Thirds and Sixths

As in other approaches to harmony, students are assumed to know the melody well before exploring thirds and sixths. Many melodies can be harmonized by the appropriate addition of thirds and sixths. With certain melodies the use of these intervals may begin with parts of the song, and eventually expand throughout the song. For example, "London Bridge" can be sung in thirds except for the next-to-last measure, where a sixth is necessary.

LONDON BRIDGE

The music series books include songs that rely heavily on thirds to introduce part singing. A song that can be sung entirely in thirds is the well-known "Polly Wolly Doodle."

POLLY WOLLY DOODLE

American Song

An interval that sounds similar to the third is the sixth, which is its inversion. After students have become accustomed to singing in parallel thirds, they can easily learn to sing in parallel sixths. Any song that can be sung in thirds can be sung in sixths. This can be illustrated with "Polly Wolly Doodle." However, when the interval is changed in this way the key must often change as well to accommodate the child's vocal range.

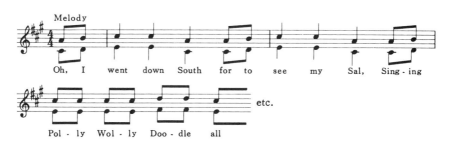

Songs such as "Lightly Row," "Goodbye," "Yankee Doodle," "To Puerto Rico," and "Catch a Falling Star" can be used in part singing through the use of thirds and sixths.

A learning sequence in part singing for students in intermediate grades follows:

1. The learning of the melody.
2. The aural comprehension of the chord structure that accompanies the melody.
3. The introduction of the new part in a manner that permits the students to hear the relation of the two parts.
4. The singing of the new part by those who are ready for part singing.
5. Balancing the two parts so that both parts can be heard by all.

When students feel secure in part-singing activities, the sight-reading of part songs can be an interesting and challenging activity. Since sight-singing is a complicated skill, neutral syllables are generally used instead of words so that the students can concentrate on the notation. The words are added when they feel secure on the parts.

The Elementary School Chorus

The elementary music program should not be based on public performance. However, special interest groups such as the orchestra, band, and chorus do offer valuable experiences for elementary children. The instrumental groups are generally the responsibility of special music teachers, but the chorus is frequently taught either by the general music specialist or a classroom teacher. Grade levels may be combined for a large-group choral experience, and children as young as age 7 can successfully participate in a school chorus. Where such a program exists, it is preferable that the chorus be offered all year during the regular school day for all students who want to participate. Otherwise students who must be bused to and from school are excluded. Because of tight scheduling in elementary schools, the choir may be limited to a six-week period each fall and spring, and culminate its work in a performance. Short, frequent rehearsals of no less than thirty minutes are preferable to longer rehearsals once a week.

Today's teachers are fortunate in having new songs written and arranged especially for the elementary school chorus. However, some of the best arrangements are often done by the teacher who knows the vocal abilities of the students. Another resource is the music series books, which include chants, descants, and countermelodies in addition to standard two- and three-part songs.

Preparation for a chorus must begin weeks before its first meeting. Songs are selected, proper keys are determined, and transpositions done where needed. A calendar of rehearsals is prepared to indicate when specific songs are to be introduced, the music concepts to be emphasized, when words are to be memorized, and when videotaping is to be done for the children's benefit. Instrumentations are devised, and lesson plans are prepared. Provisions are made for the inclusion of special students. An accompanist, selected from the teaching staff, may provide substantial assistance. However, some accompaniments can be provided by students on instruments used in general music classes. Their parts can be taught in general music classes to all the students before the chorus rehearses. Choice of players for the performance may be made by consult-

Photo by Juretta Nidever.

ing with the classroom teachers. If the group is large, other teachers of the grade levels involved can assist with roll-taking and student supervision.

There is no standard seating arrangement for these choruses. However, it is best to have the lowest and highest parts seated so that each can hear the other well. In this way the group is able to sing in tune. In choruses which have a goal of public performance, the singers are permanently assigned to one of the parts (high, middle, or low).

The general music class and the elementary chorus are not in competition. They work hand in hand to accomplish the objectives of the music program.

Activities for Singing

Relating Melody and Harmony   **Canon.** The teacher creates simple canons and writes them in numbers or syllables for the class to sing. There will be two parts. Later, some of these should be notated and sung from notation. Example:

1 1 2 3 4 5–5 4 3 2 1–
1 1 2 3 4 5–5 4 3 2 1–

Hearing Two Pitches at Once. One half of the class sustains one pitch, *do* or 1, while the other half sings other pitches as indicated by the teacher, pointing to scale degrees written in numbers or syllables on the chalkboard, or by hand signs. Later, both *do* and *so* and *la* and *mi* can be used as alternating sustained pitches.

The major scale may be constructed vertically in numbers or syllables on the chalkboard. After the teacher divides the class into two groups, each group is assigned either the teacher's left hand or right hand. Each group sings to the designated hand of the teacher as he or she points with it. The teacher points to scale degrees that produce interesting two-pitch combinations. It is advisable to start with a unison and experiment from there. Later on, the same may be done with scales other than the major. For older, experienced students, this activity can progress until both groups are singing moving parts indicated by two-hand signs given by the teacher or an advanced student. From this activity they can proceed to notation.

Round. All or part of a traditional round may be written on the chalkboard, or prepared on a transparency. Children are asked to sing rounds and to listen to them, but they seldom see them notated so that they can obtain a visual image of what a round is. First, the class should learn to sing the round in unison, then in two to four parts. After studying the score, questions such as the following can be asked. "What is the harmonic plan of this round?" Students may be given the opportunity to write a round using this same plan or another. Other rounds and their harmonic plans may be studied.

Descant, Countermelody, and Round. Students sing and play songs that have descants and countermelodies. The teacher may ask them to describe the difference between rounds and added parts. The indexes of music series books frequently include collections of rounds, songs with descants and countermelodies.

Polyphony. Sousa: *Semper Fidelis,* AM, grade 3, vol. 1. The children listen to this march to discover its distinctive melodies and how Sousa combined them.

Texture. Children develop a vocabulary of terms descriptive of texture such as light, heavy, thick, thin. Recordings can be used in which children compare thick and thin textures. Examples of contrasting textures:

Saint-Saëns, "The Swan" from *Carnival of the Animals,* AM, grade 3, vol. 2 (homophonic texture)
Ligeti, "Atmospheres" from *Space Odyssey,* Columbia MS 6733
Bach, *Little Fugue in G Minor,* AM, grade 6, vol. 1; BOL 86

Harmonic Part
Singing

Improvising Harmony. The teacher presents the class with the task of improvising parts for "Streets of Laredo," using only scale tones 3, 4, and 5. This song has been selected because it is harmonized by only two chords. I and V_7. Scale tones 3 and 5 are members of the I-chord and scale tones 4 and 5 are members of the V_7-chord. In this particular song the chords alternate regularly; this makes it easy to choose chord tones to improvise harmony parts. The class selects the pitches for each of the measures of the song and writes them on the chalkboard. The class next rehearses the melody and the new part, and revises if necessary. Next, the class adds another new part by writing it a third lower. Now the class has two new parts in parallel thirds. It then sings the three parts. The students evaluate the result and try to analyze what made it possible. In addition, this song can be sung as a round.

STREETS OF LAREDO

Cowboy Song

3. *"It was once in the saddle I used to go dashing,*
   Once in the saddle I used to go gay;
   First down to Rosie's and then to the card-house;
   Got shot in the breast and I'm dying today."

4. *"Get sixteen gamblers to handle my coffin,*
   Let six jolly cowboys come sing me a song,
   Take me to the graveyard and lay the sod o'er me,
   For I'm a young cowboy, I know I've done wrong."

5. *"Oh, beat the drums slowly and play the fife lowly,*
   Play the dead march as they carry me along,
   Put bunches of roses all over my coffin,
   Roses to deaden the clods as they fall."

6. *(Repeat Verse I.)*

Improvising Part Singing. The class explores harmonizing parts, using songs such as "Hush, Little Baby," "Good Night Ladies," "Kum Ba Yah," "Michael, Row the Boat Ashore," and "Sally Go Round."

Singing Parallel Thirds. As illustrated earlier there are some songs and parts of songs that can be sung and played in parallel thirds. Among these songs are "Hot Cross Buns," "Sally Go Round," and "Polly Wolly Doodle." The teacher first rehearses the melody thoroughly with the class, using harmonic accompaniment. Then the teacher asks part of the class to try to harmonize a third higher, and gives the new pitch to that group. The two groups begin together, and the harmonizing group makes automatic adjustments in the new part as needed. The two parts should then be revealed on the chalkboard or transparency in order that the children see the related parts. The interval of a third can be identified by sight and by sound.

Instrumental examples of harmonic intervals: thirds and sixths.

Tchaikovsky, *Italian Caprice* (a prominent theme is in thirds)

Mendelssohn: *Symphony No. 4*, First Movement (theme 2 has a two-part melody in thirds)

Charpentier, "On Muleback" from *Impressions of Italy*, AM, grade 5, vol. 1 (theme 3 has a two-part melody in thirds and sixths)

Countermelody. After singing a song with a countermelody, students select a familiar song requiring only I and V$_7$ chords for harmonization, and improvise a countermelody. The class may sing or hum the melody while a small group sings the countermelody. Several students may also want to try improvising their own countermelodies. The class may then discuss characteristics of a successful countermelody.

Dissonance. The class experiments with singing as a round a known song that is not a round. It should be a song that will result in obvious dissonances. The teacher then asks the students to analyze the reasons for the dissonances, to try to define dissonance, and to explain why some songs do not work as rounds.

Bitonality. With more advanced students, the class sings a familiar song such as "Kookaburro" while the teacher plays the accompaniment in another key. The teacher might also divide the class into two parts, and ask them to sing the song in different keys. As follow-up, they might listen to recorded examples of bitonality.

References

Articles and Books

APFELSTAD, HILARY, "Children's Vocal Range: Research Findings and Implications for Music Education," *Update* Fall 1982, 3–7.

CAMPBELL, PATRICIA S., "The Childsong Genre: A Comparison of Songs by and for Children," *Update*, 7/2 Spring 1989, 18–20.

CASSIDY, NANCY, and JOHN CASSIDY, *Kid's Songs* vols. 1 and 2. Palo Alto, Calif.: Klutz Press, 1988.

COOPER, IRVIN and KARL KUERSTEINER, *Teaching Junior High School Music: General Music and Vocal Program.* Boston: Allyn and Bacon, 1972.

COOPER, MORTON, "Prescriptions for Vocal Health," *Music Educators Journal*, February 1983, 40–59.

DAVIDSON, L., and W. G. SCARLETT, "When Is a Song a Song? The Development of Singing in Early Childhood," *Day Care and Early Education, 14/3*, Spring 1987, 30–31.

DORMAN, PHYLLIS E., "A Protest Against Musical Illiteracy," *Music Educators Journal*, November 1967, 99.

ERDIE, PETER, and KATALIN KOMLES, *150 American Folk Songs to Sing, Read, and Play*. Oceanside, N. J.: Boosey and Hawkes, 1974.

FRANKLIN, ELDA, "Monotonism," *Music Educators Journal*, March 1981, 56–58.

FRANKLIN, ELDA, and A. DAVID FRANKLIN, "The Uncertain Singer," *Update*, vol. 1, no. 3, Spring 1983, 3–5.

GOETZ, MARY, and HORII YOSHIYUKI, "A Comparison of the Pitch Accuracy of Group and Individual Singing in Young Children," *Bulletin of the Council for Research in Music Education, No. 99*, Winter 1989, 57–73.

GOULD, A. OREN, "Finding and Learning to Use the Singing Voice: A Manual for Teachers," U.S. Office of Education Bureau of Research, OEC 6-10-016, 1968.

HACKETT, PATRICIA, *The Melody Book*, 2nd ed. Englewood Cliffs, N.J.: Prentice Hall, 1991.

HACKETT, PATRICIA and CAROLYN A. LINDEMAN, *The Musical Classroom*, 2nd ed. Englewood Cliffs, N. J.: Prentice Hall, 1988.

LEVINOWITZ, L. M. "An Investigation of Preschool Children's Comparative Capability to Sing Songs With and Without Words," *Bulletin of the Council for Research in Music Education, No. 100*, Spring 1989, 14–19.

MESKE, EUNICE B, and CARROLL RINEHART, *Individualized Instruction in Music*. Reston, Va.: Music Educators National Conference, 1975.

PERSELLIN, DIANE CUMMINGS, "The Influences of Perceived Modality Preferences on Teaching Methods Used By Elementary Music Educators," *Update, 7/1*, Fall 1988, 11–15.

PHILLIPS, KENNETH H., "Training the Child Voice," *Music Educators Journal*, December 1985, 19–22.

POLISAR, BARRY LOUIS, *Noises From Under the Rug*. Silver Springs, Md.: Rainbow Morning Music Alts., 1985.

SAUNDERS, T. CLARK, "Why Do Many Young Children Sing Out of Tune? Providing a Proper Foundation for Children to Sing," *Update, 6/2*, Spring 1988, 19–21.

SWEARS, LINDA, *Teaching the Elementary School Chorus*. New York: Parker, 1985.

TUFTS, NANCY P., *The Children's Choir*, vol. 2. Philadelphia: Fortress Press. Discusses the children's choir, the boy's choir, and the handbell choir.

Songs for Children

BAILEY, CHARITY, *Sing a Song with Charity Bailey*. New York: Plymouth.

BRADFORD, LOUISE, *Sing it Yourself*. Sherman Oaks, Calif.: Alfred, 1978. American pentatonic songs.

KERSEY, ROBERT, *Just Five*. Westminster, Md.: Westminster Press. Pentatonic songs.

_____ . *Just Five Plus Two.* Westminster, Md.: Westminster Press. *Fa* and *ti* are added.

LANDECK, BEATRICE, *Songs to Grow On; More Songs to Grow On.* New York: Marks and Sloane. Recorded by Folkways Records.

SCOTT, RICHARD, *Clap, Tap, and Sing Choral Method.* Minneapolis, Minn.: Handy-Folio Music Company. For grades 2–5. Beginning with rhythm, this 48-page book takes children through sight-singing to part singing. All songs are playable on small wind instruments.

SEEGER, RUTH CRAWFORD, *American Folk Songs for Children; Animal Folk Songs for Children; American Folk Songs for Christmas.* New York: Doubleday, 1948.

Part Singing   BACON, DENISE, *46 Two-Part American Folk Songs.* Oceanside, N.Y.: Boosey and Hawkes, 1974.

BELL, LESLIE, *The Festival Song Book One.* Melville, N.Y.: Belwin-Mills. For unaccompanied voices.

BURKART, ARNOLD E., *Bicinia Americana Vol. 1.* Muncie, Ind.: Keeping Up With Music Education, 1976.

COOPER, IRVIN, *Songs for Pre-Teentime.* New York: Carl Fischer. For grades 6–7.

EHRET, WALTER, *The Youthful Chorister.* New York: Marks Music Corp. SA.

GEARHART, LIVINGSTON, *A Christmas Singing Bee.* Delaware Water Gap, Pa.: Shawnee Press.

JUREY, EDWARD B., *Mills First Chorus Album.* Melville, N. Y.: Belwin-Mills.

KENT, WILLYS PECK, *A Book of Descants.* New York: Vantage Press. For grades 5–8.

KRONE, BEATRICE, and MAX KRONE, *Our First Songs to Sing with Descants* (for upper primary); *Very Easy Descants; Songs to Sing with Descants; Descants for Christmas; Our Third Book of Descants; From Descants to Trios; Descants and Rounds for Special Days.* Park Ridge, Ill.: Neil A. Kjos Music Company.

Music Educators National Conference, *Music for Children's Choirs: A Selective Graded Listing.* Reston, Va.: The Conference, 1977. 44 pages.

PERINCHIEF, ROBERT, *Honor Your Partner Songs.* Whitewater, Wis.: Perry Publications, Inc.

SCOTT, RICHARD, *Sevenfold Choral Method.* Minneapolis, Minn.: Handy-Folio Music Company. For grades 5–7.

General Collections   ADES, HAWLEY, *One for the Melody.* Delaware Water Gap, Pa.: Shawnee Press. 26 unison songs by classic composers, with a story about each composer.

DALLIN, LEON, and LYNN DALLIN, *Heritage Songster.* Dubuque, Iowa: Wm. C. Brown. Traditional songs Americans sing.

LEISY, JAMES, *The Good Times Songbook.* Nashville and New York: Abingdon Press, 1974. For informal singing.

NYE, ROBERT E., VERNICE T. NYE, NEVA AUBIN, and GEORGE KYME, *Singing With Children,* 2nd ed. Belmont, Calif.: Wadsworth, 1970. Selected songs for teaching music to elementary school children.

Recordings   Bowmar Records, Belwin-Mills, Melville, NY 11747. *Bowmar Records Catalog.* Lists approximately 20 albums for singing, including three for children with special needs.

Children's Book and Music Center, 2500 Santa Monica Blvd., Santa Monica, CA 90404.

Classroom Materials Co., 93 Myrtle Drive, Great Neck, NY 11020. *Johnny Can Sing Too*. (K–3) Vol. 1, 2. For discovering singing voices and helping them develop. *You Too Can Sing!* (4–6) For children with singing problems. *Classroom Sing Along* (4–6) To aid the teacher in teaching songs.

Folkways Records
You'll Sing a Song and I'll Sing a Song (Ella Jenkins) FC 7664
See the Folkways Catalog for many more.

Franson Corporation, 225 Park Ave. South, New York, NY 10003. Children's Record Guild and Young People's Records.
Albums: *Let's Sing* (1–5)
Folk Songs (1–5)
Songs to Sing (1–4) activity songs

RCA Music Service, Educational Dept. A., 1133 Avenue of the Americas, New York NY 10036. *The Singing Program* (albums).

Stanley Bowmar Co., Inc., Valhalla, NY 10595
Records, Tapes, and Instructional Materials for the Classroom Catalog. Lists many records for singing activities.

Stage Productions

CASSILS, CRAIG, *Clowns.* Grades 1–5. Somerset Press, Carol Stream, IL 60187.

HAWTHORNE, GRACE, and JOHN F. WILSON, *The Electric Sunshine Man.* Upper grades. Somerset Press, Carol Stream, IL 60187.

MITCHELL, TOM, and CONNIE CROSS SMITH, *Christmas on Angel Street.* Upper grades. Jensen Publications, Inc., 2770 S. 171st St., New Berlin, WI 53151.

STURGES, KAREN, *The Pied Piper of Hamlin.* Grades 1–6. Shawnee Press, Inc., Delaware Water Gap., PA 18327.

WOOLLCOMBE, DAVID, and DAVID GORDON, *The Peace Child.* Upper grades. Jensen Publications, Inc., 2770 S. 171st St., New Berlin, WI 53151.

9 Teaching Children to Play Instruments

Using Instruments for Melodic Activities

Musical instruments may be viewed as extensions of the human body. They are used for musical performance, as a way to experiment with sound, to accompany singing and dancing, and for many other purposes. Children can expand their musical understanding in many ways while learning to play musical instruments. Because classroom instruments exist in great variety and with varying complexity, all children can have positive musical experiences playing them.

Children are characteristically interested in mechanical things. Making music by playing an instrument is attractive. Teachers need to capitalize on this interest and help students acquire the skills of playing as part of the elementary school curriculum. For example, the concept of *interval* can be made clear by seeing intervals on keyboard instruments, and by seeing and feeling them on wind instruments. The players of musical instruments must learn about key signatures, pitches, note and rest durations, and other aspects of music such as scale line, chord line, legato, and staccato.

Instruments can be used to introduce the musical traditions of various cultures. Examples are the *mbira,* or thumb piano of Africa, a variety of Latin American instruments such as the maracas, guiro and claves, and various types of bamboo flutes of cultures throughout the world. Children can also use instruments to compose melodies. Many instruments are easy to play; they can be taught by the classroom teacher. Their use combines auditory, tactile, and visual perception upon which music concepts can be realized. Some children will be more interested in trying to match tones with their voices when they produce pitches themselves on an instrument. Furthermore, the more experienced and gifted students can have additional musical experiences with instruments.

Pitched Percussion   When children have had opportunities to explore pitched percussion instruments, they can make a number of discoveries:

Long bars sound low pitches.

Short bars sound high pitches.

To play a scale going up, play from left to right.

To play a scale going down, play from right to left.

A five-note (pentatonic) scale can be played by removing certain bars.

Bars played from C to C sound the C major scale.

The tone quality of the resonating bar is affected by the way it is struck, and the type of mallet used.

Photo by Juretta Nidever.

Before children understand music notation, teachers guide them through musical activities taught by rote. First, the teacher teaches a melody by rote. Then the melody is transferred by the teacher to a pitched percussion instrument and demonstrated before the class. Next, a student may be asked to come up and mirror the actions of the teacher on the instrument.

In the early stages of instruction the teacher may use the key of C major to avoid the need for chromatic tone bars. With guidance and careful listening, young children can play songs or parts of songs in keys such as F and G major where one chromatic tone bar is necessary. The general procedure at first is to learn a song well by rote before attempting to play it.

Some teachers help children begin playing songs with the aid of numerals. Soon thereafter they are introduced to notation the teacher has prepared for them that includes the numerals written beneath (or above) the notes represented. Later, teachers prepare notation in which the numerals appear only with the beginning note of each measure, then only with the beginning note of each phrase, and finally numerals are abandoned altogether because the children have made the transition from numerals to the notes on the staff.

Pitched percussion instruments have many uses. If a classroom teacher has difficulty with his or her singing voice, an instrument can be used to teach rote songs. Difficult tonal patterns in songs can be isolated and rehearsed on the instrument. They are often employed to establish the pitch of songs by sounding the keynote, playing tones of the tonic chord, then playing the starting pitch. Special sound effects such as chimes, church bells, and sleigh bells can be imitated to enhance songs. Children can play simple parts of songs, such as the repeated rhythm patterns of ''Chimmy Chuck'' in the ''Barnyard Song.'' Introductions, codas, and interludes—all created on the instruments—can be added. Older students can write descants and other added parts to songs and play them. Pitched percussion instruments can also reinforce part singing.

BARNYARD SONG

Kentucky Folk Song

I fed my hen un - der yon - der tree.

Hen goes chim - my chuck, chim - my chuck, (etc.)

Photo by Juretta Nidever.

Students may also want to impersonate the animals in the song.

Pitched percussion instruments and keyboards are excellent audiovisual tools for teaching such musical concepts as high and low, pitch relationships and intervals, and scales. Children enjoy picking out tunes, and in doing so on keyboard instruments they see, feel, and hear demonstrations of these concepts. This activity can lead to a comprehension of the meaning of the notes on the staff—an understanding frequently lacking in children whose musical experiences have been confined to a singing approach.

Three other pitched percussion instruments are the glockenspiel, the metallophone, and the xylophone. The glockenspiel is the highest pitched of these instruments, and could be used for melodies above the children's vocal ranges. As its name indicates, the metallophone's bars are made of metal. The xylophone (Figure 9.1) is a pitched percussion instrument, the bars of which are made of wood instead of metal. *Xylo* is the greek word for wood. Because its wood strips do not vibrate as long as the metal bars of the metallophone, it has a more percussive quality. Step bells are yet another type of pitched instrument.

Figure 9.1. XYLOPHONE. Shawnee Press, Inc., Delaware Water Gap, Pa. 18327.

They are constructed in the form of stair steps which illustrate the ascending and descending pitches of the scale. Their primary function is in instruction rather than in performance.

Keyboards Keyboards can be used in connection with songs in the same ways the percussion instruments are used. Like pitched percussion instruments, keyboards provide an excellent audiovisual image of many musical concepts. They can be used as instruments of percussion, melody, harmony, and in any combination of these.

Classroom teachers do not need to be pianists to teach music through keyboard experience. They need only to be introduced to it so that they can proceed in the same way the children do. Here are some examples of such usage:

One Finger The child plays repeated single tones such as the beginning of "Jingle Bells." A tone-matching game can be played by striking a pitch that is within his or her voice range, then trying to match it vocally.

Two Fingers The child plays repeated motives in songs and can also match tones while singing such scale tones as 5 and 3 (*sol,* and *mi*).

Three Fingers The scale tones 3-2-1 can be played whenever the words "three blind mice" occur in the song of that name. The tonal pattern 1-2-3-1 can be played with the words "Are you sleeping?" in the song of that name.

Four Fingers Scale tones 4-4-3-3-2-2-1 in "Twinkle, Twinkle, Little Star" can be played when the following words appear: "How I wonder what you are." Scale tones 5-5-4-4-3-3-2 can be played along with the words, "Up above the world so high," and "Like a diamond in the sky."

Five Fingers Scale tones 5-4-3-2-1 are used at the end of "Row Your Boat" with the words, "Life is but a dream," and the scale tones 5-4-4-3-3-2-1-1 are used with the words "Ten little Indian children" at the end of that song. Songs requiring only five fingers can be played easily.

Scales Many songs are based on scales and parts of scales that can be played on the keyboard. One example is "Pussywillow."

Children can also compose songs within the limitations of three, four, and five scale tones—and both sing and play them. Eventually this activity leads to the use of more scale tones in song composition.

Other simple uses of the keyboard include the following:

playing the notes of chord roots as an easy added part to songs. Example: play F with the F chord, G with the G chord.

playing the rhythms of children's names with one tone or a series of tones; playing tones that illustrate the concepts of high and low pitch.

playing short tone patterns for tone-matching.

playing short tone patterns to add interest to songs.

playing octave intervals in songs that emphasize this interval.

playing different note values and rhythm patterns for children to reflect in movement.

playing ostinati.

Electric pianos, organs, and synthesizers can make substantial contributions to elementary music. They vary extensively in size and cost. Most can be played along with earphones without disturbing others. The more complex ones can produce a number of different tone qualities. Group instruction on keyboards is a recent trend in general music classes. It is not necessary to have an instrument for every child, though it is preferred. In such instruction the purpose is always to learn about music, not to become a pianist.

Recorder The recorder's period of greatest popularity was between the fifteenth and eighteenth centuries. In recent years there has been a strong revival of interest in it because (1) it is an instrument played with pleasure by both adults and children, (2) there is a substantial amount of excellent solo and ensemble music available for it, (3) it is comparatively inexpensive, and (4) in elementary school, the soprano recorder fits the child's hand size—the finger pads are large enough to cover its holes, and the span between notes is not too large (see Figure 9.2).

Acceptance of the recorder for upper elementary and middle school use has grown because of its low price and its good tone quality. Fingering for the soprano recorder is shown in Figure 9.3. The soprano is widely used because it is constructed in the key of C, thus having immediate use in playing the music children sing from songbooks.

The baroque recorder is preferred to the German by some teachers, despite the somewhat easier fingering of the latter, because of better pitch accuracy. While many recorders are made of wood, quite acceptable plastic instruments are available and are less expensive and more practical for elementary school

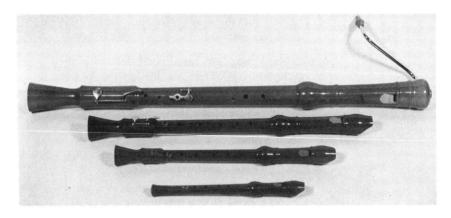

Figure 9.2. A FAMILY OF RECORDERS. Rhythm Band, Inc., Fort Worth, Texas 76101.

use. Among other things, some brands can be sterilized in the cafeteria dishwasher.

Teaching with Melody Instruments

Ostinati. Melody instruments can be used to provide ostinati which reinforce a musical phrase in a song. For example, "I love the Mountains." can be taught using the ostinato on p. 290 to teach the melody of the scat phrase "Boom de ah da." Then the ostinato can be used as an accompaniment when children sing the song.

Low-high. Students relate low and high musical pitches with left and right on the keyboard, as well as on pitched percussion instruments.

Photo by Juretta Nidever.

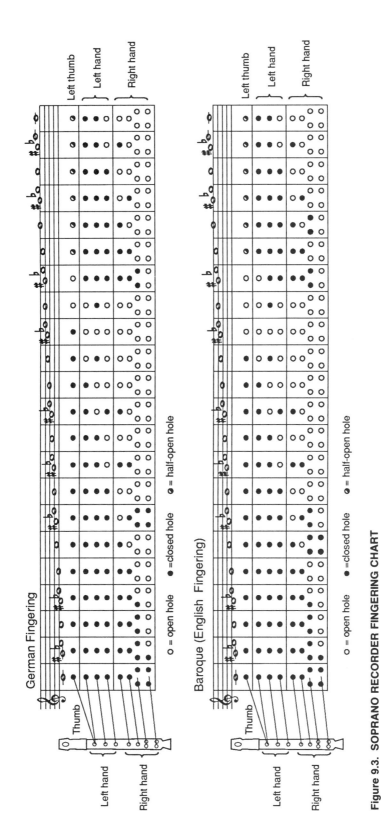

Figure 9.3. SOPRANO RECORDER FINGERING CHART

I LOVE THE MOUNTAINS

Traditional

I love the moun-tains, I love the roll-ing hills, I love the flow-ers,

I love the daf-fo-dils, I love the fire - side, When all the lights are low,

Boom de ah da, boom de ah da, boom de ah da, boom de ah___ de, boom!

ostinato

Experiment in composition. On a pitched percussion instrument, individual children select any four pitches, remove all other bars, and make up tunes on the four remaining.

Composition on black keys. Children create pentatonic melodies on the black keys of a keyboard, or on pitched percussion bars representing a pentatonic scale.

Scale. Children play scales on keyboard instruments and analyze their patterns.

Tonal relationships. A large chart of the keyboard is placed at the front of the room so that it can be used to answer questions and solve musical problems.

Ear training. The teacher plays a few consecutive scale tones on an instrument; a child is asked to reproduce the pitches on a like instrument. Later, older students can take dictation from the teacher's playing. The teacher gives the name of the first note and the key of the dictation. Then the students indicate the pitches they hear on the staff in notation, either individually on paper or collectively with a flannel or magnetic board.

Transposition. Older students learn to transpose by playing a familiar song in several keys on a melody instrument.

Improvising with keyboard. The student makes up a melody with the right hand, and then makes up an accompaniment with the left hand, all on the black keys of a keyboard instrument.

Improvising with pitched percussion. A child is chosen to improvise a free accompaniment to a pentatonic song.

Melodic improvisation based on chords. The teacher plays the chord sequence I, IV, I, V, I, and a child improvises over the chords with a pitched percussion instrument, with a recorder, or with voice.

Tonal memory. A game is played by two recorder players in which the first player performs a short series of pitches to be imitated by the second player.

Recorder melodies. Older students compose short three-note (G-A-B) melodies on the recorder, and notate them on a staff with quarter, half, and whole notes.

Bitonality. Students play a well-known song such as "Hot Cross Buns," using two keyboard instruments, each in a different key. The class considers the effect of hearing two keys at once.

Metric composition. Children compose a piece for recorder and notate it in a selected meter.

Dorian mode. Older students compose a melody for recorder in the Dorian mode. They then notate it on a transparency for class viewing, performance, and discussion. (The Dorian mode corresponds to a scale on piano white keys that begins and ends on D.)

Pentatonic mode, scale, phrase. Using recorders, students improvise answers to given phrases with tones of a pentatonic scale. Later they may improvise both question-and-answer phrases.

Tone row, polyphony, canon. Students listen to a recorded composition such as *Double Canon for String Quartet,* by Stravinsky, Columbia MS 6272. They analyze it to find that there is no tonic (home tone), that it is polyphonic, and that there is a canon. They then build their own 12-tone row with resonator bells; the row must not suggest traditional tonal music; none of the pitches are repeated. They notate the row on a staff and perform it as an ostinato. As an extension, they may even write it in inversion. When the row is inverted, the pitch direction is reversed, but the intervals remain the same.

Transposing instruments. Older children examine a band or orchestra score borrowed from the instrumental music teacher, and find that the music is written in a number of different keys. This activity leads them to discover that some instruments are built in different keys. By experimenting with notes on band instruments and comparing the resulting pitch with the keyboard, they can discover that when B ♭ instruments play written C, the pitch is B ♭, and when E ♭ instruments play C, the pitch sounded is E ♭.

Using Instruments for Harmonic Activities and Accompanying

Harmony and Texture

A child's first classroom experience with harmony comes from the simple accompaniments played by the teacher as the class sings a song. Many rote songs will have been sung without accompaniment, and when an instrument is added to provide harmonic interest the child hears both harmony and a textural change. When this occurs, the teacher discusses the event with the children so that they begin to understand the relationships between melody and harmony.

Harmony can be defined as the simultaneous occurrence of any two or more musical tones. Some combinations of tones are more pleasing to the ear, or consonant. Other combinations of tones are less pleasing, or dissonant. Both consonant and dissonant combinations of tones are called harmony. The term *musical texture* describes the relationship between melodies or a melody and its accompaniment. Traditionally, three terms are used to describe textures. They are monophonic (an unaccompanied melody), polyphonic (two or more melodies occurring together), and homophonic (a melody and an accompaniment). Many different textures can be produced in accompaniments, and children should gradually learn to recognize these differences as they hear and create them.

Autoharp and Omnichord

The autoharp is an instrument of ancient lineage which has become popular in elementary and middle schools, and is used by folk singers. The model most used today has 15 push-button bars with felts that prevent the vibration of unplayed strings. The 21-chord model is growing in popularity, as is a model that is fitted for electronic amplification (see Figures 9.4 and 9.5). A more contemporary instrument of the same general type is the Omnichord. This electronic

Figure 9.4. AUTOHARP. Oscar Schmidt-International, Inc., and Music Education Group. Northbrook, Ill. 60062.

instrument is still quite easy to play, and has the added features of selected rhythmic ostinati and other sound capabilities. Because sounds are electronically produced, it does not require tuning, a frequent challenge with autoharps.

Although some children in primary grades are able to play either of these instruments satisfactorily, it is not until the third and fourth grades that most can do so. In early primary grades teachers often press the bars while children strum the strings. It is believed that guiding children to listen carefully to autoharp chording assists the development of a feeling for harmony, which is part of the preparation for part singing. One primary purpose of the autoharp is to provide

Figure 9.5. AUTOHARP: 21-CHORD MODEL

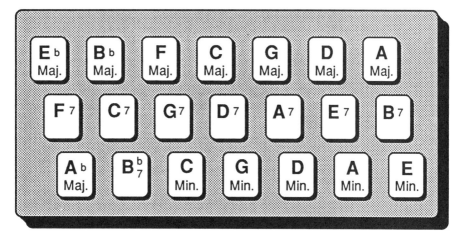

an accompaniment that is soft enough to permit children's voices to develop independence. Another is to establish the tempo and key of a song by playing introductory chords in the desired rhythm. Chording on the autoharp is also an effective way to stimulate interest in the study of chords. Hearing chord changes and playing the correct chord at the proper time are valuable for ear training, and teachers need to include these listening experiences in their efforts to develop children's musicianship.

To teach children to play the autoharp it may be necessary to separate the skills of pressing down the chord bars and strumming the instrument. To do so the autoharp is placed on a desk or table between two children who act as playing partners. One child presses firmly on the appropriate chord bar while the other child strums the full range of the strings from low to high. When the skill is mastered the children trade responsibilities. Eventually one child performs both tasks. To do so the child must be taught to use the right hand for pushing the tone bars, and the left hand for strumming. As playing ability increases, the child needs to determine chord progressions in advance, anticipate their changes, and rehearse that pattern. In most of the music suggested for autoharp there are no more than three chords, the tonic (1), the dominant seventh (V_7), and the subdominant (IV). The finger form for these chords in the keys of C major, G major, F major, D minor, and A minor is as follows:

	IV	V_7	I
left hand:	ring finger	middle finger	index finger

In some of the keys just listed, the finger pattern is straight across. In others it is triangulated. Children need to rehearse these changes in tempo before accompanying a song (see Figure 9.5).

The loud tone produced with the plastic pick that comes with the instrument is needed for most classroom singing. The soft tone produced with a felt pick is best for solo and small ensemble singing. Picks are made in different shapes and sizes. Some are worn on fingers; others are held between thumb and index finger. Rubber erasers, large paper clips, and plastic fasteners from bread wrappers may be used as substitutes.

When teaching students to play the autoharp, the teacher should use a song that has already been learned. It is usual practice to begin with songs requiring only one chord, proceeding to those requiring two chords, and then to songs in which three chords are necessary. It is desirable for the children to learn to hear the chord changes and not rely on the teacher or the printed music. Some appropriate songs for use with the autoharp are as follows:

One-chord songs:	*Key:*
"Row Your Boat," "Little Tom Tinker"	C major
"Are You Sleeping?" "Farmer in the Dell," "For Health and Strength"	F major
"Canoe Song"	D minor
"Zum Gali Gali"	G minor

"Brush Your Teeth"	E major
"All Hid"	F major
"The Rainy Round"	G major
Two-chord songs:	*key:*
"Mary Had a Little Lamb," "Sandy Land," "Looby Loo"	G major
"London Bridge," "Ten Little Indians," "Hush Little Baby," "Polly Wolly Doodle"	F major
"Old Smoky," "Oats, Peas, Beans, and Barley," "Little Red Caboose"	C major
"Down in the Valley," "Long Ago," "Bow Belinda," "Shoo Fly," "Susie Little Susie"	F major
"Nobody Home"	G minor
"Lovely Evening"	F major
"Wayfaring Stranger"	D minor
"Hokey Pokey"	G major
Three-chord songs:	*key:*
"Silent Night," Brahms' "Lullaby," "Marines' Hymn"	C major
"My Bonnie," "Jingle Bells," "Camptown Races," "Old Brass Wagon"	G major
"Red River Valley," "Twinkle, Twinkle, Little Star," "This Old Man," "Hickory Dickory Dock," "Home on the Range"	F major
"Go Down, Moses"	A minor
"Old King Cole"	D minor

Some two- and three-chord songs are not written in keys playable on the autoharp. The teacher may want to transpose them into keys that are possible on the instrument and suitable for children's voices. This procedure involves three steps:

1. determining the key on the autoharp that is closest to the written key of the song.
2. placing the fingers on the chord buttons for that key.
3. playing the primary chords of I, V_7 and IV in the new key.

It is important to keep autoharps in tune, but there is no universally accepted method for tuning the instrument. Ordinarily, tuning is done to a piano, although a pitch pipe can be used. The strings sounding the C major chord may be tuned first (all of the C's, E's, and G's), then the strings of the G_7 chord (all B's, D's, and F's—the G's having been tuned as part of the C chord), and next the F major chord (all A's—the F's and C's having been tuned as pitches belonging to the other chords). These three chords should then be played slowly to hear which of the strings need further adjusting. This procedure may need to be repeated several times. Next, the other strings may be tuned as individual tones of the chromatic scale. Then every chord of the instrument is played slowly to determine which strings need further tuning. An alternative procedure for tuning the instrument is to tune one string, and then tune subsequent strings by following the circle of fifths. To keep the instrument in tune and to protect it, it should be kept either in a case or on a protected shelf, out of the sunlight and away from sources of heat, cold, or dampness. When the instrument is subject to changes in temperature, the expansion and contraction of the strings cause changes in their tension, hence changes in pitch.

Types of autoharp accompaniments. Like any other musical instrument, the autoharp should be played with an accompaniment appropriately chosen for the song. The mood of the song indicates whether the player uses a slow relaxed stroke or a strong fast stroke. For some songs, an "um-pah-pah" style is suitable. This can be made by strumming the first beat of each measure with low-pitched strings and the other two beats with high-pitched strings. The player can make an appropriate accompaniment for some Spanish-type music by chording in the rhythm of

A bagpipe or bourdon effect is made by holding down two bars at the same time; G major and G minor, or D₇ and D minor, or A₇ and A minor. This effect is useful for pentatonic music, for some Scottish music, and for folk songs based on the open fifth of the bagpipe. Individual strings can be plucked for yet another musical effect. A zither or tamburitza effect that characterizes some Eastern European folk music can be produced by two players on the same instrument. One player presses the bars while the other strokes the strings rapidly with wooden mallets. A metal bar or object placed across the strings produces a steel guitar effect. Minor seventh chords can be sounded when two instruments are used. For example, G minor and B ♭ major chords played simultaneously sound the G minor seventh chord. A minor plus C major sounds the A minor seventh chord, and D minor plus F major sounds the D minor seventh chord. For songs of slow tempo, a skilled player can produce both the melody and the harmony. To obtain this effect, a chord is played for each tone of the melody, and the player strums the strings only as far as the melody pitch. A harp effect is obtained by reversing the usual stroke, the player beginning the stroke with the high strings and moving the pick toward the low strings.

A valuable teacher's guide to the autoharp is *Teaching Music with the Autoharp,* Washburn International, 230 Lexington Drive, Buffalo Grove, IL 60089. The book proceeds from beginning to advanced techniques for playing the instrument and includes a varied song collection.

Guitar and Ukulele

As children gain experience with the autoharp they should be introduced to the guitar. Younger children may learn to play on the upper four strings, and advanced children may use all six. Standard tuning on the guitar, from lowest pitch to highest, is E, A, D, G, B, E. To tune the instrument, the lowest pitched string should be tuned to E on an electronic tuner, or low E on the piano, a octave and a sixth below middle C. While holding the instrument appropriately the teacher should find a dot on the upper edge of the fingerboard between frets 4 and 5. By depressing the lowest string (the newly tuned E string) at that point, it sounds the correct pitch for the next string, A. The teacher strums each of these strings alternately while making tuning adjustments on the second string (A string) until the two pitches match. To tune the third string (D string), follow the same procedure, depressing the A string between the fourth and fifth frets, and tuning the D string to that pitch. The same procedure is repeated for

Courtesy of the Music Educators National Conference, Reston, Va.

the fourth string (G string). To tune the fifth string the reference point changes. The newly tuned G string is depressed between frets 3 and 4, and the fifth string (B string) is tuned to it. The last string is tuned by reverting to the original procedure; the fifth string is depressed between frets 4 and 5, and the E string is tuned to it.

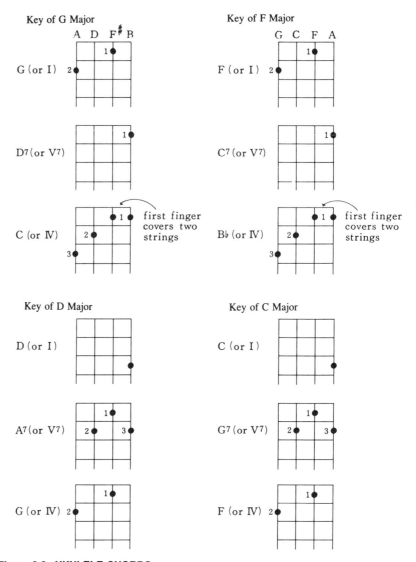

Figure 9.6. UKULELE CHORDS

To learn to play the guitar children should begin with chording on the bottom four strings (the highest pitches). The strum can be developed first by students strumming while the teacher fingers the chords. In order to be ready to play the guitar alone, the child needs to be capable of the following:

1. The hand needs to be large enough to reach around the guitar neck.
2. The fingers need to be strong enough to depress the strings securely.
3. Fine motor development must be sufficient for independent finger action.

Before the student attempts to play a chord, the fingernails of the left hand must be closely trimmed, allowing the pad of each finger to press down the string at a right angle. Learning to play a single chord is not extremely difficult. However, learning to shift from one chord to another, especially at tempo, introduces a number of problems that can be overcome only with patience and practice. Figure 9.6 illustrates a number of chords that can be played on the highest four strings of the guitar.

Eventually some students may be able to move to six-string chords. Any good guitar book illustrates fingering patterns for plucking and strumming a wide variety of chords. Figure 9.7 illustrates some common chords for all six strings.

Keyboards   Many students enjoy playing chords on the piano and other keyboard instruments. Electronic keyboards are especially fascinating. The teacher should not expect students to learn to play the keyboard with any facility unless they are studying privately. It is possible, however, for children to learn to build simple chords and use them as accompaniment for songs.

Figure 9.7. GUITAR CHORDS

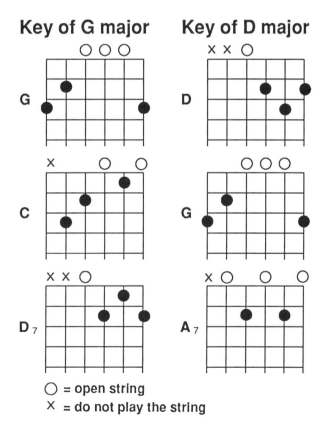

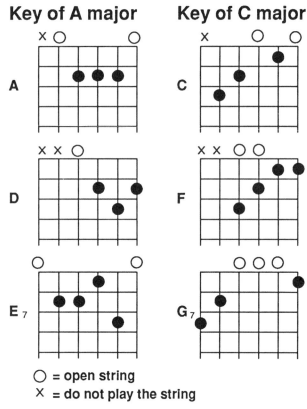

Key of A major   Key of C major

○ = open string
X = do not play the string

Figure 9.7. GUITAR CHORDS (Cont.)

The 1-3-5 chord (a triad in root position) is basic to most traditional music. With guidance the child can experiment at the keyboard, forming major and minor triads that involve no black keys.

The teacher may help the child play the chord in a steady walking tempo as the class sings a one-chord song such as "Row, row, row your boat." There are few standard songs that can be accompanied in their entirety by a single chord, but some were listed earlier in this chapter.

Songs that require two chords (1 and V_7) but that might be usable as one-chord songs include "Old MacDonald," "Farmer in the Dell," "Three Blind Mice," "Goodbye Old Paint," and "Swing Low, Sweet Chariot."

Summary of possibilities:

Play the melody with the right hand.
Play the melody with the left hand.

Sing the melody and play the chord with the left hand.

Play the chord with the left hand.

Play the chord with the right hand.

Play the chord with both hands.

Play the melody with the right hand and the chord with the left hand.

Play the melody with the left hand (in bass clef) and the chord with the right hand (in treble clef).

Play the chord in other forms, such as one note at a time.

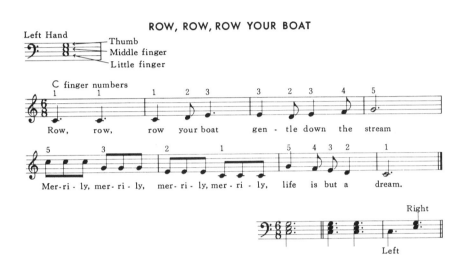

ROW, ROW, ROW YOUR BOAT

How often the chord is sounded depends on the frequency of strong beats in the song. One student may play a chord on every beat. Another may choose to sound the chord every other beat. Still another may alter the steady pattern of chords by a pause at the end of a phrase. Children should be free to be as individually creative as possible in this simple way.

When a child has learned how to build triads on different pitches such as C, F, G, and has learned to recognize the distinctive sound of the major chord, the minor triads may be easily taught. A child can soon learn that the minor triad has its own characteristic sound and that major and minor triads can be built at will. Experience will expand the concept of the difference in sound between major and minor. The physical difference between the ways major and minor triads are played is merely that the middle finger, which plays scale tone 3, is placed one half step lower in minor than in major. Few commonly known songs can be accompanied by a single minor triad, but children can compose such songs easily.

A song of Israeli origin that can be accompanied by a single minor triad (E minor) is "Zum Gali Gali."

If students have used the autoharp with songs requiring two or more different chords, the addition of the V_7 chord to permit improvising a keyboard

ZUM GALI GALI

Israeli Song

Chant

Em / Am / Em

Zum ga - li, ga - li, ga - li, Zum ga - li, ga - li.

Verse

Am / Em

1. He - cha - lutz le 'man a - vo - dah;_____
2. We will work and sing ev - ery one'_____

Am / Em

A - vo - dah le 'man he - cha - lutz.
We will work 'till our task is_____ done.

accompaniment to many familiar songs is relatively easy. A simple form of the chord change from I to V_7 and back to I is as follows:

Students may ask the question, ''Why are our fingers in the positions they are on the keyboard?'' The teacher's response may be as follows, ''What we are trying to do with our chord positions at the piano is to move our fingers as little as possible. It is more efficient. Here are the I, IV, and V chords in the root or 1-3-5 position in the C major scale'':

These can also be called C, F, and G chords because they are built on those tones. In the key of C here is the V_7 chord in root position:

Students can compare the V_7 with the V above. This chord is called V_7 because a note has been added that is seven lines and spaces above its root, G. The notes from the bottom to the top in this chord are G, B, D, and F, or 1-3-5-7. It is V_7 because G is the fifth step of the scale of C.

The following illustration shows where we obtain the simple three-finger hand position for chording:

By rearranging the G chord into another position, and by omitting the note D, which is the one we can most easily eliminate without altering the sound of the chord, we can keep the hand in the same place as in playing the I chord and move only the fingers.

The IV chord used in keyboard chording is a modified position of the original 1-3-5 arrangement of the notes of that chord:

The three basic chord positions are

In the "Blacksmith Song," these chords are outlined in the melody in root position, first inversion, and second inversion.

THE BLACKSMITH

strong, brawn - y arms free and bare; See the fire in the fur - nace a -
glow - ing, Bright its spar - kle, its flash and its glare.

2. *Blow the fire, stir the coals, heaping more on,*
   Till the iron is aglow, let it roar on!
   As the smith high his hammer keeps swinging,
   Fiery sparks fall in showers all around;
   And the sledge on the anvil keeps ringing,
   Giving out its loud clanging sound.

Using the hand position for the major triad as a starting point, the following directions apply in all major keys:

right hand: The little finger remains on the same key. The fourth finger is placed one half step higher than the third finger was. The thumb is placed one half step lower than before.

left hand: The thumb remains on the same key. The index finger is placed one half step higher than the middle finger was. The little finger is placed one half step lower than before.

The teacher can model the hand positions just described, and assist students in making the chord changes.

Many songs can be harmonized with the I and V_7 chords. Some of the most familiar were listed earlier for autoharp chording.

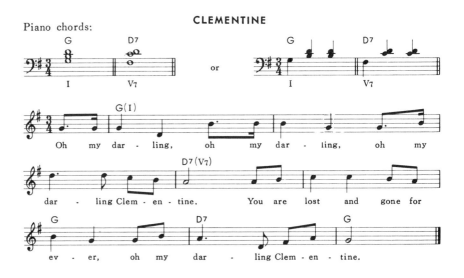

CLEMENTINE

Piano chords:

Oh my dar - ling, oh my dar - ling, oh my
dar - ling Clem - en - tine. You are lost and gone for
ev - er, oh my dar - ling Clem - en - tine.

Since most songs in minor keys are based on a scale in which the seventh tone is raised one half step, practically all minor I-V_7 chord songs have the V_7 chord played exactly the same as it is played in the major keys of the same name, that is, the V_7 chord in G minor is the same chord as in G major. Thus, the only difference in chording would be in the I chord, which in minor would have its third (the middle note) one half step lower than in the major chord. It is a simple matter, then, to play "Nobody Home" in G minor.

NOBODY HOME

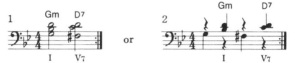

Piano chording:

or yet another way:

Suggestion: Students may compose an introduction and an ending for this round. Suitable percussion instruments and hand clapping may be added.

Other interesting songs in minor keys that use these same chords are the French carol "Pat-a-pan" and the English carol, "Dame, Get Up." Percussion instruments work well with "Pat-a-pan."

The hand position for the IV chord is easier on the keyboard than the hand position for the V_7 chord. The "rule" for the change from I to 1V is as follows:

right hand: The thumb remains on the same key. The middle finger is placed one half step higher than before. The little finger moves up one whole step.

left hand: The little finger remains on the same key. The index finger is placed one half step higher than the middle finger was. The thumb moves up one whole step.

The round "Kookaburra" provides a good introduction to this chord change. The chords are to be used as marked.

KOOKABURRA Australian Round
Words by M. Sinclair

Koo-ka-bur-ra sits on an old gum tree___

Mer-ry, mer-ry king of the bush is he___

Laugh, Koo-ka-bur-ra, laugh, Koo-ka-bur-ra,

Gay your life must be.

There are interesting similarities between the melodies of "Kookaburra" and another familiar round "Christmas Bells."

CHRISTMAS BELLS

R. E. N.   Four-Part Round

Christ-mas bells ring-ing ding dong ding. Ma-ny voi-ces be-gin to sing. Oh

ring! All the bells of Christ-mas Day, Ring a jol-ly Yule-tide song!

The IV chord in minor keys is played as shown below:

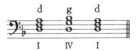

An American folk song that can be harmonized with only I and IV chords is "Wayfaring Stranger":

WAYFARING STRANGER

Examples of the many songs in major keys easily chorded with I, IV, and V_7 chords are "Oh Susanna," "Tingalayo," "Michael Row the Boat Ashore," "The First Noel," "Night Herding Song," "Eyes of Texas" (I've Been Working on the Railroad), "All Through the Night," "Sing Your Way Home," "Deck the Halls," "Happy Birthday to You," "Auld Lang Syne," "Annie Laurie," "Old Folks at Home," "Reuben and Rachel," and "The Muffin Man." Others were listed earlier for autoharp chording.

CINDY

Appalachian Mountains Song

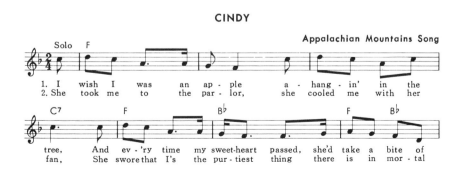

me. She told me that she loved me, she called me su - gar
man. I wish I had a nee - dle, as fine as I can

plum. She threwed her arms a - round me,___ I thought my time had come.
sew. I'd sew that gal to my coat - tail, and down the road I'd go.

Git a - long home, Cin - dy, Cin - dy, Git a - long home, Cin - dy,

Cin - dy, Git a - long home Cin - dy, Cin - dy, I'll mar - ry you some time.

Left hand
I IV I V₇ I

Right hand
I IV I V₇ I
Fingering

The use of keyboards in the classroom can enhance the variety of accompaniments available to the teacher. The electronic keyboard, or synthesizer has much better control over dynamic levels than the acoustic piano. It can easily be adjusted to avoid covering the children's voices when they sing.

If the student can chord with I, IV, and V₇ chords in major keys, it is not difficult to chord in minor keys with I, IV, and V₇. Children should be able to identify minor and major and to enjoy hearing the changes from minor to major and vice versa in songs such as "We Three Kings of Orient Are," "When Johnny Comes Marching Home," and "Minka."

For studying chords in root position and their inversions, some three-part songs in music series books for upper grades are helpful. One of these is "Jarabe," in which *passing tones* and *nonchord* tones can be discovered.

JARABE

Spirited

Mexican Song

Now the duck is in the stew pot, The bub - bles show that it is red - hot.
Ya el pa - to se está co - cien - do, En los her - vo - res de la o - lla,

Melody and words from *Spanish-American Folksongs,* collected by Eleanore Hague; published by the American Folklore Society, Inc. Used by permission. *This Is Music For Today, Book V,* by William R. Sur et al. Copyright © 1971 by Allyn and Bacon, Inc. Used by permission.

Older students can focus on songs with key changes to learn how a composer modulates (changes) from one key to another. Two such songs are ''The Erie Canal'' and ''We Three Kings of Orient Are'' in which both major and minor tonalities occur.

The keyboard provides an opportunity for hearing, seeing, and playing the chords associated with songs and for trying out new harmonizations.

Pitched Percussion

When concerned with harmony, the teacher's primary purpose for using pitched percussion instruments is as simple accompaniments based on borduns, drones, and harmonic ostinatos. These may be composed by the teacher for use by younger children, or by older students. Xylophones with wooden bars may be preferable for songs with rapid harmonic changes because of the shorter duration of their tones. Metallophones and glockenspiels, by contrast, produce longer, ringing sounds that may be more suitable for songs with less frequent chord changes.

Before children use mallets with these instruments, the teacher shows them the proper way to hold the mallets and the specific accompanying pattern for the song. The children may imitate the teacher's gestures for the pattern on their knees without the mallets, before transferring, with mallets, to the instruments.

**Teaching with
Harmonic
Instruments**

I, V₇, IV Chords. These chords are the *tonic, dominant seventh,* and *subdominant,* respectively. The teacher plays the chords slowly and repetitively on the autoharp, keyboard, or guitar. The students are asked to describe and compare the chords. When this has been done, an identification game can be played. For example, the teacher can play a series of these chords and ask students to hold up one, four, or five fingers to indicate the chord they hear.

Major, minor chords. Students can indicate the major and minor quality of chords they hear by palms up for major and palms down for minor.

Chords. Many students think of a chord as a triad of three notes, and they are correct. However, their concept of chords can be expanded by asking them to write on the grand staff the pitches of the C major chord as they are shown and sounded on the autoharp. The teacher then asks them which chord tones are repeated at octave intervals, how this might affect their definition of ''chord,'' and how this might relate to their future compositions.

Chording accompaniments. Classes can create their own accompaniments for easy two- and three-chord songs. The songs should have no chord designations to help the learners. The problem is to decide which chords to use. The teacher may have to provide assistance in determining which chords sound right. The class may discover that some songs can be harmonized in several different ways.

Chords and gestures. Students choose a different motion for each of the primary chords of a song. The tonic chord can be represented by a motion to be done in place; the dominant and subdominant chords can be represented by transversing motions. The teacher lists the choices on the board with the chords they represent. As the teacher plays a familiar song in the designated key, students show which chords is harmonizing with the melody at that time by using the appropriate gesture.

Harmonic card game. The teacher prepares small cards in geometric shapes: three shapes, each in a different color. Students are given one of each card, and informed which of the primary chords each of the cards represents. As the teacher plays a familiar song in the designated key students show which chord harmonizes with the melody at that time time by raising the appropriate card.

Tone clusters. Another technique in contemporary composition is the use of the tone cluster, a group of adjacent pitches used by composers such as Charles Ives and Henry Cowell. To make a tone cluster, place the entire palm or forearm on the keys of the keyboard. Young children might use tone clusters to imitate various sounds associated with animals or the environment.

Quartal chords. Traditional chords are constructed of thirds when in root position. Some chords used in contemporary music are constructed as a succession of perfect fourths—*quartal* chords. Several students might perform such chords at the piano with the class, then discussing how these chords might be used in compositions and for sound effects.

Harmony. The class listens to several selected recorded compositions and compares the use of harmony in each.

Composition over an ostinato. The class creates a simple pentatonic ostinato. Then individuals or small groups compose a melody to be performed over it. Examples:

McPhee, "Ostinatos" from *Tabuh Tabuhan,* Mercury MG 50103.
Cowell, "Ostinato Pianissimo" on *Concert Percussion,* Time 8000.

Accompaniment, ostinato, harmony. Students improvise an accompaniment for "Row Your Boat" using G and E on bells. The class considers whether it is an ostinato or simple harmony.

Chords, harmony. Students chord an accompaniment for a song, taking their cues from the lead-sheet notation that appears above the melody.

Cadence. Students compose a piece to demonstrate complete phrase endings (ending with a tonic chord), and incomplete phrase endings (ending with V_7 or IV chord). The phrase ending is the cadence.

Blues. The class composes a text and melody in the key of C major, using the traditional 12-bar-blues chord progression shown here. They also devise a good rhythm pattern to accompany this three-phrase song. The class might sing it with autoharp or keyboard accompaniment.

$$
\begin{array}{llll}
I & I & I & I \\
IV_7 & IV_7 & I & I \\
V_7 & IV_7 & I & I
\end{array}
$$

The teacher must remember that the lowered third and seventh steps of the major scale are features of blues music.

REFERENCES

General Copas, Lugene. "Baby Elephant Walk," *General Music Journal,* 7/2, Winter 1989, 14.

Dotson, Jeanette, "Percussion Chart," *General Music Journal,* 7/2, Winter 1989, 15.

Giles, Martha. "Recorder Ensembles—A New Wind in the Elementary Program," *Music Educators Journal,* December 1982, 41–42.

KENDALL, M. J. "Two Instructional Approaches to the Development of Aural and Instrumental Performance Skills," *Journal of Research in Music Education. 36/4,* Winter 1988, 205–219.

MORRIS, D. J., "A Different Drum: Percussion Ensembles in General Music," *Music Educators Journal,* September 1989, 30–34.

PRIEST, PHILIP. "Playing by Ear: Its Nature and Application to Instrumental Learning," *British Journal of Music Education, 6/2* July 1989, 173–191.

SCHENCK, ROBERT, "Above All, Learning an Instrument Must Be Fun!," *British Journal of Music Education, 6/1,* March 1989, 3–35.

SWEET, DEBRA. *Capsule Units for Guitar, Autoharp, Recorder, Elementary General Music,* Area Education Agency 7, Cedar Falls, Iowa, 1980. 37 pp. E0241374.

Recorder BUCHTEL, FORREST, *Buchtel Recorder Method,* Book 1. Neil A. Kjos Music Company, 525 Busse Highway, Park Ridge, IL 60068.

COX, HEATHER, and GARTH RICHARD, *Sing, Clap, and Play the Recorder,* Books 1 and 2. St. Louis, Mo.: Magnamusic-Baton, Inc.

EARLE, FREDERICK, *Trophy Elementary Recorder Method, Baroque System.* Trophy Music Co., 1278 W. 9th St. Cleveland, OH 44113.

LANAHAN, WALTER D., *Melody Method for the Recorder.* Laurel, Md.: Melody Flute Co.

NEWMAN, HAROLD, and GRACE NEWMAN, *Music Shall Live—Singing and Playing with the Recorder.* Hargail Music Press, 28 W. 38th St. New York, NY 10018. Hargail specializes in recorder.

Recorder Music Catalog. Belwin-Mills, Melville, NY 11746. Recorder music selected from many publishers.

RICHARDSON, ALLEN L., *The Breeze Easy One and All.* New York: Warner Brothers.

Sources of Classroom Instruments Continental Music, Division of C. G. Conn, Ltd., 150 Aldredge Blvd., Atlanta, GA 30336.

Lyons, PO Box 1003, Elkhart, IN 46515.

Magnamusic-Baton, Inc., 10370 Page Industrial Blvd., St. Louis, MO 63132.

Music Education Group, Oscar Schmidt, 230 Lexington Drive, Buffalo Grove IL 60089. Autoharp and all other instruments.

The World of Peripole, Inc., P.O. Box 146, Lewiston Road, Browns Mills, NJ 08015.

Rhythm Band, Inc., P.O. Box 126, Fort Worth, TX 76101.

Scientific Music Industries, Inc., 525 N. Noble St., Chicago, IL 60622.

Yamaha Music Corp. U.S.A., Clavinovia Keyboards, P.O. Box 6600, Buena Park, CA 90620.

10 Teaching Children to Listen to Music

Why We Teach Listening Skills

> Music can only be alive when there are listeners who are really alive. What we are encouraging with our students then is a more active kind of listening.
>
> AARON COPLAND

The mass media offers today's children musical snacks rather than a balanced diet of styles and kinds of music. Their sensitivity has been numbed by the bombardment of sound. Hearing is often mistaken for listening. Hearing is passive, whereas listening requires effort. Students need to become active listeners.

A varied program of listening centered on student involvement will produce more conscious, aware listeners. Opportunities exist in the elementary classroom to promote student understanding of music through the process of their acquiring actual skills in listening. A skillful teacher motivates students to listen to something in a conscious manner. At the same time attitudes and tastes are affected by the choices of music and their presentation in the classroom.

Listening Skills for the Elementary School Child

Key elements in learning to listen are awareness and interest. Awareness of the existence of a piece of music and its relationship to a particular genre occurs when a listening selection is introduced. The task of the teacher is to sharpen this awareness to include recognition of musical elements and their treatment. Simultaneously the teacher must address student interest, seeking to determine what feature will initially focus the student's interest during the first hearing. Another consideration for the teacher is how to sustain the student's interest sufficiently so that student wants to hear the music again.

Moving to music is the initial response of very young children, but it also provides an effective cue for listening and responding for older students and adults. Other skills to be developed in the elementary music program include the ability to detect musical events when they occur, and to describe those events to others. Visual materials in the form of listening maps may serve to focus student attention on the musical events. Some listening selections require prior musical experiences on the part of the students before they are ready to listen. These the teacher will anticipate.

Listening examples are available from a surprising variety of sources. Current elementary music series include musical examples on long-play records, cassettes, or compact discs. In addition, many elementary school libraries have recordings available for use, including the now out-of-print *Adventures in Music*. Any good record store has numerous commercial recordings that can be useful in designing listening lessons.

Tips for Teaching Listening

In teaching listening there are several simple axioms that help make lessons effective.

1. Use simple language.
2. Ask the students questions; do not tell them what they hear.
3. Clarify concepts by using comparison and contrast.
4. In choosing materials and approach, consider the listener's age and musical understanding.
5. Make extensive use of repetition of short musical passages.
6. Distinguish between program music and music that conveys only musical ideas.
7. Relate musical concepts to a particular work, rather than making isolated abstractions about music in general.
8. Seek visual and kinesthetic student responses as well as verbal ones.
9. Focus on active student involvement as the main goal of listening, rather than talk, study, or analysis.

Exploring the Musical Elements Through Listening

Even though listening is featured here as an independent topic, it is of central importance that the teacher integrates listening into every music lesson, whether it be focused on rhythm, dynamics, pitch, melody, harmony, or any other aspect of the program. Review the variety of lesson material in Part II to review how listening can be emphasized in those lessons, and how it plays an essential role in virtually all musical endeavors.

Rhythm
The element of rhythm was thoroughly discussed in Chapter 5. Here are two lesson plans that combine distinctive rhythm with listening:

Lesson Plan in Rhythm: FUNKY PENGUIN

Objectives:

Rhythm	The student will reflect a steady beat through movement.
Tone Quality	The student will recognize the synthesizer as the sound source for this composition.
Melody	The student will identify the melody in two forms: initially composed of eighth notes, then repeated using quarter notes.

Materials Needed:
Selection: ''Wolfgang Amadeus Penguin''
Tape: *Saving the Wildlife*, Mannheim Steamroller
Penguin picture, poster or stickers, world map

Background:
Penguins are flightless birds of Antarctica (South Pole), who are equipped with webbed feet and flippers for swimming.
Mannheim Steamroller is a contemporary group of musicians who sometimes appear in concert and record as Fresh Aire.

Student Preparation:
Awareness of the penguin, its physical characteristics, movements, and habitat.
Introduction to the sounds of the synthesizer.
Simple understanding of the concepts of rhythm, tone quality, and melody.

Teaching Suggestions:

1. The teacher introduces the penguin through a picture, a poster, or stickers.

2. Students are asked the following questions:
   — What shape repeats that of the penguin, a square, a circle, or a triangle?
   — What colors of feathers has this bird, green and yellow, black and white, or orange and black?

3. First hearing: The teacher inquires of the students whether or not the tempo is steady.

4. Second hearing: Students listen to the melody, and indicate a melody change by raising their hands. Class discusses the change that occurs as the melody is extended (use of eighth and quarter notes). The teacher may show the melody on the board in both its forms.

5. Third hearing: The teacher asks students to suggest the kind of movement a penguin might make, such as waddling, hopping, or flying. Students are directed to listen

again to the music, and to move in penguin fashion, changing their movements as the melody stretches out.

6. The teacher initiates discussion with the class regarding the choice of the synthesizer to play this music.

Extension: Students can select percussion instruments to accompany the music on an additional hearing. Their rhythmic ostinatos should reflect a steady beat.

Lesson Plan in Rhythm: BACH WITH A BEAT

Objectives:

Rhythm	The student will feel and identify an underlying beat, with a different rhythm pattern superimposed.
Tone Quality	The student will recognize by sight and hearing the following timbres in solo: trumpet, oboe, violin, flute and recorder.
Melody	The student will perform a melodic theme by singing and by playing the recorder.
Form	The student will recognize by hearing the difference between solo and tutti.

Materials:
''Brandenburg Concerto No. 2'' 3rd Movement by J.S. Bach—*The Enjoyment of Music Series*, Machlis, Side 13, #6
Also: *Music and You*. Macmillan, 1988. Grade 6 recording
Instruments to show and to play (pictures may be used if instruments are unavailable)
Worksheet

Background:
John Sebastian Bach (1685–1750)
In 1719 Bach played before the Margrave Christian Ludwig of Brandenburg. The prince was so impressed that he asked Bach to write some works for his own orchestra. Two years later Bach sent the prince six pieces that have become known as the Brandenburg Concertos. No two are alike.
In these pieces Bach has captured the spirit of the concerto grosso, in which two groups vie with each other. Notice the brilliant trumpet part. There were no valves on the trumpets in Bach's time.
In the Brandenburg Concerto No. 2, the solo group consists of a trumpet, a flute, an oboe, and a violin. The accompanying group (tutti) includes first and second violins, violas, and double bass. The basso continuo is played by cello and harpsichord. The trumpeter introduces the theme, which is next taken up by the oboe, then the violin, and finally, the recorder. A lively four-voiced fugue results, which sounds like a conversation among equals.

Student Preparation: The teacher may show the class a picture of Bach. Students can discuss the time in which he lived as suggested by his clothes and his hairstyle. Additional background may be provided by the teacher in response to student interest, but the emphasis should be on Bach's music, rather than the historical period which he represents.

Teaching Suggestions:

1. Students are taught to sing the following theme:

Bach wrote this for a prince that he knew, for Bran-den - burg, Prince Bran-den burg

2. The teacher shows and demonstrates sounds of the solo instruments. Pictures may be used when instruments are unavailable.

3. First hearing: Students listen to the music, and raise their hands when hearing the main theme.

4. Second hearing (partial): The teacher suggests that students tap the beat of the music while listening to determine whether it is fast or slow, and steady or irregular.

5. The teacher may ask students to determine which instrument plays in the highest register (the trumpet).

6. Third hearing: A worksheet is passed out to students, who listen again to respond to the questions. The teacher then reviews their answers with them in a discussion which includes consideration of the contrast between solo and tutti.

7. Students may learn to play the main theme on recorders in the key of D major.

Extension: Pictures of the solo instruments can be passed out to individual students. During a later hearing, each student may hold up his or her picture when the instrument is playing the main theme.

"Brandenburg Concerto No. 2"
Third Movement
by J. S. Bach

1. Which instrument begins and ends this music?
   a. Recorder
   b. Oboe
   c. Trumpet
2. How many times is the main melody played?
   a. 3
   b. 4
   c. 9
3. Name the solo instruments you hear:

   _____

   _____

   _____

   _____

4. The tutti, or accompanying instruments are strings and
   a. piano
   b. French horn
   c. harpsichord
5. How would you describe the tempo of the music?
   a. fast
   b. slow
   c. moderately fast
6. By what means does the composer create tension and repose in the music? (short answer)

Melody   In learning to listen, elementary students focus on melodies and the feelings of beginning, movement, and arrival that these melodies awaken. Students also begin to recognize that melodies may be broken into phrases of varying lengths, often of four measures. The important concept is not the phrase length as much as it is that melodies can be divided into logical parts called phrases. Phrase repetition and difference are found in the songs children sing and in recorded music to which they listen. Sometimes two phrases relate to each other in a special way (as antecedent and consequent phrases); these two phrases are called a *period*. They can be improvised in the classroom by the teacher singing the first phrase and students taking turns improvising the second phrase: the teacher sings a ''question,'' and the student sings an ''answering'' phrase. All of these abilities begin with the children learning to identify musical gestures as the same or different.

In learning to hear different phrases or larger contrasting sections of music, children may rely on movement, or other musical activities. Teachers select very clear examples of phrases when their objective is to help children distinguish ''same'' and ''different.'' Children are sometimes guided to portray phrases physically with gestures such as the arm movements suggested in Figure 10.1.

Students who have acquired concepts of similarity and contrast for phrases may find meaning in musical form. For example, when they discover a phrase order such as *a a b a*, or *a b a c a* and the teacher asks, ''What is there in this tune that gives us a feeling of similarity or contrast?'' and ''What is there that gives us a feeling of unity?'' the function of form becomes clear. Phrases *b* and

Figure 10.1. "ACTING OUT" PHRASES

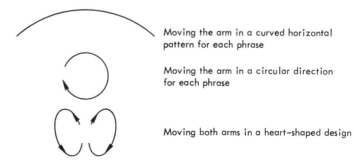

Moving the arm in a curved horizontal pattern for each phrase

Moving the arm in a circular direction for each phrase

Moving both arms in a heart-shaped design

c provide variety, and phrase *a* provides similarity with its repetitions. This principle brings meaning to the forms of students' own compositions.

Children also need to be able to hear that melodies can be extended and altered in various ways by composers. By listening to music, making music, and creating music, students discover the use of introductions, codas, and interludes. Introductions and codas are usually derived from melodies, but an interlude is often a contrasting section. Repetition is an obvious way to extend melodies. *Thematic development* is a term that describes what composers do with themes they use in their larger compositions.

Two sample listening lessons follow. They feature the principle of melodic similarity and contrast.

Lesson Plan in Melody: A RABBIT'S LULLABY

Objectives:

Melody   The student will recognize the nursery melody as a lullaby and compose appropriate lyrics for it.

Timbre   The student will identify the timbre used by the composer to accompany the story.

Materials:
Story of "The Velveteen Rabbit," narrated by Meryl Streep
Recording (same title) *Dancing Cat* (Windham Hill) Stereo DT 3007
Book (available in most elementary school libraries)
Velveteen rabbit mask (optional)

Background: George Winston is a contemporary composer of New Age Music, associated with Windham Hill Recordings.

Student Preparation:
Recognition of piano timbre upon hearing.
Familiarity with the story of "The Velveteen Rabbit."
Understanding of simple standard notation.

Teaching Suggestions:

1. The teacher introduces the music by checking student awareness of the title book, and inquiring about the characters and the story. In a class of young children, the teacher shows a rabbit mask, and inquires "What animal is this? Do you know a story about a rabbit?"

2. First hearing: The teacher plays an early portion of the tape or record, asking students to name the instrument which provides the musical setting for the story (the piano).

3. The nursery lullaby melody is played on a keyboard by the teacher. It is then taught to the students, first by rote, then transferred to standard notation. Students are asked to sing it on *la*.

4. Second hearing: The teacher replays the same portion of the tape, and asks students to raise hands when hearing the lullaby melody played by the piano.

5. The class proceeds to add lyrics to the notated melody, as the teacher draws attention to the rhythm and meter of its phrases. These lyrics may or may not rhyme. The completed lullaby is sung by the class as the teacher accompanies them on the piano.

6. Third hearing: Class may wish to hear the entire story, adding their song to the nursery lullaby when it occurs.

Extension: Students may discuss the role of the composer in stories accompanied by music.

Lesson Plan in Melody: MELODIES IN MOTION

Objectives:

Melody	The student will demonstrate awareness of different melodic lines.
Tone Quality	The student will recognize by hearing the following tone qualities: flute, finger cymbals, and guitar
Texture	The student will create a visual representation of music texture.
Form	The student will perceive melodic variation accompanied by a chordal background.

Materials:
Selection: "Variations on a Theme" by Satie
Recording: New Dimensions in Music Series (1976 ed.)
American Book Co., *Investigating Music*—Gr. 4, Record 7, Side A
Paper and colored chalk
Flute, finger cymbals, and guitar

Background: *Blood, Sweat and Tears* is a contemporary ensemble of musicians who have been performing and recording together for a number of years.

Student Preparation:
Familiarity with sight and sound of flute, finger cymbals, and guitar.
Previous experience drawing simple melodic contours and lines.
Understanding of melodic variation.

Teaching Suggestions:

1. The teacher shows the flute, finger cymbals, and the guitar to the class. Students are asked to name them, and given opportunities to initiate sounds on them.

2. Paper is passed out to each student, who then selects four different colors of chalk.

3. The tone quality of the flute is demonstrated by the teacher or a student. Students are instructed to select one color of chalk, and to note it in the corner of the paper as follows:

   _____ 1st flute

4. First hearing: Students are asked to raise hands when hearing the entrance of the first flute, and to draw the melodic line they hear with the first color as the piece is played.

5. Students are directed to take a second color of chalk and to note at the top of their papers:

_____ 2nd flute

6. Second hearing: Again students are requested to raise hands to indicate the entrance of the 2nd flute, and to draw its melodic line with the second color.

7. The teacher leads discussion about the relationship between two melodies and the kinds of variation heard. Students consider the ways in which a melody may be altered.

8. Students take a third color of chalk and note at the top of their papers:

_____ finger cymbals

9. The teacher demonstrates the tone quality of the finger cymbals in varying sizes.

10. Third hearing: Students are once more asked to raise hands to indicate the entrance of the finger cymbals, and then to show in some graphic way their frequency. Students will need to listen intently.

11. The teacher inquires about the instrument which begins, plays throughout, and ends the piece (the guitar). The class considers its function as a musical setting, and discusses ways to visually show its relationship to the melodies.

12. Students select a fourth and final color, and note it at the top of their papers:

_____ guitar

13. Final hearing: Students visually show the relationship of the guitar to the melodies of the flutes, and the interjections of the finger cymbals. Some students may wish to play finger cymbals during this hearing.

Extension: Individual interpretations of the music may be posted or displayed.

Tone Quality Learning to hear differences in tone quality begins at a very early age. Teachers may begin providing listening experiences related to this element at any time in the school program. Exploring sound sources for one's self readies the ear for distinguishing musical differences in tone quality. Teachers can help develop this aural skill by providing an enriched environment of sounds for children to manipulate. The sounds may be from the child's everyday world as well as from the world of music.

As children gain experiences through musical performance their aural acuity is developed. For example, when playing pitched percussion instruments they learn the differences in tone quality produced by felt, rubber, and plastic mallets. Or when having to choose between the sounds available on a music synthesizer, they hear a new class of musical timbres. Such cumulative experiences affect the students' musical taste and preferences throughout life.

The following lesson plan on tone quality features a variety of percussive sounds.

Lesson Plan in Tone Quality: PERCUSSION SOUNDSCAPE

Objectives:

Tone Quality   The student will identify varying tone qualities present in the percussion family of instruments.

Form   The student will recognize musical form which does not use repeated pitches or rhythmic motives but only tone color for successive musical ideas.

Materials Needed:
Ionization by Edgar Varèse
Recording: *The Enjoyment of Music Series,* Machlis, Side 17, Band 4
As many of the following instruments as are available:

claves	triangle
maracas	cowbell
gong	slapstick
cymbals	cabasa
guiro	Chinese temple blocks
drum	castanets
	sleigh bells

Background: Introduction to the percussion family

Student Preparation:
The teacher will show and demonstrate the instruments.
Students will understand and recognize the dynamic markings of piano, forte, fortissimo, crescendo, and decrescendo.

Teaching Suggestions:

1. The teacher will group different percussion instruments in several categories:
   pitched (piano, glockenspiel, chimes)
   nonpitched (claves, drums, cymbals, gongs, guiro, castanets, maracas, anvils, slapstick, triangle, and cowbell)
   Students will have opportunities to explore sounds made by these instruments.

2. First hearing: The teacher plays an early portion of the music and asks students to raise their hands when they hear the siren.

3. Second hearing: Students are asked to note icons which represent the snare drum, the maracas, and the siren on listening maps which have been passed out to them. Students follow the listening map as they listen, using the sounds of these three instruments and dynamic differences as road signs.

4. Third hearing: Students are asked to focus their listening on dynamic changes, and to indicate these with hand gestures that represent crescendo (left hand with thumb down, forming   <   ) and decrescendo (right hand with thumb down, forming   >   ).

5. The teacher facilitates class discussion of musical form in which successive musical ideas are presented.

6. Students consider the importance of a conductor for cues that indicate when players enter, and when they no longer play.

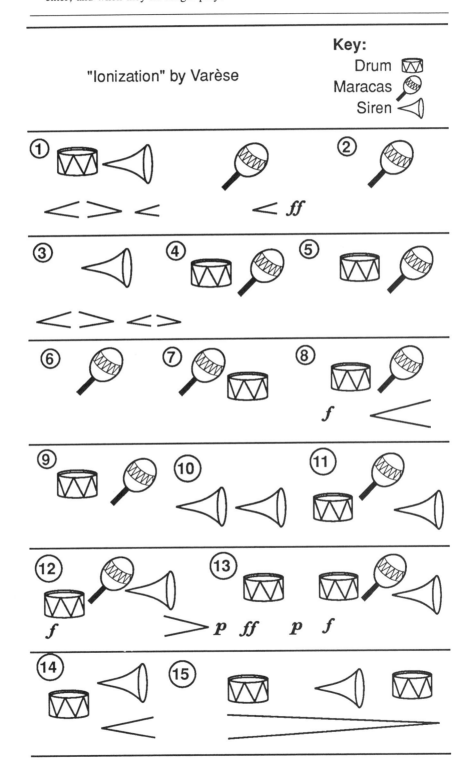

"Ionization" by Varèse

Key:
Drum
Maracas
Siren

Exploring Musical Form Through Listening

The answers to the questions, "Is the tune the same or is it different now?" and "How is it different?" guide children into learning how melodies are put together. The concepts of same, different, repetition, contrast, and variety can be reinforced through children's identifying the phrases of songs and comparing them.

Simple Forms   Three very common forms of songs are called one-part (unary), two-part (binary), and three-part (ternary) song forms. Each has many variants. The teacher and the class should expect to find songs with phrase orders which are modifications of these model forms, and songs with different forms. For a simple example, "Hole in the Bucket" has a unary form in which the same phrase is repeated. Because the phrase ends differently, it could be described as *a a'*.

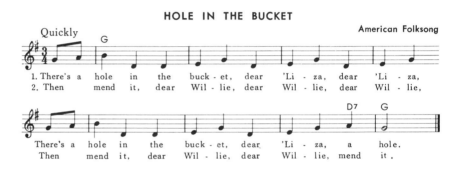

HOLE IN THE BUCKET

"Go Tell Aunt Rhody" is an example of binary form in which there are two unlike phrases, thus *a b*.

GO TELL AUNT RHODY

Another example of two-part form is "Tingalayo," which might be designated *a a' b b'* because of the phrase lengths and their repetition.

There are many examples of ternary (three-part) form, "O Tannenbaum" is one. Its form can be depicted as *a a b a*. Ternary form consists of a melodic statement, a contrasting phrase or section, followed by a restatement of the first

TING-A-LAY-O

Traditional

Ting - a - lay - o, run my lit - tle don - key run, Ting - a - lay - o, run my lit - tle don - key run. My don - key hee, my don - key haw, My don - key sleep in a bed of straw, My don - key short, my don - key wide, Don't get too close to his back side.

My donkey walk, my donkey talk,
My donkey eats with a knife and fork,
My donkey eat, my donkey sleep,
My donkey kicks with his two hind feet.

CHORUS

My donkey laugh, my donkey cry,
My donkey loves peanut butter pie,
My donkey laugh, my donkey cry,
My donkey loves peanut butter pie.

phrase. Musicians often compare the form to an arch in architecture. "O Tannenbaum" includes another interesting musical device, the *sequence,* in which part of the melody is repeated at a higher or lower pitch level. In this song measures 5 and 6 are repeated one step lower in measures 7 and 8. The song "I Love the Mountains" is another song which is sequential in character.

O TANNENBAUM (O Christmas Tree)

Firmly

Singing Game

O, Christ-mas tree, O, Christ-mas tree, How faith-ful are thy branch - es! Your boughs so green in sum-mer time, Stay green in win - ter's snow-y clime.

O, Christ-mas tree, O, Christ-mas tree How faith-ful are thy branch-es!

O, Tannenbaum, O, Tannenbaum,
Wie treu sind deine Blätter!
O, Tannenbaum, O, Tannenbaum,
Wie treu sind deine Blätter!
Du grünst nicht nur zur Sommerzeit
Nein auch im Winter, wenn es schneit.
O, Tannenbaum, O, Tannenbaum,
Wie treu sind deine Blätter!

Other examples of two- and three-part song forms follow.

Two-Part Song Form	**Three-Part Song Form**
"Du, Du, Liegst Mir im Herzen"	"Cradle Song" (French folk song)
"Go Tell Aunt Rhody"	"Lightly Row" (includes sequence)
"Li'l 'Liza Jane"	"Shoo Fly" (includes sequence)
	"Twinkle, Twinkle, Little Star"

Composers often use familiar melodies and songs in larger compositions. When a song is well known by children, their interest in listening to symphonic music is stimulated. However, identifying the melody is only a first step. Because the essence of symphonic music is thematic development, the answer to the question, "What does the composer do with the melody?" can bring forth exciting explorations. How fully students are able to reply to the question will depend upon their stage of musical development. If they have experience with the ways composers manipulate and change melodies, the teacher can help them identify these transformations as part of .their listening experience. Familiar melodies that appear in symphonic music are listed in Figure 10.2.

From the child's point of view, identifying phrases and larger sections in terms of letters of the alphabet is not as appealing as some other ways. For example, phrases *a b a* might be drawn as follows:

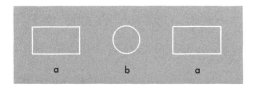

The sections of a rondo could be shown as follows:

Using colors adds more interest because color highlights the contrasts. Some students will draw objects rather than the geometric designs illustrated here. The evaluative criterion is, "Does this drawing tell us clearly what the design for the music is?" or "Does it show us all the parts in their true order?"

Larger Instrumental Forms

The principles of repetition and contrast embodied in simple forms are also manifest in larger instrumental forms. However, other compositional features are also present. One example is thematic development, or the expansion and alteration of one or more primary themes. If a tuneful phrase is presented and left unchanged, it is called a *melody*. If the phrase is manipulated it is called a *theme*. Thematic development as a means of extending musical ideas can be studied by having older students explore the beginning of Beethoven's Fifth Symphony. "What different things did the composer do with this short idea?" The first thing students may hear is the sequence Beethoven wrote.

Two-part (Binary) Form.

Ginastera, "Wheat Dance" from *Estancia*, AM, grade 4, vol. 1

Handel, "Bourrée" and "Menuetto" from *Royal Fireworks Music*, AM, grade 3, vol. 2; BOL 62.

Milhaud, "Copacabana" from *Saudades do Brazil*, AM, grade 4, vol. 2

Respighi, "Danza" from *Brazilian Impressions*, AM, grade 5, vol. 2

Bach, "Badinerie" from *Suite No. 2 in B Minor*, AM, grade 3, vol. 1

Three-Part (Ternary) Form.

Brahms, *Hungarian Dance No. 1 in C Minor*, AM, grade 5, vol. 2

Debussy, *En Bateau*, BOL 53

Offenbach, "Barcarolle" from *Tales of Hoffman*, AM, grade 3, vol. 1

Schumann, "Traumerei" from *Scenes of Childhood*, AM, grade 4, vol. 2; BOL 63

Stravinsky, "Berceuse" from *Firebird Suite*, AM, grade 1, vol. 1

Tchaikovsky, "Trepak" from *Nutcracker* Suite, BOL 58

Vaughan Williams, *Fantasia on Greensleeves*, AM, grade 6, vol. 2

Walton, "Waltz" from *Facade* Suite, AM, grade 6, vol. 2

Compound Ternary Form.

Compound ternary form is one in which each of the *A B A* sections may be a binary or ternary form within itself. It is found in the classical minuets of Haydn and Mozart.

Bizet, "Minuetto" from *L'Arlésienne* Suite No. 1, AM, grade 4, vol. 2

Haydn, "Menuetto" from *Symphony No. 6 in G Major*, BOL 63

Mozart, "Menuetto" from *Divertimento No. 17 in D Major*, AM, grade 5, vol. 2

Mozart, "Minuet" from *Symphony No. 40 in G Minor*, BOL 62

Sousa, *Stars and Stripes Forever*, AM, grade 4, vol. 2; BOL 60

Figure 10.2. SONG MELODIES IN SYMPHONIC MUSIC

Composer	Title	Song
ANDERSON	Irish Suite	"Irish Washerwoman," "Minstrel Boy," "Wearing of the Green," "The Girl I Left Behind Me"
BARLOW	The Winter's Passed	"Wayfaring Stranger," "Black Is the Color of My True Love's Hair"
BEETHOVEN	String Quartet Op. 59, No. 2	Russian hymn "Praise to God"
	Symphony 8, Second Movement, Third Theme	"The Metronome" (AM, grade 6, vol. 1)
	Symphony 9, Fourth Movement	"United Nations Hymn" ("World Anthem")
	Wellington's Victory	"For He's a Jolly Good Fellow"
BLOCH	America	"Yankee Doodle," "Old Folks at Home," "Hail Columbia"
BRAHMS	Academic Festival Overture	"Guadeamus Igitur" (BOL 76)
CAILLIET	Variations on Pop! Goes the Weasel	"Pop! Goes the Weasel" (BOL 65) (AM, grade 4, vol. 1)
CHOPIN	Fantasy Impromptu	"I'm Always Chasing Rainbows"
COPLAND	Appalachian Spring	"Simple Gifts" (BOL 75)
	Billy the Kid, Fourth Theme	"Goodbye, Old Paint"
	Lincoln Portrait	"Camptown Races," "Springfield Mountain"
	Rodeo	"Hoe-Down" (AM, grade 5, vol. 2) (BOL 55)
DOHNÁNYI	Variations on a Nursery Tune (for older children)	"Twinkle, Twinkle, Little Star" (piano and orchestra)
DVOŘÁK	Symphony 5	"Swing Low, Sweet Chariot" (First Movement, Third Theme) "Going Home" (Second Movement, First Theme)
GOULD	American Salute	"When Johnny Comes Marching Home" (AM, grade 5, vol. 1) (BOL 65)
	Cowboy Rhapsody	"Goodbye, Old Paint," "Home on the Range"
	Variations on When Johnny Comes Marching Home	"When Johnny Comes Marching Home"
GRAINGER	Londonderry Air	"Londonderry Air" (AM, grade 4, vol. 2)
GROFÉ	Death Valley Suite	"O Susanna" (AM, grade 4, vol. 1), "Old Folks at Home," "Old Black Joe"
GUION	Turkey in the Straw	"Old Zip Coon" (same tune)
HARRIS	Folk Song Symphony	"Irish Washerwoman," "Bury Me Not on the Lone Prairie," "Streets of Laredo," "Turkey in the Straw," "When Johnny Comes Marching Home"
HAYDN	"Emperor" Quartet in C Major	"Glorious Things of Thee Are Spoken" (Austrian National Hymn). Appears in several of the music series

Composer	Work	Examples
HINDEMITH	Trauermusic (Funeral Music)	"Old Hundred" Both melody and harmony are manipulated
HUMPERDINCK	Hansel and Gretel, Prelude to Act 1	"Prayer," "Song of the Gingerbread Children," "Partner, Come and Dance with Me"
IVES	Fifth Movement, Symphony 2	"Camptown Races," "Long, Long Ago," "Reveille"
KAY	Western Symphony	"Red River Valley," "The Girl I Left Behind Me," "Golden Slippers," "Jim Along Josie" (Vox Recording)
McBRIDE	Mexican Rhapsody	"Hat Dance," "Rancho Grande," "La Cucaracha"
	Pumpkin Eater's Little Fugue	"Peter, Peter, Pumpkin Eater" (BOL 65)
McDONALD	Children's Symphony	"Farmer in the Dell," "Jingle Bells" (AM, grade 3, vol. 2), "London Bridge," "Baa, Baa, Black Sheep," "Oh, Dear, What Can the Matter Be?" "Little Bo Peep"
MAHLER	First Symphony, Third Movement	"Are You Sleeping?"
MUSSORGSKY	Boris Godunov, Coronation Scene	"Praise to God"
NELSON	Kentucky Mountain Portraits	"Cindy," "Skip to My Lou," "Paw Paw Patch"
QUILTER	A Children's Overture	"Girls and Boys Come Out to Play," "St. Paul's Steeple," "Dame Get Up and Bake Your Pies," "Over the Hills and Far Away," "The Frog and the Crow," "The Frog He Would A-Wooing Go," "Oranges and Lemons," "Baa, Baa, Black Sheep"
ROSSINI	William Tell Overture	"Lone Ranger Theme" (BOL 76) (AM, grade 3, vol. 1)
SIBELIUS	Finlandia	"Song of Peace" and other titles
SOWERBY	Irish Washerwoman	"Lane County Bachelor" and other titles
R. STRAUSS	Aus Italien	"Funiculi, Funicula"
STRAVINSKY	Greeting Prelude	"Happy Birthday to You" (Columbia Record *Instrumental Miniatures*)
TCHAIKOVSKY	1812 Overture	"Russian National Hymn" and other titles
	Symphony 4, Fourth Movement	"The Birch Tree" (AM, grade 6, vol. 2)
THOMSON	"Cattle," from The Plow That Broke the Plains	"My Home's in Montana," "I Ride an Old Paint," "The Streets of Laredo" (BOL 65)
THOMSON	Fugue and Chorale on Yankee Doodle	"Yankee Doodle" (BOL 65)
VARDELL	Joe Clark Steps Out	"Old Joe Clark" (Mercury Recording)
VAUGHAN-WILLIAMS	Fantasia on Greensleeves	"What Child Is This?" ("Greensleeves") (AM, grade 6, vol. 2)

Rondo.   The principle of the rondo is a recurring theme that alternates with other themes. Children sometimes compare its scheme with a double-decker sandwich. The shortest rondo is *A B A C A*. If one compares *A* to a slice of bread and *B* and *C* to different sandwich fillings, the result is a special kind of double-decker sandwich. Longer rondos may be *A B A C A B A* or *A B A C A D A*. A beginning concept of the rondo is acquired by young children in simple ways. Five children might stand in front of the room, each positioned to play a pitched percussion instrument. The instrument might have one of the letter designations *A B A C A* in front of it. The first child (*A*) plays a 5-note phrase. The second child (*B*) plays a different 5-note phrase, and is followed by the third child (*A*), who repeats the first phrase. The fourth child (*C*) plays yet another 5-note phrase, followed by the last child (*A*) who once again plays the initial 5-note phrase. Next, the same rondo principle might be applied to rhythmic patterns played on nonpitched percussion instruments.

Rondo for Bassoon and Orchestra, Franson, YPR 1009

Beethoven, "Scherzo" from *Symphony No. 7,* BOL 62

Dvořák, *Slavonic Dance in C Minor,* AM, grade 4, vol. 2

Haydn, "Gypsy Rondo" from *Trio in G Major,* BOL 64

Khachaturian, "Waltz" from *Masquerade* Suite, AM, grade 4, vol. 2

Mozart, "Romanze" from *Eine kleine Nachtmusik,* AM, grade 4, vol. 1

Prokofiev, "Waltz on Ice" from *Winter Holiday,* AM, grade 3, vol. 2

Smetana, "Dance of the Comedians" from *Bartered Bride,* AM, grade 6, vol. 2; BOL 56

Tchaikovsky, "Waltz" from *Sleeping Beauty,* AM, grade 4, vol. 1

Kodály, "Viennese Music Clock" from *Háry János* Suite, AM, grade 2, vol. 1; BOL 81

Variation Form.   This form is an extension of the concept of altering melodies. Through listening, students find that the music can be varied in terms of its melody, rhythm, harmony, texture, tempo, dynamics, form, tone quality, and its general style. Listening to variations is somewhat like a mystery that gradually resolves itself as the listener detects which musical elements the composer changes in order to create the variation. Generally there is a theme, followed by several different treatments of it. Unity is provided by the theme, which is always present in some form; variety is provided by the changing of any of the musical elements. There are variations in which a melody or chord progression is repeated over and over, with variety coming from changes in the other elements.

Hot Cross Buns, Franson CRG 5005

Guarnieri, *Brazilian Dance,* AM, grade 6, vol. 2; BOL 55

Anderson, *The Girl I Left Behind Me,* AM, grade 5, vol. 2

Copland, "Simple Gifts" from *Appalachian Spring,* BOL 65

Cailliet, *Variations on Pop! Goes the Weasel,* AM, grade 4, vol. 1; BOL 65

Ives, *Variations on "America,"* Louisville Records

Kraft, *Variations for Percussion Instruments,* BOL 83

Gould, *American Salute,* AM, grade 5, vol. 1; BOL 65

The Cailliet *Variations on Pop! Goes the Weasel* can be useful as an example of how to help children learn the principles of variation form. Its sections are as follows:

Introduction and theme: Can the students sense the meter? Can they tell if a full orchestra is playing? Can they hear whether or not one section of the orchestra predominates?

1. Fugue   In the fugue, the same melody is played at different times by different instruments at different pitch levels, but it gives the impression of a round because of the entries of these parts. Does it sound like a round? What is the order of the entering instruments? (Six instruments are featured before the entire orchestra plays the tune.)

2. Minuet   What is the meter in this minuet? Can you hear two melodies being played at once? Which instrument plays the melody and which plays another tune? Can augmentation be heard?

3. Adagio   What elements of the music produce the mood here, and what do you think this mood is? A new tune is introduced, namely a Jewish wedding song.

4. Music box   What is a music box? What instruments are used to sound like a music box? What did the composer do to make the "oom-pah-pah" effect?

5. Jazz   What meter does the composer choose here? Listen to the trumpet with the "wa-wa" mute. What do you think the player does with the mute to make this sound? How does the composer make the music sound like jazz? What happens to the melody this time? Define "variation form" in your own words. How many ways can a melody be varied in a variation form?

Fugue.   The fugue is a rather complex polyphonic process, and is considered by some to be a form. Most simply stated, it consists of two sections that alternate, one in which there is a fugue *subject,* and one in which no subject is present. The section without a fugue subject is called an *episode.* If students should describe a two-part fugue after listening to it carefully, they might say, "It starts like a round, with the first voice stating the theme. When the second part begins the theme, the first part plays another melody (a *"countermelody"*). Then both parts leave the theme and play something else. This process goes on for a while." While the fugue is a complicated form for children to understand, it provides a clear example of a polyphonic texture, which children may enjoy.

Other fugues appropriate for elementary school music programs include the following:

McBride, *Pumpkin Eater's Little Fugue,* BOL 65
Thornson, *Fugue and Chorale on Yankee Doodle,* BOL 65

Scarlatti, *Cat's Fugue*, Keyboard Junior Recordings

Bach, *Little Fugue in G Minor*, BOL 86, AM, grade 6, vol. 1

Bizet, "Farandole" from *L'Arlésienne*, Suite No. 2, AM, grade 6, vol. 1

Sonata-Allegro Form. Sonata-allegro form is an expanded A B A form. Its plan incorporates three parts: (1) the statement of two or more themes, (2) the manipulation or development of those themes, and (3) the restatement of the themes in their original form. The first theme is often vigorous while the second theme is usually more lyrical, thus providing contrast. Often there are transitional passages between the various parts of the form. This form is used as the first movement of a symphony, sonata, concerto, quartet, and quintet, as well as appearing in some overtures and other forms.

Schubert, "First Movement" from *Symphony No. 5*, AM, grade 5, vol. 1

Mozart, "First Movement" from *Symphony No. 40*, BOL 71

Prokofiev, *Classical Symphony*, BOL 73

The Suite. The suites we hear today are often dance suites in which a series of related dances constitute the composition. Dance suites are usually made up of dances of the sixteenth and seventeenth centuries: the allemande, courante, saraband, gigue, and a number of others. Orchestral suites are based on stage works such as opera, ballet, and drama, from which selections are taken and arranged for concert performances.

DANCE SUITES

Bach, *English* Suites, *French Suites*

Handel, *Harpsichord* Suites

BALLET SUITES

Tchaikovsky, *Nutcracker* Suite, BOL 58

Stravinsky, *Petrouchka* Suite

Ravel, *Daphnis and Chloe* Suite No.2, BOL 86

Rimsky-Korsakov, *Scheherazade* Suite, BOL 77

SUITES BASED ON STAGE WORKS

Grieg, *Peer Gynt* Suite, BOL 59

Tchaikovsky, *Nutcracker* Suite

OPERA SUITES

Bizet, *Carmen* Suite

Menotti, Suite from *Amahl and the Night Visitors*, BOL 58

OTHER SUITES

Grofe, *Grand Canyon* Suite, BOL 61

Grofe, *Mississippi River* Suite, BOL 61

Tone Poem.   The symphonic poem or tone poem is a work for symphony orchestra in which the form is dictated by a story, a description, or a character.

Strauss, *Til Eulenspiegel and His Merry Pranks*
Mussorgsky, *Night on Bald Mountain,* BOL 81
Saint-Saëns;, *Danse Macabre,* BOL 81

Opera.   These are large vocal works. The opera is a stage play in which the words are sung and in which the singers are accompanied by an orchestra. There may be duets, trios, quartets, sextets, and other ensembles, a chorus, and even a ballet. The *recitative* employs a declamatory vocal style that imitates speech; an *aria* is a more songlike solo.

Menotti, *Amahl and the Night Visitors*
Humperdinck, *Hansel and Gretel*
Bizet; *Carmen*
Britten; *The Little Sweep*
Child's Introduction to Opera, Childcraft Records, Album 38 (includes *Barber of Seville, Amahl and the Night Visitors* and *Hansel and Gretel*

Exploring Cultural Differences in Music Through Listening

Black and Chicano music are integral parts of the American musical scene. Black American music has its roots in the daily lives of the slaves brought to this country from Africa. Among its earlier characteristics were the call and response, the use of pentatonic and gapped scales, frequently flatted scale tones 3, 5, and 7, complex rhythms with syncopation and shifting meters, and improvisation. Performance techniques included hand clapping, rhythmic movement, stamping, shouting, percussive vocal effects, ostinati, and story-telling in song. Some of the elements of early black music are found today in blues, jazz, rock and roll, and many other forms of music. Black folk songs are a vital element in American musical culture.

There are many recordings of early black music, including work songs, folk songs, and religious music (primarily spirituals). Students will be interested in hearing examples of these, and learning of that early culture. However, their greater interest will lie in more recent examples of music, beginning with performers such as Scott Joplin and Louis Armstrong, and continuing with such contemporary performers as Whitney Huston, Michael Jackson, and Bobby Brown. The following lesson plan introduces students to one of America's most important musicians and a unique musical form, the 12-bar blues.

Lesson Plan in Form   TWELVE-BAR BLUES

Objectives:

Form   Through a process determined by the teacher, the student will identify the 12-bar form of blues music.

Tone Quality	The student will identify scat singing as improvised imitation of an instrument.
Rhythm	The student will experience ragtime music as syncopation against a steady beat.

Materials Needed:

"West End Blues" by Louis Armstrong

Recording: *The Enjoyment of Music Series,* Machlis, Side 18, Band 2

Instruments, or pictures of a trumpet, trombone, piano, clarinet, and banjo.

Colored cards in sets of five, each set including a picture of the following instruments and combinations:

1. trumpet
2. trombone
3. piano
4. clarinet and voice
5. trumpet, clarinet, and piano

Background:

Louis Armstrong was one of the greatest trumpet players who ever lived. He played and sang jazz throughout his life, even making trips to foreign countries as America's good-will ambassador.

In this music, Armstrong's short solo intro is one of the most famous improvisations in jazz history. The music that follows consists of two primary phrases. The first is bold and brassy, including a long, loud high note. The second phrase begins in a high register, and gradually circles down. These phrases follow a straight, uncomplicated 12-bar blues form. There are five choruses: trumpet solo, trombone, clarinet and vocal duet, piano, and final ensemble.

"West End Blues" was first recorded in 1928.

Student Preparation:

Activities of improvising with various instruments, including pentatonic scales on pitched percussion instruments are suggested.

The class may also sing songs that include scat phrases. Students may want to see a picture of Louis Armstrong.

Teaching Suggestions:

1. First hearing: Students listen for the point in the music when a steady beat is established, and raise their hands to indicate it (after Armstrong's free tempo intro).
   The teacher asks students to identify the instrument heard keeping a steady beat at that point.

2. Second hearing: Students are asked to lay out their five cards in any order, and when the steady tempo begins, to reorder the cards according to the tone qualities they hear.
   Example:

Trumpet	Trombone	Clarinet & Voice	Piano	Trumpet Clarinet Piano

3. Third hearing: Students count out the uncomplicated 12-bar blues, noting its five choruses, as shown by the order of their cards.

4. The teacher clarifies this example of ragtime music, as students note the syncopated rhythms which occur against the steady beat.

5. Fourth hearing: Students prepare graphic notation using simple icons for the voice and instruments. The teacher includes discussion about its form.

Many state departments of education, county and city school systems have compiled collections of Latin American music that reflect the Spanish or Mexican-American cultures, as demonstrated by *Cancionero Alegre,* published by the Department of Public Instruction, State Capitol, Phoenix, Arizona. The music of former Africans in many North, Central, and South American nations has resulted in a merging of musical styles that has produced considerable popular music, folk music, and dance.

Country	Dance
Argentina	Tango
Brazil	Samba
Cuba	Habañera, Rhumba, Congo, Mambo, Cha-Cha
Haiti	Merengue
Mexico	Huapango
Trinidad	Limbo

In addition, the calypso, part of the popular music of Trinidad and the Bahamas, combines European melody and harmony with African rhythm. American composers who have utilized musical ideas from these sources include

Benjamin, *Jamaican Rhumba*
Copland, *El Salón México*
Gould, *Latin-American Symphonette*

One of the strong trends in music education today is an interest in music of the world. While there have been songs from Western Europe and Latin America in music textbooks, Africa and Asia have been less well represented. Efforts are now being made to learn more about the indigenous music of all peoples. The study of the music of any culture should include consideration of the following:

1. The early music in any country has a direct influence on the present and future types of music in that country.
2. The music of any country undergoes more or less constant change.

3. The music of any country reflects the people's concerns in all aspects of life—social, aesthetic, religious, political, and economic.
4. The music of most cultures has been altered and influenced by music from other cultures.
5. Folk songs in all societies undergo constant change, reflecting societal changes.
6. The music of a particular culture has a distinctive style that differentiates it from other cultures.
7. Music has multiple functions in every society, some unique to that society, others universal.
8. The music, language, literature, architecture, recreation, food, clothing, and political and social customs of a people serve to bind them together into a national or cultural unit.

Songs, dances, and instruments provide information about people's beliefs, values, and how they live. Listening to the music of various people and times may contribute to a child's sense of place in the world. New songs explain the concerns of the present day; old songs are a means of understanding the past and its influence on the present. The historian and the anthropologist consider music one important ingredient of a culture, society, or tribal organization. A practical approach to teaching world music traditions in upper elementary and middle school classes is provided in the MENC publication, *Multi-cultural Perspectives in Music Education.*

As students listen to music via television, recordings, and films, they discover that concepts of music which differ from Western music have a utility, charm, and worth of their own. Especially useful are the cassettes in the series, "Sounds of the World," recorded in the United States by immigrants dedicated to preserving their homeland traditions through authentic music. These cassettes are produced by the Music Educators National Conference.

The school music of Japanese children bears some similarity to that of American children: all authentic Japanese music is less frequently heard. Native Japanese music stems historically from Chinese culture, so Japanese children find themselves amid two cultural streams of music. The excellent film, *Folk Songs of Japan,* can be obtained from the nearest Japanese consulate (color, 29 minutes). It portrays the beauty of the Japanese countryside while taking the listener through examples of all types of folk music including a contemporary popular song performed by young people at a ski resort. The combination of Japanese and American influences in this song shows the changing nature of Japanese music. Other Japanese folk music is often based on a pentatonic scale such as those that follow:

Japanese scales (pentatonic scales with half-steps):

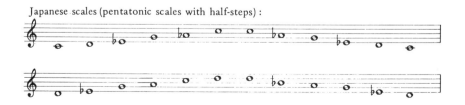

Rhythm and melody, often accompanied by a simple drone, characterize the music of India. The scale and melodic structure is found in the *raga,* of which there are hundreds. Each raga has from five to seven pitches and one or two secondary pitches. The performer elaborates and improvises on the raga. Each raga has nonmusical implications which could be some an emotion, a season, or a time of day. The music is horizontally conceived; there is no harmony as we know it—only the drone. Both melody and rhythm are more sophisticated than their counterparts in Western music; our composers are being increasingly influenced by Indian concepts of melody and rhythm. The *tala* is the rhythmic structure of Indian music, organized into a number of beats with recurring accents. Approximately thirty talas are in common use. Three popular instruments are the *sitar,* a many-stringed, fretted instrument, the *tabla,* a double drum, and the *tamboura,* a long-necked unfretted instrument with drone strings.

The music of Africa may be more diverse than the music of any other continent. The tribal music of the regions in the south has very little in common with the Muslim music of such northern countries as Egypt. Many African cultures have been influenced by music of Asia, Arabia, and the West. Conversely, the music of central and southern Africa has exerted substantial influence on the music of other countries, notably the United States and the Carribean.

When a teacher introduces music of another culture to the class, several features of the music need preliminary attention. Among those are the kinds of instruments being played, the vocal technique employed, the music's meter and texture, and finally, the function of the music in its society.

References

Articles and Books

Most collections of recordings for elementary school are accompanied by booklets which analyze the compositions presented and provide good background information for listening lessons. Another source is the Teacher's Manual that accompanies each grade in the various series books.

BAN, K. W., & J. M. JOHNSTON, "Listening: The Key to Early Childhood Music," *Day Care and Early Education. 16*/3. Spring 1989, 13–17.

FALLETTA, J., "Have We Forgotten How to Listen?," *The American Music Teacher, 38*/6, June/July 1989, 58–59.

HELLER, GEORGE N., "Listening Activities in Music Education: Some Exemplars from Historical Research," *Update, 8*/1, Fall/Winter 1989, 3–8.

POGONOWKSI, L., "Critical Thinking and Music Listening," *Music Educators Journal,* September 1989, 35–38.

SOLOMON, E. S., "Sound Ideas for Listening," *Instrumentalist, 43*/7, February 1989, 16–18.

Readings on Music From Various Cultures

AMOAKE, W. K., *African Songs and Rhythms for Children.* Mainz, W. Germany: B. Schott's Söhne, 1971. Belwin-Mills, agent.

ANDERSON, WM., and P.S. CAMPBELL, *Multicultural Perspectives in Music Education.* Reston, Va.: Music Educators National Conference, 1989.

BALLARD, LOUIS W., "Put American Indian Music in the Classroom." *Music Educators Journal,* March 1970.

COOPERATIVE RECREATION SERVICE, *World Around Songs,* Burnsville, N.C. Inexpensive songbooks concerning states, nations, and peoples of the world.

CROOK, ELIZABETH et al., *Afro-American Music and Its Roots, Country Music and Its Roots, Music of North American Indians, Spanish-American Music and Its Roots.* Morristown, N.J.: Silver Burdett, 1975. Booklets with recordings. For middle school students.

CURTISS, MARIE JOY, "India," *Music Educators Journal,* September 1969.

DEITZ, BETTY W., and MICHAEL OLATUNJI, *Musical Instruments of Africa.* New York: John Day, 1965. grades 7–12.

HAUSMAN, RUTH L., *Hawaii: Music in Its History.* Rutland, Vt.: Tuttle, 1968.

INNISS, CARLETON, "A Practical Introduction to African Music." *Music Educators Journal,* February 1974.

JARROW, JILL. *All Ears: How to Choose and Use Recorded Music for Children.* New York: Penguin Books, 1991.

KARPELES, MAUD, ed., *Folk Songs of Europe.* London: Novello, 1956. Authentic folk songs edited for the International Folk Music Council.

KEBEDE, ASHENAFI, *Roots of Black Music.* Englewood Cliffs, N.J.: Prentice-Hall, 1982.

KELLY, JOHN M., JR., *Folk Songs Hawaii Sings.* Rutland, Vt.: Tuttle, 1963.

LANDECK, BEATRICE, *Echoes of Africa in Folk Songs of the Americas.* New York: Marks 1973.

LOMAX, ALAN, *Folk Songs of North America,* New York: Doubleday, 1960. Includes historical backgrounds.

LYONS, JOHN H., *Stories of Our American Patriotic Songs.* New York: Vanguard Press, 1942.

McNEIL, ALBERT J., "The Social Foundations of the Music of Black Americans," *Music Educators Journal,* February 1974. Includes a bibliography.

MALM, WILLIAM, *Japanese Music and Musical Instruments.* Rutland, Vt.: Tuttle, 1959.

MALM, WILLIAM P., *Music Cultures of the Pacific, the Near East and Asia,* 2nd ed. Englewood Cliffs, N.J.: Prentice-Hall, 1977.

MARSH, MARY VAL et al., *The Spectrum of Music with Related Arts: Afro-American Music, Music of the Orient, Music of Latin America.* New York: Macmillan, 1975. Booklets with recordings for group and individual instruction for middle school students.

MAY, ELIZABETH, ed. *Music of Many Cultures: An Introduction.* Berkeley: University of California Press, 1981. Twenty essays by as many authors. Music, photography, recording. A scholarly, expensive book.

Music Educators Journal. November 1971, Music and Black Culture issue. October 1972, Music in World Cultures issue; includes glossary. May 1983, The Multiculture Imperative issue; includes Africa, Hawaii, Samoa, the Philippines; bibliography and recordings sources pp. 69–70.

NKETIA, J. H. KWABENA, "Music Education in Africa and the West: We Can Learn from Each Other," *Music Educators Journal,* November 1970.

PETERSON, FREDERICK A., *Ancient Mexico.* New York: Putnam, 1959. Chapter 9 describes ancient instruments and dance.

PHILLIPS, ROMEO E., "Black Folk Music: Setting the Record Straight," *Music Educators Journal,* December 1973.

RECK, DAVID, *Music of the Whole Earth,* New York: Scribner, 1977.

REEDER, BARBARA, "Afro Music: As Tough as a Mozart Quartet," *Music Educators Journal,* January 1970.

REEDER,, BARBARA, and JAMES A. STANDIFER, *Source Book of African Materials for Music Educators,* Reston, Va.: Music Educators National Conference, 1972.

SEALEY, JOHN, and KRISTER MALM, *Music in the Caribbean.* London: Hodder and Stoghton, 1982. 44 pp. Can be read by middle school students.

SEIDEMAN, LAURENCE I., "Teaching About the American Revolution Through Folk Songs," *Social Education,* November 1973, 653–64.

SOUTHERN, EILEEN, *The Music of Black Americans: A History.* New York: Norton, 1971.

SUR, WILLIAM R. et al., *This Is Music,* Book Five. Boston: Allyn & Bacon, 1967. Pages 18–161 present United States history in song.

WARRICK, MANCEL, J. R. HILLSMAN, and ANTHONY MANNO, *The Progress of Gospel Music: From Spirituals to Contemporary Gospel.* New York: Vantage, 1977.

WHITE, FLORENCE, and KAZUO AKIYAMA, *Children's Songs from Japan.* New York: Marks, 1965. Fifty songs that tell American children how Japanese boys and girls live.

WHITING, HELEN, *Negro Art, Music and Rhyme.* Washington, D.C.: Associated Publishers, 1967.

WIANT, BLISS, *The Music of China.* Hong Kong: Chung Chi Publications, 1965.

Recordings Featuring Specific Musical Concepts

MAJOR AND MINOR

Bizet, "Farandole" from *L'Arlésienne* Suite, AM, grade 6, vol. 1

Charpentier, "On Muleback" from *Impressions of Italy,* AM, grade 5, vol. 1

de Falla, "Spanish Dance" from *La Vida Breve,* AM, grade 6, vol. 1

Lecuona, "Andalucia" from *Suite Andalucia,* AM, grade 4, vol. 1

Mozart, "Romanze" from *Eine kleine Nachtmusik,* AM, grade 4, vol. 1

Mussorgsky, "Bydlo" from *Pictures at an Exhibition,* AM, grade 2, vol. 1

COMMON CHORDS

Brubeck, "Unsquare Dance" on *Time Further Out,* Columbia CS 8490

Ginastera, "Wheat Dance" from *Estancia,* AM, grade 4, vol. 1

Milhaud, "Copacabana" from *Saudades do Brazil,* AM, grade 4, vol. 2

Mozart, "Romanze" from *Eine kleine Nachtmusik,* AM, grade 4, vol. 1

TEXTURES

Bach, "Little Fugue in G Minor", AM, grade 6, vol. 1; BOL 86

Benjamin, *Jamaican Rhumba,* BOL 56

Britten, *Young Person's Guide to the Orchestra,* London 6671

Ligeti, "Atmospheres" from *Space Odyssey,* Columbia MS 6733

Saint-Saëns, "The Swan" from *Carnival of the Animals,* AM, grade 3, vol. 2

Sousa, *Semper Fidelis,* AM, grade 3, vol. 1

TONE QUALITIES

Cage, Cowell, Ussachevsky, *Sounds of New Music.* Folkways FX 6160

Kraft, *Theme and Variations for Percussion Quartet,* BOL 83, *The Science of Sound,* Folkways FX 6007

LEGATO, STACCATO
Gretry, "Ballet Music" from *Cephale et Procris,* Tambourin, AM, grade 2, vol. 1

MELODY
Bartók, "Jack-in-the-Box" from *Mikrokosmos* Suite No. 2, AM, grade 2, vol. 1

Schubert, "First Movement" from *Symphony No. 5,* AM, grade 5, vol. 1

Schuller, "Twittering Machine" from *Seven Studies on Themes of Paul Klee.* AM, grade 2, vol. 2

Shostakovitch, "Petite Ballerina" from *Ballet Suite No. 2,* AM, grade 2, vol. 1

OSTINATO
Cowell, *Ostinato Percussion,* Mainstream 5011

Kabalevsky, "Pantomime" from *The Comedians,* AM, grade 1, vol. 1

IMPROVISATION
Brubeck, *Dialogue for Jazz Combo and Orchestra,* Columbia CL 1466

Bernstein, "Improvisation I" from *Four Improvisations for Orchestra,* Columbia MS 6733

CHANGING AND LESS COMMON METERS
Brubeck, *Time Out,* Columbia CL 1397

Brubeck, *Time Further Out,* Columbia CL 1690

Tchaikovsky, "Second Movement" from *Symphony No. 6*

INTERVALS
Bartók, "Second Movement" from *Concerto for Orchestra,* Pairs at Play.

Hanson, "Bells" from *For the First Time* on *The Composer and His Music,* Mercury MG 50357

WHOLE-TONE SCALE
Debussy, "Voiles" from *Preludes,* Book 1.

Hanson, "Mists" from *For the First Time* on *The Composer and His Orchestra,* Vol. III, Mercury MG 50357

TWELVE-TONE MUSIC
Schoenberg and others, piano music (Gould), Columbia ML 5336; Schoenberg and others, orchestral pieces, Columbia ML 5616

Stravinsky, *Double Canon for String Quartet,* Columbia MS 6272

ELECTRONIC MUSIC
Cage, Cowell, others, *Sounds of New Music,* Folkways FX 6160

Mimaroglu, "Prelude XI" on *Electronic Music III,* Turnabout VOX TV 34177

Powell, *Electronic Setting,* Son Nova 1

Stockhausen, *Gesang der Jünglinge,* Deutsche Grammophon 13881 1

Ussachevsky, *Piece for Tape Recorder,* CRI 1 12

Varèse, *Poème electronique,* Columbia ML 5478

FORM

Delibes, "Swanhilde's Waltz" from *Coppelia,* AM, grade 2, vol. 2

El-Dabh, *Leilya and the Poet,* Columbia MS 6566

McDonald, "Third Movement" from *Children's Symphony,* AM, grade 2, vol. 1

Menotti, "March of the Kings" from *Amahl and the Night Visitors,* AM, grade 1, vol. 2

Mozart, Overture to *The Marriage of Figaro.* BOL 76

Pinto, *Memories of Childhood,* BOL 68 (ABA meter)

Pinto, "Run, Run" from *Memories of Childhood,* BOL 68; Haydn, "Andante" from *Symphony No. 94,* BOL 62

Prokofiev, "Waltz on Ice" from *Winter Holiday,* AM, grade 3, vol. 2

Sousa, *Stars and Stripes Forever,* AM, grade 4, vol. 1

Vaughan-Williams, "March Past of the Kitchen Utensils" from *The Wasps,* AM, grade 3, vol. 1

Recordings Featuring Music of Various Cultures

The final Contemporary Music Project *Newsletter* dated Spring 1973, contained a recommended list of recordings of Asian and African music for teaching purposes. Those preceded by one asterisk (*) are especially recommended; a second asterisk (**) indicates that extensive notes are provided to help orient the listener.

AFGHANISTAN

Music of Afghanistan, UNESCO 30L 2003

AFRICA

*Mbira Music of Rhodesia, University of Washington Press, Seattle

*The African Mbira, Nonesuch 72043

***Music of the Dan Territory,* Ocora, OCR 17

***Music of Central Africa (Musique centrafricaine),* Ocora, OCR 43

***Black Africa, Panorama of Instrumental Music (Afrique noire, Panorame de la musique instrumentale),* BAM LD 409A

***Nigeria—Hausa Music I,* UNESCO 30L 2306

Sounds of the World: African, Afro-Cuban and Haitian Traditions in U.S. MENC "Sounds of the World" series.

EAST ASIA

*Shantung Folk Music and Traditional Instrument Pieces, Nonesuch H-72051

Music of East Asia: Chinese, Korean, Japanese Traditions in U.S. MENC "Sounds of the World" series.

EASTERN EUROPE

Music of Eastern Europe: Albanian, Greek and South Slavic Traditions in the U.S. MENC "Sounds of the World" series.

INDIA

*Sarangi, Voice of a Hundred Colors, Nonesuch 72030

***The Anthology of Indian Music, Vol. 1,* World Pacific WDS 26200 (three records and extensive notes)

Drums of North and South India, World Pacific WPS 21437

Indian Drums, Connoisseur Society CS 1466

West Meets East, Ravi Shankar and Yehudi Menuhin, Angel 36418

The Sound of Subbudlakshmi, World Pacific WPS 21440

The Music of India (South), Nonesuch 72003

**Raga Jogeshwari*, Deutsche Grammophone, 2531–280

Bhavalu/Impressions, South Indian Instrumental Music. Nonesuch 72019

INDONESIA
Golden Rain (Bali), Nonesuch 72028

Gamelan Music of Bali, Lyrichord LLST 7179

The Jasmine Isle (Java), Nonesuch 72031

Gamelan Semar Pegulingan (Gamelan of the Love God) (Bali), Nonesuch H-7 2046

Music for the Balinese Shadow Puppet Plays, Gender Wayang, Nonesuch H-72037

JAPAN
Bell Ringing in Empty Sky, Nonesuch 72025. Solo flute (shakuhachi) music.

Music from the Kabuki, Nonesuch 72012

Japanese Koto Classics, Nonesuch 72008

Gagaku, Ancient Japanese Court Music, Everest 3322

LATIN AMERICA
Music of Latin America: Mexico, Ecuador, Brazil. MENC ''Sounds of the World'' series.

THE MIDDLE EAST; PERSIA (IRAN)
The Persian Santur, Nonesuch 72039

The Living Tradition: Music from Iran, Argo ZFB 51

Music from Turkey. Living Tradition, Argo ZRG 561

Music from the Middle East (Syria, Iraq, Palestine). Living Tradition, Argo ZRG 532

Music of the Middle East: Arab, Persian, Iranian, and Turkish Traditions in U.S. MENC ''Sounds of the World'' series.

SOUTHEAST ASIA
**Traditional Music of Thailand*. Institute of Ethnomusicology. UCLA, Los Angeles, CA 90046. Includes an excellent booklet by David Morten.

Music from Cambodia, UNESCO Anthology, Bahrenreiter 30L 2002

Music from Vietnam I, UNESCO 30L 2022

Music of Southeast Asia: Lao, Hmong, Vietnamese, MENC ''Sounds of the World'' series.

TIBET
**Anthology of Asian Music: Tibet*, AST 4005 (Anthology Record Corp.), 135 West 41 St., New York, NY 10036

In addition there are twelve long-playing records or cassettes produced by UNICEF. In them native groups, soloists, and children perform music, songs, and dances of forty-eight different nations, forty-three of them non-European. The music series provide some helpful recordings of ethnic music.

Films and Filmstrips   Catalogs of companies such as BFA Educational Media, Keyboard Publications, National Geographic Society, Society for Visual Education, Bowmar Records, Prentice-Hall Media (including Jam Handy Organization), National Educational Television, and Mcgraw-Hill Films are good resources. The American Music Conference, 1000 Skokie Blvd., Wilmette, IL. 60091 provides a free brochure "Film Review Service" in which current music education films are reviewed.

Discovering Form in Music, BFA Educational Media, 2211 Michigan Avenue, Santa Monica, CA 90404

Discovering Melody and Harmony, BFA Educational Media, 2211 Michigan Ave., Santa Monica, CA 90404

Elements of Composition (New York Wind Ensemble), NET Film Service, Bloomington, IN 47401

Forms of Music: Instrumental, Coronet Instructional Films, 65 E. South Water St., Chicago, IL 60601

Harmony in Music, Coronet Instructional Films, 65 E. South Water St., Chicago, IL 60601

Let's Discover the Design, EMC Corporation, St. Paul, MN. 55101

Let's Get Together, EMC Corporation, St. Paul, MN. 55101

Music, The Expressive Language, Sutherland Productions, 201 N. Occidental Blvd., Los Angeles, CA 90026

Music, Churchill Films, 662 N. Robertson Blvd., Los Angeles, CA 90069

The Metropolitan Opera Box for ages 11–18. Education at the Met, 1865 Broadway, New York, NY 10023. Ten operas with teacher's manuals, recordings, filmstrips, and handouts.

Two-Part Singing, Johnson Hunt Productions, Hollywood, CA 94105 (ages 9–11)

Young People's Concert Series (Leonard Bernstein): *What Makes Music Symphonic? What Is a Concerto?*; *What Is Sonata Form?* Mcgraw-Hill Films, 1221 Avenue of the Americas, New York, NY 10020. (60 minutes) Ages 10–Adult. Also inquire at local AT&T telephone office for possible free availability.

11 Current Approaches to Elementary Classroom Music

Émile Jaques-Dalcroze
Carl Orff
Zoltán Kodály
Education Through Music (ETM)
Edwin Gordon
Phyllis Weikart
James Froseth
References

Émile Jaques-Dalcroze

In any discussion of movement and music, the name Émile Jaques-Dalcroze (1865–1950) appears as a pioneer. Dalcroze was a Swiss musician-educator who established the Dalcroze Institute in Geneva where it continues to function today. His theories are contained in his two books, *Rhythm, Music and Education* (1921) and *Eurhythmics, Art and Education* (1930). Dalcroze found that when the learner experiences aspects of music through body movement, the expressive responsiveness engendered in the child can lead to genuine musicianship. He also believed that without such preparation in early childhood the individual may tend to respond mechanically, and that expressive musicianship may later be deficient.

Today, every teacher of early childhood education knows that children learn initially by using their bodies. Dalcroze's followers claim that eurhythmics develops the whole child physically, mentally, socially, and emotionally, as it promotes an understanding and appreciation of music. In eurhythmics the body and mind respond to what the individual hears and feels. The method stresses (1) rhythmic movement (eurhythmics), (2) ear training, and (3) improvisation. Rhythmic responses to music are commonly found in today's schools, but they are sometimes taught by people with insufficient training, and may remain isolated exercises poorly related to the rest of the curriculum.

The familiar body responses to quarter notes (walking) and eighth notes (running) form part of the Dalcroze approach. Students respond to the teacher's playing of drum or piano patterns by movement of feet, arms, or total body. Simple movements then become units within more complex responses. Eurhythmics teachers devise many rhythmic games by establishing, repeating or altering patterns of movement. Simple tunes such as "Hot Cross Buns" can be acted out with patterns such as walk, walk, step-bend for quarter, quarter, and half notes. The first motive of "Silent Night" might be felt rhythmically with a pattern of movements devised by the children, such as the following:

step-spring,   run walk   step-bend-bend

As children acquire experience with this approach, they refine their movements into those that express dynamics, pitch, phrasing, form, and style. Rhythm remains at the core of Dalcroze's approach, however, and is central to virtually every lesson. Teaching does not focus on beat, meter, or static rhythms, but rather on the constantly changing flow of motion. The concepts of rhythmic flow, tension, and release are learned through these physical responses. For example, clapping can become a graceful, shapely gesture that expresses a particular rhythm in a piece of music. At the same time, emotion and feeling may be translated into these movements.

The eurythmics teacher places the learners on a developmental course in rhythmic-musical growth. He or she improvises music on the piano while the children improvise appropriate movements. As learning progresses, children are provided opportunities to improvise rhythm patterns on one or more pitches, or on nonpitched percussion instruments. They may also improvise spontaneous melodies. A simple example would be improvisations on "Hot Cross Buns."

Solfège, or singing with syllables, is an important part of this approach, as it sharpens the sense of pitch and the understanding of relationships between tones. Dalcroze recommended using the *fixed-do* approach to pitch. Through this training, students learn to hear harmonies, to read music, and to improvise vocally.

The primary aim of eurythmics is to develop good musicianship. Dalcroze used the music of a variety of cultures to achieve this purpose, focusing on the rhythmic movements inherent in each. He believed that musicality can be encouraged by consciously using one's body movement in association with keen hearing. Furthermore, he planned his procedures to assist young and old, gifted and handicapped, as well as the average person. There are extensions of the Dalcroze method into dance, physical education, and therapy.

The Dalcroze method provides a unique combination of eurythmics, improvisation and solfège. In recent years there has been a resurgence of interest in eurythmics, and it is becoming more important in the preparation of elementary music specialists. As this occurs, certification programs are becoming more readily available.

Carl Orff
Carl Orff (1895–1982), a German composer-educator, agreed with Dalcroze's insistence on rhythm as a foundation for musical growth. He developed an educational approach that begins with speech rhythms and leads to a creative, improvisatory learning process. He grouped the children in low and high speaking voices to produce better dramatic effects. Orff believed, as did Dalcroze, that the study of standard musical instruments should begin only after the learner acquires the skills of hearing, moving to music, recognizing and playing basic rhythms, and discerning and singing basic tonal patterns and intervals. Unlike Dalcroze, who used the piano extensively, Orff considered other instruments to be better suited for children's music. As a result he designed musical instruments of high quality that still carry his name today, and are used widely in children's musical instruction.

Speaking, moving, and singing are regarded as a composite act, illustrative of how young children engage in music when undirected. Orff organized improvisation in ways to make it easy for children to create their own music. The common pentatonic (5-tone) mode, tones 1, 2, 3, 5, and 6 of the major scale, is used in the beginning, followed by ostinato patterns (repeated rhythmic or melodic fragments) and borduns (the open-fifth interval and variations constructed from it). Children can create music on pitched percussion instruments that is truly their own, and not an imitation of adult music. When children have learned to make music within the pentatonic framework, they move on to major, minor, and modal tonalities.

Orff advocated, as did Zoltán Kodály, the use of folk songs and children's traditional rhymes and melodies. Children were encouraged to use rhythmic and melodic ideas from songs to compose introductions, codas, interludes, and accompaniments. He created instrumental ensembles that consisted of glockenspiels (soprano and alto), metallophones (soprano, alto, bass), and xylophones (soprano, alto, bass) with removable tone bars, assisted by recorders and the cello. Such ensembles produces a sound similar to that of the Indonesian gamelan (Figure 11.1).

soprano glockenspiel	sounds two octaves higher than written
alto glockenspiel	sounds one octave higher than written
soprano metallophone	sounds one octave higher than written
soprano xylophone	sounds one octave higher than written
alto metallophone	sounds as written
alto xylophone	sounds as written
bass metallophone	sounds one octave lower when written in the treble clef
bass xylophone	sounds one octave lower when written in the treble clef

The continuing popularity of the Orff approach and of these fine quality instruments has led to their manufacture both in Europe and in the United States.

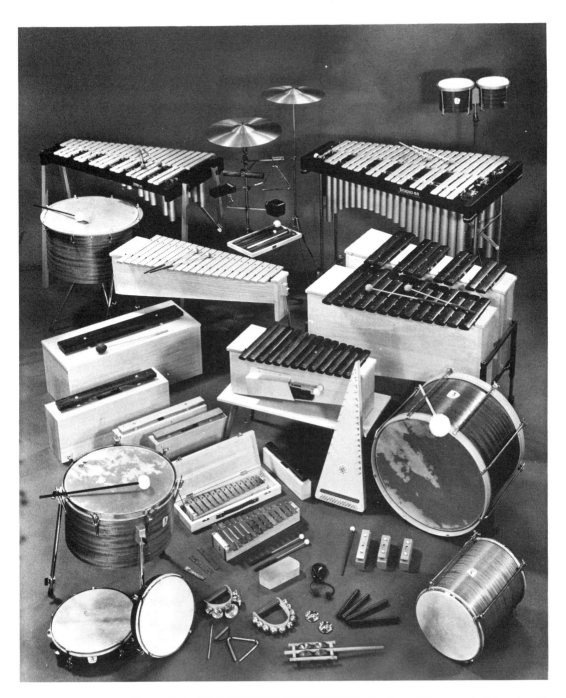

Figure 11.1. ORFF-DESIGNED INSTRUMENTS. Courtesy of Magnamusic Baton, Inc., St. Louis, Missouri 63132.

Sonar and Studio 49 are respected European manufacturers. In this country nearly all the suppliers of percussion instruments and autoharps sell Orff-type instruments.

Both Orff and Kodály used the descending minor third with chanting as a tonal beginning for young children. The tones of the chant form part of the pentatonic scale, which is employed because it requires no harmonization. Pentatonic melodies can be played or sung canonically or in combination, making satisfying musical performance within the capabilities of young children.

Basic to Orff's process is the progression from rhythmic speech to accompanied movements—clapping, finger snapping, stamping, and patschen and substituting percussion instruments for these. Nursery rhymes, chants, names of children, animals, geographical places, plants, and any speech designation of interest can grow into musical activities. Improvised dance is another possibility, perhaps a culminating one. Through a creative approach to speech, concepts of phrasing, dynamics, repetition, contrast, and simple form can be learned and then applied to musical pitch in logical sequence.

The following example illustrates the use of well-known verse to create a pentatonic song.

Lit - tle Miss Muf - fet   sat   on a tuf - fet,   etc.

Courtesy of the Music Educators National Conference, Reston, Va.

The following borduns and ostinati may be used with the preceding melody:

Ostinati can be heard in pieces such as the following:

Grieg, "Anitra's Dance" from *Peer Gynt* Suite
Guarnieri, *Brazilian Dance*
Bizet, "Carillon" from *L'Arlésienne* Suite
Herbert, "Dagger Dance" from *Natoma*
Pierné, *Entrance of the Little Fauns*

Orff and Gunild Keetman, an associate, wrote a series of books, *Music for Children,* containing examples of the activities comprising the Orff approach. The books, written in German, were adapted by Canadians Doreen Hall and Arnold Walier for use in English-speaking countries. The Orff-Keetman books are valuable references, but much of the material is not arranged sequentially. Orff intended his examples to be germinal rather than prescriptive because he wanted children and teachers to create their own. American music educators have developed three levels of skills using sequenced American materials, and have succeeded in communicating these concepts to an ever larger number of teachers. The American Orff-Schulwerk Association has provided leadership in organizing teacher training programs on the three levels, with certificates granted upon completion of the work at each level. *The Orff Echo* is the association's official magazine and the address of both is Cleveland State University, Department of Music, Cleveland, OH 44115.

The Orff procedure is one of guided exploration of sound, space, and form within a given structure. Orff and Kodály concepts of music education agree in part and are complementary to some degree, and thus many teachers use Orff-Kodály in their teaching. Both use solfège syllables. However, Kodály places greater emphasis on singing and on note reading.

Zoltán Kodály   Kodály, the distinguished Hungarian composer-educator (1882–1967), created a method for teaching music that is based upon the Hungarian language and authentic verse and folk music of that nation. It has become the national music education program of Hungary. The method includes a carefully sequenced vocal curriculum with specific materials of instruction and activities. Stress is put on good singing and music literacy—the ability to read music fluently. When adapted for use in other countries, the language and authentic folk songs of each particular nation provides the foundations of the method.

Techniques from the method became known in the United States before the method as a whole, in part due to the adaptation made by Mary Helen Richards in her *Threshold to Music* charts (Fearon-Pittman Publishers). Teachers were attracted to the prenotation symbols, such as drawings of objects and note stems without heads, then to the transition to notation in a setting that made learning music more of a game. The apparently successful use of Latin syllables and Curwen hand signs led to a renewed interest in those devices in many American schools. The way Kodály organized his method is a good example for music teachers. He first established objectives, then felt free to borrow, seek, and create the means to reach them. In this sense he was eclectic in his approach.

The following description is of the Kodály program for music in early childhood and first grade.

Rhymes and children's game songs in the children's native tongue are selected for specific purposes;

Body movement is an important means for learning music, including aspects of form;

Conforming to the regular beat is emphasized;

Songs are selected with the pitch configuration to be learned, such as *sol-mi, mi-re-do, sol-la-mi, sol-mi-re-do, do-la-sol, mi-re-do-la*;

Inner hearing (thinking pitches silently) is stressed;

Learning is based on games and songs, which merge into simple dance;

Sequencing of learning steps is held to quite ridgily in order for the proper foundation of musical knowledge to be built;

Instrumental accompaniments are rarely used in singing;

Live musical performance is preferred to listening to recordings;

Daily singing is recommended;

Teachers may add songs and listening experiences to the established curriculum;

Songs within a range of a sixth are frequently used.

The Kodály program through the elementary and middle school years has been called *The Kodály Choral Method*. When applied to the children's chorus, there have been exceedingly successful results in choral performance in this country that equal those in Europe. Kodály composed excellent music and exercises for children to sing. The current music series books contain applications of the Kodály method, as they do Orff-Schulwerk. American adaptations differ from the Hungarian in song material, rhythm patterns (from English speech), rhymes and folklore, and technical aspects such as learning of compound meters and the seventh degree of the major scale. A leading writer of Kodály music education is Lois Choksy.

Hand Signs. In the Kodály method, pitch discrimination and the concepts of high and low are explored by beginning with the descending interval of a minor third, 5–3 or *sol-mi*. Many names, nursery rhymes and other poems or words are sung on the two pitches. Hand signs may be performed by the children in response to them (see Figure 8.1). The teacher sings *sol* or *mi,* and the children learn to identify either pitch as high or low and to use the appropriate hand signs. After children have learned the hand signs they think the pitches and give signs, which the class can sing as pitches. Next, *la,* (6) is added, and the three pitches are used in many ways such as improvising short songs, for learning the hand signs, and seeing the relation of the pitches to notation. Eventually *re* and *do* are added, and a similar series of activities follows. With the addition of these two tones, the five pitches of the common pentatonic scale have been introduced.

Rhythm patterns performed with body and percussion sounds can be utilized throughout this process; the learning of notation and its description of the duration of pitch (note values) can be applied throughout the experience. Children can discover that rhythm and melody are integrally related, that one cannot have a melody unless the pitches are assigned duration.

The low *do* is the lowest hand signal. The signs move upward step by step, as the teacher makes sure that all signs are visible to members of the class (see Figure 11.2).

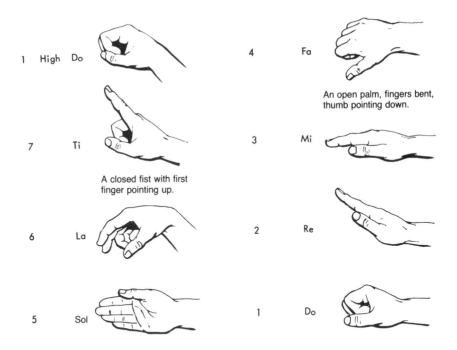

1	High	Do	
7		Ti	A closed fist with first finger pointing up.
6		La	
5		Sol	

4		Fa	An open palm, fingers bent, thumb pointing down.
3		Mi	
2		Re	
1		Do	

Figure 11.2. KODÁLY HAND SIGNS

To illustrate how rhythm syllables, Latin syllables, and hand signs are used by many teachers, the following excerpt is reproduced from *Twenty-Two Music Lessons,* published by the Nova Scotia Department of Education, part of a Kodály-inspired sequence.

LESSON 15

Using Roll-Call to Reinforce *Sol-Mi* and Hand Signs

1. Teacher says, "I will clap the rhythm pattern of someone's name. I would like that person to stand and answer by saying and clapping it." (There may be several people whose names have the same rhythm pattern—they may all respond at once.) Then the whole class responds by clapping and saying the rhythm syllables (ta ti-ti).

Examples:

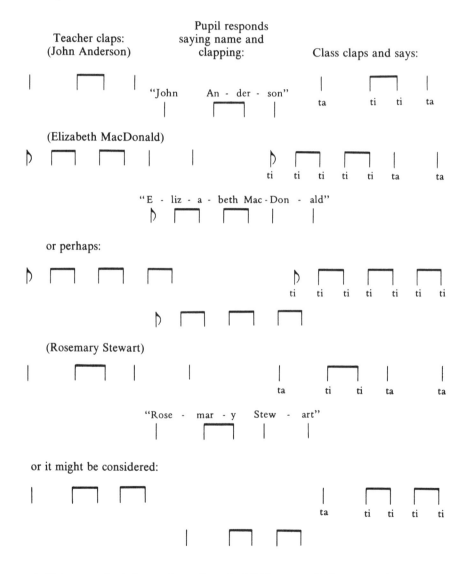

2. Using *so* and *mi*, the teacher calls each child by name (full name preferably), and each child echoes, as in the examples below:

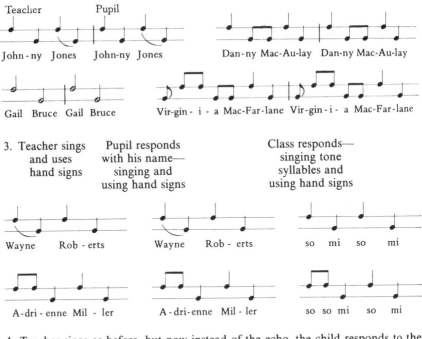

Teacher   Pupil

John-ny Jones   John-ny Jones   Dan-ny Mac-Au-lay   Dan-ny Mac-Au-lay

Gail Bruce Gail Bruce   Vir-gin - i - a Mac-Far-lane   Vir-gin - i - a Mac-Far-lane

3. Teacher sings   Pupil responds   Class responds—
     and uses   with his name—   singing tone
     hand signs   singing and   syllables and
                   using hand signs   using hand signs

Wayne   Rob - erts   Wayne   Rob - erts   so   mi   so   mi

A - dri - enne Mil - ler   A - dri-enne Mil - ler   so so mi   so   mi

4. Teacher sings as before, but now instead of the echo, the child responds to the
teacher's question, singing and using hand signs. The class responds, as in (3):

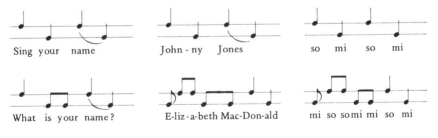

Sing your   name   John - ny   Jones   so   mi   so   mi

What   is   your   name?   E-liz-a-beth Mac-Don-ald   mi   so so mi   mi   so   mi

Education Through Music (ETM)

Mary Helen Richards is a pioneer adapter of Kodály concepts to the English-speaking world. She organized the Richard's Institute of Music Education and Research. Certain principles gleaned from research are being continuously studied and applied. Richards advised teachers to utilize the language and songs native to the people living in the United States and the British Isles. Consequently, folk songs and games were selected that reflect the rhythm, accents, and inflections of English as spoken in the United States. Kinesthetic experience is stressed in many games with songs. Through body motions the child is led to discover repeated words, rhythm patterns, phrases, and tonal patterns. These patterns, both rhythmic and vocal, are related to musical notation, thus encouraging sight-singing, a Kodály objective. The Curwen hand signs and the corresponding syllables are employed.

ETM is noteworthy for its emphasis on a game approach that involves the learner physically. Each singing game has a clearly defined educational purpose congruent with ETM's position that children learn by physical activity, an idea shared with Dalcroze, Orff, and Kodály. ETM's music learning stimulates thought processes by means of games, purposeful movement, and simple dramatization. Aural discrimination, sequencing, evaluation, comparing, and contrasting are all important cognitive skills that can be acquired by means of this approach. Relationships to language arts, mathematics, and social growth are claimed. The publications of ETM are available from The Institute of Music Education and Research, 149 Corte Madera Road, Portola Valley, CA 94025.

Edwin Gordon Edwin Gordon is best known for his many years of research related to music education, and his music aptitude tests. He collaborated with David Woods to develop a music program that spans kindergarten through middle school. This program is a carefully sequenced curriculum designed to adapt to the individual needs of all students, and is published under the name *Jump Right In!* The authors advertise the program as a complete music curriculum. It includes activity books, rhythm and tonal register books and pattern cards, a song collection, transparencies, cassettes, and other appropriate materials. Among its strengths is the inclusion of methods for evaluating student progress. In addition to the music curriculum, Gordon and Grunow publish an instrumental series under the same title, *Jump Right In!* (G.I.A. Publications, 7404 Mason Ave., Chicago, IL, 60638).

Phyllis Weikart Phyllis Weikart's approach focuses on movement as the core activity of elementary music. It is her premise that many people today have inadequate rhythmic coordination and lack awareness of the beat. Out of this concern Weikart has developed a sequential approach to rhythmic movement that has proven successful with individuals of all ages. For example she differentiates between nonlocomotor and locomotor movements, and articulates a sequence in each that progresses from simple to complex. She also stresses the use of language as the impetus for these movements.

Among Weikart's objectives are the building of basic timing through beat awareness and body coordination, and developing the ability to decode various signals aurally, visually, and kinesthetically. Her interest in developing these various movement skills has led to a focus on international folk dance, and the production of numerous authentic recordings of folk-dance music. Materials for Weikart's approach are available from High/Scope Educational Research Foundation, 600 North River Street, Ypsilanti, MI 48198.

James Froseth James Froseth has developed a comprehensive approach to music instruction that involves creative movement and the active use of multiple senses in acquiring musical competence. The initial stimulus is non-verbal and is provided through recorded music, to which children respond either in imitation of the teacher or another student. These movements progress from easy to difficult, and anchor the kinesthetic skills which, along with listening, are central to his program. Further steps in the program include associating listening with verbal skills, visual skills, and music reading skills. His program includes singing and the playing of instruments at various levels. He also has an extensive training program for music teachers in learning to diagnose problems with students' techniques of playing instruments.

In addition, Froseth's program provides materials for recorders, strings, band instruments, guitar, and other instruments, all under the title *The Comprehensive Music Instructor,* The sequence of activities for each of these is listen, move, sing, and play. He has conducted studies in creative musicianship and written books on the topic. Further information about these books, flash cards, records, and cassettes is available from Music Learning Research, Division of G.I.A. Publications, Inc., 7404 South Mason Avenue, Chicago, IL 60638.

References

BACON, DENISE, *50 Easy Two-Part Exercises.* Clifton, N.J.: European American Music Distributors Corp.

_____ , "Kodály and Orff: Report from Europe," *Music Educators Journal,* April 1969, 53–56.

BENNETT, PEGGY, "From Hungary to America: The Evolution of Education Through Music," *Music Educators Journal,* September 1987, 37–45.

BIRKENSHAW, LOIS, *Music for Fun, Music for Learning.* Toronto: Holt, Rinehart and Winston of Canada. Obtainable from Magnamusic-Baton, 10370 Page Industrial Blvd., St. Louis, MO 63132. Magnamusic-Baton is a good source of materials concerning Orff Schulwerk.

BURNETT, MILLIE, *Melody, Movement and Language.* San Francisco: R and E Research Associates, 1973.

CARLEY, ISABEL, ed., *Orff Re-Echoes.* Cleveland: American Orff-Schulwerk Association, 1977. A collection of excerpts from the *Orff Echo,* the association's magazine.

CHOKSY, LOIS, *The Kodály Context.* Englewood Cliffs, N.J.: Prentice Hall, 1981.

_____ , *The Kodály Method: Comprehensive Music Education from Infant to Adult.* Englewood Cliffs, N.J.: Prentice Hall, 1974. Describes the method, adapts it for American schools, and includes 153 songs.

CHOKSY, LOIS, ROBERT ABRAMSON, AVON GILLESPIE, DAVID WOODS. *Teaching Music in the Twentieth Century.* Englewood Cliffs, N.J.: Prentice Hall, 1986.

CHOKSY, LOIS, DAVID BRUMMITT, *Singing Games and Dances for Elementary Schools.* Englewood Cliffs, N.J.: Prentice Hall, 1987.

Dalcroze School of Music, 161 E. 73 St., New York, NY 10021

DANIEL, KATINKA S., *The Kodály Approach*, vols. 1, 2, and 3. Belmont, CA: Fearon. Sequentially written workbooks for the primary grades.

FINDLAY, ELSA, *Rhythm and Movement:: Applications of Dalcroze Eurhythmics.* Evanston, Ill.: Summy-Birchard, 1971.

FROSETH, JAMES O., AND ALBERT BLASER, *Music for Movement.* Music Learning Research Division, G. I. A. Publications, Inc., 7404 Mason Avenue, Chicago, IL 60638

GILL, RICHARD, et al., *Singing, Dancing, Playing*. St. Louis: Magnamusic-Baton, Inc. Six cassette tapes and teacher's guide.

GORDON, EDWIN and DAVID WOODS, *Jump Right In: The Music Curriculum*. Chicago: G.I.A., 1990.

JAQUES-DALCROZE, ÉMILE, *Rhythm, Music and Education*. Translated by Harold F. Rubenstein. 1921. Reprint. New York: Arno Press, 1976.

KEETMAN, GUNHILD, *Elementaria*. Translated by Margaret Murray. London: Schott, 1974. An introduction to Orff techniques.

Kodály Center of America. 1326 Washington St., West Newton, MA 02165.

Kodály Music Training Institute. University of Hartford, Hartt School of Music, West Hartford, CT 06117.

KODALY, ZOLTAN, *The Selected Writings of Zoltan Kodály*. Edited by Ferenc Bonis. Translated by Lili Halapy and Fred Macnicol. London: Boosey and Hawkes, 1974.

LANDIS, BETH, and POLLY CARDER, *The Eclectic Curriculum in Music Education: Contributions of Dalcroze, Kodály, and Orff*. Reston, Va.: Music Educators National Conference, 1972.

Magnamusic-Baton, 10370 Page Industrial Blvd., St. Louis, MO 63132. Magnamusic-Baton is a good source of materials concerning Orff Schulwerk.

MOLL, BETSY, and CHRISTINE KUNKO, eds. *The Kodály Envoy*. Pittsburgh, Pa.: School of Music, Duquesne University. Official journal of the Organization of Kodály Music Educators.

NASH, GRACE C., et al., *The Child's Way of Learning, Do It My Way*. Sherman Oaks, Calif.: Alfred, 1977.

ORFF, CARL and GUNILD KEETMAN, *Music for Children*. Mainz: B. Schott's Sons, 1960. English adaptation by Doreen Hall, vol. I–V *American Edition*, Book 2, primary, 1977; Book 3, upper elementary, 1980.

PERINCHIEF, ROBERT, and LORNA ZEMKE, *Kodály Transparencies*. Whitewater, Wisc.: Perry Publications. An eight-level program of supplementary teaching aids.

RICHARDS, MARY HELEN, *Aesthetic Foundations for Thinking*. Portola Valley, Calif.: Richards Institute of Music Education and Research, 1977. *Education Through Music, Part II*, 1978; *Part III*, 1979.

RICHARDS, MARY HELEN, and ANNA P. LANGNESS, *The Music Language: Section One*. Portola Valley, Calif.: Richards Institute of Music Education and Research, 1982.

Silver Burdett Music, *Kodály Curriculum Guide for Grades One Through Six*, Morristown, N.J.: Silver Burdett, 1983.

STRINGHAM, MARY, *Orff-Schulwerk, Background and Commentary*. St. Louis, Mo.: Magnamusic-Baton, 1976.

Recordings   WEIKART, PHYLLIS, *Rhythmically Moving* (series of recordings). The High/Scope Press, 600 North River Street, Ypsilanti, MI 48198.

WILLOUR, JUDITH, "Beginning with Delight, Leading to Wisdom: Dalcroze," *Music Educators Journal*, September 1969, 72–75.

Appendix A

Books for Elementary School Children

Biographies   CONE, MOLLY. *Leonard Bernstein*. Crowell, 1970.
     Well-written biography describing the life and career of this contemporary composer and conductor.

CORNELL, JEAN GAY. *Louis Armstrong: Ambassador Satchmo*. Garrard, 1972.
     Biography conveys the exuberance of Satchmo's trumpet and the vitality of his contribution to jazz.

_____ . *Mahalia Jackson: Queen of Gospel Song*. Garrard, 1974.
     The moving story of Mahalia Jackson's rise from poverty to renown. Includes her activities in the civil rights movement, and emphasizes how she sang about her beliefs from the heart.

EVANS, MARK. *Scott Joplin and the Ragtime Years*. Dodd, Mead, 1976.
     A thorough account of Joplin's involvement in the development of ragtime. Joplin's pieces are traced historically from early compositions to the release of the film *The Sting*.

*GREENFIELD, ELOISE. *Paul Robeson*. Crowell, 1975.
     Reflects the dynamic spirit of Robeson's life and accomplishments in his fight for freedom.

IVERSON, GENIE. *Louis Armstrong*. Crowell, 1976.
     Explains jazz through "Satchmo's" life story.

*Suggested by the Oregon State Department of Education, Delmer Aebischer, Music Consultant.

KRISHEF, ROBERT K. See various titles. Lerner, 1978.
Series tracing the development of country music. Straightforward accounts of entertainers' lives illustrated with excellent photographs. Each includes table of contents and index.

The Carter Family—Country Music's First Family

Comedians of Country Music

The Grand Ole Opry

Hank Williams

Jimmie Rodgers

Loretta Lynn

The New Breed

Western Stars of Country Music

MATHIS, SHARON BELL. *Ray Charles*. Crowell, 1973.
Clearly written biography of this world-famous blues, gospel, and jazz entertainer.

MCDERMON, KAY. *Mahalia: Gospel Singer*. Dodd, Mead, 1976.
The life of Mahalia Jackson, a voice for freedom and an inspiration for people of all races.

MONTGOMERY, ELIZABETH R. *Duke Ellington: King of Jazz*. Garrard, 1972.
A lively account of Ellington's dedication to music, years of practice, his work with jazz, success, and his honor at being named "Musician of Every Year."

SCHAFF, MARTHA E. *Duke Ellington: Young Music Master*. Bobbs-Merrill, 1975.
Beautifully told story of Duke's life; his early interest in sports, art, and music, and his success as a conductor and composer.

SILL, HAROLD D. *Misbehavin' with Fats*. Addison Wesley, 1978.
The life story of singer, organist, pianist and composer Fats Waller, who wrote over 400 songs before his death at 39.

TERKEL, LOUIS. *Giants of Jazz*. Crowell, 1975.
Details the lives of many jazz musicians. The final chapter sums up the history of jazz to 1974.

TOBIAS, TOBI. *Marian Anderson*. Crowell, 1972.
A look at the emotions and feelings of Marian Anderson in a way that young children can understand. Beautifully illustrated.

*Ventura, Piero, *Great Composers*. Putnam, 1989.

Folk Music AGAY, DENES. *Best-Loved Songs of the American People*. Doubleday, 1975.
An anthology of popular songs from "Yankee Doodle" to "The Impossible Dream." Piano arrangements, guitar chords, and historical notes are included in this spiral-bound volume.

BERGER, MELVIN. *The Story of Folk Music*. Phillips, 1976.
Songs and information about folk music and instruments, the role of folk music in politics, and how folk music relates to young people today.

BIERHORST, JOHN. *Songs of the Chippewa*. Farrar, Straus and Giroux, 1974.
Beautiful songs of the Chippewa Indians arranged for piano and guitar.

*Bryan, Ashley. *Walk Together Children: Black American Spirituals*. Atheneum, 1977.
A collection of spirituals (melody only), complemented with striking woodcut illustrations.

CAMPBELL, PATRICIA S., and NGUYEN, PHONG THUYET. *From Rice Paddies & Temple Yards: Traditional Music of Vietnam*. World Music Press, 1989. Il 4–6

CROFUT, WILLIAM. *The Moon on the One Hand*. Atheneum, 1975.
Poems by well-known poets set to music. Useful for language arts and music teachers.

DE CESARE, RUTH. *Myth, Music & Dance*. Alfred, 1988.

*DISNEY, WALT. *The Walt Disney Song Book*. Golden, 1971.
Thirty-four Disney songs illustrated by Disney Productions. Simple piano arrangements and large type make it particularly useful with younger children.

*FOWKE, EDITH. *Sally Go Round The Sun*. Doubleday, 1969.
A collection of 300 singing games, fun songs, and jumping rhymes. Guitar chords and some piano arrangements.

GLASS, PAUL. *Songs and Stories of the North American Indians*. Grossett and Dunlap, 1968.
Songs of many Indian tribes: sacred, dream, legends, games. History of each tribe included.

Go In and Out the Window: An Illustrated Songbook for Young People. Metropolitan Museum of Art, 1987.

HOUSTON, JAMES. *Songs of the Dream People*; *Chants and Images from the Indians of North America*. Atheneum, 1972.
Songs, chants, and poetry of the Eskimos and North American Indians.

JOHN, TIMOTHY. *The Great Song Book*. Doubleday, 1978.
A large collection of folk tunes ranging from nursery rhymes and lullabies to Christmas songs. All include guitar chords, many piano accompaniment.

*JOHNSTON, RICHARD. *Folksongs North America Sings*. Caveat, 1984.

LANGSTAFF, JOHN. *Hot Cross Buns and Other Old Street Cries*. Atheneum, 1978.
An illustrated collection of short street cries. Some arranged as rounds and part songs.

————— . *The Season for Singing: American Christmas Songs and Carols*. Doubleday, 1974.
A collection of American Christmas songs. All arranged for piano and guitar. Notes on history included.

————— . *Shimmy Shimmy Coke-A-Pop! A Collection of City Children's Street Games and Rhymes*. Doubleday, 1973.
Games and chants under eleven headings: name calling, ball bouncing, sidewalk drawing games, circle games, who's it?, tag games, jump rope, action games, follow the leader, hand clapping, dramatic play.

————— . *Sweetly Sings the Donkey: Animal Rounds for Children to Sing or Play on Recorders*. Atheneum, 1976.
Collection of thirteen ancient and modern rounds with music, each printed on a double-page illustration of medieval life.

LEWIN, OLIVE. *Dandy Shandy: 12 Jamaican Folk Songs for Children*. Oxford, 1975.
Twelve folk songs from Jamaica arranged in two-part harmony.

POSTON, ELIZABETH. *The Baby's Song Book*. Crowell, 1972.
Eighty-four nursery songs and Mother Goose rhymes from all over the world, each with simple piano arrangement. English translations with foreign language songs.

Rise Up Singing. Sing Out, 1988.

ROBINSON, ADJAI. *Singing Tales of Africa*. Scribner, 1974.
Seven African tales with active parts for listeners, and a moral. Chants introduce each tale. Woodcut illustrations.

_____ . *American Folk Songs for Children in Home, School and Nursery School; A Book for Children, Parents and Teachers*. Doubleday, 1948.
Ninety selections for singing and acting out. Introductory chapters explain how to use the music, and its value as an activity.

*SERWADDA, W. MOSES. *Songs and Stories from Uganda*. Crowell, 1974.
A collection of songs and stories in Luganda, the language of Uganda, with English translations. Red and black woodcuts enhance the East African flavor.

Songs of Praise. Harcourt Brace Jovanovich, 1988.

Tom Glazer's Treasury of Songs for Children. Doubleday, 1988. IL 1–6

World's Best Funny Songs. Sterling, 1988.

History and Origin

DAVIS, MARILYN K. and ARNOLD BROIDO. *Music Dictionary*. Doubleday, 1956.
Excellent format and illustrations. Easy to read and use.

DAVIS, MAY, and ANITA DAVIS. *All About Music*. Oxford University Press, 1975.
Excellent explanation of basic music theory. Good for individualized music stations.

*GILDER, ERIC. *The Dictionary of Composers*. Paddington, 1978.
Excellent resource publication.

INGMAN, NICHOLAS. *The Story of Music*. Taplinger, 1976.
A comprehensive history of music. Colorfully illustrated.

SCHOLES, PERCY A. *The Oxford Junior Companion to Music*. Oxford University Press, 1954 (reprinted 1977).
Short articles about composers, instruments, musical terms, and so on. Well illustrated.

Instruments

*DIAGRAM GROUP. *Musical Instruments of the World*. Paddington, 1976.
Informative and well-illustrated book describing instruments from around the world. Excellent reference.

BAILEY, BERNADINE. *Bells, Bells, Bells*. Dodd, Mead, 1978.
History of bells, casting, tuning, handbell ringing, and carillon playing. Stories of famous bells, such as Big Ben and the Liberty Bell, generously illustrated with photographs.

*BLACKWOOD, ALAN. *Musical Instruments*. Bookwright Press, 1987.

ETKIN, RUTH. *Playing and Composing on the Recorder*. Sterling, 1975.
An excellent "how-to" book, information about music theory, composition, notation, rhythm bands, and how to make a recorder case. (ESLC)

*GUSTAFSON, SCOTT. *Animal Orchestra: A Counting Book*. Contemporary Books, 1988.

*KUSKIN, KARLA. *The Philharmonic Gets Dressed*. Harper & Row, 1982. IL 1–3

*LILLEGARD, DEE. *Brass: An Introduction to Musical Instruments*. Children's Press, 1988.

*_____ . *Strings: An Introduction to Musical Instruments*. Children's Press, 1988.

SURPLUS, ROBERT W. *The Beat of the Drum*. Lerner, 1963.
History and cultural significance of drums, with specific information on percussion instruments used today. Special section on South American percussion.

WHEELER, TOM. *The Guitar Book*. Harper & Row, 1974. IL
Although this book may be too difficult for elementary grade students, it is an excellent teacher resource. Contains many illustrations, complete information about guitars, performers, history, and styles of playing.

YOLEN, JANE. *Ring Out! A Book of Bells*. Seabury, 1974. IL Historic information on bells sacred and secular, their significance, and usage.

Opera　　*MENOTTI, GIAN CARLO. *Amahl and the Night Visitors*. Morrow, 1986. IL 3–6

MONTRESOR, BENI. *Cinderella*. Knopf, 1965.
Montresor's beautiful illustrations enliven this retelling of Rossini's opera *Cenerentola*.

SPENDER, STEPHEN. *The Magic Flute*. Putnam, 1966.
A retelling of Mozart's opera with impressionistic illustrations by Montresor.

Sound and Music　　*ARDLEY, NEIL. Knopf, 1989.

*BERGER, MELVIN. *The Science of Music*. Crowell, 1989. IL 3–6

BRANLEY, FRANKLYN M. *High Sounds, Low Sounds*. Crowell, 1967.
Experiments using spoons, strings, and straws help the young reader understand sound.

FAULHABER, MARTHA, and JANET UNDERHILL. *Music: Invent Your Own*. Whitman, 1974.
Basic musical concepts of rhythm, timbre, melody, and dynamics inventively presented.

HAWKINSON, JOHN, and MARTHA FAULHABER. *Music and Instruments for Children to Make*. Whitman, 1969.
Rhythm and sound experiments and how to make rhythm instruments.

————— . *Rhythms, Music and Instruments to Make*. Whitman, 1970.
How to make wind, string, and percussion instruments; good teacher resource for upper grades.

KIRSHEF, ROBERT K. *Playback: The Story of Recording Devices*. Lerner, 1974.
A history of recording equipment from Thomas Edison's first phonograph to the record player of today.

*McLEAN, MARGARET. *Make Your Own Musical Instruments*. Lerner, 1988.

*SNOW, BARBARA. *Index of Songs on Children's Recordings*. Staccato Press, 1988.

Stories　　*ARNOLD, CAROLINE, *Music Lessons for Alex*. Clarion, 1985.

*BARRIE, CARSON, and TURNER. *I Like Music*. Warwick, 1989.

BRAND, OSCAR. *When I First Came To This Land*. Putnam, 1974.
Song-story of an American homesteader. Musical score included.

*CHILD, LYDIA MARIA. *Over the River and Through the Wood*. Coward, McCann and Geoghegan, 1974.
Beautiful illustrations help tell the story of a trip to grandparents' house for Thanksgiving.

*DISNEY, WALT. *Peter and the Wolf*. Random House, 1974.
Beautifully illustrated version of Prokofiev's famous adaptation of the story of a boy and a wolf.

Fantasia Pictorial. See various titles. Gakken, 1971.

Stories of famous musical compositions, with unusual illustrations combining many textures and materials.

Carnival of the Animals	*The Nutcracker*
Coppelia	*Peter and the Wolf*
Hansel and Gretel	*The Sorcerer's Apprentice*
Invitation to the Dance	*Swan Lake*
A Night on Bald Mountain	*William Tell*

KROSKE, ROBERT. *America The Beautiful*. Garrard, 1972.

Stories about patriotic songs and why they were written. Includes "America the Beautiful," "Yankee Doodle," "Star-Spangled Banner," "God Bless America," and "America."

_____ . *Oh, A-Hunting We Will Go*. Atheneum, 1977.

Piano and guitar arrangements accompany this story of this old folk song.

_____ . *Over in the Meadow*. Harcourt, Brace, 1967.

Story of ten meadow families in folk song. Melody arrangement included.

L'ENGLE, MADELEINE. *Prelude*. Vanguard, 1968.

Fictional story of a young girl's struggles to become a concert pianist.

*PAINTER, WILLIAM M. *Musical Story Hours: Using Music with Storytelling and Puppetry*. Library Professional Publications, 1989.

*PAOLO, TOMIEDE. *Pages of Music*. Putnam, 1988.

PECK, ROBERT NEWTON. *King of Kazoo*. Knopf, 1976.

Fun book to read, can also be performed. With lyrics, scores, and staging suggestions.

QUACKENBUSH, ROBERT. *Old MacDonald Had A Farm*. Lippincott, 1972.

End result of this add-on song book is a barnyard full of animals!

SCHICK, ALICE and JOEL SCHICK. *Viola Hates Music*. Lippincott, 1977.

Viola, the dog, doesn't like music, but then becomes a music lover when she learns to play the bagpipes.

*SCHROEDER, ALAN. *Ragtime Trumpie*. Joy Street Books, 1989.

SPIER, PETER. *The Erie Canal*. Doubleday, 1970.

Watercolor illustrations enliven this old folk song. History and music included.

_____. *London Bridge Is Falling Down*. Doubleday, 1967.

History, lyrics, and score, complemented by colorful illustrations.

_____ . *The Star-Spangled Banner*. Doubleday, 1973.

Spier's outstanding illustrations dramatize the first four stanzas of the American national anthem. Score and historical information included.

VAN LAMSWEERDE, JOYCE. *Ziggy and His Music*. Ideals, 1968.

Introduces music in terms of everyday sounds. Beautifully done in rhyme.

Appendix B

Alphabetical Listing of Composers in ADVENTURES IN MUSIC (AM)

Anderson: Irish Suite—"The Girl I Left Behind Me," grade 5, vol. 2

Arnold: English Dances—
Allegro Non Troppo, grade 2, vol. 2
Grazioso, grade 1, vol. 2

Bach:
Cantata No. 147—Jesu, Joy of Man's Desiring, grade 5, vol. 1
Little Fugue in G Minor (arr. by L. Cailliet), grade 6, vol. 1
Suite No. 2—Badinerie, grade 3, vol. 1
Suite No. 2—Rondeau, grade 2, vol. 2
Suite No. 3—Gigue, grade 1, vol. 1

Bartók:
Hungarian Sketches—"Bear Dance," grade 3, vol. 2
Hungarian Sketches—"Evening in the Village," grade 5, vol. 2
Mikrokosmos Suite No. 2—"From the Diary of a Fly," grade 1, vol. 2
Mikrokosmos Suite No. 2—"Jack-in-the-Box," grade 2, vol. 1

Beethoven: Symphony No. 8—Second Movement, grade 6, vol. 1

Berlioz: The Damnation of Faust—Ballet of the Sylphs, grade 1, vol. 1

Bizet:
L'Arlésienne Suite No. 1, —Minuetto, grade 4, vol. 2
L'Arlésienne Suite No. 2, —Farandole, grade 6, vol. 1
Carmen—"Changing of the Guard," grade 3, vol. 2
Carmen—"The Dragoons of Alcala," grade 2, vol. 2
Children's Games—"The Ball"; "Cradle Song"; "Leap Frog"; grade 1, vol. 1

Borodin: *On the Steppes of Central Asia,* grade 6, vol. 1

Brahms: *Hungarian Dance* No. 1, grade 5, vol. 2

Cailliet: ''Pop! Goes the Weasel''—Variations, grade 4, vol. 1

Carpenter: *Adventures in Perambulator*—''The Hurdy-Gurdy,'' grade 5, vol. 2

Chabrier:
    España Rapsodie, grade 5, vol. 1
    Marche Joyeuse, grade 4, vol. 1

Charpentier: *Impressions of Italy*—''On Muleback,'' grade 5, vol. 1

Cimarosa: *Cimarosiana*—Non Troppo Mosso, grade 2, vol. 2

Coates: London Suite—''Knightsbridge March,'' grade 5, vol. 2

Copland:
    Billy the Kid Ballet Suite—''Street in a Frontier Town,'' grade 6, vol. 1
    The Red Pony Suite—''Circus Music,'' grade 3, vol. 1
    The Red Pony Suite—''Dream March,'' grade 2, vol. 2
    Rodeo—''Hoe-Down,'' grade 5, vol. 2

Corelli-Pinelli: Suite for Strings—Sarabande, grade 6, vol. 2

Debussy:
    Children's Corner Suite—''The Snow Is Dancing,'' grade 3, vol. 1
    La Mer—''Play of the Waves,'' grade 6, vol. 2

Delibes:
    Coppelia—''Waltz of the Doll,'' grade 1, vol. 1
    Coppelia—''Swanhilde's Waltz,'' grade 2, vol. 2
    The King Is Amused—''Lesquercarde,'' grade 1, vol. 2

Dvořák: *Slavonic Dance* No. 7, grade 4, vol. 2

Elgar:
    Wand of Youth Suite No. 1—''Fairies and Giants,'' grade 3, vol. 1
    Wand of Youth Suite No. 1—''Sun Dance,'' grade 2, vol. 2
    Wand of Youth Suite No. 2—''Fountain Dance,'' grade 2, vol. 1

Falla: *La Vida Breve*—Spanish Dance No. 1, grade 6, vol. 1

Fauré: *Dolly*—Berceuse, grade 2, vol. 1

German: *Henry VIII* Suite—''Morris Dance,'' grade 1, vol. 2

Ginastera: *Estancia*—''Wheat Dance,'' grade 4, vol. 1

Gliére: *The Red Poppy*—''Russian Sailors' Dance,'' grade 6, vol. 2

Gluck:
    Armide Ballet Suite—Musette, grade 2, vol. 2
    Iphigenie in Aulis—''Air Gai,'' grade 1, vol. 1

Gottschalk-Kay: *Cakewalk* Ballet Suite—''Grand Walkaround,'' grade 5, vol. 1

Gould: *American Salute,* grade 5, vol. 1

Gounod: *Faust* Ballet Suite—Waltz No. 1, grade 3, vol. 1

Grainger: ''Londonderry Air,'' grade 4, vol. 2

Gretry:
    Cephale et Procris—Gigue (Arr. by Mottl), grade 1, vol. 1
    Cephale et Procris—Tambourin (Arr. by Mottl), grade 2, vol. 1

Grieg:
    Lyric Suite—''Norwegian Rustic March,'' grade 4, vol. 1
    Peer Gynt Suite No. 1—''Anitra's Dance,'' grade 1, vol. 2
    Peer Gynt Suite No. 1—''In the Hall of the Mountain King,'' grade 3, vol. 2

Griffes: *The White Peacock,* grade 6, vol. 1

Grofé: *Death Valley* Suite—"Desert Water Hole," grade 4, vol. 1

Guarnieri: Brazilian Dance, grade 6, vol. 2

Handel:
    Royal Fireworks Music—Bourrée, Minuetto No. 2, grade 3, vol. 2
    Water Music—Hornpipe, grade 2, vol. 1

Hanson: *For the First Time*—"Bells," grade 1, vol. 2
    Merry Mount Suite—"Children's Dance," grade 3, vol. 1

Herbert:
    Babes in Toyland—"March of the Toys," grade 2, vol. 1
    Natoma—"Dagger Dance," grade 3, vol. 1

Holst: *The Perfect Fool*—"Spirit of the Earth," grade 6, vol. 2

Howe: "Sand," grade 2, vol. 2

Humperdinck: *Hansel and Gretel*—Prelude, grade 5, vol. 2

Ibert:
    Divertissement—"Parada," grade 1, vol. 1
    Histories No. 2—"The Little White Donkey," grade 2, vol. 1

Kabalevsky:
    The Comedians—March, "Comedians Galop," grade 3, vol. 1
    The Comedians—"Pantomime," grade 1, vol. 1
    The Comedians—Waltz, grade 1, vol. 2

Khachaturian:
    Gayne Ballet Suite—"Dance of the Rose Maidens," grade 1, vol. 2
    Masquerade Suite—Waltz, grade 4, vol. 2

Kodály:
    Háry János Suite—"Entrance of the Emperor and His Court," grade 4, vol. 2
    Háry János Suite—"Viennese Musical Clock," grade 2, vol. 1

Lecuona: *Suite Andalucia*—"Andalucia," grade 4, vol. 1

Liadov: Eight Russian Folk Songs—Berceuse, grade 1, vol. 2

Lully: Ballet Suite—March, grade 3, vol. 2

MacDowell: *Second (Indian) Suite*—"In Wartime," grade 5, vol. 1

Massenet: *Le Cid*—"Aragonaise," grade 1, vol. 1

McBride:
    Pumpkin Eater's Little Fugue, grade 2, vol. 2
    Punch and the Judy—"Pony Express," grade 1, vol. 2

McDonald:
    Children's Symphony (1st Movement)—*"London Bridge," "Baa, Baa Black Sheep,"* grade 3, vol. 2
    Children's Symphony (3rd Movement)—*"Farmer in the Dell," "Jingle Bells,"* grade 2, vol. 1

Menotti:
    Amahl and the Night Visitors—"March of the Kings," grade 1, vol. 2
    Amahl and the Night Visitors—"Shepherds' Dance," grade 4, vol. 2

Meyerbeer: *Les Patineurs*—Waltz, grade 2, vol. 1

Milhaud:
    Saudades do Brazil—"Copacabana," grade 4, vol. 2

Saudades do Brasil—"Laranjeiras," grade 2, vol. 1
Suite Provençale—"Modéré No. 1," grade 1, vol. 2

Moore: Farm Journal—"Harvest Song," grade 1, vol. 2

Mussorgsky:
Pictures at an Exhibition—"Ballet of the Unhatched Chicks" (Orchestrated by Ravel), grade 1, vol. 1
Pictures at an Exhibition—"Bydlo" (Orchestrated by Ravel), grade 2, vol. 1
Pictures at an Exhibition—"Promenade" (Orchestrated by Ravel), grade 1, vol. 2

Mozart:
Divertimento No. 17—Menuetto No. 1, grade 5, vol. 2
Eine kleine Nachtmusik—Romanze, grade 4, vol. 1
The Little Nothings, No. 8, grade 1, vol. 2

Offenbach: *The Tales of Hoffmann*—Barcarolle, grade 3, vol. 1

Pierné: *Cydalise* Suite No. 1—"Entrance of the Little Fauns," grade 2, vol. 2

Prokofiev:
Children's Suite—"Waltz on the Ice," grade 3, vol. 2
Lieutenant Kije—Troika, grade 2, vol. 2
Summer Day Suite—March, grade 1, vol. 1
Winter Holiday—"Departure," grade 2, vol. 1

Ravel:
Mother Goose Suite—"The Conversations of Beauty and the Beast," grade 5, vol. 1
Mother Goose Suite—"Laideronnette, Empress of the Pagodas," grade 4, vol. 2

Respighi:
The Birds—Prelude, grade 2, vol. 2
Brazilian Impressions—Danza, grade 5, vol. 2
Pines of Rome—"Pines of the Villa Borghese," grade 4, vol. 1

Rimsky-Korsakov:
Le Coq d'Or Suite—"Bridal Procession," grade 4, vol. 1
The Snow Maiden—"Dance of the Buffoons," grade 2, vol. 2

Rossini: *William Tell* Overture—Finale, grade 3, vol. 1

Rossini-Britten:
Matinees Musicales—Waltz, grade 1, vol. 2
Soirées Musicales—Bolero, grade 2, vol. 2
Soirées Musicales—March, grade 1, vol. 1

Rossini-Respighi:
The Fantastic Toyshop—Can-Can, grade 2, vol. 1
The Fantastic Toyshop—Tarantella, grade 3, vol. 2

Saint-Saëns:
Carnival of the Animals—"The Elephant," grade 1, vol. 2
Carnival of the Animals—"The Swan," grade 3, vol. 2

Scarlatti-Tommasini: *The Good-Humored Ladies*—Non Presto ma a Tempo Di Ballo, grade 4, vol. 2

Schubert: Symphony No. 5—First Movement, grade 5, vol. 1

Schuller: Seven Studies on Themes of Paul Klee—"The Twittering Machine," grade 2, vol. 2

Schumann: *Scenes from Childhood*—Traumerei, grade 4, vol. 2

Shostakovich:
Ballet Suite No. 1—"Petite Ballerina," grade 2, vol. 1
Ballet Suite No. 1—"Pizzicato Polka," grade 1, vol. 1

Sibelius: *Karelia* Suite—Alla Marcia, grade 5, vol. 1

Smetana: *The Bartered Bride*—"Dance of the Comedians," grade 6, vol. 2

Sousa:
Semper Fidelis, grade 3, vol. 2
Stars and Stripes Forever, grade 4, vol. 2

Strauss, R.: *Der Rosenkavalier*—Suite, grade 6, vol. 1

Stravinsky:
The Firebird Suite—Berceuse, grade 1, vol. 1
The Firebird Suite—"Infernal Dance of King Kastchei," grade 5, vol. 2
Petrouchka—"Russian Dance," grade 1, vol. 2

Taylor: *Through the Looking Glass*—"Garden of Live Flowers," grade 3, vol. 2

Tchaikovsky:
Nutcracker Suite—"Dance of the Sugar Plum Fairy," "Dance of the Reed Pipes," grade 1, vol. 2
The Sleeping Beauty—"Puss-in-Boots and the White Cat," grade 3, vol. 1
The Sleeping Beauty—Waltz, grade 4, vol. 1
Swan Lake—"Dance of the Little Swans," grade 1, vol. 1
Symphony No. 4—Fourth Movement, grade 6, vol. 2

Thomson:
Acadian Songs and Dances—"The Alligator and the 'Coon,' " grade 3, vol. 2
Acadian Songs and Dances—"Walking Song," grade 1, vol. 1

Vaughan-Williams:
Fantasia on "Greensleeves," grade 6, vol. 2
The Wasps—"March Past of the Kitchen Utensils," grade 3, vol. 1

Villa-Lobos: *Bachianas Brasileiras* No. 2—"The Little Train of the Caipira," grade 3, vol. 1

Wagner: *Lohengrin*—Prelude to Act III, grade 6, vol. 1

Walton: *Facade* Suite—Valse, grade 6, vol. 2

Webern: Five Movements for String Orchestra—Sehr Langsam, grade 2, vol. 2

Appendix C

Compositions in the BOWMAR ORCHESTRAL LIBRARY(BOL)

Series 1 ANIMALS AND CIRCUS (BOL 51)

CARNIVAL OF THE ANIMALS, Saint-Saëns. (Introduction, Royal March of the Lion, Hens and Cocks, Fleet-Footed Animals, Turtles, The Elephant, Kangaroos, Aquarium, Long-Eared Personages, Cuckoo in the Deep Woods, Aviary, Pianists, Fossils, The Swan, Finale)

CIRCUS POLKA, Stravinsky

UNDER THE BIG TOP, Donaldson. (Marching Band, Acrobats, Juggler, Merry-Go-Round, Elephants, Clowns, Camels, Tightrope Walker, Pony Trot, Marching Band)

NATURE AND MAKE-BELIEVE (BOL 52)

MARCH OF THE DWARFS, Grieg

ONCE UPON A TIME SUITE, Donaldson. (Chicken Little, Three Billy Goats Gruff, Little Train, Hare and the Tortoise)

THE LARK SONG (*Scenes of Youth*), Tchaikovsky

LITTLE BIRD, Grieg

DANCE OF THE MOSQUITO, Liadov

FLIGHT OF THE BUMBLE BEE, Rimsky-Korsakov

SEASON FANTASIES, Donaldson. (Magic Piper, The Poet and His Lyre, The Anxious Leaf, The Snowmaiden)

TO THE RISING SUN (Fjord and Mountain, Norwegian Suite 2), Torjussen

CLAIR DE LUNE, Debussy

PICTURES AND PATTERNS (BOL 53)

PIZZICATO (*Fantastic Toyshop*), Rossini-Respighi

MARCH—TRUMPET AND DRUM (*Jeux d'Enfants*), IMPROMPTU—THE TOP (*Jeux d'Enfants*), Bizet

POLKA (*Mlle. Angot* Suite), GAVOTTE (*Mlle. Angot* Suite), Lecocq

INTERMEZZO (*The Comedians*), Kabalevsky

GERMAN WALTZ-PAGANINI (*Carnaval*), Schumann-Glazounov

BALLET PETIT, Donaldson

MINUET, Mozart

A GROUND, Handel

CHOPIN (*Carnaval*), Schumann-Glazounov

VILLAGE DANCE, Liadov

EN BATEAU (In a Boat), Debussy

HARBOR VIGNETTES, Donaldson (Fog and Storm, Song of the Bell Buoy, Sailing)

MARCHES (BOL 54)

ENTRANCE OF THE LITTLE FAUNS, Pierné

MARCH, Prokofiev

POMP AND CIRCUMSTANCE No. 1, Elgar

HUNGARIAN MARCH (*Rakoczy*), Berlioz

COL. BOGEY MARCH, Alford

MARCH OF THE LITTLE LEAD SOLDIERS, Pierné

MARCH (*Love for Three Oranges*), Prokofiev

CORTEGE OF THE SARDAR (*Caucasian Sketches*), Ippolitov-Ivanov

MARCHE MILITAIRE, Schubert

STARS AND STRIPES FOREVER, Sousa

THE MARCH OF THE SIAMESE CHILDREN (*The King and I*), Rodgers

DANCES, PART I (BOL 55)

DANCE OF THE CAMORRISTI, Wolf-Ferrari

DANCA BRASILEIRA, Guarnieri

GAVOTTE, Kabalevsky

SLAVONIC DANCE No. 1, Dvořák

HOE-DOWN (Rodeo), Copland

FACADE SUITE, Walton (Polka, Country Dance, Popular Song)

HUNGARIAN DANCE No. 5, Brahms

SKATER'S WALTZES, Waldteufel

MAZURKA (*Masquerade* Suite), Khatchaturian

GALOP (*Masquerade* Suite), Khatchaturian

DANCES, PART II (BOL 56)

FOLK DANCES FROM SOMERSET (*English Folk Song* Suite), Vaughan-Williams

JAMAICAN RHUMBA, Benjamin

BADINERIE, Corelli

DANCE OF THE COMEDIANS, Smetana

CAN CAN (*Mlle. Angot* Suite), Lecocq

GRAND WALTZ (*Mlle. Angot* Suite), Lecocq

TRISCH-TRASCH POLKA, Strauss

TARANTELLA (*Fantastic Toyshop*), WALTZ (*Fantastic Toyshop*), Rossini-Respighi

ESPAÑA WALTZES, Waldteufel

ARKANSAS TRAVELER, Guion

RUSSIAN DANCE (*Gayne* Suite No. 22), Khatchaturian

FAIRY TALES IN MUSIC (BOL 57)

CINDERELLA, Coates

SCHERZO (*Midsummer Night's Dream*), Mendelssohn

MOTHER GOOSE SUITE, Ravel (Pavane of the Sleeping Beauty, Hop o' My Thumb, Lai-
deronette, Empress of the Pagodas, Beauty and the Beast, The Fairy Garden)

STORIES IN BALLET AND OPERA (BOL 58)

SUITE FROM AMAHL AND THE NIGHT VISITORS, Menotti (Introduction, March of the Three
Kings, Dance of the Shepherds)

HANSEL AND GRETEL OVERTURE, Humperdinck

NUTCRACKER SUITE, Tchaikovsky (Overture Miniature, March, Dance of the Sugar-Plum
Fairy, Trepak, Arabian Dance, Chinese Dance, Dance of the Toy Flutes, Waltz of
the Flowers)

LEGENDS IN MUSIC (BOL 59)

DANCE MACABRE, Saint-Saëns

PEER GYNT SUITE No. 1, Grieg (Morning, Asa's Death, Anitra's Dance, In the Hall of the
Mountain King)

SORCERER'S APPRENTICE, Dukas

PHAETON, Saint-Saëns

UNDER MANY FLAGS (BOL 60)

THE MOLDAU, Smetana

LAPLAND IDYLL (Fjord and Mountain, Norwegian Suite No. 2), Torjussen

FOLK SONG (Fjord and Mountain, Norwegian Suite No. 2), Torjussen

LONDONDERRY AIR, Grainger

FINLANDIA, Sibelius

LONDON SUITE, Coates (Covent Garden, Westminster, Knightsbridge March)

AMERICAN SCENES (BOL 61)

GRAND CANYON SUITE, Grofé (Sunrise, Painted Desert, On the Trail, Sunset, Cloudburst)

MISSISSIPPI SUITE, Grofé (Father of Waters, Huckleberry Finn, Old Creole Days, Mardi
Gras)

Series 2   MASTERS IN MUSIC (BOL 62)

JESU, JOY OF MAN'S DESIRING, Bach

BOURRÉE FROM FIREWORKS MUSIC, Handel

VARIATIONS (from *Sunrise* Symphony), Haydn

MINUET (from Symphony No. 40), Mozart

SCHERZO (from Seventh Symphony), Beethoven

WEDDING DAY AT TROLDHAUGEN, Grieg

RIDE OF THE VALKYRIES, Wagner

TRIUMPHAL MARCH (*Aïda*), Verdi

HUNGARIAN DANCE No. 6, Brahms

THIRD MOVEMENT, SYMPHONY No. 1, Mahler

CONCERT MATINEE (BOL 63)

CHILDREN'S CORNER SUITE, Debussy (Doctor Gradus ad Parnassum, Jumbo's Lullaby, Serenade of the Doll, The Snow Is Dancing, The Little Shepherd, Golliwog's Cakewalk)

SUITE FOR STRING ORCHESTRA, Corelli-Pinelli (Sarabande, Gigue, Badinerie)

MINUET (from *Surprise* Symphony), Haydn

ANVIL CHORUS (*Il Trovatore*), Verdi

NORWEGIAN DANCE IN A (No. 2), Grieg

TRAUMEREI, Schumann

MINIATURES IN MUSIC (BOL 64)

CHILDREN'S SYMPHONY, Zador

THE BEE, Schubert

GYPSY RONDO, Haydn

WILD HORSEMEN, Schumann

HAPPY FARMER, Schumann

LITTLE WINDMILLS, Couperin

ARIETTA, Leo

MUSIC BOX, Liadov

FUNERAL MARCH OF THE MARIONETTES, Gounod

DANCE OF THE MERRY DWARFS (*Happy Hypocrite*), Elwell

LITTLE TRAIN OF CAIPIRA, Villa-Lobos

MUSIC, USA (BOL 65)

SHAKER TUNE (*Appalachian Spring*), Copland

CATTLE & BLUES (*Plow That Broke the Plains*), Thomson

FUGUE AND CHORALE ON YANKEE DOODLE (*Tuesday in November*), Thomson

PUMPKIN EATERS LITTLE FUGUE, McBride

AMERICAN SALUTE, Gould

POP! GOES THE WEASEL, Cailliet

LAST MOVEMENT, SYMPHONY No. 2, Ives

ORIENTAL SCENES (BOL 66)

WOODCUTTER'S SONG, Koyama

THE EMPEROR'S NIGHTINGALE, Donaldson

SAKURA (folk tune), played by koto and bamboo flute

FANTASY IN MUSIC (BOL 67)

THREE BEARS, Coates

CINDERELLA, Prokofiev (Sewing Scene, Cinderella's Gavotte, Midnight Waltz, Fairy Godmother)

MOON LEGEND, Donaldson

SLEEPING BEAUTY WALTZ, Tchaikovsky

CLASSROOM CONCERT (BOL 68)

ALBUM FOR THE YOUNG, Tchaikovsky. (Morning Prayer, Winter Morning, Hobby Horse, Mamma, March of the Tin Soldiers, Sick Doll, Doll's Burial, New Doll, Waltz, Mazurka, Russian Song, Peasant Plays the Accordion, Folk Song, Polka, Italian Song, Old French Song, German Song, Neapolitan Dance Song, Song of the Lark, Hand-Organ Man, Nurse's Tale, The Witch, Sweet Dreams, In Church)

OVER THE HILLS, Grainger

MEMORIES OF CHILDHOOD, Pinto (Run, Run; Ring Around the Rosie; March; Sleeping Time; Hobby Horse)

LET US RUN ACROSS THE HILL, Villa-Lobos

MY DAUGHTER LIDI, TEASING, GRASSHOPPER'S WEDDING, Bartók

DEVIL'S DANCE, Stravinsky

LITTLE GIRL IMPLORING HER MOTHER, Rebikov

Series 3   MUSIC OF THE DANCE: STRAVINSKY (BOL 69)

FIREBIRD SUITE (L'Oiseau de Feu) (Koschai's Enchanted Garden, Dance of the Firebird, Dance of the Princesses, Infernal Dance of Koschai, Magic Sleep of the Princess Tzarevna, Finale: Escape of Koschai's Captives)

SACRIFICIAL DANCE from "The Rite of Spring" (*Le Sacre du Printemps*)

VILLAGE FESTIVAL from "The Fairy's Kiss" (*Le Baiser de la Fée*)

PALACE OF THE CHINESE EMPEROR from *The Nightingale (Le Rossignol)*

TANGO, WALTZ, AND RAGTIME from *The Soldier's Tale (L'Histoire du Soldat)*

MUSIC OF THE SEA AND SKY (BOL 70)

CLOUDS (Nuages), Debussy

FESTIVALS (Fêtes), Debussy

MERCURY from *The Planets,* Holst

SEA PIECE WITH BIRDS, Thomson

OVERTURE TO "THE FLYING DUTCHMAN" (*Der fliegende Holländer*), Wagner

DIALOGUE OF THE WIND AND SEA from *The Sea (La Mer),* Debussy

SYMPHONIC MOVEMENTS, NO. 1 (BOL 71)

FIRST MOVEMENT, SYMPHONY No. 40, Mozart

SECOND MOVEMENT, SYMPHONY No. 8, Beethoven

THIRD MOVEMENT, SYMPHONY No. 4, Tchaikovsky

SECOND MOVEMENT, SYMPHONY No. 4, Schumann

THIRD MOVEMENT, SYMPHONY No. 3, Brahms

FOURTH MOVEMENT, SYMPHONY No. 3, Saint-Saëns

SYMPHONIC MOVEMENTS, NO. 2 (BOL 72)

FIRST MOVEMENT, SYMPHONY No. 9 (*From the New World*), Dvořák

FIRST MOVEMENT, SYMPHONY No. 5, Beethoven

FIRST MOVEMENT (Boisterous Bourrée), A SIMPLE SYMPHONY, Britten

SECOND MOVEMENT, SYMPHONY No. 2, Hanson

FIRST MOVEMENT, SYMPHONY No. 2, Sibelius

SYMPHONIC STYLES (BOL 73)

SYMPHONY No. 99 (*Imperial*), Haydn (Adagio: Vivace Assai, Adagio, Minuetto, Vivace)

CLASSICAL SYMPHONY, Prokofiev (Allegro, Larghetto, Gavotte: Non troppo allegro, Molto vivace)

TWENTIETH-CENTURY AMERICA (BOL 74)

EL SALON MEXICO, Copland

DANZON from *Fancy Free,* Bernstein

EXCERPTS, SYMPHONIC DANCES from *West Side Story,* Bernstein

AN AMERICAN IN PARIS, Gershwin

U.S. HISTORY IN MUSIC (BOL 75)

A LINCOLN PORTRAIT, Copland

CHESTER from NEW ENGLAND TRIPTYCH, Schuman

PUTNAM'S CAMP from *Three Places in New England,* Ives

INTERLUDE from FOLK SYMPHONY, Harris

MIDNIGHT RIDE OF PAUL REVERE from Selections from McGuffey's Readers, Phillips

OVERTURES (BOL 76)

OVERTURE TO "THE BAT" (*Die Fledermaus*), Strauss

ACADEMIC FESTIVAL OVERTURE, Brahms

OVERTURE TO "THE MARRIAGE OF FIGARO," Mozart

ROMAN CARNIVAL OVERTURE, Berlioz

OVERTURE TO "WILLIAM TELL," Rossini (Dawn, Storm, Calm, Finale)

SCHEHERAZADE BY RIMSKY-KORSAKOV (BOL 77)

The Sea and Sinbad's Ship, Tale of the Prince Kalendar, The Young Prince and the Princess, The Festival at Bagdad

MUSICAL KALEIDOSCOPE (BOL 78)

ON THE STEPPES OF CENTRAL ASIA, Borodin

IN THE VILLAGE FROM CAUCASIAN SKETCHES, Ippolitoff-Ivanov

EXCERPTS, POLOVETSIAN DANCES FROM "PRINCE IGOR," Borodin

RUSSIAN SAILORS' DANCE FROM "THE RED POPPY," Glière

L'ARLÉSIENNE SUITE No. 1, Bizet (Carillon, Minuet)

L'ARLÉSIENNE SUITE No. 2, Bizet (Farandole)

PRELUDE TO ACT 1, "CARMEN," Bizet

MARCH TO THE SCAFFOLD, from *Symphonie Fantastique,* Berlioz

MUSIC OF THE DRAMA: WAGNER (BOL 79)

LOHENGRIN (Overture to Act 1, Prelude to Act 3)

THE TWILIGHT OF THE GODS (*Die Götterdämmerung*) (Siegfried's Rhine Journey)

THE MASTERSINGERS OF NUREMBERG (*Die Meistersinger von Nürnberg*) (Prelude, Dance of the Apprentices, and Entrance of the Mastersingers)

TRISTAN AND ISOLDE (Love Death)

PETROUCHKA BY STRAVINSKY (BOL 80)

COMPLETE BALLET SCORE WITH NARRATION

ROGUES IN MUSIC (BOL 81)

TIL EULENSPIEGEL, Strauss

LIEUTENANT KIJE (Birth of Kije, Troika), Prokofiev

HÁRY JANÓS, Kodály (Viennese Musical Clock, Battle and Defeat of Napoleon, Intermezzo, Entrance of the Emperor)

MUSICAL PICTURES: MUSSORGSKY (BOL 82)

PICTURES AT AN EXHIBITION (Promenade Theme, The Gnome, The Old Castle, Tuileries, Ox-Cart, Ballet of Chicks in Their Shells, Goldenberg and Schmuyle, The Market Place at Limoges, Catacombs, The Hut of Baga Yaga, The Gate of Kiev)

NIGHT ON BALD MOUNTAIN

ENSEMBLES, LARGE AND SMALL (BOL 83)

YOUNG PERSON'S GUIDE TO THE ORCHESTRA, Britten

CANZONA IN C MAJOR FOR BRASS ENSEMBLE AND ORGAN, Gabrieli

CHORALE: AWAKE, THOU WINTRY EARTH, Bach

FOURTH MOVEMENT, "TROUT" QUINTET, Schubert

THEME AND VARIATIONS FOR PERCUSSION QUARTET, Kraft

THEME AND VARIATIONS from SERENADE FOR WIND INSTRUMENTS, Mozart (K. 361)

CONCERTOS (BOL 84)

FIRST MOVEMENT, PIANO CONCERTO, Grieg

FOURTH MOVEMENT, PIANO CONCERTO No. 2, Brahms

THIRD MOVEMENT, VIOLIN CONCERTO, Mendelssohn

SECOND MOVEMENT, GUITAR CONCERTO, Castelnuovo-Tedesco

THIRD MOVEMENT, CONCERTO IN C FOR TWO TRUMPETS, Vivaldi

MUSICAL IMPRESSIONS: RESPIGHI (BOL 85)

PINES OF ROME (Pines of the Villa Borghese, Pines Near a Catacomb, Pines of the Appian Way)

FOUNTAINS OF ROME (The Fountain of Valle Giulia at Dawn, The Triton Fountain at Morning, The Trevi Fountain at Midday, The Villa Medici Fountain at Sunset)

THE BIRDS (Prelude)

FASHIONS IN MUSIC (BOL 86)

ROMEO AND JULIET (Fantasy-Overture), Tchaikovsky

LITTLE FUGUE IN G MINOR, Bach

SUITE NO. 2 FROM "DAPHNIS AND CHLOË," Ravel

ROMANZE FROM A LITTLE NIGHT MUSIC (*Eine kleine Nachtmusik*), Mozart

PERIPETIA FROM FIVE PIECES FOR ORCHESTRA, Schoenberg

Appendix D

Compositions in The Enjoyment of Music Series by Joseph Machlis

Armstrong: *West End Blues*   Side 18, Band 2
    Louis Armstrong and his Hot Five, featuring Earl Hines

Bach: from Cantata No. 140, *Wachet auf*
    Chorus, *Wachet auf*   Side 14, Band 1
    Chorale, *Zion hört die Wächter singen*   Band 2
    Chorale, *Gloria sei dir gesungen*   Band 3
        Vienna Academy Chorus and Orchestra; Hermann
        Scherchen, Conductor

Bach: Organ Fugue in G minor (''Little'')   Side 13, Band 1
    E. Power Biggs, Organ

Bach: from Suite No. 3 in D major
    Air   Side 13, Band 2
    Gigue   Band 3
        Jean-François Paillard Chamber Orchestra; Jean-François
        Paillard, Conductor

Bach: Brandenburg Concerto No. 2 in F major
    First movement, Allegro   Side 13, Band 4
    Second movement, Andante   Band 5
    Third movement, Allegro assai   Band 6
        Anthony Newman and Friends (Soloists: Martin Berin-
        baum, Trumpet: Shelley Gruskin, Recorder: Ronald Rose-
        man, Oboe: Ani Kavafian, Violin: Anthony Newman,
        Harpsichord Continuo)

Bartók: First movement from *Music for Strings, Percussion, and Celesta*

The BBC Symphony Orchestra; Pierre Boulez, Conductor   Side 16, Band 2

Beethoven: Piano Sonata in C minor, Op. 13 ("Pathétique")

First movement, Grave—Allegro di molto e con brio   Side 9, Band 1
Second movement, Adagio cantabile   Band 2
Third movement, Rondo: Allegro   Band 3
     Rudolf Serkin, Piano

Beethoven: Symphony No. 5 in C minor, Op. 67

First movement, Allegro con brio   Side 10, Band 1
Second movement, Andante con moto   Band 2
Third movement, Allegro   Band 3
Fourth movement, Allegro
     The Cleveland Orchestra; George Szell, Conductor

Berg: Scenes 4 & 5 from *Wozzeck*, Act III   Side 17, Band 1

Walter Berry, Wozzeck; Albert Weikenmeier, The Captain; Carl Doench, The Doctor; Children's Chorus of the Paris Opera directed by Jean Pesnaud; Paris Opera Orchestra; Pierre Boulez, Conductor

Berlioz: Fourth movement from *Symphonie Fantastique*   Side 2, Band 2

The Toronto Symphony; Seiji Ozawa, Conductor

Billings: *Chester*   Side 17, Band 2

The Gregg Smith Singers; Gregg Smith, Director

Brahms: Third movement from Symphony No. 3 in F major   Side 2, Band 3

The Cleveland Orchestra; George Szell, Conductor

Carter: Etudes 4, 5 and 8 from Eight Etudes and a Fantasy   Side 18, Band 5

Members of the Dorian Woodwind Quintet (Karl Kraber, Flute; Charles Kuskin, Oboe; William Lewis, Clarinet; Jane Taylor, Bassoon)

Chopin: Etude in A minor, Op. 25, No. 11   Side 1, Band 8

℗ 1972 Polydor International
Maurizio Pollini, Piano

Chopin: Mazurka in C-sharp minor, Op. 6, No. 2   Side 1, Band 7

Charles Rosen, Piano

Chopin: Prelude in E minor, Op. 28, No. 4   Side 2, Band 1

Murray Perahia, Piano ℗ 1975 CBS INC.

Copland: Opening Scene from *Billy the Kid*   Side 17, Band 5

London Symphony Orchestra; Aaron Copland, Conductor

Crawford: Andante from String Quartet (1931)   Side 17, Band 6

The Composers Quartet (Matthew Raimondi & Anahid Ajemian, Violins; Jean Dupouy, Viola; Michael Rudiakov, Cello) ℗ 1973 Nonesuch Records

Crumb: First movement from *Ancient Voices of Children*   Side 18, Band 6
Jan DeGaetani, Mezzo-Soprano; Michael Dash, Boy Soprano;
Contemporary Chamber Ensemble; Arthur Weisberg, Conductor

Davidovsky: *Synchronisms No. 1*   Side 18, Band 7
Samuel Baron, Flute; tape realized at Columbia-Princeton
Electronic Music Center
℗ 1974 Nonesuch Records

Debussy: *Prelude to "The Afternoon of a Faun"*   Side 16, Band 1
New Philharmonia Orchestra; Pierre Boulez, Conductor

Dufay: *Alma redemptoris mater*   Side 11, Band 5
Capella Antiqua, Munich; Konrad Ruhland, Conductor

Dvořák: Symphony No. 9 in E minor ("From the New World")
First movement, Adagio—Allegro molto   Side 4, Band 1
Second movement, Largo   Band 2
Third movement, Scherzo: Molto vivace   Band 3
The Cleveland Orchestra; George Szell, Conductor

Dvořák: Symphony No. 9 in E minor ("From the New World")
Fourth movement, Allegro con fuoco   Side 5, Band 1
The Cleveland Orchestra; George Szell, Conductor

Ellington: *Blue Light*   Side 18, Band 3

Ellington: *Subtle Lament*   Band 4
Duke Ellington and his Orchestra

Handel: from *Messiah*
Overture   Side 14, Band 4
Comfort ye; Ev'ry valley   Band 5
Hallelujah   Band 6
Ryland Davies, Tenor; English Chamber Orchestra Choir;
English Chamber Orchestra; Raymond Leppard, Conductor

Haydn: Symphony No. 94 in G major ("Surprise")
First movement, Adagio—Vivace assai   Side 7, Band 1
Second movement, Andante   Band 2
Third movement, Minuet and Trio: Allegro molto   Band 3
Fourth movement, Allegro di molto   Band 4
The Cleveland Orchestra; George Szell, Conductor

Ives: *Putnam's Camp* from *Three Places in New England*   Side 17, Band 3
The Philadelphia Orchestra: Eugene Ormandy, Conductor

Josquin: *Déploration sur la mort d'Ockeghem*   Side 12, Band 1
℗ 1973 Polydor International
London Pro Cantione Antiqua; Bruno Turner, Director

Josquin: *Scaramella*   Side 11, Band 6
Nonesuch Consort; Joshua Rifkin, Director

Machaut: *Kyrie* from *Notre Dame Mass*   Side 11, Band 4

Mahler: Fourth movement from Symphony No. 4   Side 15, Band 2
Judith Raskin, Soprano; The Cleveland Orchestra; George
Szell, Conductor

Mendelssohn: First movement from Violin Concerto in E minor   Side 2, Band 4
Isaac Stern, Violin; The Philadelphia Orchestra; Eugene
Ormandy, Conductor

Monteverdi: Scene from *Orfeo,* Act II   Side 12, Band 4
Eric Tappy, Tenor; Vocal Ensemble of Lausanne; Edward Tarr
Brass Ensemble; Instrumental Ensemble of Lausanne; Michel
Corboz, Conductor

Mozart: *Eine kleine Nachtmusik*
First movement, Allegro   Side 8, Band 1
Second movement, Romanze: Andante   Band 2
Third movement, Menuetto: Allegretto   Band 3
Fourth movement, Allegro   Band 4
The Cleveland Orchestra; George Szell, Conductor

Mozart: from *Don Giovanni*
Catalogue Aria   Side 8, Band 5
Ezio Pinza, Bass; Metropolitan Opera Orchestra;
Bruno Walter, Conductor
Là ci darem la mano   Band 6
Anna Moffo, Soprano; Antonio Campo, Baritone; Aix
Festival Orchestra; Hans Rosbaud, Conductor

Mozart: from Symphony in G minor, K. 550
First movement, Molto allegro   Side 11, Band 1
Fourth movement, Allegro assai   Band 2
The Cleveland Orchestra; George Szell, Conductor
Introit: *Gaudeamus*   Band 3

Palestrina: *Sanctus & Benedictus* from *Missa Ascendo ad*   Side 12, Band 2
Patrem
The Singers of Saint-Eustache; Emile Martin, Director

Puccini: Scene from Act I of *La Bohème* (from Mimi's entrance   Side 6, Band 2
to the end of the act)
Bidù Sayáo, Soprano; Richard Tucker, Tenor; Orchestra of
the Metropolitan Opera Association; Giuseppe Antonicelli,
Conductor

Purcell: *Dido's Lament* from *Dido and Aeneas*   Side 12, Band 5

Schoenberg: *A Survivor from Warsaw*   Side 18, Band 1
John Horton, Narrator; CBC Symphony Orchestra; Festival
Singers of Toronto; Robert Craft, Conductor

Schoenberg: from *Pieces for Orchestra*, Op. 16
No. 1, *Vorgefühle* (Premonitions)   Side 16, Band 3
No. 2, *Vergangenes* (The Past)   Band 4
Robert Craft conducting The Cleveland Orchestra

Schubert: *An Sylvia* Side 1, Band 5
Hermann Prey, Baritone; Karl Engel, Piano

Schubert: *Erlkönig* ℗ 1970 Polydor International Side 1, Band 4
Dietrich Fischer-Dieskau, Baritone; Gerald Moore, Piano

Schubert: Fourth movement from Quintet in A major ("Trout") Side 9, Band 4
Rudolf Serkin, Piano; Jaime Laredo, Violin; Philipp Naegele,
Viola; Leslie Parnas, Cello; Julius Levine, Bass

Schumann: *Mondnacht* ℗ 1968 Polydor International Side 1, Band 6
Christa Ludwig, Mezzo-Soprano; Erik Werba, Piano

Smetana: *The Moldau* Side 3, Band 1
New York Philharmonic; Leonard Bernstein, Conductor

Stravinsky: from *The Rite of Spring*
Opening Scene Side 15, Band 3
Sacrificial Dance Band 4
    The Cleveland Orchestra; Pierre Boulez, Conductor

Stravinsky: First movement from *Symphony of Psalms* Side 5, Band 3
Igor Stravinsky conducting the CBC Symphony Orchestra;
The Festival Singers of Toronto, Elmer Iseler, Director

Tchaikovsky: *Romeo and Juliet,* Overture-Fantasy Side 3, Band 2
The Philadelphia Orchestra; Eugene Ormandy, Conductor

Tchaikovsky: from *The Nutcracker Suite*
March Side 1, Band 1
Arabian Dance Band 2
Dance of the Toy Flutes Band 3
    Philadelphia Orchestra; Eugene Ormandy, Conductor

Varèse: *Ionisation* Side 17, Band 4
Robert Craft, Conductor

Verdi: *Dies irae* (opening section) from *Requiem Mass* Side 15, Band 1
George London, Bass; Westminster Choir; The Philadelphia
Orchestra; Eugene Ormandy, Conductor

Verdi: Violetta's Scene from *La Traviata,* Act I Side 6, Band 1
℗ 1963 Polydor International
Renata Scotto, Soprano; Gianni Raimondi, Tenor; Orchestra
of Teatro alla Scala; Antonino Votto, Conductor

Wagner: Prelude to *Tristan und Isolde* Side 5, Band 2
The Cleveland Orchestra; George Szell, conductor

Webern: from *Pieces for Orchestra,* Op. 10
No. 3, *Sehr langsam und äusserst ruhig* Side 16, Band 5
No. 4, *Fliessend, äusserst zart* Band 6
    London Symphony Orchestra; Pierre Boulez, Conductor

Weelkes: *As Vesta was descending* Side 12, Band 3
The Purcell Consort of Voices; Grayston Burgess, Director

Appendix E

Supplementary Song Sources in Three Current Music Textbook Series:
Silver Burdett & Ginn, World of Music, 1991
Holt, Rinehart and Winston, Music, Music, 1991
Macmillan, Music & You, 1991

Song	Silver Burdett	Holt	Macmillan
All Hid			
Barney's Tune			
Barnyard Song			Gr. 2, p. 52
Beautiful Day			
Bingo	Gr. 1, p. 152	Gr. 1, p. 123	Gr. 2, p. 57
Blacksmith, The			
Brush Your Teeth	Gr. 1, p. 128		
Cindy	Gr. 4, p. 16	Gr. 6, p. 208	Gr. 5, p. 52
Clementine	Gr. 4, p. 18 Gr. 5, p. 290		
Clouds Are Up High			
Come, Follow, Follow		Gr. 6, p. 72	Gr. 6, p. 16

Song	Silver Burdett	Holt	Macmillan
Come, Ye Thankful People, Come	Gr. 3, p. 197 Gr. 4, p. 275 Gr. 5, p. 231 Gr. 6, p. 225		Gr. 5, p. 66
Count, The			
Down by the Bay		Gr. 4, p. 144	
Down by the Station			
Down in the Valley	Gr. 1, p. 160 Gr. 3, p. 102		
Ducklings, The			Gr. K, p. 187 Gr. 1, p. 216
Fish and Chips			
Five Little Skeletons			
Flea!			
Follow On			
Gerikina			Gr. 6, p. 218
Go Tell Aunt Rhody	Gr. K, p. 90 Gr. 1, p. 212 Gr. 2, p. 243 Gr. 4, p. 494	Gr. 2, p. 130	
Hickory Dickory Dock	Gr. K, p. 18		
Hokey Pokey	Gr. K, p. 114		
Hole in the Bucket		Gr. 3, p. 115	
I Can Reach High			
If You're Happy	Gr. K, p. 59	Gr. 1, p. 13	Gr. 1, p. 168 Gr. 2, p. 17
I Have a Little Bird			
I Love the Mountains	Gr. 4, p. 112 Gr. 5, p. 284	Gr. 3, p. 48	Gr. 4, p. 100
Jarabe			
Jennie Jenkins			
Kookaburra	Gr. 4, p. 58	Gr. 4, p. 16	Gr. 6, p. 249
Kum Ba Yah	Gr. 5, p. 127 Gr. 6, p. 278		
London Bridge	Gr. K, p. 16		
Lone Star Trail	Gr. 2, p. 17	Gr. 3, p. 42	

Song	Silver Burdett	Holt	Macmillan
Looby Loo	Gr. 1, p. 264		Gr. K, p. 130 Gr. 2, p. 42
Love Somebody	Gr. 1, p. 201 Gr. 3, p. 261 Gr. 5, p. 283 Gr. 6, p. 272		Gr. 1, p. 209 Gr. 4, p. 139
He Manu Rere			
Michael, Row the Boat Ashore	Gr. 2, p. 91 Gr. 4, p. 316 Gr. 6, p. 108		Gr. 2, p. 258
Mister Sun	Gr. 2, p. 96		
My Hat	Gr. 2, p. 137		
New Shoes			
Nobody Home			
Old MacDonald			Gr. K, p. 175 Gr. 1, p. 51
Old Texas	Gr. 4, p. 46 Gr. 5, p. 57 Gr. 6, p. 270	Gr. 4, p. 145	Gr. 4, p. 203
One, Two, Three			
O Tannenbaum (O Christmas Tree)			
Polly Wolly Doodle	Gr. 2, p. 98 Gr. 3, p. 124	Gr. 4, p. 42	
Pussy Willow Song			
Rainy Round, A			
Red Birds Flying			
Rig-a-Jig-Jig			
Round in a Circle			
Row Your Boat	Gr. 5, p. 549	Gr. 2, p. 31	Gr. 2, p. 205 Gr. 6, p. 197
Sailing			
Sally Go Round the Sun	Gr. K, p. 205		
Sandy Land	Gr. 2, p. 78 Gr. 3, p. 108, 112 Gr. 5, p. 288		
Scarborough Fair	Gr. 6, p. 102		

Song	Silver Burdett	Holt	Macmillan
Silent Night	Gr. 2, p. 217 Gr. 6, p. 231		
Skinnamarink	Gr. 1, p. 202		
Sleep, Baby, Sleep			
Space Ship			
Streets of Laredo	Gr. 4, p. 293 Gr. 5, p. 122	Gr. 5, p. 155	
Sunshiny Day			
That's the Way Tunes Go			
This Train	Gr. 4, p. 42 Gr. 5, p. 118		Gr. 6, p. 145
Tinga Layo	Gr. 3, p. 65		
To Puerto Rico			
Toooh the Zooo			
Trampin'		Gr. 2, p. 72	Gr. 3, p. 226 Gr. 5, p. 247
Wayfaring Stranger			
When the Saints Go Marching In	Gr. 1, p. 134 Gr. 5, p. 119 Gr. 6, p. 87	Gr. 5, p. 154 Gr. 6, p. 214	Gr. 5, p. 174
Zum Gali Gali		Gr. 4, p. 118	

Appendix F

Copyright Law

A concern of every teacher when gathering materials of instruction is the copyright law, which protects copyrighted materials. Under Section 107 of the Copyright Act, unfair use is determined if the photocopied material is used commercially and for profit, if more than a portion of the work is copied, or if it reduces the copyright owner's market for the material. In an MENC *Newsbrief* dated July 1983, guidelines state that a single copy for research, teaching, or preparation to teach may be made of a chapter from a book; a periodical or newspaper article; a short story, essay, or poem; or a diagram or picture. Allowed are multiple copies, not more than one copy per pupil in class, of a 250-word poem, a 2,500-word article, a 1,000-word excerpt, and special works shorter than 2,500 words. Not allowed are more than one piece or two excerpts from the same author, more than nine multiple copies for one course during one term, and copying that replaces collective works. The preceding refers primarily to words; the music teacher is concerned primarily with making photocopies of music. Incidentally, most music series publishers and some other sources offer materials that can be reproduced freely; this fact is stated clearly in the materials and no teacher need worry about these. In an emergency situation, a teacher may reproduce copyrighted songs or instrumental music if such copies will be promptly replaced with those purchased from the copyright owner or agent thereof. This refers to music for performance. For academic (nonperformance) purposes multiple copies of *excerpts* of works may be made, provided that such excerpts do not comprise a part of the whole that would be considered a performable unit such as a section, movement, or aria, but in any case more than 10 percent of the whole work. The number of copies shall not exceed one copy per pupil. Printed copies that have been purchased may be edited or simplified provided that the fundamental character of the work is not distorted or the lyrics altered or lyrics added if none exist. Thus, teachers may not write new versions of a copyrighted song and photocopy them for classroom use without permission from the copyright owner. A single copy of recordings of performances by students may be made for evaluation or rehearsal purposes and may be retained by the school or individual teacher. A single copy of a sound recordings such as a tape, disc, or cassette of copyrighted music may be made from sound recordings owned by the teacher for the purpose of constructing aural exercises or examinations and may be retained by the school or teacher. (This pertains only to the copyright of the music itself and not to any copyright which may exist in the sound recording.) Prescott and Gary (1982) state that the following are prohibited:

> Copying to create or replace or substitute for anthologies, compilations, or collective works.
>
> Copying of or from works intended to be "consumable" in the course of study or of teaching, such as workbooks, exercises, standardized tests, and answer sheets and like material.
>
> Copying for purpose of performance, except as in an emergency for public performance.
>
> Copying for the purpose of substituting for the purchase of music, except in emergency situations.
>
> Copying without inclusion of the copyright notice, which appears on the printed copy.

Because the copyright law is complex, an informed person (such as a librarian) should be appointed to keep records, to seek permission to copy, and to keep copies of correspondence relating to obtaining permissions, thus protecting teacher and school districts from lawsuits.

References

Copyright Basics. Washington, D.C.: Copyright Office, Library of Congress, 1981.

Highlights of the New Copyright Law. Washington, D.C.: Copyright Office, Library of Congress, 1981.

PRESCOTT, MICHAEL P., and CHARLES L. GARY, "Copyright in the Legal Spotlight," *Music Educators Journal,* March 1982, 25–27.

The United States Copyright Law: A Guide for Music Educators. Reston, Va.: Music Educators National Conference. Single free copies available.

Index of Songs

General Index

A

Accent, lesson plan for teaching, 156–58
Accidentals, 216–17
Accompaniments:
  for autoharp, 296
  chording, 310
  harmony and, 292
  and keyboards, 308
Adventures in Music recordings, 122,
    314, 363–67
Agogo bells, 175
American Indian, music of, 188
Articulation, 130–32, 201
Arts, relating music to, 6
Assertive discipline, 103
Associative-process thinking, 65
Attitudes, 14–15
  assessment of, 112–13
Augmentation, 140
Autoharp, 70, 178, 292–96
  accompaniments, types of, 296
  chording on, 13, 294
  tuning, 295

B

Ballet suites, 332
Banjo, 178
Baroque recorders, 287–88

B

Basic education, 3
Bassoon, 182
Beat, 120–22, 201
  divisions of, 127–28, 200
Behavioral approach, to classroom
    management, 103
Billings, William, 3
Bitonality, 278, 291
Blues, 311
Bongo drum, 169
Books, music-related, 357–62
Boston Academy of Music, 4
Bowed instruments, *See* Stringed
    instruments
Bowmar Orchestral Library, 122–23,
    368–74
Boys' voices, 240, 245
Brass instruments, 182–84
Bruner, Jerome, 25–26, 42
Bugle, 182

C

Cabasa, 175
Cadence, 311
Call-and-response songs, *See* Dialogue
    songs
Canons, 225, 258–61, 275, 291
Castanets, 172
Celesta, 179

music learning activities, 31–33
philosophy, 37–41
Cymbals, 70

D

Dalcroze, Emil Jacques, 5, 17, 344–46
Dance suites, 332
Data, 42–43
  application of, 12–13
  interpretation of, 12
Descants, 13, 225, 265–67, 276
Dewey, John, 2
Dialogue songs, 258
Diminution, 140
Discovery learning, 26
Disjunctmotion, 214
Dominant seventh chords, 209
Dotted notes, 128–30
Double bass, 178–180
Double stops, 179
Dreikursian approach to classroom
    management, 103
Dreikurs, Rudolf, 103
Drums, 70, 168–69
  drum beaters, 168
Drum talk, 188
Duration, 25, 130–31, 201
Dynamics, 25, 63–64, 201, 252
  See also Tempo and dynamics

E

Ear training, 290
Echo-clapping, 119–20, 124–27, 138
Educable retarded students, 92–93
  mainstreaming tips, 96
Education Through Music (ETM), 353–54
Eight Ages of Man (Erickson), 27
Electronic keyboards, *See* Keyboards
Elementary schools:
  band and string programs in, 203–4
  chorus, 274–75
Emotionally disturbed students, 93–94
  mainstreaming tips, 97
Enjoyment of Music Series (Machlis),
    375–79
Environmental sounds, studying tone
    quality of, 166–67
Erikson, Erik, 27

Ethnic scales, 218
Evaluation, 46, 106–17
  of music program, 113–15
  purposes of, 106–7
  of songs, 11–12
  student evaluation, 107–13
  teacher self-evaluation, 115–16
Experiments in Music Creativity
    (CMP/MENC), 191
Exploratory improvisation, 194–196

F

Finger cymbals, 70, 173
Finger snapping, 133, 167, 192
Flexitone, 175
Flugelhorn, 183
Flutes, 181, 182, 283
Foot stamping, 133, 167, 192
Formal operations stage, 24
Forms, 62–63
  fugue, 331–32
  lesson plans for teaching, 158–59,
    333–37
  one-part (unary), 324
  opera, 333
  rondo, 330
  sonata-allegro, 332
  suite, 332
  three-part (ternary), 324–27
  tone poem, 333
  two-part (binary), 324, 326–27
  variation, 330–31
Fowler, Charles, 3
Free exploration of sound sources, 193,
    195
French horn, 182, 183
Froseth, James, 354–55
Fugue, 331–32

G

Gapped scale, 210
Generalizations, 25, 43–44, 65
Gifted students, 94–95
  mainstreaming tips, 97–98
Glockenspiel, 285, 309
Gongs, 70, 174
Gordon, Edwin, 109, 354
Gordon syllables, 128

Guided exploration of sound sources, 193, 195–96
Guiro, 173, 283
Guitar, 70, 178, 180
    chords, 13, 298, 299–301
    teaching children to play, 296–98

H

Hand clapping, 119, 121, 133, 188, 192, 219
Hand signs, 211, 228, 229
    Curwen, 350, 353
    Kodály, 350–353
Harmonic card game, 310
Harmonic endings/freeze tones, 268–69
Harmonic instruments, teaching with, 309–11
Harmonics, 178–79
Harmony, 25, 60–61, 224–27, 310
    accompaniments and, 292
    chord changes, learning to hear, 225–26
    contemporary, 226–27
    relating melody and, 224–25
    See also Part singing
Harp, 179
Harpsichord, 179
Hearing impaired students, 90–92
    mainstreaming tips, 96
Heel-clap, 188
Homophonic music, 61, 225
Hunt, J. McVickar, 22

I

Improvisation, 228, 229
    based on chords, 291
    of harmony, 276–77
    with keyboard, 290
    of part singing, 277–78
    with pitched percussion instruments, 290
Independent singing, 252
Individualized instruction, 79–85
    Job Cards, 81–85
    learning stations, 80, 84–85
    physical environment for, 79–80
    room plan, 81
    See also Classroom management

Inner hearing, concept of, 228
Instructional programs, designing, 37–58
    music content areas, 41–42
    philosophy/goals/objectives, 37–41
    program content, selecting, 42–44
Instruction, delivery of, 68–105
    classroom management, 98–104
    learning environment, 68–77
    organizing for, 77–98
Instruction, organizing for, 77–98
    computer-assisted instruction, 85–86
    individualized instruction, 79–85
    large groups, 77–78
    small groups, 78–79
    special learners, 86–89
Instrument playing, as motor skill, 13
Instruments:
    teaching children to play, 282–312
    transposing, 291
    using for harmonic activities and accompanying, 292–311
Intervals, 219–21, 278, 282, 285
Intrinsic motivation, 20
Invented scales, 231

J

Japanese, music of, 336–37
Japanese scale, 218
Jingle bells, 70, 174
Jingle clogs, 174

K

Keyboard instruments, 179–80
Keyboards, 210, 254, 286–87
    teaching children to play, 286–87, 298–309
Key signatures, 214, 230
Kodály, Zoltan, 5, 6, 346, 349–53
    hand signs, 350–53
    Kodály Choral Method, 350

L

Large-group instruction, 75, 77–78
Leading tone, 213

Music experiences, for four- to five-
year-old children, 31
Music learning center, 71
Music normal institutes, 4
Music program, evaluation of, 113–115

N

National Commission on Excellence in
Education, 1
Natural minor, 231
Nonpitched percussion instruments, 167
Notation, 126, 129, 130, 139, 188,
201, 202, 256

O

Oboe, 182
Omnichord, 70, 292–94
One-part (unary) form, 324
Opera, 333
Opera suites, 332
Orff, Carl, 5, 6, 17, 133, 176, 346–49
Orff-type instruments, 70, 176–77
Organizational plans, 71–72
Organs, 287
Orthopedically handicapped/spastic
students, 89
mainstreaming tips, 95
Ostinati, 202, 225
composition over, 310
melody instruments and, 288

P

Parallel thirds, singing, 278
Part singing:
bitonality, 278, 291
chants, 261–65
chord changes, learning to hear, 272
chord roots, 269–72
countermelodies and descants,
265–67, 278
dialogue songs, 258
dissonance, 278
elementary school chorus, 274–75
harmonic, 276–78
harmonic endings/freeze tones, 268–69
improvisation, 277–78
of harmony, 276–77

intervals, 278
parallel thirds, 278
partner songs, 267–68
pitched percussion instruments and,
284
rounds and canons, 258–61
thirds and sixths, 272–74
vocal chording, 269–72
Patschen, 121, 133, 167, 192, 219
Pentatonic scales, 210, 230, 291
tonal activity of, 214
Percepts, 10
Percussion instruments, 119, 133
nonpitched, 167
pitched, 176–78
Phrases, 252, 291, 318–19
Physical environment, 69–71
Piaget, Jean, 23–24
Pianos, 179, 254, 287
chording on, 13
Piccolo, 181, 182
Picks, 294
Pitch, 25, 133, 209–10, 275–76
establishing for singing, 245–46
Pitch discrimination:
and learning to sing, 240–48
lesson plans for teaching,
227–29
Pitched percussion instruments,
176–78, 210
harmony and, 309
teaching children to play, 283–86
Planned improvisation, 194, 196–97
Polyphony, 25, 61, 224, 276, 291
Preoperational stage, 23–24
Preverbal stage, 23
Primacy Measures of Music Audiation
(Gordon), 109
Program content, selecting, 42–44
concepts, 43
data, 42–43
generalizations, 43–44
Program evaluation, 113–15
Psychomotor skills, 13

Q

Quartal chords, 310
Questioning, and learning, 18

R

Recorders, 167, 181
  baroque, 287–88
  melodies for, 291
  soprano, 70, 287, 289
  teaching children to play, 287–88
Repetition, 200, 201
Resonator bells, and tone row, 218
Rest, teaching concept of, 127
Rhythm, 59
  activities for teaching, 141–42
    lesson plans, 149–59
    selected songs for experimentation, 144–59
  beat, 120–22, 127–28
  compositional devices, 140–41
  conducting, 135
  duration, 25, 130–31, 201
  dynamics, 63–64
  lesson plans for teaching, 153–56, 315–18
  meter, 132–33, 135–38
  pitch, 133
  rest, 127
  rhythm patterns, 138–40
  tempo, 63
Rhythm sticks, 70, 139, 170
Rhythm syllables, 126
Richards, Mary Helen, 350, 353–54
Rondo, 202, 330
Rote teaching:
  music concepts and, 252
  selecting songs for, 249–52
Rounds, 13, 225, 258–61, 276

S

Sandblocks, 70, 171
Saxophone, 182
Scales, 210–13, 230–31, 285, 290
  chromatic, 216–17
  ethnic, 218
  invented, 231
  Japanese, 218
  key signatures, 214
  lesson plan for teaching, 230–31
  major, 210–12
    tonal activity of, 213
  minor, 212–13

pentatonic, 210
  tonal activity of, 214
tone row, 218–19
whole-tone, 216–17, 231
Self-contained classroom, definition of, 72
Sensorimotor stage, 23
Sight barriers, 80
Singing:
  activities for, 275–78
  child's voice, 234–40
  creating songs, 254–58
  as motor skill, 13
  part singing, 258–75
  pitch discrimination in, 240–48
  rote songs, teaching, 249–52
  See also Tone matching
Slap stick, 175
Sleigh bells, 284
Small-group instruction, 78–79
Sonata-allegro form, 332
Songs:
  chants, 261–65
  countermelodies and descants, 265–67
  creating, 254–58
  dialogue songs, 258
  evaluation of, 11–12
  partner songs, 267–68
  recordings of, 253–54
  rounds and canons, 258–61
Soprano recorders, 70, 287, 289
Sounds of the World (MENC), 137
Sound sources, 167–76, 190–203
  brass instruments, 182–84
  drums, 168–69
  exploratory improvisation, 194, 196
  free exploration of, 193, 195
  guided exploration of, 193, 195–96
  metal instruments, 173–74
  nonpitched percussion instruments, 167
  pitched percussion instruments, 176–78
  planned improvisation, 194, 196–97
  special effects instruments, 175
  stringed instruments, 178–81
  synthesizers/computers, 184–87
  unconventional, 187–89
  voices, 176
  wooden instruments, 170–73
  woodwind instruments, 181–82

V

Variation form, 330–31
Vibraslap, 175
Vibrato, 178
Violin/viola/violoncello,
    178, 180
Visually impaired students, 89
    mainstreaming tips,
    95–96
Vocal chording, 269–72
Voice:
    boy voice, 240, 245
    changing, 245
    child's, 176, 234–40
    range, 235–36
Voice substitutes, 254

W

Weikart, Phyllis, 354
Whole-tone scales, 216–17, 231
Woodblocks, 70, 139, 172
Wooden instruments, 170–73
Wood kameso, 175
Woodwind instruments, 181–82
Word-rhythms, 123–24, 135, 200
Written test, sample of, 109

X

Xylophone, 210, 285, 309

Z

Zither, 178